MARXISM AND THE MORAL POINT OF VIEW

MARXISM AND THE MORAL POINT OF VIEW

Morality, Ideology, and Historical Materialism

Kai Nielsen

Westview Press
BOULDER & LONDON

Published in 1989 in the United States of America by Westview Press, Inc., 5500 Central Avenue, Boulder, Colorado 80301

Library of Congress Cataloging-in-Publication Data
Nielsen, Kai, 1926–
  Marxism and the moral point of view : morality, ideology, and
historical materialism / Kai Nielsen.
    p. cm.
  Includes index.
  ISBN 0-8133-0653-1
  1. Communist ethics. I. Title.
BJ1390.N465 1989
171′.7—dc19   88-14146
                                                                              CIP

Printed and bound in the United States of America

The paper used in this publication meets the requirements of the American National
Standard for Permanence of Paper for Printed Library Materials Z39.48-1984.

10   9   8   7   6   5   4   3   2   1

For Jocelyne

Contents

1

Introduction

Marxism and the Moral Point of View attempts to say what consistent Marxists working within the parameters of the canonical conceptions of Marxism should say about morality. This includes what they should say about the function of morality in society, about the extent of moral comment they can justifiably make, and about freedom, equality, and justice, including the justice of whole social formations.

Karl Marx—and most Marxists follow him—was opposed to all moralizing. Marxists have, in opposition to utopian socialism, sought to put socialism on a scientific footing and have stressed the importance of developing a critique of capitalism that was scientific, not moral—that is, not simply or even primarily moral.

Morality, Marxists have claimed, is a form of ideology. A morality—specifically, the actual moralities in a given society—will have a certain character generally congruent with a particular stage of development of the modes of production. The pervasively held moral views of any society are deeply conditioned by the mode of production of that society and (where it is a class society) by the dominant class interests of that society. Our extant moralities function to reinforce and legitimate the class interests of the dominant class while purporting to answer in an impartial manner to the interests of everyone alike. Very extensively, we are sufficiently mystified to believe that our moral beliefs somehow reflect eternal truth when in reality they standardly reflect the class interests of the dominant class.

This is the iconoclastic side of Marx and Marxism, where the stress is on morality as ideology. But the writings of Marx, and of Marxists

1

more generally, are replete with moral judgments—in particular with stern moral condemnations of capitalism. Moral judgments such as these make it look as if Marx and Marxists have rejected morality at the same time as they have deeply appealed to it in criticizing capitalism. This, of course, is hardly a comfortable position in which to be.

I seek to give an interpretation of Marxism that, without challenging the canonical conceptions of Marxist theory and practice, shows that in reality there is no conflict here. I provide a reading of the concept of ideology and an interpretation of the claim that morality is ideology that frees them of any epistemological or ontological claim that moral ideas cannot but be subjective and mystifying. (The reading and the interpretation also do this without committing themselves to the opposed claim of moral realism.[1]) I also argue that historical materialism tenders a sociological account of morality compatible with a contextualist objectivism that would allow for a rational assessment of the justice of whole social formations, including that of capitalism and socialism. In this fundamental way I side with the Marxist moralism of G. A. Cohen, Norman Geras, and Jon Elster and against the Marxist antimoralism of Robert Tucker, Allen Wood, and Richard Miller, whose accounts I critically examine in some detail. I argue that neither Marx nor Marxism revolutionized 'the foundations of ethics' or showed that morality could not have a rational foundation or point. (Whether indeed it does or even whether such metaphorical talk makes any coherent sense is another matter—a matter about which Marxists can remain, without undermining Marxist moralism, utterly agnostic!) Rather, Marxism provides us with a sociological account of the function(s) of morality, with a critique of moralizing, and with a demonstration of the importance of taking morality seriously without engaging in moralizing or going on a quest for the rational foundations of morality.

II

In the chapters that follow, there are several recurrent themes, although each has different stresses and nuances.

1. The ambivalence concerning morality is in Marx and the Marxist tradition generally. Marx was one of the great denouncers of all time, yet he detested all forms of moralism. According to Marx, communism will break the staff of all morality, and we must recognize that morality is through and through ideological. But Marx also adjudged capitalism to be an inhuman system that has outlived its historical usefulness and is destined to be replaced by a socialist system representing a truly human society in which there is the possibility for greater human flourishing for everyone.[2] So we have on Marx's part both a palpably negative evaluation of capitalism and a positive evaluation of socialism concomitant with a rejection of moralizing and a claim that morality is only ideology. Plainly there is tension and ambivalence here. Within

the Marxist tradition and by Marxologists there have been various responses to it. All have agreed that Marx at least consciously rejected moralism—namely, the belief that ideas, including sound moral arguments and clear and humane moral ideals, will be the main causative factors in changing the world. Although they agreed on that, they disagreed about whether Marx made or Marxists should make a moral critique of capitalism and a defense of the ethical superiority of socialism. Some have taken the line that has come to be called Marxist anti-moralism and have argued that Marx rejected, and contemporary Marxists should reject, appeals to morality in appraising whole social formations or modes of production or in formulating strategic political reasoning about what is to be done. Instead, in class struggles the thing is to attend closely to the class interests involved and to be aware of what is and what is not feasible in a given historical situation. Marxist moralists, on the other hand, while not downplaying the importance of class interests and class struggle, have argued that Marx, among other things he did, made a moral critique of capitalism and a moral defense of socialism and that it is vital for Marxists to refine and develop that critique and defense.

Both of these views easily lead to caricature. However, it is important to realize at the outset that neither Marxist anti-moralism nor Marxist moralism, in spite of what the word 'moralism' suggests, is a silly view. Marxist anti-moralism, as we shall see, is a humane view without being a moral perspective and not at all an advocation of bloodthirsty *realpolitik* or cynical manipulation. And Marxist moralism is not naïve about our moral powers or simplistically idealistic about how the world can be changed. It also, almost as fully as Marxist anti-moralism, stresses the ideological function of moralities in class societies.

I will ultimately side with a version of Marxist moralism, but I shall first show how the aforementioned tension in Marxist thought can be relieved. Marxists can, I shall argue, consistently criticize (and from a moral point of view) capitalism and defend socialism while stressing that morality is ideology. Stated in this way, such a remark, of course, sounds paradoxical. It will be an underlying rationale of this book to provide a reading and an understanding of that claim to relieve that paradox and to show it to be something to which it is reasonable to assent. However, in understanding what is involved here and in coming to see that and why the Marxist tradition has made a vital contribution to our understanding of morality, it is essential that we follow out the often complicated lines of reasoning of both Marxist anti-moralism and Marxist moralism. Both have had insightful and carefully reasoned formulations, and both are onto something vital in Marxist thinking about morality. Indeed—or so I shall argue—both consider things that should be a part of reflective thought on morality generally. A Marxist moralism without a full cognizance of the rationale and impact of the anti-moralist challenge would be an impoverished view.

2. I discuss historical materialism and ethics in the various chapters, from several angles, with somewhat different stresses. I seek to clearly articulate what historical materialism is, and I argue that historical materialism, even if it is a sound view of epochal social change, does not undermine belief in the objectivity of morals. There *may* be some distinctively philosophical reasons to reject the belief that moral claims can be objective, a viewpoint held by David Hume and updated more recently by Edward Westermarck and J. L. Mackie. Be that as it may and contrary to many popular misunderstandings, historical materialism does not afford a sound basis for rejecting the belief that some moral claims can have an objective foundation. It is, however, understandable that students of Marx might come to think that historical materialism does undermine morality. I argue that this is a mistake and that a belief that some moral claims can be objectively warranted is perfectly compatible with an unqualified acceptance of historical materialism.

I return to this from different angles and in one way or another in almost all of these chapters, but I introduce the topic in Chapter 2 and probe the issue most extensively in Chapters 7, 8, and 11. However, in Chapter 2, in introducing the topic, I argue that historical materialism *may* sanction a version of meta-ethical relativism. If that form of meta-ethical relativism is accepted it would, or at least should, lead a historical materialist, who accepts that form of meta-ethical relativism, to the view that people would only be justified in making mode-of-production-dependent judgments of what is right or wrong, just or unjust. It *may* be the case that if historical materialism is true, there could be no ground for asserting a transhistorical set of moral principles. I try to show the plausibility of that claim in Chapter 2, but I also point out that it is at least as reasonable to believe, as Friedrich Engels did, that the historical materialist may instead have a belief in moral progress incompatible with any recognizable version of meta-ethical relativism, and that instead presupposes a contextualistic form of fallibilistic objectivism. In morals, as well as in some other human domains, there can be objectively justified beliefs. Such a view, I argue, is at least as compatible with historical materialism as any form of relativism, squares better with the general Enlightenment orientation of Marx and Engels, fits better with our reflective hopes, and is at least as reasonable as its relativist, subjectivist, or nihilist alternatives. I leave open, vis-à-vis their compatibility with historical materialism, both the non-objectivist and objectivist stances in Chapter 2, but in Chapters 7, 11, and 12 I argue for the objectivist option.

What might on a quick reading appear to be a conflict between Chapter 2 and Chapter 7 arises from the fact that in the former, I do not as definitively try to close off certain relativistic possibilities as I do in the latter. However, in trying to canvass a range of at least prima facie possibilities, I do attempt to show in Section IV of Chapter 2 how strong the case is for meta-ethical relativism vis-à-vis historical materialism and how difficult the case is for moral progress. Still, while I argue that it is difficult, it is not impossible, and there are, against the fashion of our age, grounds for sharing Engels's belief in moral progress.

3. Marx, and Marxists generally, spoke of morality being ideology or as being ideological. This, of course, cries out for interpretation, and it poses problems somewhat similar to those posed by historical materialism for ethics. I articulate and defend a distinctive Marxist conception of ideology in Chapter 5 and contrast it with more typical Marxist conceptualizations as well as with more global non-Marxist ones. In Chapter 6, more extensively than elsewhere, I apply this characterization to the thesis that morality is ideology. I argue that while all ideological conceptions are superstructural, not all superstructural conceptions are ideological. This leaves conceptual space for the existence of ideas, such as some new creative ideas about our social life, that are not ideological, although they are, innocently enough given the Marxist typology, superstructural.[3] I also argue that the mark of the ideological—that is, what identifies something as being ideological—is that it answers to class interests, not, as is typically argued in Marxist circles, that it distorts. Ideologies, I contend, are *distortion prone,* but they do not *necessarily* distort. What makes a belief or practice ideological is that it answers to class interests.[4] I also argue that the claim that morality is ideology should be understood as a thesis in the sociology of morals and not as a thesis in the ontology or epistemology of morals or as a meta-ethical thesis. So understood, it is of immense importance in understanding morality and in critiquing ideology. Understood in any of the latter senses the claim, 'Morality is ideology' or 'Moral beliefs are ideological' is itself mystificatory. These three theses taken together, I argue, give us a perspicuous representation of morality and ideology and help resolve the tensions and ambivalences I referred to earlier.

All of this is, I hope, articulated clearly in Chapters 5 and 6, but some of my remarks in other chapters (most notably Chapter 2) *may* appear to be in conflict with what I say about morality and ideology in Chapters 5 and 6. In these other chapters, for certain tolerably evident pedagogical and dialectical reasons, I stick with the standard Marxist characterization of ideology: To be an ideology, an ideology, on this conception, must distort. Working with that standard characterization rather than my own, I examine certain consequences of the thesis that morality is ideology. But there is no clash between what I argue there and what I argue in Chapters 5 and 6, for while in my own preferred characterization of ideology I deny that ideology necessarily distorts our understanding of ourselves or our social life, I also stress, in giving that characterization, that ideology is distortion prone and that most, indeed perhaps all, ideologies do give us a distorted picture of ourselves, our possibilities, and the nature of our societies. Let me repeat—answering to class interests, rather than being distortive, is the mark of the ideological, and it is not, to suggest a more complex criterion, the two together.

However, in arguing thusly I do stress—and such a stress is important for my conception of the ideological functions of morality—how standardly and pervasively ideologies do distort and how useful this is to the class whose interests the ideology serves. But in some places, I write as if the more typical Marxist characterization were being followed, where being distortive is a necessary feature of being an ideology. Suppose, in that vein, we define ideology as G. A. Cohen did: "as thinking that is not just incorrect but that is systematically deflected from truth because of its conformity to the limited vision and sectional interests of a particular social class."[5] Working, in places, with such a more typical Marxist conception of ideology, I argue that not all morality need be ideological and that a Marxist need not, and indeed should not, assert that it must be. But I also argue that even where ideology (if pace the standard characterization that were ever the case) does not distort, there is no good reason to believe that all moral ideas are ideological or that Marxists must think, to be consistent, that they are. But in particular it is crucial to see that even when we stick with the canonical conceptions of Marxism, we are not justified in believing that if something is a moral belief, it must be ideological and distortive of our understanding. It is important to see not only are we not justified in holding that belief but for an adequate Marxist self-definition, if that is what we want, we must deny it.

III

The chapters collected here were drafted between 1980 and 1987 for different occasions with different audiences and for varying purposes. Chapters 2, 3, and 8 were among the earliest, and Chapters 10, 11, and 12 were the latest. It would not be surprising if, more than I am aware, some tensions exist between the earlier and later chapters, particularly in view of important emerging literature—indeed a kind of growth industry—and my repeated efforts to sort out the conflicting claims of Marxist anti-moralism and Marxist moralism. I have already addressed some of these claims, but I want now to address others as well as problems some readers have had previously with this material.

I use a number of concepts without defining them, and this has troubled some readers. I hoped that these concepts would be clear from the context, but because they have caused trouble before, they may do so again, so let me give some detailed definitions in this introduction.

Let me turn to the first, and what may be the most troubling, one. I utilize a contextualism in a coherentist model of justification that I contrast with absolutism and a belief in eternal moral truths or principles, which comprise a battery of conceptions characteristic of the model of objectivity appealed to by ethical rationalists. I claim, against such a rationalistic tradition, that this contextualism gives us a perfectly adequate conception of objectivity, and I would claim as well, although I do not do so in this book, that at least in moral domains and the like this contextualism gives us the only plausible conception of objectivity we are going to get. However, it is not unreasonable to ask: What is this contextualism, and what more exactly is the related conception of objectivity? Relatedly, my talk of moral truisms, eternal moral principles, historicism, relativism, and the like has caused trouble. Thus, some definitions, elucidations, and categorizations are necessary.

I shall try to gain some purchase on these matters by first characterizing different forms of relativism, all of which contrast with contextualism. Contextualism, it is important to see, is none of these things. However, relativism, like contextualism, is a term of art, and different people mean somewhat different things by it. But I think my characterizations have captured the main varieties, although (of course) not everyone would characterize them in exactly the way I have.

Cultural relativism (sociological relativism, descriptive relativism) is simply the empirical and at least putatively factual thesis that different peoples (different cultures or civilizations) often have moral standards that differ and sometimes even conflict in a very fundamental way.

Ethical relativism (normative ethical relativism) is the normative claim that what is right or good for one individual or society need not be right or good for another even when the situations involved are similar. The ethical relativist is not simply (or necessarily even at all) making a factual statement about the differences in moral beliefs between people; rather, the ethical relativist is making the moral claim that what is really right or good in the one case need not be so in the other. He or she is making a claim in normative ethics and not a claim, or not simply a claim, about moral behavior or language.

Meta-ethical relativism is the thesis that there are no objectively sound procedures for justifying one moral code or one set of moral judgments. Two moral codes may be equally "sound," and two moral claims may be equally "justified" or "reasonable." There is no way of establishing what is the true moral code or set of moral beliefs.

Conceptual relativism is the thesis that different cultures have different concepts and that indeed some of their concepts are so fundamentally different that people within these different cultures see the world differently in certain crucial respects. Conceptual relativists also claim that there is no neutral or culturally ubiquitous way in which the world can be described against which these different and incommensurable conceptual systems or schemes can be graded or measured. Moreover, there is no right way of seeing the world or viewing the world. It is a conceptual confusion or ethnocentric arrogance or both to assume that one's own society's understanding of things is the correct one. (This is not to say that any other society is in or can be in a better or worse position.) We have no idea what must be so (what must obtain) for us to justifiably assert what it would be like for any given conceptual scheme to be the correct one—that is, that it, and not some other quite different ones would, if we utilized it, tell us what the world is like or how best to live.

There are the related but distinct conceptions of ethical nihilism and ethical skepticism.

Ethical nihilism is the thesis that there is no right and wrong. These conceptions are confused, erroneous ideas without any validity or warrant. 'That is wrong' and 'This is right' are meaningless or always mistaken. Thus, all moral conceptions are either meaningless or in error.

Ethical skepticism is the thesis that no one can ever say with any justification that something is good or bad, right or wrong. Some actions may be right and others may be wrong, but there is no way of knowing which they are.

I shall argue that there is nothing in the canonical core of Marxism that commits Marxists to any of these theses or conceptions. Marxists have no need for them, and if any Marxist wishes to accept any of them, he or she must do so on grounds that are independent of the canonical elements of Marxism. Similarly, and more to my immediate purpose, contextualism is distinct from all of the above six conceptions or any conceptions bearing a family resemblance to them.

Contextualism (as applied to morality) is the thesis that what is required morally varies, almost without exception, in some considerable measure with the context. Contextualism is not the claim that what is right or wrong or good or bad is determined by one's attitudes, commitments, or whatever universalizable prescriptions one will accept; rather, right or wrong, good or bad, is in considerable measure determined by the objective situation in which people find themselves. Thus, contextualism is not relativism in any form for what is right or wrong is not determined by what a person, culture, class, or whatnot believes to be right, how each happens to conceptualize things, or what canons of justification each will accept. Right or wrong instead is determined largely by what needs people have and by the objective situation in which they find themselves.

An illustration might help to distinguish contextualism from relativism. Just as it is rationally necessary for a person living in the Yukon in the winter to have a heavy coat while no such requirements can rationally be made of people living near the Amazon, so it is morally irresponsible for people who do not know each other very well to have sex without using a condom in our society now, while it would not be morally irresponsible in a society with a fail-safe vaccine and an easy and fail-safe cure for AIDS. In both cases, people's needs and something (objectively discernable) in the situation ground both the non-moral evaluation and the moral evaluation.[6] It is not people's attitudes, their being members of a certain culture or class, or having a certain conceptual scheme that determines and indeed justifies their making certain evaluations or having certain moral beliefs. If an Amazonian came to live in the Yukon, it would be reasonable for him or her to get a heavy coat, and if we come to live in an AIDS-protected world, it would not be unreasonable or immoral (under many circumstances) for us to no longer use condoms.

Situations change and, contextualists argue, it is not infrequently the case that our moral beliefs should change with them. However, there is nothing relative about this because something ascertainably objective in the situation, not our thinking or cultural belief-system, justifies the change in belief. I ought to give money to starvation funds for Ethiopia, but if I am starving myself, that is a different matter.

There is a superficial resemblance between contextualism and relativism because what is right or wrong varies in part with the situation. Nevertheless, the rationale is completely different for the contextualist than for the relativist. For the contextualist, a changed objective situation justifies the change; for the relativist, attitudes; the societal, class, or individual belief-system; a cluster of distinctive commitments; or some distinctive conceptual scheme justifies or at least explains the different moral beliefs or evaluative sets. The first is something plainly objective; the second is not.

Contextualists, unlike cultural relativists, do not commit themselves to the claim that there are different moral beliefs that *conflict in a fundamental way,* for contextualists think that differences, where they do not rest on objectively ascertainable confusions, rest on the different situations people encounter and would justifiably converge as their situations converge. This would also be true for what contextualists would say about what some might call mode-of-production relativism (a variant of cultural relativism).

Unlike meta-ethical relativists, who claim there are no objectively sound procedures for justifying one moral code or one set of moral judgments over another, contextualists make no such claim at all. They could very well accept a common procedure for justifying moral claims or moral codes but still claim that the very same procedures will justify moral claims or perhaps even moral codes with somewhat different contents, including even general moral principles, in objectively different situations.[7] Contextualists will not deny that one situation can be better than another; that this could, at least in principle, be ascertained by any reasonable person in either situation; and that a person in the objectively less desirable situation could discern it and reasonably advocate, where the situation could be changed, that the situation ought to be changed so that moral beliefs appropriate for the objectively better situation could become applicable.

This contextualism is a far cry from conceptual relativism, something that should fall before Davidsonian arguments.[8] Conceptual relativism claims that we have different conceptual systems with incommensurable moral beliefs and, indeed, other beliefs that preclude any objective appraisal of the comparative adequacy of different moral codes, different moral belief-systems, or different attitudinal sets. All these forms of relativism, nihilism, and skepticism (cultural relativism aside) tell us in one way or another that objectively there is, morally speaking, no right way of seeing the world. Contextualism firmly rejects this conclusion. There is, contextualists maintain, a right way of seeing the world and acting in it, although what that right way is involves a complex, contextually specific articulation. Specifically, *what* we would justifiably say is right or wrong will typically vary from context to context, although these judgments themselves are not context relative. That is to say, in principle at least, people in quite different contexts and with quite different backgrounds can come to a reflective and informed consensus about what should be said—and typically somewhat different things will and should be said—in these different contexts. But that there are such judgments; that they vary in just these ways; and that these judgments are correct is something about which there can be such a reflective consensus. These judgments have cross-cultural validity.

Does not the belief in moral progress accepted by my contextualism require a belief in *some* very general transcultural and transhistorical moral beliefs? I expect it does and this is where my account of moral truisms comes into play. But this appeal in turn has seemed problematic to some, which occasions the following explanation and argument. To move extensionally before I move intensionally, moral truisms are beliefs—such as the belief that suffering and degradation are bad; that servitude is bad; that an inability to use one's non-destructive powers is bad; that health is good; that pleasure is good; that kindliness is good; that mutual concern and respect are good; that human autonomy is good; that it is a good thing for people to live lives in which their non-destructive needs are met and in which their wants are satisfied when they are neither self-destructive nor harmful to others. These judgments, like all moral judgments, take ceterus paribus clauses, are in certain respects vague and indeterminate, and can sometimes usefully take philosophical clarification. But it would be more reasonable to accept these judgments than to accept any philosophical theory or belief that would reject them or require their rejection. In that way common sense, including common moral sense, is prior to philosophy.

Why do I call these judgments truisms? Because they are commonplaces that only a good dose of philosophy (including some conceptual confusion) or some bizarre religiosity would ever lead one to doubt. It is in this sense that they are truisms, and not in the sense that they are trivial, although it is indeed true that just to assert them out of the blue would be to utter commonplaces and thus to utter trivialities. It would be like uttering—unless some metaphysician were around—

"There is a world out there and it's got trees in it." However, in some bizarre philosophical context where these moral truisms were actually being denied, their utterance would not be trivial; that such beliefs (commonplaces although they be) are, as I assert, actually held is not a trivial matter.

Following Engels I inveigh against eternal moral principles or eternal moral truths. Still, it might be responded, are not my moral truisms just such eternal principles, and does not this make my contextualism pretty ersatz: a contextualism that presupposes eternal moral principles? It does not, and my moral truisms are not just another name for eternal moral principles.

How can I, or can I, coherently and correctly claim that these moral truisms (or at least some of them) are non-ideological and transhistorical moral beliefs and then deny that they are eternal moral truths or principles? Moral truisms apply to all societies. But then aren't they eternal moral principles? No, that does not follow—for moral principles to be eternal they would have to apply to *all possible societies in all possible worlds,* regardless of what human nature and the scheduling of human needs turned out to be. Moral truisms make no such transcendent, universalistic claims but only claim to apply to this world and to human beings as they recognizably are. We do not ask what should be said if human beings had entirely different needs or a radically different scheduling of needs or if humans grew metallic exoskeletons so that they could not be physically harmed in the usual ways.

Moral truisms, which are also trivial in the sense of being non-controversial, differ from eternal principles or eternal moral truths (assuming we know what that means) in not being a priori truths (analytic or synthetic, if such there be) and in not being self-evidently certain moral truths or moral principles. Moral truisms can be denied without asserting or implying anything contradictory, and they cannot in some incorrigible manner just be seen, noted, or adverted to as being unquestionably true. Rather, in good coherentist and fallibilist fashion, they are, as John Rawls might put it, provisional fixed points among our considered judgments—that is, they are the most firmly fixed of our considered judgments. Moral truisms will withstand a close examination of the facts about ourselves and our situation and about alternative feasible possibilities; they are not extinguished by cognitive psychotherapy or by sustained, non-evasive reflection, when we are in a cool hour, adequately informed, and the like. They could, in theory or in principle, wither away, but in fact they do not, and there is no reason to expect they would in any psychologically or sociologically feasible changed circumstances. But, for all of that, à la Immanuel Kant, Henry Sidgwick, or Alan Gewirth, they are not synthetic a priori truths.

My contextualism is not only fallibilistic; it is also coherentist. I, as I have argued in detail elsewhere, use a moral methodology basically similar to that of John Rawls and Norman Daniels where I seek to show that a cluster of moral beliefs or principles is justified if these beliefs can be shown to be in wide reflective equilibrium.[9] This means, crudely expressed, that we have been able to show that we have gotten a cluster of considered moral judgments (including abstract moral principles that are also considered judgments), factual beliefs, background, social, and other relevant empirical theories, and conceptions about the role and import of morality into a consistent and coherent set that squares, after this perspicuous coherentist representation is articulated, with our reflective moral sensibilities and our beliefs about what the world is like and can become.

The 'us' and 'our' are naturally worrisome here. Indeed, this worrisomeness starts with the 'our' of our particular culture (where else, for us, could it *start?*), but, as Charles Taylor pointed out, it is not locked in the ethnocentricism of our culture, for we, where we are, as we often are, in a position to learn about other cultures, learn about their considered convictions and their moral practices.[10] To learn about them in any coherent way we must start from our own considered judgments and our own practices and reflectively compare and contrast considered judgments and accounts about considered judgments. Just as we as individuals, if we are not stuck in our infantile omnipotence, so compare and confront *intra-culturally* our own individually held considered convictions with those of others; alterations sometimes taking place as a result of that dialectic, so we, *inter-culturally,* can make similar comparisons and confrontations. That is to say, we *can* do the same thing and sometimes *do* do the same thing, although often with great difficulty, across cultures. Again, both in the intra-cultural case and the inter-cultural case, it is a matter of repairing the ship at sea. There is (pace David Gauthier) no ahistorical Archimedean point of pure practical rationality, and we can have no a priori guarantees that we will attain consensus in wide reflective equilibrium. Perhaps instead we will have several incompatible or at least distinct equilibria. In that eventuality we would not have achieved a consensus of considered judgments in *wide* reflective equilibrium, and we would not have achieved a moral consensus that can be sustained, or at least confidently or fully sustained, rationally. But there are no a priori roadblocks to again contrasting and comparing the whole wide range of beliefs and commitments had by the people who are at loggerheads to see if we could discover or alternatively forge an agreement of considered judgments in wide reflective equilibrium. This obtains even when we are parties to that disagreement. There is, of course, no guarantee that we will get such agreement, but there is also no guarantee that we will not. To recognize this as inescapably our situation is not skeptical, but fallibilistic.

It is in this manner that we widen the net from an ethnocentric 'we' to an ever wider 'we' that in the ideal case will encompass all humanity. And if this is historicism, then so be it. Such historicism is a long way from relativism, subjectivism, nihilism, or ethnocentricism, although it does involve a rejection of some ahistorical Archimedean point where sub specie aeternitatis we can view the world from nowhere. Perspectivism is inescapable, but without knowing what it would be like to find the absolute, we can attain ever wider perspectives. There is neither an a priori end point or stopping point here, nor need there be to gain objectivity. To have objectivity, we need not go on a quest for certainty.

I need to say something about the principles of distributive justice I articulate perhaps most fully and clearly in the last chapter. I do argue, and contend that Marxists should argue, that such principles, in good contextualist fashion, vary with the changing modes of production. Thus, the principles of justice that are appropriate where capitalism is firmly entrenched and for a considerable time stable are of one sort, while the principles of justice for socialism in similar conditions of appropriate mode-of-production stability are different, and for communism the principles will be still different. The same thing obtains for the other modes of production. However, while ideology makes it difficult for us to see that the foregoing is so, this can in theory at least be recognized by anyone living in a society with any of these modes of production. (The farther these modes of production are from each other, the more difficult it will be to make such comparative judgments. The person living in a primitive hunting and gathering society can hardly be expected to have an idea about capitalism. But even here such comparisons are not in principle ruled out.) So a person living in a capitalist society can come, although admittedly with difficulty, to see that it would be better, when possible, to shift to a socialist society for there would be more human flourishing and autonomy there and a more adequate system of justice. A person could see all those things while continuing to affirm, where that capitalist mode of production is firmly entrenched, that a different set of capitalistically oriented principles of justice is the most adequate system of justice for this society. This, again, is not relativism or subjectivism but contextualism.

It is indeed true that in order to articulate such principles of justice, which are mode-of-production dependent for their appropriateness, and to articulate a related conception of moral progress, I must presuppose the acceptance of some moral truisms, which, while not being eternal moral truths, have a transhistorical acceptability. But this is not at all to gainsay my claim concerning the mode-of-production dependency of the principles of justice I articulate and defend. When I say in a later chapter, "Marxists do not think there is a set of substantive principles we can simply appeal to anywhere and at any time," I am referring to principles of distributive justice and other moral principles of a similar scope and thick substance. I do not refer there to moral truisms, including some commonplaces of justice, such as, 'Give every person her due.' In my contextualism I must appeal to moral truisms *and* changing circumstances, but the reigning principles of justice that result are mode-of-production dependent without being relativistic or subjective principles.

IV

In Chapter 4 I give an interpretive description and elucidation of Marx's arguments about justice, rights, morals, and strategies in class struggles in his *The Critique of the Gotha Programme* (1874). I also give a similar interpretive description and elucidation of Engels's and Lenin's discussion of Marx's *Critique*. I point out the difficulties involved in taking the distributive principles Marx stated there as principles of justice, let alone as *critical* distributive principles of justice, as I would take them to be. These difficulties notwithstanding, I argue, as did Engels and Lenin, that these principles should be taken as principles of justice (if you will, critical principles of justice) applicable, separately and distinctively, to the distinctive social formations of capitalism, socialism, and communism. In Chapters 8 and 9, against Wood's careful arguments to the contrary, I mount a defense, linked with a critique of Wood, for taking these principles as principles of justice. In the final three chapters I return from various angles to that claim. In Chapter 12, I try to provide a strong case for so regarding these principles and, most particularly, for regarding an emendation of Marx's needs principle as a principle of justice for a communist society.

The chapters herein contain, as I have remarked, considerable overlap. They return again and again, from different angles and with different stresses, to the aforementioned themes. They perhaps reflect the obsessional concerns of a philosopher with certain moral problems that are in large measure also conceptual. We know from Ludwig Wittgenstein's obsessions with quite different problems how relentless and demanding this can be. I want to present a perspicuous representation of classical Marxist views about morality that would relieve them of paradox and ambivalence and show, compatible with a belief in the objectivity of morals and without falling into historical idealism, how there is a set of Marxist moral beliefs that can provide a useful *ancillary* critique of capitalism—that is, a critique ancillary to the socio-economic critique of capitalism provided by Marx in *Capital* and elsewhere.

Marx and later Marxists also sought to provide a defense of socialism along with its transition to communism. I seek to show, where these movements are regarded as through and through democratic, that this defense has an ethical side, although surely not an ethical entirety. I go some way toward articulating this ethical side and demonstrating its reasonableness and thus toward making a strong moral case, given the truth or approximate truth of certain empirical claims, for socialism and eventually for communism. If Marx's descriptive-interpretive-ex-planatory account, a thoroughly empirical and at least putatively scientific account of the social world, is near to the mark, then we have, I argue, good reasons for accepting socialism and communism. I try to show how Marx's empirical account does not yield moral nihilism, subjec-tivism, indifference to morality, or any form of relativism. I also try to show how we can be good contextualist, fallibilist, moral objectivists without ceasing to be consistent Marxists. More than that, if Marx's empirical account of the world is approximately correct, then his view of how things are and plausibly can become, together with Marxist conceptions of morality, including conceptions of justice, autonomy, and equality, presents us with an account of human emancipation that is both humanly attractive and reasonable.

I want now, in bringing this section to a close, to place the chapters that follow in this overall scheme of things. Chapter 2 starts by posing a series of questions for Marxism and morality. The chapter shows how historical materialism and ideology pose acute problems for morality, how a series of Marxists writing during the first quarter of the twentieth century responded to these issues, and how I would respond (at least preliminarily). Chapters 3 and 4 take a historical turn but a turn that is essential for the subsequent discussion and argument. Chapter 3 gives a sympathetic interpretive account of Engels's views of morality as derived principally from his *Anti-Dühring*. The importance of such an account proceeds from the fact that Engels wrote more extensively and more systematically on morals than did Marx or any of the classical Marxists, and Engels's views are the closest we get to an extended treatment of morality by one of the founders of Marxism. This is followed in Chapter 4 by a similar account of Marx's own views about rights, justice, and equality from *The Critique of the Gotha Programme,* the last extended piece he wrote and the most closely knit writing from Marx on these topics. The discussion of Marx is rounded out in this chapter with an account of Engels's and Lenin's remarks about *The Critique of the Gotha Programme* and with a preliminary general discussion of this topic. These chapters set the stage for and provide an essential background to what is to follow.

Chapter 5 is a discussion of different conceptions of ideology and culminates in an articulation and defense of a distinctive Marxist account of ideology. Chapter 6, perhaps the most central chapter, adapts this conception of ideology to the discussion of morality. In doing so, the chapter shows how Marx and, more generally, Marxists did not even obliquely gesture at some normative ethical theory or meta-ethical theory with some epistemology or ontology of morals; rather, when Marx spoke of morality being ideology or ideological he was tendering a sociology of morals that sought to depict the function of moralities in class societies and to criticize those moralities for the way they distort our understanding of ourselves and our world and the way in which they further ruling class hegemony. I show how this can and should be done without undermining the reasonableness of taking the moral point of view. Chapter 7 extends that general claim with particular reference to historical materialism and the widespread belief that its acceptance commits one to some form of relativism or immoralism.

Chapters 8, 9, and 10 together provide the core of my elucidation and appraisal of Marxist immoralism. I try to give Marxist immoralism, which is a powerful, if somewhat paradoxical view, a run for its money, for it is in many respects a persuasive view. It is a view that takes Marx and consistent Marxists to be critics of morality who have rejected the hegemony of the moral point of view and have utterly dismissed the very possibility of or need for a critical morality. In Chapter 7 I examine the influential claims of Robert C. Tucker and Allen Wood that this can be established as a Marxological point. I argue that although the issue is much more complicated than it usually is thought to be, Tucker and Wood have not been able to defeat Marxist moralist alternatives and that the Marxist moralist alternatives in themselves and as Marxological positions are the more plausible. (Marxist moralist alternatives and Marxological positions could, of course, be one without being the other.) Chapters 9 and 10 turn to an examination of a battery of powerful arguments, made somewhat differently but with a significant overlap by Richard Miller and Allen Wood, to the effect that, Marxological arguments aside, a consistent Marxist will be a Marxist immoralist— that is, whatever Marx's own views about morality may have been, this is what a consistent Marxist should think. I am particularly concerned in Chapter 9 with Miller's arguments that a consistent Marxist, accepting historical materialism and realizing the depth and pervasiveness of class conflict, will reject a commitment to general norms, to an impartial assessment of the moral point of view, and to human equality. I argue against Miller and Wood that both Marx and Engels were egalitarians; that Marxists should be as well; and that for Marxists, adopting a moral point of view can be consistent with accepting historical materialism and the centrality of class and class struggle. They have no need to make such hard choices here. In Chapter 10 I examine and critique Wood's further, distinctive, and in a way compelling arguments about class and justice. This cluster of considerations, culminating around the class interests thesis and the class interests argument, I regard as the high point of Marxist immoralist philosophical argumentation. I try to bring out their full force and still show how a Marxist moralism can account for everything sound in them while defending the adoption of a moral point of view and arguing for principles of justice that are compatible with Marxism. The chapter ends with a volte face in which I contend that G. A. Cohen's arguments for a rights-based Marxist moralism have serious defects and do not face the depth of the challenge of Marxist immoralism.

In Chapters 11 and 12, returning to the central themes of Chapters 6 and 7, I seek to develop and refine my own case for Marxist moralism.

Building on some arguments of G. A. Cohen, Steven Lukes, and Jon Elster, and utilizing some of the Hegelian roots of Marx's views on morality in the service (pace Wood) of Marxist moralism, I seek to show in Chapter 11 the central importance of Hegel's criticism of morality viewed simply as *Moralität* and how essential it is, in understanding morality, to understand morality as well and very essentially as *Sittlichkeit*. I then show how this distinction is vital for understanding the moral point of view; what a Marxist rational reconstruction of the Hegelian conception of *Sittlichkeit* would look like; and how it is supportive of Marxist moralism.

Finally, in Chapter 12, building on distinctions drawn and elucidated in Chapter 11 and Chapter 6, I articulate a context-sensitive, mode-of-production-sensitive, hierarchical conception of justice that specifies what moral progress comes to and what principles of justice are appropriate to different modes of production and to different perspectives within those modes of production. This conception also shows how, where we move from capitalism to socialism to communism, we can get progressively more adequate conceptions of justice that can only have an actual exemplification (have a social existence as functioning normative principles) within these distinctive modes of production. Here we have a conception of moral progress and moral objectivity together with an empirical sociological account of how such ideals are to be achieved.

V

Marxism and the Moral Point of View, as I initially remarked, attempts to say what a Marxist working within the parameters of the canonical conceptions of Marxism should say about morality. In this book, for the purposes of my distinctive concerns here, I take for the most part the canonical core of Marxist conceptions as given. Thus, I ask, what should we say about ethics if the descriptive-explanatory-interpretive claims of Marxism are approximately true? But it is at least equally important to ask which ones, if any, of these Marxist canonical claims are true or approximately true or could be made so by an appropriate, textually responsible rational reconstruction. We should also ask if that system, our best efforts at rational reconstruction to the contrary notwithstanding, really is in ruins, as John Gray was one of the latest to think. If that is so, then what should be said about ethics and about ethics and socialism? (We should not forget that it is possible to be a socialist without being a Marxist.[11]) Does it make much sense to speak of a purely ethical socialism, an ethical Marxism, or of Marxism as moral vision without a sociological and economic underpinning?[12] I do not attempt the formidable task of answering such questions in this book. My intention, rather, is to determine if we can make plausible moral and political sense out of Marxism. How much truth there is in

Marxism is a task I want on some later occasion to turn to, and it is a task to which some analytical Marxists, most notably Jon Elster, have already turned.[13] I want, in bringing this initial chapter to an end, to say something terribly provisional about that.

As was brilliantly exemplified in G. A. Cohen's *Karl Marx's Theory of History: A Defense* (1978), analytical Marxists initially attempted to use analytical philosophy to defend central Marxist positions. In Cohen's case this came to a fairly orthodox articulation and defense of historical materialism, although the techniques of this elucidation were those of analytic philosophy (principally, ordinary language philosophy). Social theorists interested in the issue expected that analytically derived, rational reconstruction would result in a certain amount of revision, but they also expected, or at least hoped, that the revisions would not be too deep. Nevertheless, the discussion among analytical Marxists and others since Cohen's book was published indicates that "clarification has revealed vulnerabilities—prompting development, revision, and in some cases abandonment of traditional Marxian claims. Over the past decades it has become clear that relatively little that Marx wrote can be accepted as is."[14] But this should hardly be surprising to anyone, Marxist or non-Marxist. Marx was, after all, a nineteenth century figure. For him to have escaped that fate would have required him to be different than any other human being in history. The interesting question is whether or not there is enough left intact of a rationally reconstructed, developed, critically pared down core of Marxism to supply a sound body of theory to guide revolutionary socialist practice.

In this context, Jon Elster's *Making Sense of Marx* (1985) was important. It was a massive blockbuster of a book that many (including G. A. Cohen and Andrew Levine) took to be exemplary for the latest development of analytical Marxism. Coming eight years after Cohen's book, *Making Sense of Marx* stood in marked contrast to it. Cohen's book, as I have remarked, was an elucidation and defense of a crucial part of the canonical core of Marxism. Elster's book was encyclopedic in scope and ranged over the whole canonical core of Marx and more. But Elster's text was hardly meant as a defense. If only a reasonable portion of Elster's criticisms are sound, they still visit considerable devastation on orthodox Marxism. And if he is more extensively right, there is almost nothing left of the canonical core even in a developed, rationally reconstructed form. Moreover, Elster was as ironic and dismissive as either Karl Popper or Leszek Kolakowski were about the very possibility of scientific socialism.[15]

However, Elster, as Levine remarked, "remains radical and sympathetic to the marxian project."[16] Be that as it may, what, given Elster's accounting, is left of the Marxian project that could show socialism to be superior to capitalism? It is, Elster claimed, socialism's conception of distributive justice, its commitment to economic democracy, and its capacity for affording greater opportunities than capitalism for self-realization in work.[17] But this does not appeal to the canonical core conceptions of Marxism and relies on what orthodox Marxists (including Marx and Engels) have called utopian ethical socialism, which is unsupported by what they took to be a scientific theory of society that included a scientific account of the workings of capitalism.[18] Perhaps belief in such a science of society, on any plausible reading of 'science,' is just a scientistic myth that deserves the derision Elster directed at it. Perhaps, in our time, knowing what we know, we can only base socialism on such moralistic conceptions and on the resultant organizational conceptions (for example, a commitment to industrial democracy) based on them. This, of course, is significant, but a return to such an ethical socialism is a return to utopian socialism, which puts very great weight on its moral vision and abandons the classical Marxist hope that we could develop a science of society that could enable us to understand how societies work; how they may be changed; and what forms of social organization we could attain with changed forms of economic organization. Moreover, this would enable us to understand what forms of economic organization in a given epoch were feasible and were the most emancipating. We want to understand, if we can, who we are, were, and might become. Orthodox Marxism held out a hope in this regard. Elster simply derided the whole idea of scientific socialism. There is, he believed, nothing like this to be had. To think otherwise is just a bit of what he called Marxist fundamentalism, which, like the other fundamentalisms, should be left to the religiose.

Indeed Marxist fundamentalism is as pitiful as orthodox Thomism. Neither honors Karl Marx nor Thomas Aquinas. But there is a plain point, including a moral point, in trying to gain, if we can, a science (in some recognizable sense of the word) of society and a systematic critical theory of society.[19] Marxism (and Marx), where it is not fundamentalism and thus a pseudo-science, offers us what appears at least to be something of a start on which we might hopefully build. Is it as much a system in ruins as Elster seemed at least to think, and is this the verdict of analytical Marxism or analytical philosophy or analytical philosophy aligned with the most advanced techniques of contemporary social science?

Elster's work, among others, forces us to ask whether, and if so in what sense, it is still possible to be a Marxist in the late twentieth century. How much, if anything, is left of the canonical core? Can a knowledgeable economic theorist accept the labor theory of value as a central element in the science of economics? Can a philosopher who knows anything at all say with a straight face that the only proper logic is dialectical? Do we even understand what this means? Are we justified in believing that historical materialism is the correct theory of epochal social change? Is there a proletariat that through class struggle will achieve its own self-emancipation and usher in a classless

society? Is socialist revolution a live option in the advanced capitalist
countries? If not, can socialism be exported over time from the Third
World periphery to the industrial center? Is there a coherent and correct
Marxist theory of the state or of democracy? Is the falling rate of profit
working out in the way Marx predicted? Is there any good probability,
let alone an inevitability, that in anything like the foreseeable future
capitalism, with or without revolutionary activity, will collapse and
that its post-capitalist replacement will be socialism? Elster looked
hard at these questions and answered them in a way that undermined
Marxist orthodoxy. On his account there is next to nothing of the
canonical core left. What is left is a rationally reconstructed form of
Marx's critique of exploitation and alienation and what Elster took to
be Marx's related moral vision of a better society where all human
beings could do what only human beings can do—namely, create,
invent, and imagine other worlds.

Was Elster justified in believing that analytical philosophy, together
with an exacting, up-to-date social science, has wreaked havoc on
Marxism? It is hard yet to say; whether there is as little that can be
rationally reconstructed and developed as Elster believed is unclear.
I believe that Allen Wood, in discussing Elster, was justified in claiming
that "the commonest fault" of *Making Sense of Marx* "is that it is
occasionally unsympathetic to Marx, to the point of distorting his views
in the way that professionally anti-Marxist writers have customarily
done."[20] What we need instead from analytical Marxism, in trying to
sort out what, if anything, is sound in Marx or alive in Marxism, is to
give Marx and Marxists the most maximally sympathetic reading compatible with responsibility to the text. That done, at least in an initial
way, analytical Marxists should then critically inspect those sets or
clusters of theories and claims and, where they are found wanting,
seek first to make still another rational reconstruction of the wanting
part and then determine if this articulation of Marxism escapes these
difficulties. Analytical Marxists then, in turn, should subject that refined
account to renewed, distinctly varied, critical inspection. This process
should be repeated until a rationally reconstructed version will stand
or until it becomes apparent that there is no such account in the
offing. (Note here we have combined theory construction with critique.
Marx, before Karl Popper, stressed the imperative necessity of engaging
in relentless criticism.)

When this has been done, what is left, which is viewed now as a
whole, should be compared to other social theories of similar scope
(say Weberian theories) that have been similarly treated. If the rationally
reconstructed Marxist theory, although deeply scarred, comes off better
than its relevant alternatives, then there is some reason to stick with
it as, for the nonce, the best game in town. If the reconstructed theory
is too deeply scarred, the reasonable response might instead be a
thorough skepticism about all grand theories.[21] Unfortunately, Elster's

Making Sense of Marx did not do these things, but this is exactly the sorting out we need from analytical Marxism. Elster had, as Wood noted, a penchant for taking too short a way with dissenters.

We need, I believe, a double skepticism here. Elster and most analytical Marxists only had half of it. They were rightly skeptical about classical Marxism with its deeply embedded Hegelian methodology and mode of expression. Analytical Marxists also were rightly skeptical of Continental readings of and buildings upon Marx, including Althusserian and Habermasian constructions. But these same analysts also tended to accept rather uncritically a certain orthodoxy in analytical philosophy (as Alan Ryan commented wryly, an analytical philosophy practiced thirty years ago) and what they took, rather selectively, to be the cutting edge of social science.[22] Elster's attitude was paradigmatic of this incomplete skepticism. Good social scientists, he told us, must be methodological individualists. Likewise, he held that functional explanations without micro-foundations of a methodologically individualist sort are useless; game theory is a very useful social science tool; and rational preference theory and rational choice Marxism are the tools for a social theorist who wishes to avoid obscurantism.[23] These are the reigning assumptions of his uncritically held methodological commitments. An analytically sophisticated Marxism, Elster believed, as did John Roemer, needs to use the tools of contemporary logic (including modal logic), mathematics, and sophisticated model building. Using these tools and then moving to far higher levels of abstraction than those with which historically centered and politically centered Marxists are wont to operate, we are to search for the foundations, indeed the micro-foundations, that underlie Marxian judgments. This may well be the way to go, but it is far more problematical than Elster or Roemer led us to believe.

Other analytical Marxists have made careful challenges to these methodological individualist claims by contending that they require an unrealistic and unachievable reductionism.[24] This stance has a more general theoretical backing in the anti-reductionism of such leading philosophers working out of the analytical tradition as Hilary Putnam, Donald Davidson, and Richard Rorty. Similar skepticism about the tools and the dominant social science methods is deep in the social sciences themselves and in the writings of some philosophers commenting on the social sciences, for example, Charles Taylor and Alastair MacIntyre.[25] And from within analytic philosophy itself (think here of Ludwig Wittgenstein, Gilbert Ryle, and John Austin) there is deep skepticism about such Elsterian confidence in theory, and with this there is a stress on the need to translate, where abstract claims are being made, into the concrete. What, in fine, is very problematic Elster took as given and used uncritically as a yardstick to criticize Marx and Marxism.[26] What we need is more skepticism all around. We need, by repeatedly translating abstract claims into the concrete and working with live examples from the social terrain, to compare and contrast Marxian and non-Marxian accounts; to cultivate a sensitivity to the depth of ideological penetration on all sides that prompts us unwittingly to cook the books; to seek out a more adequate science of society. In doing this, whether our turn is Marxist or non-Marxist, the methodology we use should be just good scientific methodology, but while not backing off at all from this, we need to recognize in the human sciences how deeply contested that very conception is. We cannot use the tools utilized by Elster and Roemer in such an unself-conscious and uncritical manner. We need, that is, a double skepticism—namely, to share their skepticism as well to be skeptical about those aspects of analytical philosophy and the dominant types of social science about which Elster and Roemer were not skeptical.

Analytical Marxism does not have to have such high flown theoretical commitments and such confidence in the power of new analytical tools. (It could use some Rortyish skepticism here.[27]) I see myself as an analytical Marxist and, as can be seen from this book, I do not employ such fancy analytical tools; neither in fact did such important analytical Marxists as G. A. Cohen, William Shaw, Andrew Levine, or Richard Miller. We, more in the tradition of Ryle, Austin, and Wittgenstein, work with theoretically unramified tools; we remain confident of the reliability of plain speech and plain statement and of our capacity to draw important distinctions, clarify important ambiguities, and detect conceptual confusions that are often doing ideological work. Our task is also to detect and puncture philosophical pomposities, which often are of a thoroughly confused sort. (Contrast here the way Cohen and Levine worked with the way Louis Althusser or Roy Bhashar worked.) Operating with a relatively low level of theory, we aim to clarify ambiguities, to set out Marx, Marxist, or Marxian claims and arguments in a clear and perspicuous manner and to inspect their soundness. In doing this we should be very wary indeed of high theory, whether it is Althusserian or game theoretic. (G. A. Cohen's discussion of ideology and ordinary language is a model example in microcosm of what I have in mind.[28])

I do not want to rule out, particularly in an a priori way, the use in such critical and clarificatory contexts of the kind of theoretical tools utilized by Elster and Roemer. That would indeed be stupidly Luddite. Perhaps game theory is a good tool for Marxian analysis, and rational preference theory may be a good thing, but Austin-like or Moore-like skepticism is in order, which stresses that we use these tools with extreme caution and that we remain as skeptical of such shiny new tools as we are of structuralism. By now we should have lost our innocence concerning the prospect of some new methodological tools taking us to the promised land. We are not going to get such a fix.

A less theoretically ramified analytical Marxism seems to me plainly a good thing, particularly in the face of Continental obscurities and the obscurities endemic to the Hegelian heritage of classical Marxism. (I do not mean for a moment by that that all is dross in Hegel.) Working from this, if you will, 'Moorean Marxism' we once again need to inspect the Marxian corpus, particularly the canonical parts of Marxist theory, to see what, if anything, can stand the heat in the kitchen. I am confident that anti-Marxist writers, such as Sidney Hook, Karl Popper, and Leszek Kolakowski, will think that this is like reinventing the wheel. But, as Elster and the rest of the analytical Marxists have realized and stressed, there are challenging and telling components in the Marxian project that cry out for analyses and development, and, as Allen Wood put it, "Capitalist oppression is just as real today as it was a century ago."[29] Its forms have changed and the alternatives are more problematic. But we need just as much as we ever did an emancipatory science of society, if we can get one, that will guide our political practice. Marx's account has played, for good or for ill, a key role here and, practically speaking, continues to play that role. We need a perspicuous representation of Marx's theory or Marxist theory to help determine how much, if any, of it we can utilize in trying to articulate a theory of an emancipatory practice. A modest analytical Marxism is, I believe, vital here, at least at the stage in which we now find ourselves. Perhaps, instead, we should go in a more Habermasian direction or, if we are more deeply suspicious of theory, we should go in an antinomian Foucaultian direction. But it seems to me solid common sense, for anyone socialistically inclined, to first see if we can carefully sort out what is alive and dead in Marxist theory and practice. Here a modest analytical Marxism is essential, at least as a starting point.

Notes

1. Alan Gilbert defended a Marxian moral realism in the following three articles: Alan Gilbert, "Marx's Moral Realism: Eudaimonism and Moral Progress," in Terence Ball and James Farr (eds.), *After Marx* (Cambridge: Cambridge University Press, 1984), pp. 154–183; "Historical Theory and the Structure of Moral Argument in Marx," *Political Theory* 9 (1981):173–205; and "An Ambiguity in Marx's and Engels's Account of Justice and Equality," *The American Political Science Review* 76 (1982):126–146. I contrast that view with Richard Miller's Marxist immoralism and criticize it in my "The Rejection Front and the Affirmation Front: Marx and Moral Reality," *Journal of Indian Council of Philosophical Research* 4, 1 (Autumn 1986):123–138. I am centrally concerned there to show that Marxists need take no position at all about moral realism in order to make sense of moral claims or to sensibly believe that some of them could be objectively justified.

2. This may sound like a commitment to a teleological scheme of things that for the reasons Jon Elster (among others) brought out is, to understate it, suspect. See Jon Elster, *Making Sense of Marx* (Cambridge: Cambridge University Press, 1985), pp. 7–8, 107–118; and Jon Elster, *An Introduction to Marx* (Cambridge: Cambridge University Press, 1986), pp. 139, 157, 180. For

me it is a hyperbolic and metaphorical way of speaking; no grand teleological unfolding of things is intended. For a similar conception to my own on such matters see Andrews Levine, Elliott Sober, and Erik Olin Wright, "Marxism and Methodological Individualism," *New Left Review* 162 (March/April 1987):67–84.

3. John McMurty argued clearly for that in his *The Structure of Marx's World-View* (Princeton, N.J.: Princeton University Press, 1978), pp. 123–156.

4. Joe McCarney, *The Real World of Ideology* (Brighton, England: Harvester Press, 1980); and his "Recent Interpretations of Ideology," *Economy and Society* 14, 1 (1985):77–93.

5. G. A. Cohen, "Are Disadvantaged Workers Who Take Hazardous Jobs Forced to Take Hazardous Jobs?" in Gertrude Ezorsky (ed.), *Moral Rights in the Workplace* (Albany: State University of New York Press, 1987), p. 60.

6. On the relevance of needs to morality see David Braybrooke, *Meeting Needs* (Princeton, N.J.: Princeton University Press, 1987).

7. Kai Nielsen, "Searching for an Emancipatory Perspective: Wide Reflective Equilibrium and the Hermeneutical Circle," in Evan Simpson (ed.), *Anti-Foundationalism and Practical Reasoning* (Edmonton, Alberta: Academic Printing and Publishing, 1987), pp. 143–164; Kai Nielsen, *Equality and Liberty: A Defense of Radical Egalitarianism* (Totowa, N.J.: Rowman and Allenhend, 1985), Chapter 2; Kai Nielsen, "On Needing a Moral Theory: Rationality, Considered Judgements and the Grounding of Morality," *Metaphilosophy* 13, no. 12 (1982):97–116; and Kai Nielsen, "Considered Judgements Again," *Human Studies* 6 (1982):109–118.

8. Donald Davidson, "On the Very Idea of a Conceptual Scheme," in his *Inquiries into Truth and Interpretation* (Oxford: Oxford University Press, 1984), pp. 183–198.

9. See references in footnote 7.

10. Charles Taylor, "Understanding and Ethnocentricity," in his *Philosophy and the Human Sciences: Philosophical Papers,* vol. 2 (Cambridge: Cambridge University Press, 1985), pp. 116–133.

11. Michael Walzer, "What's Left of Marx?" *New York Review of Books* 32, no. 18 (November 21, 1985):46.

12. Many of the old arguments about revisionism are relevant here. Edward Bernstein, in effect collapsing socialism into something that is indistinguishable from welfare state capitalism (capitalism, Swedish style, with a human face), came close, in spite of his dislike of utopian socialism, to taking socialism to be essentially a set of ethical ideals. Sometimes Elster sounded, in this respect, very much like a latter-day Bernstein. Karl Kautsky, Rosa Luxemburg, and V. I. Lenin, their other differences notwithstanding, with their stress on the need for scientific socialism, argued that in addition to a moral vision there must be the underpinning of a sound systematic and empirically corroborated social theory with a linked conception of praxis. It is, of course, easy to make sport, as Elster did, of scientific socialism, and there have indeed been silly claims made on its behalf. For a sensible and plausible conceptualization of it see Andrew Collier, "Scientific Socialism and the Question of Socialist Values," in Kai Nielsen and Steven Patten (eds.), *Marx and Morality* (Guelph, Ontario: Canadian Association for Publishing in Philosophy, 1981), pp. 121–154. See, as well, my "Coming to Grips with Marxist Anti-Moralism," *The Philosophical Forum* 19, no. 1 (Fall 1987):1–22.

13. See the references in footnote 2, and see G. A. Cohen, *Karl Marx's Theory of History: A Defence* (Oxford: Clarendon Press, 1978); Allen Wood,

Karl Marx (London: Routledge & Kegan Paul, 1981); Richard Miller, *Analyzing Marx* (Princeton, N.J.: Princeton University Press, 1984); John F. Roemer, *Analytical Foundations of Marxian Economic Theory* (Cambridge: Cambridge University Press, 1981); John Roemer, *General Theory of Exploitation and Class* (Cambridge: Cambridge University Press, 1982); John Roemer (ed.), *Analytical Marxism* (Cambridge: Cambridge University Press, 1986).

14. Andrew Levine, "Review of *Making Sense of Marx*," *The Journal of Philosophy* 83, no. 12 (December 1986):728.

15. Note particularly Elster's responses to what he regarded as his Marxist fundamentalist critics in Jon Elster, "Reply to Comments," *Inquiry* 29, no. 1 (March 1986):69–71. See also his discussion of Kolakowski in "Clearing the Decks," *Ethics* 9, no. 4 (July 1981):634–644.

16. Levine, "Review of *Making Sense of Marx*," p. 728.

17. Elster, "Reply to Comments," p. 76. See also his "Clearing the Decks."

18. See references in footnote 9.

19. Kai Nielsen, "Emancipatory Social Science and Social Critique," in Daniel Callahan and Bruce Jennings (eds.), *Ethics, the Social Sciences and Policy Analysis* (New York: Plenum Press, 1983), pp. 113–157; Kai Nielsen, "Can There Be Progress in Philosophy?" *Metaphilosophy* 18, no. 1 (January 1987):1–30; Kai Nielsen, "Scientism, Pragmatism and the Fate of Philosphy," *Inquiry* 29, no. 3 (September 1986):277–304; Kai Nielsen, "Philosophy as Critical Theory," *Proceedings and Addresses of the American Philosophical Association* 61 (September 1987):89–108.

20. Allen Wood, "Historical Materialism and Functional Explanation," *Inquiry* 29, no. 1 (March 1986):12.

21. Frederick Crews, *Skeptical Engagements* (New York: Oxford University Press, 1986), pp. 159–178.

22. Alan Ryan, "Can Marxism Be Rescued?" *London Review of Books* 17 (September 1987):10.

23. See Elster, *Making Sense of Marx*, particularly Chapter 1.

24. Levine, Sober, and Wright, "Marxism and Methodological Individualism"; and Miller, *Analyzing Marx*, pp. 271–313.

25. Charles Taylor, *Philosophy and the Human Sciences* (London: Cambridge University Press, 1985); and Alasdair MacIntyre, *After Virtue* (Notre Dame, Ind.: University of Notre Dame Press, 1981), Chapters 7 and 8.

26. Sean Sayers, "Jon Elster's New Clothes," *Radical Philosophy* 46 (Summer 1987):40–41.

27. See Richard Rorty, "Philosophy in America," in his *The Consequences of Pragmatism* (Minneapolis: University of Minnesota Press, 1982), pp. 211–230.

28. Cohen, "Are Disadvantaged Workers Who Take Hazardous Jobs Forced to Take Hazardous Jobs?" pp. 60–64.

29. Wood, "Historical Materialism and Functional Explanation," p. 11.

2

Marxism, Morality
and Moral Philosophy

I

Neither Karl Marx nor Frederick Engels tried to construct a moral
theory resembling the type we find in classical moral theories such
as those of Plato, Aristotle, Kant, Bentham, J. S. Mill or Sidgwick.
Indeed they made no attempt to construct a moral theory at all.[1] Marx
and Engels do indeed make scattered remarks about morality but they
do not try to construct a moral theory or, like Nietzsche, to forge a
'new morality' or even write anti-foundationalist treatises on moral
philosophy after the fashion of Hume, Westermarck or Dewey. In this
they have been followed by the great Marxist theoreticians who constitute
the core of the classical Marxist tradition. (I refer here to Luxemburg,
Lenin, Trotsky, Gramsci and Lukács.) The closest thing we get to
anything like the articulation of a moral theory among the classical
Marxists is in Leon Trotsky's pamphlet *Their Morals and Ours,* and
even there Trotsky's work is in part very much a tract for the times
in which he defends himself against a variety of charges including
that of 'Bolshevik amoralism,' though in the course of doing so he
articulates a series of theoretical claims of no small significance.[2] Indeed
even *Their Morals and Ours,* interesting as it is, is hardly an exception.

This essay was originally published in Joseph P. DeMarco and Richard M. Fox, eds.,
New Directions in Ethics: The Challenge of Applied Ethics (New York: Routledge &
Kegan Paul, 1986), pp. 92–112. Reprinted by permission.

It is not one of Trotsky's major works; it was written near the end of his life when he was isolated and politically rather impotent and it is very taken up with the polemics of the time. However, Marx and Engels, and Lenin as well, did in passing make moral comments and they had a coherent conception of the place of morals in the structure of life that is both threatening and deeply challenging to our common conceptions of morality and the variety of views held by most moral philosophers and theologians.[3]

Other less central figures, though by no means insignificant, have in diverse ways taken up the conceptions of the Founding Fathers and have developed, challenged, modified and rejected their views in various ways. It is not part of my task here to tell this history, though I will where it is germane give some fragments of it. What I shall try to do instead is to show how Marxism poses a challenge for morality, how in turn morality poses problems for Marxism, and how a variety of contemporary Marxists have responded to these problems. In doing this I shall also argue my own Marxist response to these challenges. I shall examine considerations that naturally arise when we both think carefully about the human prospect and take Marxism seriously. I shall also try to show that a Marxist is not committed to nihilism or to the belief that all moral reflection, including his own, can be nothing but ideological twaddle.[4]

II

We will start by asking the following cluster of questions, questions we will consider in various sections of this essay. Does Marxism require a moral theory and if so what sort? Can it coherently do so? Indeed, should it do so? Some Marxists have said that morality is a form of ideology and that, since any given morality arises out of a particular stage of the development of the productive forces and relations and thus (or so not a few Marxists have said) is relative to a particular mode of production and to particular class interests, there can be no objective system of moral beliefs.[5] Yet, Marx and Marxists roundly condemn capitalism. They see it as an inhuman, though historically necessary, exploitative system that must, and indeed will, be replaced by a truly human communist society which they plainly judge to be a better society than capitalist society or any of the other previous social formations. How can these two sets of beliefs go together or, if they can't, which should give way and why? We need also to ask in this context: what is ideology and is morality unavoidably ideological? Moreover, is the issue as to whether morality is ideological an epistemological thesis or some other kind of thesis? If historical materialism is true does morality, any morality at all, totter? I shall try to make some headway with these and related questions.

In addition to the social scientific theory of Marxism and to the social critique that is integral to Marxism, there has again and again in the history of Marxism been the demand for a systematic and coherent articulation of what has been called 'the moral foundations of Marxism.' This, for those dissident Marxists who take that route, has involved the claim that a Marxist moral theory be constructed. To this more mainstream Marxists have responded with a denial that anything like this is either possible or, even if it were possible, necessary.

Given such a controversy, we should ask whether there should be or even could be a Marxist ethical theory and if so what sort of an ethical theory should it be? Marxism does indeed proffer a sociology of morals and a theory of ideology but this is a very different thing from proffering an ethical theory or a foundational claim for morals. In trying to think through what is involved here, it is vital to ascertain the bearing of the theory of ideology and the sociology of morals on the question of the possibility of a moral theory or of moral knowledge. Marx certainly thought that his own social theory raised fundamental doubts about traditional moral thinking. Does Marx's anti-moralism commit him to some form of relativism in ethics or to some form of moral skepticism or nihilism that would deny the very possibility of objective moral evaluations?

These issues are under renewed discussion today particularly by social theorists and philosophers who hold progressive views and yet, at the same time, perhaps through the reading of Marx or Freud, have come to be very wary of moralistic approaches to social criticism.[6] They want to know whether Marx and Engels did in fact base their critique of capitalism on moral considerations or whether they sub-scribed explicitly or implicitly to any moral views or any moral theory. They also want to know to what extent, if at all, a Marxist social theory and Marxist criticisms of capitalism, no matter what Marx may have thought about the matter, require a moral critique of capitalism or even a distinctively Marxist morality?[7] Rather than requiring it, they may not even be compatible with it. It is most fundamentally this issue that we need to sort out.

III

Issues very similar to this came under intense discussion in the first quarter of the twentieth century. The *dramatis personae* here are some of the relatively major figures in the attempt to further develop or revise Marxism after Marx. Edward Bernstein, Karl Vorlander, Karl Kautsky, Georg Plekhanov, Max Adler, Otto Bauer, and Georg Lukács count centrally among their number. There, more than in contemporary discussions, the long shadow of Kant fell and the problem about the relation of fact to value—the possibility or impossibility of deriving an ought from an is—took center stage. Marx, squarely in that respect in the Hegelian tradition, tried to set that question aside and firmly rejected a fact/value dualism.[8] Edward Bernstein and Karl Vorlander tried to meld their versions of Marxism with a Kantian conception of science which, if it were to be genuine science, must be normatively neutral.[9] They took very seriously indeed Henri Poincaré's famous dictum that from premises in the indicative mood we could never draw a conclusion in the imperative mood. Although Vorlander's position was the most extreme, it is a position towards which many people who have had some philosophical training and who have become sympathetic with Marx's social criticism would, at least initially, quite naturally gravitate. Vorlander argued that socialism cannot be based on an objective normatively neutral social science or simply on political practice but must be grounded in a distinctive set of socialist values and a Marxist moral theory.

This 'ethical socialism,' seconded by Edward Bernstein, was very influential with the revisionist and reformist wing of the Second International. It was opposed by what was widely taken at the time to be the 'Orthodox Marxism' of Karl Kautsky and Georg Plekhanov.[10] Surprisingly, in the light of Marx's own Hegelianism here, both Kautsky and Plekhanov accepted the Kantian fact/value distinction. But in opposition to Vorlander and Bernstein, and here closer to Marx himself, they refused to ground socialism in either moral philosophy or morality. It was sufficient for Marxist social theory to reveal the economic law of development of modern society. This is the central task of social theory and it must not, as Kautsky argued in his *Ethics and Materialist Conception of History,* if it is to remain a genuinely scientific theory, speak, as Vorlander did, of the moral point of view in *Capital.*

Both Kautsky and Plekhanov concluded that empirical trends in the world confirmed Marx's theory of history. The historical development of capitalist societies was inexorably toward socialism. But this fact (putative fact), in itself, or in relation with any other set of facts, did not enable us to conclude that we had an obligation to struggle to attain socialism or even to approve of this development. Kautsky and Plekhanov see Marx as a social scientist who tells us who we were, who we are now and what it is likely we will become. He also, and in a powerful way, condemned capitalism for the inhuman system it is, but this, Kautsky and Plekhanov claim, is not a part of Marx's scientific theory. Strictly and accurately understood it says nothing about whether the development from capitalism to socialism to communism is good or bad.

The next stage in the development of this argument came from two Austro-Marxists, Max Adler and Otto Bauer.[11] They, like the other parties to the dispute, continued to accept a Kantian conception of the autonomy of morals. They saw themselves, however, as mediators in this dispute. They sided with the 'Orthodox Marxists' in rejecting any attempt to find a moral basis for socialism. In taking this position they realized—and indeed stressed—that what brings most socialist militants to socialism in the first place and often what nourishes them and helps them remain in the struggle is a conviction about the badness (to put it mildly) of capitalism and the conviction that socialism offers humankind a better future. With the possibility of socialism there is hope in the world; without it there isn't. The choice between socialism and capitalism or a technocratic replacement of capitalism is often seen as the choice between barbarianism and a possibly decent future. These Austro-Marxists did not, for a moment, in taking their anti-moralist stance, deride these ideas or argue that they, as moral ideas, reflected an ideologically based false consciousness. But, that notwithstanding, they still sided firmly with 'Orthodox Marxism' in viewing Marx as a social scientist who is telling us, as Adler put it, that "socialism will not be achieved because it is justified from an ethical point of view, but because it will be the result of a causal process."[12] They were as adamant as Kautsky in repudiating any search for the moral basis for socialism in Kant, in utilitarian theory or elsewhere. Such a fashion of establishing socialism, Adler wrote, "must be . . . energetically repudiated, and precisely from a Marxist point of view. Marxism is a system of sociological knowledge. It bases socialism on causal knowledge of the processes of social life. Marxism and sociology are one and the same thing."[13]

This perhaps overly scientistic conception of Marxist social theory was in turn resisted by Georg Lukács in his *History and Class-Consciousness,* and later by Lucien Goldmann.[14] They both, many believe, brought Marxist theory closer to its Hegelian roots. They stressed the unity of theory and practice in Marx and challenged the legitimacy of the Kantian assumption of a sharp distinction between facts and values. Like John Dewey, they rejected the standard belief that scientific inquiry dealt only with the factual and could not, while remaining faithful to its vocation, make claims about what is good or bad, right or wrong. They rejected this view as an unjustified dualism as well as Max Adler's view that Marxism was social science and nothing else. Such a conception utterly neglected, they argued, the very central Marxist conception of the unity of theory and practice.

Lukács and Goldmann took evaluative discourse and factual discourse to be ineradicably intertwined and denied that there is any clear, or at least any rigid, distinction between the is and the ought. Lukács and Goldmann argued that Marx believed—and indeed rightly believed—that social theory and social critique run in tandem and, in any proper social theory, understanding, explanation and evaluation are so closely linked that the value judgments, including the moral judgments, which cannot but remain in any interpretive-explanatory richly descriptive discourse, are not autonomous and independent of the facts.[15] In any social theory rich enough to have explanatory value or critical thrust, statements of value, interpretations and statements of fact are indissolubly linked. We cannot atomize the situation and usefully look at these items separately, accepting the facts of Marx's social theory and rejecting the interpretations or the value judgments, or accepting the latter and rejecting his factual picture of the world. We must take them as a gestalt. The conception of the science that goes with Marx's social theory and social critique cannot be the scientistic conception of a normatively neutral social science.

Neither Marx nor Marxists should give us 'the ethical foundations' of Marxism. Such a conception is both illusory and unnecessary, but it also—and this is just the other side of the coin—should not seek to give us a 'cleaned up' social science which makes no moral claims. Lukács and Goldmann argue, that such a restricted social science will neither have extensive explanatory power nor have the emancipatory role of social critique. The error made in common, they argue, by the revisionists Vorlander and Bernstein, the 'Orthodox Marxists' Kautsky and Plekhanov and the Austro-Marxists Bauer and Adler, but not by Marx or Engels, was to accept the Kantian dualism of fact and value.

IV

Contemporary Anglo-American philosophers who have taken Marx seriously have for the most part fought shy of taking firm stands on the relation of fact to value. There was around a decade ago a very extensive debate about whether in any significant sense an ought can be derived from an is.[16] From the rise of analytic philosophy to about mid-century a belief in the autonomy of ethics and Poincaré's maxim had become a fixed dogma among Anglo-American philosophers. That dogma was forcefully challenged and an extensive debate followed, the result of which was inconclusive.[17] Perhaps as a result, Marxist philosophers, who are also in some way part of the analytical tradition, have been understandably reluctant to take a stand on such matters.[18]

Andrew Collier in his masterful "Scientific Socialism and the Question of Socialist Values" captures the substance of what Lukács and Goldmann were about and indeed what Marx was about, *vis-à-vis* values, without assuming that there is no categorial distinction between facts and values or that there is an entailment relation between factual statements and fundamental evaluative utterances.[19] While avoiding Bernstein's and Vorlander's appeal to an ethical socialism and claims about distinctively socialist values, Collier does acknowledge that normative conceptions have a place in socialism.

There are a number of rather secular values, connected principally with conceptions of human flourishing and need satisfaction, that have come into common currency since the Enlightenment.[20] Certain very severe religious thinkers aside, there is by now, in societies which have gone through what Max Weber called the process of modernization, a very considerable consensus about these values: a consensus that is reflected in the thought of modernizing intelligentsia in a spectrum from Bentham to Nietzsche. (It is, of course, though often in rather inchoate forms, widely abroad in the culture.) If someone were to challenge the justifiability of this consensus either from outside this modernizing group or in a purely speculative way, I do not know how we could prove or establish those moral truisms, as I shall call them, beyond appealing to considered judgments in wide reflective equilibrium and pointing to the untenability of foundationalism.[21]

A socialist, even a Marxist anti-moralist, has those values available to him, and they will, and should, guide his practice. What divides him from the liberal or indeed from most conservatives as well, is his political sociology. That is to say, his disagreement with them is about the facts—about what is the most perspicuous representation of the facts—and about what in a particular historical situation, including most importantly our situation, is possible (empirically feasible).

Liberals typically would have it that fundamental political disagreements are deep moral or normative disagreements—often tragic disagreements—that cannot be rationally resolved. Collier argues that this is false. Fundamental political disagreements, he carefully argues, turn finally on factual disagreements about what is the case and most importantly about what can become the case. Such disagreements can, at least in principle, be resolved, though the strength of various ideological defenses make their rational resolution extremely difficult. But there is neither conceptual imprisonment nor an ultimate disagreement over fundamental values here. To so view political argument is to misunderstand it.

Even if we cannot derive fundamental moral judgments from plain matters of fact, it does remain the case—and this is what is actually important—that we can, do and indeed should, base moral judgments on the facts. In most situations, for a person about to step off a curb, the fact that there is a car coming is a good reason to stop. The value judgment "You ought to stop" is based on the fact that there is a car coming.

No matter how autonomist we are about ethics we have to realize that repeatedly in everyday life value judgments are based on the facts. Marx's analyses of capitalism and other social formations, his remarks about how social change takes place and the relations of power between the classes, and his claims about how these relations could change and what could replace them all give us at least a putatively perspicuous representation of the facts and what is empirically possible. If so then for people who accept what I have called moral truisms, the set of factual-cum-theoretical claims that Marxists make are of the utmost moral relevance. In speaking of 'moral truisms' I am referring to the belief that human autonomy is a good thing, that suffering and degradation are bad things, that it is a good thing for people to stand in conditions of fraternity and mutual respect, that it is a good thing for people to live lives in which their needs are met and their wants are satisfied (which are neither self-destructive nor harmful to others) and it is a good thing that people stand in relations of rough equality in which one person or group of persons cannot dominate others. For people who accept these beliefs (as almost all of us do) the Marxist factual claims, if true, are of a not inconsiderable moral relevance. A Marxist critique of society proceeds not by way of presenting new moral tablets but by way of showing people with ordinary human feelings and moral beliefs how societies really function and what the world could become with the development of the productive forces.[22]

Marxist social science is also, as we have seen Lukács and Goldmann stressing, an emancipatory social science functioning as critique, but its critique (including its motivating import to change the world), Collier stresses, is by way of telling it like it is and by showing us what the human possibilities are.[23] For neutral spectators, it would have only explanatory value; it would not serve as a guide for what to do or what to struggle against. But human beings are not neutral spectators. They are agents who intervene in the world and react to the world, who care about their lives and the lives of others. For people who have tolerably mundane commonsensical moral beliefs, the Marxist picture of the world is emancipatory. The important thing, Marxists rightly believe, is to see if it is *an approximately true and comprehensive picture of the world*. If that picture is approximately true, the moral evaluations will take care of themselves. We do not need to spell out a distinctive set of socialist values or give a Marxist foundationalist account of morality.

V

What, however, are we to make of Marx's claim that historical materialism breaks the staff of morality and his repeated claims that morality is through and through ideological? *The Communist Manifesto* echoes earlier remarks in *The German Ideology* to the effect that morality is ideology, that morality in capitalist society, along with law and religion, is a collection of disguised bourgeois prejudices masking and rationalizing bourgeois domination in class society. The thing to do, according to Marx, is to strip morality of all the mystification created by moralizing and to come to see morality for what it is, namely as an ideology in which the class interests of the dominant class are, through mystification, insinuated as being in the interests of the society as a whole. People are seduced by moral ideology into accepting their domination as their rightful or at least inescapable station with corresponding duties, to which they should subordinate their wants and interests.[24] Yet Marx and Engels's suspicion of moralizing, their hostility towards moral theorizing, and their reception of the ideological nature of morality went hand in hand with their readiness, throughout their lives—in their pamphleteering, in their theoretical work and in their private correspondence—to perfectly unselfconsciously make moral evaluations which they gave no sign at all of regarding as ideology, as class biases or as subjective. This would lead us to think that their accounts of morality are contradictory. Without abandoning historical materialism or any of Marx's strong and, I believe, basically correct claims about the ideological functions of morality, I will attempt in the remainder of this essay to establish that Marx's claims are neither contradictory nor incoherent and are indeed powerful and plausible claims that deserve serious consideration.

An acceptance of the perspective on morality I have portrayed does not entail, or even suggest, a rejection of the reality of moral conceptions, though historical materialism does entail the denial of their causal primacy, particularly where epochal social change is at issue. (But this, note, is not to deny them any causal efficacy.) Far from believing in the unreality of moral notions Engels did say baldly in *Anti-Dühring* that it cannot be doubted that there has been progress in morality. These considerations, however, are not decisive, for it is perfectly natural to reply that, if Marx and Engels had thought through the implications of historical materialism and of their sociology of morals (including their beliefs about ideology), they would have rejected a belief in the objectivity of morals or of the possibility of moral truth claims. Their accounts of historical materialism and ideology are incompatible with a belief in moral knowledge. This is the central issue with which I must come to grips.

Morality, on any Marxist account, must be part of the superstructure and hence, it is natural to say, it must be ideological. And if morality is ideological, it cannot be objective, since ideological beliefs cannot be justified. All we can do is explain how moral beliefs arise. (Keep in mind here that an ideology is typically a system of illusory beliefs reflecting in a disguised way the interests of a determinate class.)

What we need first to recognize is that it is consistent with historical materialism to distinguish, within the moral realm itself, between ideological beliefs and non-ideological beliefs and that, on Marx's own account, it is not true that all forms of consciousness, including all forms of self-consciousness, are ideological.[25] If they were Marx would have hoisted himself by his own petard.

Being superstructural is only a *necessary* condition for being ideological. It is *not sufficient.* There can be superstructural beliefs which are not ideological. While all ideological beliefs are superstructural not all superstructural beliefs are ideological.[26] In many, but not all, contexts, the following moral beliefs (expressed in the five sentences below) are non-ideological, though this is not to deny, what is plainly true, that they *can* be embedded in moral theories or in moralities which are ideological. But from the fact that they *can* be so embedded it does not follow that they *must* be so embedded.

1. Pleasure is good.

2. Health is good.
3. Freedom is good.
4. Servitude is bad.
5. Suffering is bad.[27]

These beliefs can be held in such a way that they are not supportive of any particular class interests. They neither directly favor the interests of the dominant class nor the interests of the challenging exploited class. These beliefs need not mystify social reality: they need not express false consciousness or false beliefs, and they need not rest on rationalizations. Moreover, they are beliefs which would not be extinguished, if we came to know what caused us to hold them. They need not be beliefs which are expressive of dominant class interests or of any class interests. This can be seen to be true because it would be reasonable to continue to hold those beliefs in a classless society. They would not wither away with the ending of capitalism, the complete disappearance of all elements of a capitalist mentality, the withering away of the state and the achievement of communism. If the moral theories in which they are embedded are ideological, as they typically are, it is crucial to recognize that these moral beliefs themselves can have a life of their own outside these ideological theories. There is no good reason to believe that these moral beliefs are *per se* ideological.

VI

A Marxist sociology of morals shows that moral beliefs have a tendency to function ideologically. But it is not committed to the thesis—a strange kind of *a priori* thesis, probably rooted in some questionable moral epistemology—that they all do or all must. Indeed, acceptance of that thesis would make nonsense out of many, though surely not all, of the critical remarks Marxists direct against capitalism. Consider, for example, claims about the dehumanizing effects of capitalist work relations. They are plainly moral beliefs, though in the way I pointed out in the previous section, they are moral beliefs based on factual beliefs articulated by and argued for by Marxist social theory. To accept such an *a priori* thesis about all moral beliefs being necessarily ideological and distorting of our understanding of ourselves would render all such remarks ideological and unjustifiable. We should keep firmly in mind in this context that it is one thing to deny that Marx's social science is a treatise on social ethics or a moral critique and it is another thing again to deny legitimacy to the moral remarks that are liberally distributed throughout his scientific work simply on the grounds that they are moral judgments or value judgments.

What we need to see is how a fuller accounting of what it is for a belief to be ideological makes it evident how some moral beliefs can be superstructural without being ideological. It is our various publicly articulated forms of self-consciousness that are the primary subject matter of ideology. It is here where we have that which in class societies is necessarily ideological. But it is not the case that any belief or any self-conception a person has must be ideological, though such beliefs, in class societies, are ideology-prone. Ideological beliefs are most paradigmatically the *public* conceptions we have about ourselves; they are in their most paradigmatic instances *the socially* sanctioned self-images. They typically are conceptions on the social level which, like purely individual rationalizations, involve mystification. Typically they are the social rationalizations of the ruling class, but sometimes these public conceptions have such a publicly approved status only within a challenging class. But what is crucial for us to see here is that not all ideas or ideals *must* involve such a collective rationalization and mystification of social relations. Moreover, this is not true of all ideas or beliefs as such, even when they are, as moral ideas must be, superstructural.

It cannot be the case that all our beliefs about man and society are ideological because we all must suffer from some grave epistemological malady. This is not even a coherent possibility, for, if it were so, nothing conceptualized could count as an unmystified idea. The very notion of an 'ideological belief' would be unintelligible, for then we could not even recognize that certain belief-systems mystify social reality.[28] Indeed, only if we can draw a conceptual distinction between 'a mystified idea' and 'an unmystified idea' could we go on to show how pervasively ideological most moral thinking actually is.

It is vital to avoid turning ideology or being ideological into an *epistemological* category about how or what we can know, or about what can be true or false. Ideologies are our *public* conceptions of ourselves and should not be taken as referring to *all* our beliefs or even to all our self-images or philosophical or moral conceptions. Ideology is not a term referring to an all-inclusive range of cognitive or affective phenomena.[29] Rather ideology is the *official currency* of self-consciousness in class societies. This explains why the extant moralities—the moralities of the various tribes and classes—will all be ideological.

Most private forms of cognition are also very likely to conform in one way or another and, to a greater or lesser degree, to the ideology of the class society in which the person lives and sometimes is a member. But it does not follow that all individual or even all group thinking must so conform to an ideological pattern. There is conceptual and epistemological space for moral conceptions and beliefs which are non-ideological. These remarks show why Marxism itself need not be ideological.

VII

There remain 'relativistic problems' about Marxism *vis-à-vis* ethics which might show that if historical materialism is true morality totters. I think it is evident enough that a Marxist need not endorse any version of *ethical* relativism, namely the doctrine that an action or practice X is morally right in society S if and only if X is permitted (approved) by the conventions of S or by the dominant class in S. Historical materialism is a thesis about what generates and sustains moral beliefs in a society and the related Marxist doctrine of ideology explains how moral beliefs function in class society. It is probably the case that these doctrines do not commit one to any assertion about what is right or wrong. But, whether or not that is so, they do not commit one to saying that, because a moral belief is deemed right by the conventions of the society or by the ruling or dominant class in the society, that moral belief is therefore right in that society or indeed in any society. At most, it would require the historical materialist to say that if it is *believed* to be right by the ruling class of that society, it will generally be believed to be right in that society. But that anthropological observation is perfectly compatible with denying that it is therefore right in that society, or with a skepticism about whether we could ever determine what is right or wrong period. And that, whatever it is, is not ethical relativism.

Moreover, if a Marxist committed himself to ethical relativism, he would have to say that if Society S were a capitalist society and action X were a revolutionary act designed to overthrow capitalism that he, the Marxist, would be committed to believing that it is wrong to do X in Society S, for X is not approved by the conventions of S or by its ruling class, unless (perhaps) he could show that the production relations in S no longer suit the productive forces. But no Marxist need say that. He could, and in my view should, stick to the innocuous and trivial thesis in descriptive ethics that such acts would be generally *believed* to be wrong in Society S and he could use historical materialism and its correlated theory of ideology to explain why it was believed to be wrong. But this is to assert nothing at all about what is right or wrong, let alone to assert that, if it is generally *believed* to be wrong in Society S, it is wrong in Society S.

To assert anything like this ethical relativist thesis is entirely contrary to the spirit of Marxism and is not required by historical materialism. Historical materialism sees the dominant moralities in a society as cultural 'legitimizing' and stabilizing devices in that society. They are devices functionally required by a given mode of production. But to make such a claim is not to imply anything about what is or is not right, or to claim that what is functionally required by a given mode of production ought to obtain.

However, ethical relativism is not the only kind of relativism there is. There is also meta-ethical relativism. It is the view that there are no objectively sound procedures for justifying one moral code or one set of moral judgments against another moral code or another set of moral judgments. For all we can ascertain, two moral codes may be equally 'sound' and two moral claims may be equally 'justified' or 'reasonable.' There is no way of establishing what is 'the true moral code' or set of moral beliefs. Indeed it may not even make sense to say that there could be a true moral code. Someone who believes that historical materialism commits her to meta-ethical relativism, and who also accepts historical materialism, will also claim that, if historical materialism is true, judgments of what is right or wrong, just or unjust, become mode-of-production dependent. Taking meta-ethical relativism and historical materialism together, she will assert that there is no possible Archimedian point in morality—there is nothing that could be properly called a "true morality"—and thus it is not even possible for there to be an objective certification of moral principles. There is no method that all rational, properly informed and conceptually sophisticated people must accept for fixing moral belief.

VIII

Does historical materialism actually entail or contextually imply the non-availability of an Archimedian point or cluster of developing Archimedian points in moral philosophy? Neither the diversity of actual moral beliefs nor the diversity of methods for establishing moral beliefs will show that no Archimedian point is possible. Such diversities do not show that all are equally sound. Moreover, the relative appropriateness of certain moral conceptions to historically determinate modes of production would not show that there could not be progress towards the greater adequacy of a mode of production over previous modes of production, or that perfectly objective judgments could not be made. We could show that certain norms were appropriated to capitalism and still quite consistently assess capitalism as a general advance over feudalism and as less advanced than socialism.[30] There is no inconsistency at all here in making these diverse assessments. We could not only show that certain norms were functionally appropriate to certain modes of production but that whole modes of production—later more developed modes of production—make possible a way of organizing social life that is better than previous organizations which were also functionally appropriate to their modes of production.

Historical materialism is clearly committed to contextualism, not relativism or subjectivism. It does not rule out a belief in moral progress. Indeed, it would appear at least to commit one, as Engels was committed, to a belief in moral progress through the development of moral ideas from one mode of production to another as the productive forces develop and as we gain a greater control over the world and a more extensive rationalization of our lives.

We should also recognize that the causal genesis of moral beliefs does not undermine their validity. We can recognize that people have moral beliefs because of the distinctive production relations of the society in which they live without thereby thinking that their moral beliefs must be unjustified and subjective.

> An elementary distinction can be drawn between the cause of a person (class, society) holding a certain belief and the evidence for that belief or, alternatively, between the reasons for which one believes and the reasons which justify belief. A fundamental tenet of Marxist class analysis is that one's class position, one's particular location in a specific type of economic structure, strongly conditions one's outlook, moral and otherwise. But it is a simple truth of logical analysis that the origin of a belief is not relevant to its evaluation as true or false. Thus, there is nothing inconsistent in a Marxist maintaining (say) both that the value judgments of the proletariat are socially determined and that they tended to be more veridical than the judgments of other classes.[31]

We need to distinguish between the origin of moral beliefs, their rationale and their justification.

We need, however, to be careful about applying such genetic fallacy arguments in such an unequivocal way. As Richard Miller points out, it is not always the case that "ideas are debunked simply by tracing their origins to social interests."[32] It was false to say, as was said above, that the origin of a belief is not at all relevant to its evaluation as true or false. Miller points out that tracking moral beliefs can be vitally important. He gives the following example:

> A strong duty to be hospitable to strangers is accepted by traditional Eskimoes because of a common interest in such hospitality in a semi-nomadic society where any family may be struck down in the constant battle with Nature. This explanation does not debunk. If anything, it justifies.[33]

Here, pointing to the origin of the moral belief reveals a rationale that otherwise might not have been obvious, but it is also true that simply pointing to the origin of the belief does not even start to justify. Moreover, and more relevantly to the standard genetic fallacy arguments, we cannot simply prove a belief to be mistaken by pointing to its origin. But if the belief can be shown to have a rationale, then we have at least some start on a justification. If we can exhibit a rationale, we have at least a *prima facie* case for claiming it is justified. The fact that our moral outlook is dependent on general economic conditions does not show that there is no independent justification for that outlook. There might not be one, but that could not be determined by simply finding out how moral outlooks arise.

The above notwithstanding, it still does look like historical materialism may be committed to a meta-ethical relativism in the following rather distinctive sense: if historical materialism is true there could be no ground for asserting a trans-historical set of moral principles. As Engels stressed, we cannot justifiably say that there is a set of *eternal* moral principles. However, we may be able to say that at time t1 in context X such and such moral principles are correct, and that at time t2 in context Y that such and such moral principles are correct.

These judgments are general and can be made across modes of production. Moreover, historical materialism allows, though it may not require, the judgment that there is rational progress from t1 to t2 to t3 such that it is, *ceteris paribus,* better for human beings to go through that development rather than remain fixed at t1. This shows a moral understanding, a moral way of viewing things, which is non-relativist, contextual, and yet compatible with historical materialism. If such moral progress is an illusion, historical materialism does not and does not attempt to show that it is. There is no good reason to believe that if historical materialism is true morality totters.

Notes

1. The closest thing to an extended account in one work comes in Karl Marx, *Critique of the Gotha Programme,* C. P. Dutt (ed. and trans.), (New York, NY: International Publishers, 1938), and in Frederick Engels, *Anti-Dühring,* Emile Bruns (trans.), (New York: International Publishers, 1939), chapters IX–XI.

2. Leon Trotsky, *Their Morals and Ours* (London: Plough Press, 1968). The original publication date of the Russian text was 1938.

3. Though I demur from some of his key conclusions, it should be remarked that Richard Miller brilliantly brings out what Marx is up to here. Richard Miller, *Analyzing Marx,* (Princeton University Press, 1984), pp. 15–97.

4. Kai Nielsen, "Justice as Ideology," *Windsor Yearbook of Access to Justice,* vol. 1 (1981), pp. 165–78.

5. David Levin provides a powerful and sophisticated example of such a defense. David S. Levin, "The Moral Relativism of Marxism," *The Philosophical Forum,* vol. XV, no. 3, (Spring 1984), pp. 249–78.

6. Anthony Skillen, *Ruling Illusions,* (Sussex: Harvester Press 1977) and Richard Norman, *The Moral Philosophers,* (Oxford: Clarendon Press, 1983), pp. 173–201.

7. This may sound paradoxical to some. How could a Marxist set aside things that Marx said and still remain a Marxist? Very easily indeed, for there are many things that Marx said that are hardly central to his core theory and indeed some of the things he said may be incompatible with it. There is no need for a Marxist to go around defending everything Marx believed. But he must make some judgments about what is canonical to Marx's theory (say historical materialism, the theory of classes, the labour theory of value) and concerning these matters there is, of course, room for intelligent dispute. That is why there is a perennial dispute over what is essentially Marxist. The worry about whether a Marxist critique of capitalism requires for its rounding out a moral critique and perhaps even a moral theory is the worry about whether the theory really is incomplete without it or whether the insights embedded in the canonical core would be undermined or in any way compromised if such an ethical rounding out were made. For a masterful discussion of the notion of a canonical core see Marx Wartofsky, "The Unhappy Consciousness," *Praxis International* (1981), pp. 288–306. For three significant attempts to weld an ethical critique to Marxism see Maximilien Rubel, *Rubel on Karl Marx: Five Essays,* Joseph O'Malley and Keith Algozin (eds and transl.), (Cambridge University Press, 1981), pp. 26–81. Svetozar Stojanovic, *Between*

Ideals and Reality, (New York: Oxford University Press, 1973) and Douglas Kellner, "Marxism, Morality and Ideology," *Marx and Morality* in Kai Nielsen and Steven Patten (eds), (Guelph, ON: Canadian Association for Publishing in Philosophy, 1981), pp. 93–120.

8. See the stress on this by Lucien Goldmann and Bertell Ollman in their discussions of Marx on morality. Lucien Goldmann, "Y a-t-il une sociologie marxiste?", *Les Temps Modernes,* vol. 13 (1957), pp. 729–51 and Bertell Ollman, *Alienation,* second edition, (Cambridge University Press, 1976), pp. 41–51.

9. Kurt Vorlander, *Kant and Marx* (Tubingen: 1926). Edward Bernstein, *Evolutionary Socialism,* Edith Havey (trans.) (New York: Schocken Books, 1961).

10. Karl Kautsky, *Ethik und materialistiche Geschichtsauffassung* (Stuttgart: 1926) and Georg Plekhanov, *Selected Philosophical Works,* (Moscow: 1961).

11. Max Adler, *Der soziologische Sinn der Lehre von Karl Marx* (Leipzig: 1914) and Otto Bauer, "Marxismus und Ethik," *Die Neue Zeit,* vol. 24 (1905–6), pp. 485–99.

12. Max Adler, *Kant und der Marxismus,* p. 141.

13. Ibid.

14. Georg Lukács, *History and Class-Consciousness,* Rodney Livingstone (trans.), (London: Merlin Press, 1968). See note 8 and Lucien Goldmann, *The Hidden God,* Philip Thody (trans.), (London: Routledge & Kegan Paul, 1964), Chapter 5, and his *The Human Sciences and Philosophy,* Hayden V. White (trans.), (London, Jonathan Cape, 1969).

15. This has also been argued powerfully from the liberal side by Isaiah Berlin and Charles Taylor. Isaiah Berlin, *Concepts and Categories* (Oxford University Press 1980), pp. 103–42 and "Rationality of Value Judgments," *Nomos* VII, Carl J. Friedrich (ed.), (New York: Atherton Press, 1964), pp. 221–3. Charles Taylor, "Neutrality in Political Science," in *Philosophy, Politics and Society,* (third series), P. Laslett and W. G. Runciman (eds.), (Oxford: Basil Blackwell, 1967), and "Interpretation and the Sciences of Man," *The Review of Metaphysics,* vol. 25 no. 1 (September 1971).

16. On the traditional autonomist side perhaps the most significant figures were R. M. Hare, Karl Popper and J. L. Mackie; the chief nonautonomist challengers were John Searle, Charles Taylor, Max Black and Philippa Foot. A reasonable sampling of the significant literature is brought together in *The Is/Ought Question,* W. D. Hudson's (ed.), (London: Macmillan 1969). But see also the two essays by Charles Taylor cited in footnote 15, Richard Norman, "Seeing Things Differently," *Radical Philosophy,* No. 1 (January 1972), pp. 6–13 and Philippa Foot, "Morality as a System of Hypothetical Imperatives," *Philosophical Review,* vol. 81 (July 1972), pp. 305–16.

17. See the references in the previous footnote.

18. I both review the literature and take an autonomist stand in my "On Deriving an Ought from an Is: A Retrospective Look," *The Review of Metaphysics,* vol. XXXII, no. 3 (March 1979), pp. 487–514. (Useful additional bibliographical references occur in the first two footnotes.) I also try to show, in a way that meshes well with Andrew Collier's Marxist arguments, that non-derivability (the core autonomist claim) entails no significant substantive conclusion for we still in moral reasoning back up our moral judgments by an appeal to facts. See also on this, Peter Singer, "The Triviality of the Debate Over 'Is/Ought' and the Definition of 'Moral,'" *American Philosophical Quarterly,* vol. 10 (January 1973), pp. 51–6.

19. Andrew Collier, "Scientific Socialism and the Question of Socialist Values," in *Marx and Morality,* Kai Nielsen and Steven Patten (eds.), (Guelph: Canadian Association for Publishing in Philosophy, 1981), pp. 121–54 and his "Positive Values," *The Aristotelian Society* supplementary vol. LVII (1983).

20. I am not here giving to understand that these values were invented by the Enlightenment. There were certainly such beliefs floating around before and they were sometimes passionately held by some people. But that cluster of values came to have a very deep and pervasive consensus only after the ethos of the Enlightenment took hold.

21. Kai Nielsen, *Equality and Liberty* (Totawa, NJ: Rowman & Allenheld, 1985), Chapter 2. Norman Daniels, "Wide Reflective Equilibrium and Theory Acceptance in Ethics," *The Journal of Philosophy,* vol. 10 (1979), pp. 256–82, and his "Reflective Equilibrium and Archimedean Points," *Canadian Journal of Philosophy,* vol. 10, no. 1 (March 1980), pp. 83–104. Jane English, "Ethics and Science," *Proceedings of the XVI World Congress of Philosophy* (1979).

22. This is convincingly argued by Andrew Collier in his "Positive Values."

23. Ibid.

24. Anthony Skillen and Andrew Collier skillfully bring out this side of Marx and Marxism in Skillen, "Marxism and Morality," *Radical Philosophy,* vol. 8 (1974) and Collier, "Truth and Practice," *Radical Philosophy* 5 (1973) and in his "The Production of Moral Ideology," *Radical Philosophy* 9 (1974).

25. This has been well articulated by John McMurty in his *The Structure of Marx's World-View* (Princeton University Press, 1978), pp. 123–56.

26. Ibid.

27. I do not mean to give to understand that these moral beliefs are little nuggets of eternal moral truth to be uncovered after all the layers of ideology have been peeled away. The very notion of 'moral truth' is not unproblematic. What these are, are moral truisms that take somewhat different readings in different contexts; still each of these utterances are not without a common content, e.g. health means something different from culture to culture but *not* completely different. If you want to call these 'eternal moral truths' you can but this is using an enriched moral language for the commonplace. There is no good reason to go on like that.

28. Alasdair MacIntyre, "Ideology, Social Science and Revolution," *Comparative Politics,* vol. 5, no. 5 (April 1973), pp. 321–42.

29. McMurty, op. cit., pp. 123–56.

30. 'Advanced' here, for Weberian reasons, might cause trouble. Much of the sense here (a sense Weber would sanction) can be cashed in terms of the greater development of the modes of production of certain societies and thus the capacity for those societies to more fully satisfy human wants and needs.

31. William Shaw, "Marxism and Moral Objectivity," *Marx and Morality,* Kai Nielsen and Steven Patten (eds), (Guelph: Canadian Association for Publishing in Philosophy, 1981).

32. Richard Miller, "Marx and Morality," *Nomos,* vol. XXVI (New York University Press, 1983), pp. 18–19.

33. Ibid.

3

Engels on Morality
and Moral Theorizing

I

Friedrich Engels wrote more fully and perhaps more adequately about
morality than did Karl Marx, though, indeed, many of the Engels'
disparagers would deny the latter part of that claim. My interest here
is neither to affirm nor to deny that but to try to see what Engels'
views about morality were and something of their import. I shall try
here clearly to articulate what they were and spot their underlying
rationale. I shall present a sympathetic view of Engels' account as well
as a view which will attempt, where the text is vague, both to note
that vagueness and to place as plausible an interpretation on the text
as the text will reasonably yield. A critique of that view, as well as
an examination of whether anything useful can be built from it, will
have to await another occasion.

With Engels, as with any other theorist of at least putative stature,
I think it is well to proceed on a principle of interpretative charity.
Where an unstrained but reasonable interpretation can be put on a
text put that interpretation on it. See how much sense it can reasonably
yield. This is precisely what I shall attempt to do in my account of
Engels on morality and moral theorizing.

This essay was originally published in *Studies in Soviet Thought* 26 (1983): 229–248.
Copyright © 1983 by D. Reidel Publishing Company. Reprinted by permission of Kluwer
Academic Publishers.

II

Engels' views on morality and moral philosophy can be usefully related to his appropriation of a reaction to the Enlightenment. He, more than Marx, stresses his indebtedness to the Enlightenment.[1] In the first paragraph of *Anti-Dühring,* Engels remarks that modern socialism is, on its theoretical side, linked with the Enlightenment. He sees it as "a further and ostensibly more consistent extension of the principles established by the great French philosophers of the Eighteenth Century" (p. 23). They, Engels remarks, did yeoman's service in "clearing the minds of men for the coming revolution" and indeed they, as Engels put it, acted themselves "in an extremely revolutionary fashion" (p. 23). And here, though Engels has just referred to the importance for socialism of class struggle and of economics, he also refers to something very superstructural indeed, namely, to ideas. The philosophers of the Enlightenment, he remarks, acted in an exemplary revolutionary fashion by recognizing "no external authority of any kind." They relentlessly subjected "religion, conceptions of nature, society, political systems, everything to the most merciless criticism: everything had to justify its existence at the bar of reason . . . " (p. 23). Principles arrived at by untrammeled, rigorously pursued human ratiocination are to provide "the basis of all human action and association" (p. 23).

There was something both giddy and emancipatory about this, yet, on Engels' view, it was hyperbolic as well. The following quotation well captures the flavor of his view of the Enlightenment:

> All previous forms of society and government, all the old ideas handed down by tradition, were flung into the lumber-room as irrational; the world had hitherto allowed itself to be guided solely by prejudices; everything in the past deserved only pity and contempt. Now for the first time appeared the light of day; henceforth, superstition, injustice, privilege and oppression were to be superseded by eternal truth, eternal justice, equality grounded in Nature and the inalienable rights of man (p. 23).

Engels makes it very clear that he regards this as both a progressive move and an important bit of bourgeois ideological mystification. In the very next paragraph after the one quoted above Engels remarks:

> We know today that this kingdom of reason was nothing more than the idealised kingdom of the bourgeoisie; that eternal justice found its realisation in bourgeois justice; that equality reduced itself to bourgeois equality before the law; that bourgeois property was proclaimed as one of the essential rights of man; and that the government of reason, the Social Contract of Rousseau, came into existence and could only come into existence as a bourgeois democratic republic. No more than their predecessors could the great thinkers of the eighteenth century pass beyond the limits imposed on them by their own epoch (p. 24).

But in this social world, with all its social mystifications, class struggle continued and took a new turn. There was, of course, the struggle between the feudal nobility and the bourgeoisie; but there was also the emerging struggle between the bourgeoisie (the exploiters) and the proletariat (the exploited, toiling poor). The moral ideology of the bourgeoisie was in this circumstance a useful one: they represented themselves as speaking for "the whole of suffering humanity" (p. 24). Yet this ideology did not go unchallenged even then. The idea that the bourgeoisie with their values and their outlook represented the "interests of the different sections of the workers" was challenged by Thomas Münzer, Babeuf and the Levellers. Indeed this challenge was not just talk but involved "revolutionary armed uprisings of a class which was as yet undeveloped" and, paralleling this practical activity, there was the theoretical activity of the great utopian socialists (Saint-Simon, Fourier and Owen). They, going beyond the *philosophes,* made claims for equality which were "no longer limited to political rights but were extended also to the social conditions of individuals . . . " (p. 24). It was not only class privileges that were to go but the very existence of class distinctions themselves. This radically egalitarian social ideal was related directly to a consciously materialist world-view (p. 25).

However, unlike Marx and Engels, these utopian socialists did not, in articulating their theories and ideals, put themselves forward as "representatives of the interests of the proletariat"; like "the philosophers of the Enlightenment, they aimed at the emancipation not of a definite class but of all humanity" (p. 25). They, like the *philosophes,* wanted to establish "the kingdom of reason and eternal justice"; but, unlike the *philosophes,* they took the bourgeois world, and certain central moral conceptions of such *philosophes* reflecting and rationalizing that world, to be "irrational and unjust" (p. 25). Yet they remained thorough utopians and historical idealists, for, as Engels ironically puts it, "if pure reason and justice have not hitherto ruled the world, this has been due to the fact that until now men have not rightly understood them" (p. 25). To change the world, these historical idealists argued, we need men of genius to recognize the true nature of reason and justice and perspicuously to articulate such a conception of the world. These utopians believed that such persons, with luck, can come along almost any time, and, when this happy accident occurs, humanity will in short order be emancipated.

This view, Engels remarks, is the view of all early socialists. For them " . . . socialism is the expression of absolute truth, reason and justice, and needs only to be discovered to conquer the world by virtue of its own power; as absolute truth is independent of time and space and of the historical development of man, it is a mere accident when and where it is discovered" (p. 25).

So far Engels has been giving us social history, though indeed, an interpretative social history, spiced with descriptive ethical remarks.

That is to say, he is making some remarks which could occur in a work in descriptive ethics. Without developing in this part of *Anti-Dühring* moral arguments of his own or expressing moral views of his own, except perhaps by indirection, Engels displays the moral conceptions of the *philosophes* and the utopian socialists and shows us something of the role they played in the social history of the time and something of the import their work had for the development of socialism.

However, Engels contrasts his and Marx' attempts to set socialism on a sound scientific basis with utopian socialism and criticizes the utilization of moral arguments by the utopians.[2] The great defect of their arguments was their subjectivism. Indeed there is in their work much talk of absolute truth, reason and justice, but each socialist group has a different conception of these notions. Each utopian's "special kind of absolute truth, reason and justice is in turn conditioned by his subjective understanding, his conditions of existence, the measure of his knowledge and intellectual training . . . " (p. 26). So we have here only the sectarian illusion of objectivity rather than a genuine objectivity. What can be distilled from such a tower of babel is "a kind of eclectic average socialism" (p. 26). And it is indeed this bland variety of socialism that has come to dominate "the minds of most socialist workers in France and England . . . " (p. 26). This can, Engels argues, only confuse the workers in their struggle for emancipation (p. 26). What, by contrast, must be done, to give us an effective tool in the struggle for our emancipation, is to set socialism on a solid scientific foundation.

I shall not comment here on Engels' conception of scientific socialism save to say that it must, on his view, be both dialectical and empirical and see the world as an ever-changing and in some way unified and developing world in which we no longer content ourselves with "observing natural objects and natural processes in their isolation" detached from a changing vast interconnection of things (p. 27).[3] Sound common sense, Engels argues, inclines us very strongly to take a synchronic view and to look at things as discrete objects in isolation from each other and to take things as relatively fixed and unchanging. This atomistic way of viewing things found its intellectual defense in British empiricism—a view which Engels derisively refers to as a metaphysical rather than a scientific way of viewing things. Science, by contrast, Engels claims, breaks with this sturdy common sense and notes carefully the interconnections between things, looks at things holistically and never forgets that "everything is in flux" (p. 27).[4] (Engels, in speaking of the 'dialectics of nature,' even contrasts a dialectical view of reality with a metaphysical one [p. 29].) Moreover, as we learned from Hegel, we should not only look at things diachronically, we should look at them teleologically as well. We, if we wish to be genuinely scientific, should no longer see history "as a confused whirl of senseless deeds" but, following Hegel, "as the process of development of humanity itself" (p. 30). We should seek, in a careful, rigorously empirical and systematic fashion, to trace in society the "regularities running through all its apparently fortuitous phenomena" (p. 30).

Engels, against the Hegelian system, took the scientific attitude to be a thoroughly fallibilistic one. But, no more than Peirce or Dewey, did he think that this forced him into a relativism. Engels put the matter quite unequivocally: "A system of natural and historical knowledge which is all-embracing and final for all time is in contradiction to the fundamental laws of dialectical thinking; which however, far from excluding, on the contrary includes, the idea that the systematic knowledge of the external universe can make giant strides from generation to generation" (p. 31).

Engels moved away, as did Marx as well, not only from conceptions of 'absolute truth' to a fallibilism; he moved from a historical idealism to a historical materialism as well.

However Engels, revolutionist that he was, did stress a kind of evolutionary picture of the development of society and, beyond a historical materialism, he also argued for a materialism in the sense that many philosophers in Anglo-American societies are now materialists. "Modern materialism," Engels remarked, "sees history as the process of the evolution of humanity, and its own problem as the discovery of laws of motion of this process" (p. 31). He takes this modern materialism as embracing the essential advance of natural science—a view which sees nature as having a history—and, as being, as Engels put it, "essentially dialectical" (p. 31).

He also had a view of what philosophy would become in this essentially dialectical-materialist world perspective which in important ways is like that of the positivists. We have in such a world perspective no longer a need of "philosophy standing above the other sciences" (p. 31). From there, Engels goes on to remark in a very positivist manner, "As soon as each separate science is required to get clarity as to its position in the great totality of things and of our knowledge of things, a special science dealing with this totality is superfluous. What still independently survives of all former philosophy is the science of thought and its laws—formal logic and dialectics. Everything else is merged in the positive science of Nature and history" (p. 31).[5]

However, in the very next paragraph, after reminding us again of the present state of the class struggle and adverting to its pervasiveness in all societies up to the present time, Engels reasserts the importance for a scientific socialism, and for a scientific account of society generally, including our understanding of the role of morality in society, of historical materialism or what he called "a materialist conception of history." A clear view of the history of civilization would direct us to focus on the conflicting material interests of the different antagonistic classes. With this focus, we would come to recognize that *all* past history was the history of class struggles, that these warring classes of society are always the product of the conditions of production and exchange, in a word, of the *economic* conditions of their time; and therefore the economic structures of society always forms the real basis from which, in the last analysis, is to be explained the whole superstructure of legal and political institutions, as well as of the religious, philosophical, and other conceptions of each historical period (p. 32).[6]

Historical idealism explains man's "being by his consciousness"; historical materialism reverses it and explains his "consciousness by his being" (p. 32).[7] It is in this stress on historical materialism and dialectics that scientific socialism makes a considerable advance on moralizing utopian socialism (p. 32). Utopian socialism indeed did criticize "the existing capitalist mode of production and its consequences" but its criticism was essentially a *moral* one. It "could only simply reject them as evil" (p. 33). Scientific socialism, by contrast, does not just give a critical account [of] the moral perspective of the capitalist system but explains it and so provides the intellectual basis for gaining a mastery over it (p. 33). It will enable us to see how capitalism arises and must persist for a given time but it will also enable us to see how, with the development of the productive forces and with the intensification of class struggle, capitalism must in time collapse (p. 33). By understanding how exploitation works through understanding how surplus value is extracted, and by understanding historical materialism, workers will have put in their hands key intellectual weapons to use in their struggle for emancipation. This, more than any portrayal of what are plainly the evils of capitalism, will move forward the struggle against capitalism.[8]

III

Engels begins his chapters on morality in *Anti-Dühring* with a critique of what we would now call ethical rationalism and a statement of a fallibilistic world-outlook: a view which captures what is important about relativism and historicism without becoming entrapped in its paradoxes and without (or so I shall argue) committing its errors (pp. 94–104). His immediate target is Dühring but his critique would apply to an important ethical rationalist such as Kant or Sidgwick and to contemporary versions of ethical rationalism such as Alan Gewirth's or Alan Donagan's and, less directly, but still correctly, to philosophers such as Aquinas, Descartes and Locke. The extreme ethical rationalist claim is that there are moral truths which have the same validity or a very similar validity to mathematical truths. They are, that is, truths which are said to have a categorical authoritativeness and a final and ultimate validity. There are, such rationalists claim, substantive moral truths of absolute certainty which are also eternal truths that no rational agent can deny (pp. 103, 93). The moral world has its permanent principles and utterly certain foundational claims. Moreover, the argument goes, such claims are not only true but it is also the case that without such a belief we are subject to a mordant skepticism or led to chaos and nihilism (pp. 95, 100–1).

Engels thinks that this rationalist claim is at best a confusion and at worst pompous nonsense. Against such ethical rationalism and such a quest for certainty generally, Engels contrasts a realistic view which sees people making such "unconditioned" knowledge claims against the background of being a particular people of a distinctive class and social group at a particular time and with a necessarily limited, culturally and historically determinate, group of background beliefs plainly circumscribed by a culturally and historically skewed information base. "Individual human beings with their extremely limited thought" are, with a lack of self-awareness or a lack of sense of history and cultural space, unselfconsciously claiming that the character of human thought is absolute (p. 97). Despite all this, Engels asks, are there not any truths "which are so securely based that any doubt of them seems to us to amount to insanity" (p. 97)? Engels answers quite unequivocally, "Certainly there are" (p. 97). In rejecting ethical rationalism, he is not at all driven to skepticism or nihilism. Unlike the skeptic, or even an extreme historicist, Engels is perfectly willing to accept "*eternal truth*" (p. 97).

However, they are not such truths as would be of any comfort to rationalists—including ethical rationalists. To see what Engels has in mind here it is worthwhile attending closely to his discussion in the first part of Chapter 9 of *Anti-Dühring* (pp. 97–101). If we consider the "three great departments of knowledge"—(1) mathematics and the natural sciences, (2) the biological sciences and (3) the historical sciences (what we would now call the human sciences)—we will find, for the most part, Engels claims, a changing, growing, developing body of warranted beliefs most of which are anything but certain and certainly not something which, taken together, constitutes a body of final ultimate truths. "Often enough discoveries such as that of the cell in the biological sciences are such as to compel us to make deep revisions in our understanding of biological phenomena." Where in biology, as elsewhere, we get "pure and immutable truths," we will have to be content with platitudes such as "All men are mortal," "All female mammals have lacteal glands," "A man who gets no food dies of hunger," "Paris is in France" and the like (pp. 97, 99). Those platitudes, together with analytic platitudes, such as "Twice two makes four" and "The three angles of a triangle are equal to two right angles" are our "eternal, final and ultimate truths" (p. 98). But most scientific knowledge is not of that character, though these platitudes can be trotted out to counter the epistemological skeptic. We can rightly claim that we are more confident of their truth than we can be of any skeptical philosopher's claim that, appearances to the contrary notwithstanding, we do not after all really know these things.

However, none of these truths—these commonplaces—are moral truths and turning more in the direction of what possibly could turn up as some roughly analogous 'moral truths' we find Engels, quite plausibly, saying of the historical sciences that there "our knowledge is more backward than" in other domains of knowledge (p. 99). (But, note, morality is being conceived of as a domain of knowledge.) In studying "human life, social relationships, forms of the law and the state," we do not have the regularities that we have in physics and biology. Because of this, the historical sciences are in a far worse plight than the biological or natural sciences (p. 99). "Knowledge," Engels remarks,

> is here essentially relative, inasmuch as it is limited to the perception of relationships and consequences of certain social and state forms which exist only at a particular epoch and among particular people and are of their very nature transitory. Anyone therefore who sets out on this field to hunt down final and ultimate truths, truths which are pure and absolutely immutable, will bring home but little, apart from platitudes and commonplaces of the sorriest kind—for example, that generally speaking man cannot live except by labour; that up to the present mankind for the most part has been divided into rulers and ruled; that Napoleon died on May 5, 1821, and so on (p. 100).

Nevertheless, even here, we gain some platitudes which, though not *a priori,* still give us some 'absolute, eternal and ultimate truths.' But again they are not even remotely sufficient to build a science of man on and they are not moral or normative truths. We do not have anything that forms a basis for ethical rationalism.

Engels notes that philosophers play a comforting trick on themselves. They note that there are these platitudes which are eternal, absolute truths of various sorts, to wit "Birds have beaks" and "Twice two makes four" and then, by a kind of hat trick, they conclude that there must also be "eternal truths in the sphere of human history—eternal morality, eternal justice and so on—which claim a validity and scope equal to those of the truths and deductions of mathematics" (p. 100). But we have not been shown that there are any such truths. What we in reality have is a tower of Babel of the philosophers and theologians each claiming, in various ways and in various idioms, that they have such truths and that all the others are quite mistaken. Most of them believe that they, with a new Copernican turn, have in their "bag, all ready made, final and ultimate truth and eternal justice" (p. 100). Of such claims to an Archimedean point, Engels remarks with a thoroughly realistic worldweariness: "That has all happened so many hundreds and thousands of times that we can only feel astonished that there should be people credulous enough to believe this, not of others, but of themselves" (p. 100). But the fact is there are such people and that they typically fly "into high moral indignation when other people deny that any individual whatsoever is in a position to hand out to us the final and ultimate truth" (p. 100). Of this Engels remarks: "Final and ultimate truths" in the domain of morals are very sparsely sown indeed: even more so than in the domain of factual truth. "The conceptions of good and bad have varied so much from nation to nation and from age to age that they have often been in direct contradiction to each other" (p. 103). Moreover, we get no place at all with the truism "Good is good and evil is evil." At most this reminds us that there are moral matters we care about and care about deeply. What we want and of course do not get from anything like that is a criterion for choosing between the various extant moralities.

We have Catholic-Christian moralities and Protestant-Christian moralities. And we have more modernizing moralities such as bourgeois morality and the "proletarian morality of the future." To know that "Good is to be done and evil avoided" and that "Good is good and bad is bad" is not going to help us choose between them. Indeed they do not, being tautologies, function as action-guides at all.

What we want to know is how are we going to choose between these positive moralities. Which, if any one, is the true one or the approximately true one and how would we decide? Engels makes it quite clear that an ethical rationalism will not help us here. There is no showing that one of them or some new philosophical morality created by some super-Dühring will help us here. There is no showing that they have any kind of absolute prescriptivity. But this does not justify our taking a relativist or subjectivist turn, for some of these moralities have, in Engels' words, more "durable elements" than others. They are not all on a par such that you must just plump for which one to accept. You will not find Engels supporting anything like the contemporary liberal shibboleth that in the domain of ultimate values decision is king. But he is not defending a morality of categorical prescriptivity either. Still, his denials here do not lead him to relativism or skepticism. The proletarian morality has, as Engels sees it, "the maximum of durable elements" (p. 104). It has a coherent vision of a future proletarian emancipation: an emancipation that will lead to a general human emancipation and to the construction of a human and classless society without exploiter and exploited, master and slave, ruler and ruled.

Engels rejects any moral absolutism with ultimate changeless moral truths and principles. But he does not think that anything goes morally or that there can be no progress or development in our moral thinking.[9] He does not defend ethical subjectivism or skepticism. That there are no ultimate truths in morality does not mean that there are no proximate truths (p. 104).

As an explanation of why this is so historical materialism is important and Engels brings it into play at just this juncture. The above theses in descriptive ethics could be asserted and established to be true. But these are all statements of empirical fact about people's moral beliefs; they are not themselves moral or normative utterances. Moreover, while historical materialism would not justify this developmental non-absolutism in ethics, it could explain it and that is exactly how Engels does utilize it.[10] He utilizes it in this way but he also utilizes it critically as well as a ground for rationally rejecting ethical rationalism. If an ethical rationalist tries to legitimate a claim that such and such is an ultimate moral truth or set of such truths on the ground that the "moral world . . . has its permanent principles which transcend history and the differences between nations," historical materialism is, if true, a very effective counter. For with it one can show that that rationalist claim does not square with the actual or realistically possible structure or design of the moral world: moralities and "moral theories are the product, in the last analysis, of the economic stage which society" has reached at "a particular epoch" (p. 105). These societies, as the productive forces develop, change by means of class struggle. Societies in the past have been class societies and they will remain so up until the thorough consolidation of socialism (p. 105). And the moralities of these class societies are class moralities.

The "three classes of modern society, the feudal aristocracy, the bourgeoisie and the proletariat, each have their special morality." Engels concludes from this "that men, consciously or unconsciously, derive their moral ideas in the last resort from the practical relations on which their class position is based—from the economic relations in which they carry on production and exchange" (p. 104).

'Derive' could mean here 'logically deduce' or "causally spring." I take it that Engels means the latter for (a) on the first reading the thesis is absurd, (b) the latter reading squares with the causal explanatory role of historical materialism and (c) the latter reading has plausibility and point. (I am here operating with the rather standard maxim of interpretative charity.) "That group X are members of the feudal aristocracy" does not entail that "group X ought to have a Christian-feudal morality." But what is at least plausible to say is that most members of a feudal aristocracy will as a matter of fact be committed to a Christian-feudal morality and that people standing in these productive relations will naturally and, indeed, generally speaking almost unavoidably come to have a distinctive morality which matches with and tends to help reinforce and to preserve for a time that distinctive set of production relations: production relations which in periods of social stability neatly match with moral conceptions which function to maintain them. In turn these production relations provide the causal basis for these moral ideas having, for a time, though surely not forever, a solid social exemplification.

Still, during a given historical period there will be common elements shared by the different class moralities (p. 104). In our epoch, Christian morality, bourgeois morality and proletarian morality "represent three different stages of the same historical development, and have therefore a common historical background, and for that reason alone they have much in common" (p. 104).

Engels states his case in even stronger terms. "In similar or approximately similar stages of economic development moral theories must of necessity be more or less in agreement" (p. 104).[11] Societies with the institution of private property need a widely recognized and socially inforced injunction "Do not steal" for them to function effectively. (I take it the above 'must' is a causal and not a logical or moral 'must' and I take 'moral theories' here importantly to include 'moralities.') Except in periods of revolution some given class or temporarily co-operating cluster of classes will be dominant in any society. But even the contending antagonistic classes of a class society will have, even with their clashing moralities, moralities with some common content with that of the morality of the dominant class. This common content will result from their common historical background and from the need of those moralities, in one way or another, to support to some degree at least the economic relations of that society. Bases need superstructures. We can speak here of the functional role of these moralities.

Moralities and moral theories function as moral ideologies in class societies. They have "either justified the domination and the interests of the ruling class, or, as soon as the oppressed class has become powerful enough, it has represented the revolt against this domination and has been expressive of the future interests of the oppressed" (p. 105). Moralities have purported to be systems of eternal moral truth while in reality they have supported class interests, including very typically the interests of the ruling class. They have done the typically mystifying ideological work of supporting class interests while representing themselves as purveyors of a higher truth answering to the interests of all humankind.

However, notwithstanding his recognizing very clearly the ideological role of morality, Engels also believes that, emerging out of these class struggles, there has been moral progress, giving the lie to the rather common belief that Marxists, or at least one very prominent Marxist (the first Marxist after Marx, as it were), thought that in the very nature of the case moral conceptions were so distorting and mystifying that there could be no coherent sense in speaking of moral progress or of one moral conception of things or way of organizing society being more adequate than another. There have been nihilists or moral skeptics who have thought that, but there is no good textual warrant for saddling Engels (or for that matter Marx) with the view that all moral conceptions are without any coherent sense or are, in the nature of the case, subjective or rest on some kind of error. Engels, quite confidently, without the least ambivalence, asserts that "there has on the whole been progress in morality, as in all other branches of knowledge . . . " (p. 105). That, he tells us, "cannot be doubted" (p. 105).

However, even with this progress, Engels continues, we have "not yet passed beyond class morality." Though note that this clearly indicates that he believes that there can be moralities that are not class-bound (p. 105). Engels goes on to say, echoing a phrase from Marx's *Paris Manuscripts* and ending with a remark that resonates with their *Critique of the Gotha Programme,* "A really human morality which transcends class antagonisms and their legacies in thought becomes possible only at a stage of society which has not only overcome class contradictions but has even forgotten them in practical life" (p. 108).

This shows, as clearly as can be, how Engels, while rejecting ethical rationalism, and accepting a fallibilistic world-view, did not regard *all* morality as subjective or as a form of moral ideology, distorting our understanding of ourselves and of our society. A lot of morality does just that and should be unmasked as ideology, but it is not something which is essential to all morality everywhere, at all times. At least Engels is not claiming that and there is nothing in Engels' text which implicitly warrants that claim.

IV

Engels next in Chapter 10 of *Anti-Dühring* turns to a discussion of equality. He first points out that there is a lot of ideological twaddle in much of our talk of equality and inequality (pp. 107–112). On the one hand, talk of mental and moral inequalities has been used ideologically to 'justify' "crimes of civilized robber states against backward peoples" and, on the other, contracterian talk of equality has mystified the actual hierarchical relations between people in which one class has dominated another (pp. 112 and 108–110). Indeed sometimes what in reality has been the brutal subjugation and repression of one people or class by another has been justified in the name of attaining equality. Some have decided that others are afflicted with "superstition, prejudice, brutality and perversity of character" while they, 'the enlightened ones,' have, in the name of attaining equality, 'adjusted' these malformed people (p. 112). The tides of ideology are running high, Engels claims, when equality comes to "adjustment by force" (p. 112). Some are where such conceptions reign, to "attain equal rights through subjection" (p. 112).

However, while philosophers like Dühring have in effect made a charade out of talk of equality, nonetheless the idea itself is an extremely important one. Engels acknowledges the importance of Rousseau's articulation of equality both theoretically and in a practical sense in the French Revolution (p. 113). "Even today," Engels continues, it "still plays an important agitational role in the socialist movement of almost every country" (p. 113). However, it is only after we have been able to determine with greater exactitude its "scientific content" that we will be able to "determine its value for proletarian agitation" (p. 113).[12]

What is the 'scientific content' of equality? It is not the primeval conception that men have some common characteristics and that it is in virtue of these common characteristics that they are equal (p. 113). Rather "the modern demand for equality is something entirely different from that . . . " (p. 113). It consists in "deducing from those common characteristics of humanity, from that equality of humans as humans, a claim to equal political or social status for all human beings, or at least for all citizens of a state or all members of a society" (pp. 113–114). (Engels here should have said 'attempting to deduce' rather than 'deducing.' However, it is clear from the context that he does not think any valid deduction can be made. He was speaking above in a sociological mode.) It is worth noting, however, that it took thousands of years for this modern idea, i.e. the idea that "all men should have equal rights in the state and in society," to take hold and to come to seem "natural and self-evident" (p. 114). For millenia "women, slaves and strangers" were "excluded from this equality as a matter of course" (p. 114). It is only with the rise of the bourgeoisie that we get the modern demand for equality described above (p. 115).

Here Engels uses his conception of historical materialism to show how such a class arose and how, with the development of capitalist relations of production, such an idea of equality became historically possible and how it, in turn, helped the stabilization of such relations of production and facilitated the development of these relations of production (pp. 115–116). There was in such a cultural environment much emphasis on equal legal and political rights, but the firmest form of equality under capitalism was that of the "equal status of human labor" (p. 116). This conception found its "unconscious but clearest expression in the law of value of modern bourgeois economics according to which the value of a commodity is measured by the socially necessary labor embodied in it" (p. 116). It is to this, Engels argues, that we should trace the modern idea of equality. In doing so we are tracing it back "to the economic conditions of bourgeois society" (p. 116). Unlike the guild restrictions of feudal society, capitalist production relations "required freedom and equality of rights." For capitalism to flourish all artificial barriers to the development of manufacture must be done away with. However, once set in motion this demand for equality was hard to contain or circumscribe. "It was a matter of course that the demand for equality should assume a general character reaching out beyond the individual state. . . . " It was a matter of course, with this economic development, "that freedom and equality should be proclaimed as *human* rights" (p. 117). There was, of course, room for all kinds of double-mindedness here. The American Constitution, for example, was the first to recognize the rights of man, yet, as Engels put it, "in the same breath" it "confirmed the slavery of the colored races in America . . . " (p. 117). What it did was to "proscribe class privileges while sanctifying race privileges . . . " (p. 117).

However, this is not, for Engels, the full story of equality or the only thing that the development of the forces of production was bringing into being. As the burghers of the feudal period "developed into a class of modern society, it was always and inevitably accompanied by its shadow, the proletariat" (p. 117). And, as there emerged a bourgeois demand for equality, so too there emerged a proletarian demand for equality (p. 117). As Engels puts it in a famous passage:

> From the moment when the bourgeois demand for the abolition of class *privileges* was put forward, alongside of it appeared the proletarian demand for the abolition of the *classes themselves*—at first in religious form, basing itself on primitive Christianity, and later drawing support from the bourgeois equalitarian theories themselves. The proletarians took the bourgeoisie at their word: equality must not be merely apparent, must not apply merely to the sphere of the state, but must also be real, must be extended to the social and economic sphere. And especially since the time when the French bourgeoisie, from the Great Revolution on, brought bourgeois equality to the forefront, the French proletariat has answered it blow for blow with the demand for social and economic equality, and equality has become the battle-cry particularly of the French proletariat (p. 117).

For the proletariat the demand for equality came to have a double meaning. Its first sense was that of an ideological weapon of the struggling proletariat. It was, as Engels put it, "the simple expression of the revolutionary instinct and finds its justification in that, and only in that" (p. 117). This simple expression of revolutionary instinct is "the spontaneous reaction against the crying social inequalities, against the contrast of rich and poor, the feudal lords and their serfs, surfeit and starvation . . . " (p. 117). Secondly, and very importantly, we must recognize another ideological role in the class struggle of the proletarian demand for equality. This proletarian demand for equality draws "more or less correct and more far-reaching demands from this bourgeois demand" and serves "as an agitational means in order to rouse the workers against the capitalists . . . " (p. 118). Yet it is a demand "which is made on the basis of the capitalists' own assertions . . . " (p. 117). It does not require a *distinct* moral content or conception. It is, I take it, at least in part this that Engels has in mind when he remarks, somewhat enigmatically, that this proletarian demand "stands and falls with bourgeois equality itself" (p. 117). Presumably that means that it must (1) presuppose this bourgeois norm in order to extend itself beyond the bourgeois demand and (2) that it is causally dependent on that demand since it arises from it and (3) that if the bourgeois demand is not justified it is not justified.

Now, as the 'scientific content' of the demand for *bourgeois* equality is the demand that the value of a commodity, any commodity, including labor-power, be measured by the socially necessary labor embodied in it, so the scientific content of the *proletarian* demand for equality, taking into consideration both of its meanings, is "*the demand for the abolition of classes*" (p. 118, italics mine). Engels adds, in a remark that is vital for an understanding of a socialist conception of equality, "Any demand for equality *which goes beyond that of necessity passes into absurdity*" (p. 118). Engels appears, at least, to have contradicted himself in these passages. He first says that proletarian conceptions of equality have the same content as bourgeois ones and then says they have a different content, i.e. the demand for the abolition of classes. What I think he should have said, and what he seems at least to intend, is that they have a similar content, a content that is both rendered more determinate and is extended as proletarian class consciousness develops. As the social formation distinctive of Communism is consolidated, equality would come to have a quite different content. It would come to mean the attainment of a thorough classlessness.

Engels concludes Chapter 10 of *Anti-Dühring* by relating this talk of equality to his earlier critique of self-evident, eternally true moral ideas and to his historical-materialist methodology (p. 118). We need to recognize that the idea of equality, whether in its bourgeois or proletarian forms, is not an eternal truth or an axiomatic truth (p. 118). They are rather both historical products, brought about by historical conditions "which in turn themselves presuppose a long previous historical development" (p. 118). That in one sense or another equality is taken by the general public with the development of capitalism to be almost a self-evident axiomatic truth does not at all show that it is anything of the kind.[13] Rather—and here Engels is very much a child of the Enlightenment—it is the "result of the general diffusion and the continued appropriateness of the ideas of the eighteenth century" (p. 118). This remark, interestingly, is both empirical and sociological (he speaks of 'the general diffusion') and normative (he speaks of 'the continued appropriateness').

V

I have now completed my characterization of the central places where Engels speaks of moral ideas and morality in *Anti-Dühring*: to wit Chapters 1, 9 and 10. I shall turn in this section to some further scattered remarks in *Anti-Dühring* where he speaks of liberty and its relation to equality.

In the context of discussing liberty, Engels, fitting well with his overall Enlightenment orientation and his sense of how societies historically develop, remarks that "English law with its quite exceptional developments" has safeguarded "personal liberty to an extent unknown anywhere on the Continent" (p. 124). In talking of liberty and freedom, Engels did not mean to deny the truth of determinism. He develops what would now be called a compatibilist position on the 'free will controversy,' though it is a compatibilism with a very Hegelian and ultimately a Spinozist flavor. "Freedom is the appreciation of necessity." We are unfree to the extent that we do not understand the ways the laws of nature and society work. "Freedom does not consist in the dream of independence of natural laws, but in the knowledge of these laws, and in the possibility this gives of systematically making them work towards definite ends" (p. 125). Against the indeterminist, Engels argues that "freedom . . . consists in the control over ourselves and over external nature which is founded on knowledge of natural necessity" (p. 125). This self-mastery increases as our knowledge increases and is plainly "a product of historical development." The 'freedom' of the indeterminist (incompatibilist), even if it were possible, would be no genuine freedom at all. A decision made in uncertainty and founded on ignorance—"an arbitrary choice among many different and conflicting possible decisions"—shows "precisely that it is not free" (p. 125). Rather, 'freedom of the will,' if it means anything at all, "means nothing but the capacity to make decisions with real knowledge of the subject" (p. 125). We have that capacity and with the development of science and the forces of production generally, we have an ever greater opportunity to exercise that freedom. "The first men who separated themselves from the animal kingdom were in all essentials as unfree as the animals themselves, but each step forward in civilization was a step towards freedom" (pp. 125–126). It is, in Engels' view, the extensive development of "powerful productive forces" which "alone makes *possible* a state of society in which there are no longer class distinctions or anxiety over the means of subsistence for the individual, and in which for the first time there can be talk of real human freedom . . . " (p. 126).

Here we have a crucial claim for Marxism and for egalitarianism. Liberty and equality are tightly linked. Liberty, the control over ourselves and over external nature, is always a matter of degree, but, for it to flourish, it requires the development of the productive forces. Until scarcity is overcome, nature tamed and general social wealth is considerable, freedom cannot be extensive. It cannot, without such social wealth, except perhaps for a few, flourish to the fullest extent possible. It is also the case that freedom will not flourish until there are no longer class distinctions. Until, that is, there is no longer a situation in which one group of people in very crucial ways can coerce others. But this means that liberty requires equality. Indeed, Engels is making the striking claim that it goes both ways: *liberty requires equality and equality requires liberty.* The real content of equality is classlessness, but there can be no human freedom for all without classlessness, for without classlessness some will always be in the control of others. So equality cannot exist without liberty and extensive liberty, liberty for all (the ideals of the French Revolution), can only exist with equality (classlessness).

Notes

1. The central work here is his *Anti-Dühring*, though there are scattered references throughout his work to ethics, moralizing and moral theory. References to *Anti-Dühring* will be given in the text and the page citations will be to an English translation. Frederick Engels, *Anti-Dühring*, translated by Emile Burns, New York, International Publishers, 1939.

2. There is a natural tendency to be very wary of talk of 'scientific socialism.' Andrew Collier in his masterful "Scientific Socialism and the Question of Socialist Values" shows how skepticism here can be dispelled and how much good sense can be made of this scientistic sounding notion. Andrew Collier, "Scientific Socialism and the Question of Socialist Values," in *Marx and Morality*, Kai Nielsen and Steven C. Patten (eds.), Guelph, Ontario, Canadian Association for Publishing in Philosophy, 1981, pp. 121–154.

3. See here Ted Benton, "Natural Science and Cultural Struggle: Engels and Philosophy and the Natural Sciences," in *Issues in Marxist Philosophy*, Vol. II, edited by John Mepham and David-Hillel Ruben, Sussex, England, 1979, pp. 101–142 and Terrell Carver, 'Marx, Engels and Dialectics,' *Political Studies* XXVIII (1980), 353–363. See also his *Engels*, New York, Hill and Wang, 1981.

4. Terrell Carver, "Marx, Engels and Dialectics" and Roy Edgley, "Marx's Revolutionary Science," in *Issues in Marxist Philosophy*, Vol. III, John Mepham and David-Hillel Ruben (eds.), Sussex, England, 1979, p. 5–26.

5. Benton sees Engels as setting out a non-speculative metaphysics and ontology. It is, as he puts it, based in "some as yet undefined sense" on "scientific knowledge." Indeed, he sees "Engels' ontology" as "the product of philosophical reflection on what is presupposed by the recent development of the sciences." Benton, "Natural Science and Cultural Struggle," p. 125. I think Engels' description of what he is doing here is innocuous enough but in some of his practice about the 'dialectics of nature' he was doing the kind of speculative work that he, in his programmatic statements, wisely eschewed. For a contrast between Engels and Marx here see Terrell Carver, "Marx, Engels and Dialectics."

6. George G. Brenkert, "Marx, Engels and the Relativity of Morals," *Studies in Soviet Thought* 17 (1977), 201–224. See also Andrew Collier, "Scientific Socialism and the Question of Socialist Values."

7. Contrast here Allen Wood, "Marx and Equality," in *Issues in Marxist Philosophy*, Vol. IV, John Mepham and David-Hillel Ruben (eds.), Harvester Press, Sussex, England, 1981, pp. 195–220. I intend on some other occasion to argue that Wood both underplays the importance of conceptions of equality in the work of Marx and Engels and underplays its importance in social life.

8. Contrast here Marxist anti-moralism. See Andrew Collier, "Truth and Practice," *Radical Philosophy* 5 (1973); "The Production of Moral Ideology," *Radical Philosophy* 9 (1974); "Scientific Socialism and the Question of Socialist Values" and see, as well, Anthony Skillen, "Marxism and Morality," *Radical Philosophy* 8 (1974), "Workers' Interests and the Proletarian Ethic; Conflicting Strains in Marxian Anti-Moralism," in *Marx and Morality* and A. Skillen, *Ruling Illusions*, Harvester, Sussex, England, 1977, pp. 122–177.

9. But what moral progress comes to requires a reading. It may not be as straightforward as it seems in Engels' work. See here Brenkert, op. cit., pp. 215–219.

10. Brenkert, mistakenly I believe, thinks it justifies it as well. *Ibid.,* pp. 210–12 and 219–221.

11. This sentence indicates that Engels, however unwittingly, was committed to what is now called cognitivism in ethics.

12. Engels' mode of speech sounds overly scientistic. It would perhaps be better if he substituted 'factual content' or 'rational content' for 'scientific content.'

13. In our time, as the neo-conservative reaction exhibits (e.g., Kristol, Nozick, Hayek, Friedman, Flew and Nisbet), it is no longer generally thought to be even true, let alone self-evident.

4

Marx, Engels and Lenin on Justice: *The Critique of the Gotha Programme*

I

The Critique of the Gotha Programme is a polemic, turned against certain of Marx's opponents in the German social-democratic movement.[1] It is a vitriolic, sarcastic indictment of what Marx takes to be bad utopian political thinking on the part of the Eisenachers, the German followers of Ferdinand Lassalle. These matters are better left to the dustbin of history and I shall not be concerned with them here.

However, Marx does say things there about justice, equality and about a future communist society which are both hard to interpret and suggestive. I shall stick close to his text and see what account of these matters emerges from a close reading of it. (I shall in my characterization and explication of it, for the most part, deliberately put aside the sometimes fascinating recent interpretations of Marx on justice.)[2]

Early on in his *Critique of the Gotha Programme,* Marx makes some remarks which are clearly enough integral to his overall social theory and would fit as well with his revolutionary strategy, but which are

This essay was originally published in *Studies in Soviet Thought* 30 (1986): 23–63. Copyright © 1983 by D. Reidel Publishing Company. Reprinted by permission of Kluwer Academic Publishers.

plainly empirical statements which also have a moral force. Marx notes, against the Lassalleans, that "labour is not the source of all wealth" for "nature is just as much the source of use values" as is labour (p. 3). Indeed human labour power is itself the manifestation of a natural force. Material wealth consists in the amassing of use values and they come from nature and labour (p. 3).

Marx then remarks significantly, and thoroughly in harmony with his labour theory of value, that, if the only thing a person owns is his own labour power, then, under all conditions of society and culture, he must remain a *slave* to other men who have made themselves the owners of the material conditions of labour. In using the word 'slave' here, Marx has clearly flagged that he is making a moral judgment and indeed whether he thought of it in these terms is immaterial, for the very term 'slave,' used in such a linguistic environment, clearly indicates a moral judgment is being made. But Marx, in making that claim, is *also* making an empirical statement of fact, though in a vocabulary which is somewhat theory-laden, and that claim will not be thought to be appropriate unless some central bits of his social science are believed to be approximately correct. But the use of 'slave' does not make Marx's remarks here subjective, merely emotive or even tendentious, if his empirical social analysis is correct, anymore than the use of 'cheated' makes the following empirical statement merely emotive, subjective, or tendentious if what it asserts is true. "He cheated her. The tickets are only two dollars and when she gave him a twenty dollar bill, he only gave her back sixteen dollars." Sometimes the use of terms with a certain emotive and normative force are exactly the appropriate terms to use in making an empirical statement of fact that is accurate and true.[3] A statement, to count as a genuine statement of fact, need not be normatively neutral.

A few pages later Marx makes another cluster of statements that are both empirical and have a plain moral force. They are, however, statements which are not brutely empirical, for they are statements which are very theory-dependent and use the vocabulary and forms of conceptualization which are integral to Marx's overall social theory. But this, again, we should not forget, is a social theory which at least sets out to be an empirical theory.

Marx reminds us that as labour develops socially and becomes more complex and requires more co-operative labour (though the division of labour in the workplace generally becomes more acute), it becomes an ever greater source of wealth and culture in the society. But, as it so develops, "poverty and neglect develop among the workers, and wealth and culture among the non-workers" (p. 5). Again we have an empirical statement which is subject to all the empirical constraints that all empirical statements are subject to; but, still, talk of poverty and neglect in such a context also makes it a moral utterance, though one which is plainly true—empirically true—if Marx's political sociology here is accurate.

Marx goes on to say that when we recognize that this has been "the law of history hitherto" and further recognize how extensively the productive forces have developed under capitalism, we will come to see that "the material conditions" in society "have at last been created which will enable and compel the workers to lift this social curse" (p. 5). Again with the use of the phrase 'social curse,' we have a powerful normative phrase with clear emotive overtones; but, we also have an empirical statement making a prediction about what will happen in the future and that statement is perfectly open to confirmation or disconfirmation. Moreover, if the conditions of poverty and neglect of the working class are as Marx says they are, if (for example) Engels' description of the conditions of working class life in Manchester are even in part accurate, and the development of the productive forces make such poverty, degradation and inhuman working conditions unnecessary, then the phrase 'social cause' is both morally appropriate and empirically apt for the characterization of the situation.

II

Marx's first remark about justice comes in his comment on the third proposition of Part One of the Gotha Programme. The Eisenachers' proposition speaks of the "equitable distribution of the proceeds of labour" (p. 6). Marx asks: "What is 'equitable distribution'?" Applying both his historical-materialist methodology and the keen eye of a social scientist for the diversity of moral beliefs, Marx remarks, "Do not the bourgeois assert that the present-day distribution is 'equitable'? And is it not, in fact, the only 'equitable' distribution on the basis of the present-day mode of production? Are economic relations regulated by legal conceptions or do not, on the contrary, legal relations arise from economic ones? Have not also the socialist sectarians the most varied notions about 'equitable' distribution?" (p. 6)

Marx shows his awareness that within the socialist movement itself people, including militants, have all sorts of different moral conceptions and beliefs about what is just and what is unjust. Moreover, they often have very different notions about what some philosophers would call the logical status of these claims and have, as well, varied conceptions about how, if at all, they can be validated. He also, employing his own materialist methodology, makes a claim that he makes in *Capital* as well, namely that what we would correctly judge to be just or unjust at a given time is fixed by the level of development of economic relations at that time. If at time *T* we judge *A* to be just or equitable, if we mean anything sensible at all, we must mean something contextual, namely that, with respect to the set of production relations *Z,* we mean that *A* was just or unjust. The judgment we would make about the justice of distribution of food to the aged in a primitive hunting and gathering society living under marginal life conditions—say the ab-

origines in the anthropological present in Tasmania—and the judgment
we would make about the justice of distribution of food to the aged
in a contemporary Switzerland will not be the same, if we are informed
and reasonable. We could not rightly say the same thing about both
societies. But this is not at all a form of relativism but a contextualism
which is perfectly compatible with a belief in moral objectivity.[4] What
it does appeal to is a recognition that material conditions and the
economic organization of social life strongly condition what we can
rightly say is just or unjust in a particular circumstance or even during
a particular epoch in a particular society.

There is also the steadfast assertion that bases determine superstructures and not the other way around. Legal and presumably moral
relations arise out of economic ones and are regulated by them. (Note
here how Marx naturally sees justice-talk as a part of legal talk and
not as distinctively moral.)[5]

Marx next remarks that in the Lassallean program there is a lot of
loose talk about 'the equal rights of all members of society' and
'undiminished proceeds of labour.' He sees the kernel of the conceptions
underlying such talk as amounting to the claim that, given the Lassallean
conception of a communist society, in such a society every worker
must receive the "undiminished" proceeds of his labour (p. 7).

Marx argues that such an 'axiom of justice,' if that is the right word
for it, cannot reasonably stand as it is given. The "undiminished
proceeds of labour" must become the "diminished proceeds of labour"
(p. 8). However, it is important to recognize that, even with the
'diminished proceeds,' there is an overall gain for workers here. What,
because of these diminished proceeds, an individual producer is
deprived of in his capacity as a private individual, he receives back
in things which "benefit him directly or indirectly as a member of
society" (p. 8). In talking in this context of the proceeds of labour,
we are talking of the product of labour and the co-operative proceeds
of labour are the total social product. Speaking of this product, before
we can even reasonably begin to talk about the part of the total product
to be divided up for individual consumption, we need to make the
following types of deductions: we must (1) allow "for the replacement
of the means of production used up," (2) "allow for expansion of
production" and (3) allow for a "reserve fund to provide against
misadventures, disturbances through natural events" and the like. Here
we are talking about economic necessities and how we are reasonably
to respond to them. "Their magnitude," Marx remarks, "is to be
determined by available means and forces, and partly by calculation
of probabilities, but they are in no way calculable by equity." I want
to note here in passing that it is not so evident that this is completely
so. I could imagine at least a materially very wealthy society in which
it would be a real question of equity as to whether or not to expand
production. Some people, with one scheduling of needs, would want

more and others with a different scheduling of needs would rather have less and do instead less work. They would not, that is, be for an expansion of production. It would be a real question of equity whether or not to continue to expand production and if so by how much.

Be that as it may, and to return to our characterization of Marx, once we have made those deductions from the total social product, we still have further deductions to make before we get to what is left from the total product that can rightly be divided into consumer items. Before we can do that, we have to allow for the general costs of administration, we have to make deductions for the meeting of social needs (what Marx calls the communal satisfaction of needs) such as schools, health services, day-care centres, parks and the like. And we must, as well, set aside from the product, funds for those unable to work, i.e. the aged, the disabled, mental defectives and the like. So we cannot sensibly and literally think of dividing up the total social product among individuals as we might divide up a pie.

Moreover, the Lassalleans, socialistic though they intend to be, still see things, Marx argues, too much in a capitalist way. In the future Communist society, we will no longer talk about or conceive of the individual getting the proceeds of his labour. "Within the co-operative society based on common ownership of the means of production, the producers do not exchange their products; just as little does the labour employed on the products appear here as the value of these products, as a material quality possessed by them, since now, in contrast to capitalist society, individual labour no longer exists in an indirect fashion but directly as a component part of the total labour" (p. 8).

What Marx, in effect, does here is to draw out some of the analytical connections of what the communist society of the future would look like in its various phases. He is not describing something which is but he is saying what in general terms, if we ever have a communist society, that society must be like.[6] This is partly definitional but it is also partly empirical in a way analogous to a biologist's description of what he would predict to be a likely future mutation of a given species. The biologist is telling us that if the present environment of that species is changed in some substantial way, then that species in time will very likely come to have certain characteristics that it does not have now. Marx is saying similar things about societies only he is saying that certain societies will change in certain ways and he is giving us to understand as well—and here is the definitional part—that if, contrary to his expectations, they do not change in that way, then they would not be communist societies. Perhaps his claims also reflect, as many have thought, a distinctive moral vision, but that claim need not be invoked to make Marx's point here. We have empirical propositions here, though we also have a recognition that in such a future society of abundance we would no longer distribute according to contribution but instead according to need.

III

However, Marx, social realist that he always was, at least in his mature writings, reminds us of what have come to be called the problems of the transition.[7] What counts as a just treatment or an equitable treatment of people in early phases in communist society would not be the same as what would count as just or equitable treatment in later phases of communist society. (The same distinction is sometimes made in different terminology in speaking of the transition from socialist society to a later communist society.)

What we need to recognize, Marx tells us, is that we must, standing where we are, start with a society emerging out of a capitalist society with all the problems and limitations that that brings:

> What we have to deal with here is a communist society, not as it has developed on its own foundations, but, on the contrary, as it emerges from capitalist society; which is thus in every respect, economically, morally and intellectually, still stamped with the birthmarks of the old society from whose womb it emerges. Accordingly, the individual producer receives back from society—after the deductions have been made— exactly what he gives to it. What he has given to it is his individual amount of labour.

In this early stage of communism, remuneration is determined by individual contribution. Marx remarks that intensity of labour will also be taken into consideration as well as his labour time in determining what a worker shall receive. Still, what he shall receive is principally determined in a society where every able-bodied adult is a worker, by his labour time. "The same amount of labour which he has given to society in one form, he receives back in another" (p. 8). (How labour contribution is to be computed is actually very complex, much more complex than Marx hints at here. How we could compute intensity, for example, is not evident.) Be that as it may, here in this early phase of communism we still have something very like exchange of commodities in capitalism. Still there is this important difference: in communism no one can give anything except his labour; "nothing can pass into ownership of individuals except individual means of consumption" (p. 9). (This includes, of course, consumer durables like cars and houses.) But we still have, as we have in capitalism, labour exchanging at equal value. I get ten chits for ten hours work and I can take from the common stock of means whatever would be produced by ten hours of labour. "Hence," Marx remarks, "equal right here is still in principle, *bourgeois right,* although principle and practice are no longer in conflict . . . " (p. 9). That is, there really is an exchange of equivalents and not just in theory.

Marx now makes a remark, as reasonable as it is, which does not seem to me a remark that could be a remark of *wertfrei* (a normatively neutral) social science. He sees the moral and social relations he has just described as unavoidable, given the way, as a matter of fact, early communism must emerge out of capitalism. But he thinks, though they are unavoidable, that they are still *flawed.* "The equal right" of workers in early communism "is still stigmatised by a bourgeois limitation" (p. 9). What he has in mind is that "the right of the producers is *proportional* to the labour they supply; the equality consists in the fact that measurement is made with an *equal standard,* labour" (p. 9). But why, according to Marx, are such social relations flawed? We indeed will by now be living in a classless society in the straightforward and objective sense that every able-bodied adult in the society is a worker, but the individuals in the society—that is all of us—are still, in terms of the division of labour, viewed only as workers, *sic* as personifications of economic categories. That they have different needs is ignored in the distribution to them of their share of the total social product.[8] We ignore from this perspective considerations such as that one is married and another is not, that one has more children than another, that one is ill and the other well. The measure is not in terms of need but *entirely* in terms of labour contribution measured by its duration and intensity.[9] "Thus with an equal output, and hence an equal share in the social consumption fund, one will in fact receive more than another, one will be richer than another" (p. 10). The maxim of justice, or at least of distribution, for early communism is 'From each according to his labour contribution, to each according to his labour contribution.' (Think here of problems in measuring that contribution.)[10]

In a statement which is both characteristic and famous Marx tells us:

> These defects are inevitable in the first phase of communist society as it is when it has just emerged after prolonged birth pangs from capitalist society. Right can never be higher than the economic structure of society and the cultural development thereby determined (p. 10).

Again there are clearly value-judgments at work here. But they are value-judgments based on his historical-social analysis and on an empirical theory about the relation of base to superstructure. If that analysis and that theory are approximately true, then Marx's moral evaluations follow rather trivially. Only if certain moral truisms presupposed by Marx, and by almost everyone else as well, are not accepted would his moral evaluations here not be accepted if his empirical analysis is accepted. But that is true as well of "Duck! There's a sniper!"[11]

IV

Marx next turns to a discussion of what would be just distribution and equitable treatment in "*a* higher phase of communist society

. . . "¹² (p. 10). A passage here is so famous and so crucial that I shall quote it in full:

> In a higher phase of communist society, after the enslaving subordination of individuals under division of labour, and therewith also the antithesis between mental and physical labour, has vanished; after labour, from a mere means of life, has itself become the prime necessity of life; after the reproductive forces have also increased with the all-round development of the individual, and all the springs of co-operative wealth flow more abundantly—only then can the narrow horizon of bourgeois right be fully left behind and society inscribe on its banners: from each according to his ability to each according to his needs! (p. 10)

Note that Marx is telling us—and this is a *wertfrei* scientific bit of the sociology of morals—that the earlier phase of communism will have a fundamental principle of justice 'From each according to his ability to each according to his labour contribution' and that a later phase will have a quite different fundamental principle of justice 'From each according to his ability, to each according to his needs' and that these different principles of justice arise from and support and in turn are supported by different material conditions and different forms of economic organization. Given a certain development of productive forces and a consequent development of production relations, we get one principle; given another development of the productive forces and a consequent development of production relations, we get another.

Marx, however, also refers to these earlier and later phases of communist society as higher and lower phases of communism and this clearly connotes that one phase is a better state of affairs than the other. And it is evident enough that this is something which plainly Marx firmly believed. He did not think, as many bourgeois intellectuals now think, that progress is an illusion. In short, there is here a moral judgment, though it seems to me a perfectly reasonable one, on Marx's part. And again we have gone beyond *wertfrei* social science.¹³ (In his attitude toward progress Marx's conceptions are plainly at odds with those of Max Weber.)

Marx also talks, appropriately enough it seems to me, of a higher phase of communist society, escaping "the enslaving subordination of individuals under the division of labour," escaping the antithesis between mental and manual labour, where people of one class and status do one kind of job and people of another class and status do another kind of job. Work, in capitalist societies, and in the early phase of communism, will be under the realm of necessity. Much of the work will not be satisfying, will not be fulfilling. But, with the extensive development of technology, with democratic control of the workplace, with the rationale of production becoming the meeting of unmanipulated human needs, work will become increasingly less dehumanizing and less a matter of drudgery—a mere means of life—and will become instead a meaningful and indeed an important necessity of life as it is for some fortunately placed people now. With the development of the productive forces and with the greater leisure this makes possible and with the existence, for everyone, of a more extensive and more varied education and, at least the possibility of a greater variation in work, a more 'all-around development of the individual' becomes possible and a greater self-realization for more and more people becomes a genuine possibility. This all, of course, requires a high degree of economic development, a state of affairs where "the springs of co-operative wealth flow more abundantly" than they do now or in the earlier phases of communism. It is only when the productive capacity of the society is very fully developed that this state of affairs can obtain so that "the narrow horizon of bourgeois right" can be, and will be, "fully left behind and society" will "inscribe on its banners from each according to his ability, to each according to his needs" (p. 10).

We have in Marx's account here some 'moral description' in indirect discourse that might be construed as the descriptive discourse of the sociology of morals, but there is also talk, which plainly is directly moral, e.g. talk of the "enslaving subordination of individuals." There Marx is speaking in his own voice as a moralist—I did not say as a moral philosopher—and is not doing *wertfrei* social science. There is the judgment that one form of society is higher than another, because it is more liberating, more conducive to human self-realization and to a maximal satisfaction of human needs. (We can see here how both the self-realizationist and the utilitarian can claim him.)[14] Such claims on Marx's part do not at all justify the claim that Marx was here developing a moral philosophy or some 'rational foundation' for ethics, whatever exactly that means, but he does show here something of a vision of a good society and of a humanly more adequate way of distributing things.[15] The earlier phase or phases of communism were an improvement in this respect over capitalism and the later phase or phases of communism are an improvement over the earlier phase or phases.

With the stress here on altered patterns of distribution and conceptions of right, albeit changes which come with changes in the mode of production, I do not see why it is not at least plausible to conclude that Marx believed, though he did not actually say this, that with a greater increase of social wealth, with the development of productive forces and with an alteration of economic relations to relations which match more adequately these developed productive forces, there will be a growth of justice in the world, though it will not always be a direct growth and it will not be without its temporary setbacks. (Still, is 'a growth of justice' the right way to describe this growth?) Certainly if things go in that direction a more humane society is coming into being and there is an increased human flourishing, but do we want to say that with such changes, we have a more just or a fairer society?

Here Allen Wood's argument should be borne in mind. Still, it does *not* seem to me a mistake to say that we have a fairer society, as well or a more human society. If Wood would resist and we would drop terms like 'fairer' or 'juster' would it matter very much? We still have a judgment about one society being better than another.[16]

Marx goes on to stress, in the paragraphs following the famous passage cited above, that it is a "mistake to make a fuss about so called 'distribution' and put the principal stress on it" (p. 10). This is almost a corollary of central theses in his labour theory of value and historical materialism. But it is still not at all to deny the moral reality of what was described above. It is rather again to put stress on how meaningful moral argument is circumscribed by determinate historical possibilities and specifically on how questions of distribution are subordinate to questions of production, since the "distribution of the means of consumption at any time is only a consequence of the distribution of the conditions of production themselves" (p. 10). Where the "material conditions of production are the co-operative property of the workers themselves then this results in a different distribution of the means of consumption from the present one (p. 11). The crucial thing in defending a socialist construction of society is to stress the co-operative ownership and control of the means of production. That development of the mode of production will produce a better distributive pattern answering more readily to the interests and needs of the vast majority of the people. That is—or so at least Marx believes—automatic.

It is a mistake—in effect playing into the hands of bourgeois ideology—to consider questions of distribution as if they were independent of questions of production and to see socialism as principally an alternative system of distribution of the social product.[17] The crucial question is the question of industrial democracy: the question of who owns and controls the means of production.[18] It is only with that control that workers can gain autonomy and win the battle for democracy. Here we have claims which have a moral force but are still claims which have empirical truth-conditions and are part of an empirical social science.

V

Marx also makes a characteristic remark, a remark echoed in several places by Engels and again much later by Lenin, when he contrasts his position on equality with that of the Lassalleans.[19] The Lassalleans (the Eisenachers) had called for establishing, by the legal means of a 'free state,' the "removal of all social and political inequality" (p. 14). Marx says such indefinite and loose talk should be dropped from the programatic statement of a worker's party and emphasis should be placed instead on class struggle and the attainment through such struggle of classlessness. Instead of talk of "removal of all social and political inequality" and the establishment of a 'free state,' the worker's program should spell out to the workers that their agitation and struggle should be for a liberation from class society, and that "with the abolition of class differences all the social and political inequality arising from them would disappear of itself"[20] (p. 16).

That last remark is ambiguous in various ways, but I take it that Marx means by it that the really troublesome and morally objectionable inequalities are caused by society being divided into classes and that when class society is firmly overcome these inequalities will just disappear.

Engels says, in greater detail, similar things in his *Anti-Dühring*. (It is important that we have a look at Engels here for his remarks on morality are more extensive and systematic than anything Marx ever gave. It was written in 1878 while the *Critique of the Gotha Programme* was written in 1875. Thus they are of the same period.) Engels remarks there that in different places and at different times the demand for equality has meant different things[21] (pp. 113–4). In modern times, with the rise of the bourgeois order, it has meant most essentially that human beings, women and men, "should have equal rights in the state and in society" (p. 114). But this is still, important as it is, a limited and inadequate kind of equality. To show this, Engels goes on to point out that when the bourgeoisie developed into a class in modern society, they brought into existence another class, the proletariat. Both classes demanded equality, but their demands were distinct. The bourgeoisie demanded an end to class *privileges* but the proletarians demanded the "abolition of the classes themselves" (p. 117). The proletarians took the bourgeoisie at their word: "equality must not be merely apparent, must not apply merely to the sphere of the state, but must also be real, must be extended to the social and economic sphere" (p. 117). So, as a battle cry for the proletariat, the demand is not merely for political and legal equality but for socio-economic equality as well.

In a famous passage Engels sets forth, more fully than does Marx, but in harmony with Marx's remark cited above, the characteristic Marxist position on equality.

The demand for equality in the mouth of the proletariat has therefore a double meaning. It is either—as was especially the case at the very start, for example in the peasants' war—the spontaneous reaction against the crying social inequalities, against the contrast of rich and poor, the feudal lords and their serfs, surfeit and starvation; as such it is the simple expression of the revolutionary instinct, and finds its justification in that, and indeed only in that. Or, on the other hand, the proletarian demand for equality has arisen as the reaction against the bourgeois demand for equality, drawing more or less correct and more far-reaching demands from this bourgeois demand, and serving as an agitational means in order to rouse the workers against the capitalists on the basis of the

capitalists' own assertions; and in this case it stands and falls with
bourgeois equality itself. In both cases the real content of the proletarian
demand for equality is the demand for the abolition of classes. Any
demand for equality which goes beyond that, of necessity passes into
absurdity (pp. 117–118).

The most crucial thing to see here is that Engels treats the key core
of the communist demand for equality to be the demand for the end
of class society. Meaningful, morally supportable, demands for equality
are demands, *not* for the obliteration of all human differences, something
which, even if achievable (as it is not), would be morally monstrous,
but for the abolition of class differences.[22] The demand for equality,
where sensible, is now the demand for the end to a society divided
into social classes with their great inequalities of power and control
in the living of one's life. In the modern era, the struggle for equality
and the struggle for socialism come to the same thing. This, I think,
is the most crucial thing to see in Engels' passage. If that claim of
Engels had been duly noted, much strawman criticism of egalitarianism
could have been avoided.

However, it is also worth noting that Engels there regards, in certain
circumstances, the appeal to equality as a useful agitational weapon
in the class struggle. And it is also useful to note how this appeal so
functions. It is not so much a matter of designing a clearly crafted,
clearly articulated principle of equality, à la Ronald Dworkin, but of
drawing out the appropriate implications of the bourgeois conception.[23]
The thing is, looking at things from the standpoint of workers, to make
the capitalists eat their own words by making evident that in reality
their own professed commitment to equality cannot be realized.[24] It
cannot be realized because political and social inequalities cannot but
exist if the economic inequalities, unavoidable in class society, exist.
It is not so much that we need to unearth some deeper understanding
of the equality of human beings than that articulated by the best
bourgeois thinkers; rather what we principally need is a more realistic
understanding of the conditions under which the achievement of this
equality would be possible. (Though we do need to know that economic
equality is pivotal here.)

To round out this discussion of Marx's arguments about the Lassallean
claims about equality and to shed further light on what Engels is
claiming, it is useful to quote Engels' 1875 letter to August Bebel,
where he discusses Marx's response to the Lassalleans about such
matters. Engels comments on the Second General principle of the
Gotha Programme.

> The removal of all social and political inequality is also a very questionable
> phrase in place of "the abolition of all class differences." Between one
> country and another, one province and another and even one place and
> another, there will always exist a certain inequality in the conditions of

life, which can be reduced to a minimum but never entirely removed. Mountain dwellers will always have different conditions of life from those of people living on plains. The idea of socialist society as the realm of equality is a one-sided French idea resting upon the old "liberty, equality, fraternity"—an idea which was justified as a stage of development in its own time and place, but which, like all the one-sided ideas of the earlier, socialist schools, should now be overcome, for they only produce confusion in people's heads and more precise modes of presentation have been found.[25]

Here we see Engels stressing that there are certain inequalities which have nothing to do with classlessness which cannot be removed and which we should not attempt to remove. At any given time some will have to live in places like Brandon or Kansas City while some live in Victoria or Portland, some will be more energetic and creative than others, some will be better looking than others. It would be the height of absurdity to have everyone undergo plastic surgery in order to produce a uniform look. There are inequalities that are harmless and some that we should rejoice in because they are the cause of cultural richness and there are some that we just have to live with and try to reduce their ill effects to a minimum. Not everyone will be able to marry the person he or she wants to marry; to insist on equality here makes no sense. Rather the inequalities most persistently to be struggled against and to be overcome are the political, social and economic inequalities which stem from the existence of class society and which deeply affect, through resulting differentials in power, people's autonomy.

Engels also stresses that egalitarianism can be and has been, as it has come out of the French Enlightenment, a one-sided ideal. To try to construe equality as *the* notion of what a socialist society is about is to miss the complexity of conception that is built into the very idea of a socialist society and of a future communist society, though to say this is not to deny that there is in socialism a conception of equality of condition partly captured in the bourgeois conception of an equality of political and social rights and more fully captured in the socialist idea of classlessness. It is also important to recognize that some such conception of an equality of condition would have to be part of a vision of the communist society of the future.[26]

VI

For contemporary thinkers as diverse as John Rawls and Robert Nozick talk of freedom and of the role of the state in society is closely related to discussions of justice. Marx does not directly link his talk of freedom and the state to talk of justice but, there appears at least to be an implication there, for such talk does occur in Parts III and IV of his *Critique of the Gotha Programme,* just after his discussion of equality and only two sections after his discussion of justice. The thread of the argument there is continuous. Marx there derides the Lassalleans' naive talk of the 'freedom of the state' and their reliance on state action, within capitalist society, to establish workers' co-operatives and by new state loans to build a new society just as the state might instigate and support the building of a new railway (p. 16). Marx will have nothing of what later will be labelled revisionist ideas (p. 16). It is a mistake, Marx argues, to ignore class struggle. We must recognize its import and we must further recognise that it must be channelled in the direction of a revolutionary transformation of society. Instead the Lassalleans simple-mindedly look to the state in capitalist society to transform society into a society of producer's co-operatives (p. 16). Class-conscious workers will not be so hoodwinked and will work instead to revolutionize the present conditions of production and this "has nothing in common with the foundation of co-operative societies with state aid" (p. 17). Such a revisionist stress, whatever the intentions of the authors, is in reality reactionary and supportive of the *status quo,* for it will, where it gains currency, deflect the worker's attention away from the necessity of militant class struggle culminating in a revolution in which they will seize the state apparatus and run the state in a transformed form in their own interests. That is the state will be run by workers for workers. We should not fail to note here *vis-à-vis* any moral assessment we might want to make about this that these interests are those of the vast majority of people. Still, until such time as the last remnants of bourgeois opposition and bourgeois consciousness have withered away, there will be the need for a coercive *workers* state. But when the last remnants of such bourgeois opposition is gone, the repressive state apparatus can be replaced by an administrative apparatus designed to administer things in the interest of everyone alike.

This also points the way to what Marx takes freedom to be, namely "converting the state from an organ standing above society into one completely subordinate to it . . . " (p. 17). The state in bourgeois society is an instrument for the control of the vast majority of people by a few. These few men constitute a pinnacle of power of the capitalist class. It is they, sometimes in subtle and indirect ways, who control the vast majority of people. Freedom will be obtained only when that control is broken and when even the state comes to be completely subordinate to society as a whole, that is to say, subordinate to the people acting together democratically.

A preliminary partially liberating idea is to come to see through the common ideological view that the state is "an independent entity that possesses its own *intellectual, moral and free basis*" (p. 17). Moreover, we must recognize that in the period of revolutionary transformation between capitalist and communist society when the proletarians have gained control of the state apparatus but where the economic institutions are still in a period of transition "the state can be nothing but the revolutionary dictatorship of the proletariat" (p. 18).

We must be careful how we proceed here for this is one of the most misunderstood remarks of Marx and one, given the modern sense of 'dictatorship,' that has understandably caused alarm.[27] Marx meant by 'dictatorship of the proletariat' the 'rule by the vast majority of the people,' i.e. the workers, in the interests of the vast majority of the people,' i.e. the workers. He was speaking here of mass and popular democracy. 'The dictatorship of the proletariat' is meant to refer to the rule of this huge class in a period of transition when it was still contending with the threat of the capitalist class, but this proletarian class rule was the rule of a class which was to put itself out of business by finally ending all class society. When the last remnants of bourgeois resistance and distinctively bourgeois thought are gone and we have a society of people who are all workers and who think of themselves as workers, then the need for rule by a class would also be gone and with that the dictatorship of the proletariat, like the state itself, would wither away. This could not be what the anarchists so feared, namely 'Dictatorship *over* the proletariat' for to be the dictatorship that Marx spoke of it *must* be rule *by* the proletariat itself.[28] What the anarchists worried about might transpire, but if it were to happen what we would have would not be a dictatorship of the proletariat. If, contrary to Marx's expectations, a 'dictatorship *over* the proletariat' were the upshot of what started out as a socialist revolution, then the socialist revolution would have failed and we would have the transition from a capitalist society—a dictatorship of the bourgeoisie—to some distinct kind of authoritarian society, perhaps, depending on its exact form, to a fascist society or some modern form of technocracy. This might very well not be an ending of 'the dictatorship of the bourgeoisie' but a transforming of it to meet modern conditions. The transition state in the revolutionary move from capitalism to socialism, must be a dictatorship of the proletariat. But to talk of a 'dictatorship of the proletariat' is to talk of a democratic workers state. It is not to talk of the domination of the many by the few, though it is to talk of the domination by the proletariat of the bourgeois. We must remember that we still are in a state of class war.

Marx also addresses himself to questions about freedom of education, science and conscience. He points out that around these notions there is not an inconsiderable amount of bourgeois subterfuge and ideological distortion. If we want to have free education, he argues, it better not be education by the state. It is his belief that "government and church should rather be equally excluded from any influence on the school" (p. 21). The state should not be the educator of the people; the education of the people should remain in the democratic control of the people[29] (p. 21).

In his attitude toward 'Freedom of Conscience,' Marx's distance from liberalism can be clearly seen. He saw the talk and the preoccupation with freedom of conscience as an unfortunate diversion that, particularly in Bismarck's Germany, divided the working class along religious lines and stimulated a superficial bourgeois anti-clericalism. Marx saw the stress on "bourgeois 'freedom of conscience'" as "nothing but the toleration of all possible kinds of religious freedom of conscience." The stress in socialism should not be here but should be placed instead on liberating "the conscience from the spectre of religion" (p. 21). Here Marx was one with Ludwig Feuerbach. But this is not to say, or to give to understand, that in a transitional society, or any society, where there are Jews, Protestants and Catholics, as well as atheists, that all but the atheists should be interfered with or repressed such that religious folk should not be allowed to engage in their religious practices. There are, as Marx recognized, both practical and moral reasons for not doing that. But it is to say that a workers state, without being oppressive about these matters, will not be neutral in its approach to religion and that it will actively promote atheism as something which is in the workers' interest. Communists will recognize, and under many circumstances stress, that religion is *generally,* in one way or another, an ideological prop for the old society. But to actively promote atheism—and indeed to use the workers state to actively promote—is one thing; to suppress freedom of conscience is another. Aside from recognizing that freedom of thought and conscience is itself a good, it is also the case that such a policy is misguided (a) because under suppression religion is likely to be strengthened and (b) left to itself, where people have greater wealth, security and education, the religious impulse will gradually wither away.

What I think we can see here in Marx's *Critique of the Gotha Programme* is not the development of a theory of justice or even a theoretical articulation of a sociology of morals but, in the light of certain empirical-cum-theoretical social beliefs—the articulation of a political sociology, if you will—a critique of bourgeois ideology in the form of the critique of certain bourgeois conceptions of justice, equality and freedom and the substitution for them of a more adequate conception of these moral notions, freed from their distorting ideological context and resting on a more adequate empirical-cum-theoretical understanding of the world that would satisfy, for the most part, though, as we have seen, not entirely, Weber's criteria for a *wertfrei* social science.

There is no reason to think of Marx's own understanding of morality here as ideological or of his own moral judgments as being ideological.[30] How far Marx was from seeing them as ideological expressions can be seen from his unself-consciously moral remarks about the regulation of prison labour at the very end of his *Critique of the Gotha Programme.* He notes there, without any suggestion that this should be construed as a bit of ideology—as something which distorts our understanding of social reality, as something which is class biased or as something which is subjective—that "it *should* have been clearly stated that there is no intention from fear of competition to allow ordinary criminals *to be treated like beasts,* and especially that there is no desire to *deprive* them of their sole means of *betterment,* productive labour. This was *surely* the least one might have expected from socialists" (p. 22, underlining mine).

VII

Robert Tucker and Allen Wood argue that it is a mistake to think of Marx as defending some particular conception of justice (some distinctive principles of justice which provide us with an Archimedean point [from] which we could assess the institutions of society) or as developing even the kernal of a moral theory, though it is the case that, in accordance with his historical materialism and his conception of ideology, Marx develops a sociology of morals.[31] This Tucker-Wood thesis, as I remarked initially, has occasioned much discussion and I shall turn to an examination of it on another occasion. Here I want to examine how Engels and Lenin took Marx's argument in his *Critique of the Gotha Programme* about what they took to be justice. They took Marx's remarks at face value as stating principles of justice, for both a transitional socialist society (a workers state in the early phases of building socialism) and as providing, as well, principles of justice for a higher phase of communist society, where the springs of social wealth flow freely. As we shall see in the next section, an economist-political [philosophy] team, Edward and Onora Nell, interpret and assess Marx's argument understood in this very natural way Engels and Lenin took them. We shall see in the next section what their critical arguments, taking into account contemporary argument over such matters, come to. (Even *if* this is an anachronistic, mistaken reading of Marx's intent and execution, it is significant to examine it as an argument in its own right as to what could be made of those claims.)

Let us start by discussing Engels. In a series of letters, some of them written in 1875 and others written in 1891, Engels, perfectly straightforwardly, with utter seriousness and without even a touch of irony, makes moral remarks about what it is his duty to do, what people's rights are, what the right thing to do is, what the obligations of the *International* are and of the people working in solidarity with it. He speaks freely of what ought and ought not to be the case and he speaks of a "colossal moral defeat for our party" when it was "converted to the Lassallean confession of faith" (p. 39). (See Engels in *The Critique of the Gotha Programme,* pp. 29, 37, 39, 43–4.)

There can be no doubt that Engels regarded *much* moral-talk as ideological twaddle, but if he had regarded all moral-talk, or all moral discourse, simply in virtue of what moral discourse is, as ideological twaddle, he could hardly, without gross inconsistency and a double-mindedness between his theory and practice, have made the straightforward, everyday moral remarks he unself-consciously made above. (Remember many of these were in private letters where he was expressing his moral conviction to trusted comrades.) The contradiction is just so patent that no principle of interpretive charity would allow us so to read Engels, if we can find a reading of him (and Marx as well), which will not commit them to such a conflict between theory and practice. And there is in fact a ready one: namely that in speaking, in doing the sociology of morals, of morality as ideology, they were making the empirical claim that very frequently, indeed almost always, morality is ideological, and indeed for very good reasons, but that that notwithstanding there is nothing in the very nature of moral discourse itself which made it necessarily ideological so that anyone who ever made a moral comment, no matter how informed or how sensitive he was about the role and extent of ideology in life, must be making an ideological remark because that is what morality essentially is. Marx's and Engels' sociology of morals requires no such meta-ethical backdrop and there is no independent evidence that they made any such assumption. They repeatedly and unself-consciously made moral judgments and there is no reason not to take them for what they are: to wit moral judgments either reasonably made or not so reasonably made.[32]

I shall turn next to V. I. Lenin's comments about Marx's remarks about both the first phase and a higher phase of communism and about justice and equality generally in Marx's *Critique of the Gotha Programme.* (Lenin, like Marx, was known to have made some very snappy remarks about moralizing and about moral-talk.) There are brief remarks in Lenin's notebooks on Marxism and the state and detailed remarks, indeed much more detailed than Marx' own, in Chapter V of his *State and Revolution.*[33] I am struck here by the faithfulness of Lenin's account to that of Marx and how it perceptively draws out of Marx' account what is implicit in it and what would result from a rigorous application of the method of historical materialism to the problems Marx discusses.[34]

Lenin here no more does moral philosophy than does Marx, though he does make remarks about what under the first phase of communist society and what under the higher phase of communist society just distributions and a morally and humanly appropriate form of equality would look like.[35] Yet this discussion is thoroughly meshed with a discussion of what the state of development of the productive forces is, what the historical possibilities are and the like. Like those of Marx and Engels, Lenin's moral judgments and assessments about the appropriateness of various social arrangements are always made with such considerations firmly in mind.[36]

To start first with something very general: Lenin, as we can see from his notebooks on *Marxism on the State,* accepted, and accepted *as a principle,* 'From each according to his ability, to each according to his needs.' He took it to be a principle which was to be a fundamental governing principle in *The Higher Phase of Communist Society.*[37] (p. 56). Here, it seems to me, Marx's, Engels' and Lenin's positions are identical. Lenin stressed in his notebooks, and again in *State and Revolution,* that in the lower phase of communist society—a phase often called socialism—there would still be a form of compulsion. The Biblical 'He who does not work, neither shall he eat' will be one of the principles of justice rooted in a conception of fairness appropriate to that situation[38] (p. 59). Indeed, Lenin follows Marx in claiming that in such a society the articles of consumption will be distributed proportionately according to "the quantity of labour contributed by each to society." In such a circumstance, Lenin remarks, inequality of distribution will still be considerable (p. 59). In this transitional workers society with a workers state we will be able effectively to transcend the horizons of bourgeois society, and to pass over into a higher phase of communism only (a) when "the antagonism between mental and physical labour has disappeared," (b) when the habit of working has become the rule and is seen as meaningful and desirable and is engaged in without compulsion as a *"prime necessity of life"* and (c) when the productive forces have developed sufficiently such that we all live in a society of abundance.

Lenin develops these points in detail in *State and Revolution.* In discussing socialism or the first phase of communist society, Marx, Lenin avers, "makes a sober estimate of exactly how socialist society will have to manage its affairs" (p. 78). He contrasts this favorably with the hazy and obscure moralizing of the Lassalleans. Marx, while remaining morally reflective, applies his materialist methodology to specific historical situations and makes "a concrete analysis of the conditions of life of a society" (p. 78). We are speaking, recall, of a "society which has just come into the world out of the womb of capitalism and which, in every respect, bears the birthmarks of the old society . . . " (p. 78). Still, it is already a society in which a socialist revolution has taken place. The state, in such a society, is in the hands of the workers; the military and police are made up of armed workers militias and the "means of production are no longer the private property of individuals" but "belong to the whole of society" (p. 78). Distribution is carried out in the following way:

> Every member of society, performing a certain part of socially-necessary labour, receives a certificate from society to the effect that he has done such and such an amount of work. And with this certificate, he draws from the social stock of means of consumption, a corresponding quantity of products. After deduction of the amount of labour which goes to the public fund, every worker, therefore, receives from society as much as he has given it (p. 78).

Marx, on Lenin's reading, thinks of this as the most just and equitable (fair) social arrangement in *that historical circumstance,* but he does not think of it as the goal of equality that communist society should aim for. It still involves a lot of inequality that, though necessary in that circumstance, is a state of affairs that it would be desirable to overcome as the social wealth comes to flow more freely as the productive forces expand. Such a world of moderate scarcity, before the springs of social wealth flow freely, will be a world in which every able-bodied adult is a worker and every person "having performed as much social labour as another, receives an equal share of the social product," after the deductions Marx discusses are made. Yet there should be no blinking at the fact that this will still result in a kind of inequality, for people are in various ways different: their needs are not all the same, their propensities and abilities differ, they are in different situations (some are married, some are not, some have children, some do not, some live in different parts of the world in quite different circumstances). So while they receive the same certificates to draw from the social stock of means of consumption depending on whether they make the same labour contribution, this equal measure will still have the effect of making some better off than others. There will in reality, operating in accordance with 'From each according to his labour contribution,' develop not inconsiderable inequalities though they will not be so severe or so unjust as the inequalities under capitalism.

Lenin's remarks here are important and reveal his willingness to make moral judgments in the course of his analysis without regarding them as bits of a distorting ideology:

> Hence, the first phase of communism cannot yet produce justice and equality; differences, and unjust differences, in wealth will still exist, but the exploitation of man will have become impossible, because it will be impossible to seize the means of production, the factories, machines, land, etc., as private property. In smashing Lasalle's petty-bourgeois, confused phrases about "equality" and "justice" in general, Marx shows the course of development of communist society, which, at first, is compelled to abolish only the "injustice" of the means of production having been seized by private individuals, and which cannot at once abolish the other injustice of the distribution of articles of consumption "according to the amount of labour performed" (and not according to needs) (p. 79).

Even with the abolition of private productive property, and the ending of the exploitation that goes with it, there will still remain unjust inequalities; that is, there will be inequalities to be overcome as long as products must still be divided according to the amount of work performed. But in the situation of moderate scarcity of early communism (socialism)—the first phase of communism—it is an unavoidable necessity. We need such incentive schedules and the husbandry of what is accumulated to attain the development of the productive forces which would make possible the abundance that would allow us to distribute according to needs (pp. 79–80). In certain respects early communism will face problems like those of capitalism and will operate under some similar constraints. One of them is the imperative necessity to speed the development of the productive forces. In early communism our maxims of justice are almost puritanical, though not without reason, e.g. "He who does not work neither shall he eat" and "An equal amount of labour for an equal amount of products." We still do not, nor can we, distribute according to needs; we are not yet able to follow the rule of procedure of a higher stage of communism which, in Lenin's words, "gives to unequal individuals, in return for an unequal (actually unequal) amount of labour, an equal amount of products" (p. 80). (To stick with Marx, we would have to add something about 'where these needs are the same'.)

Lenin, like Marx and Engels, insists on political realism: " . . . if we are not to indulge in utopianism, we must not think that having overthrown capitalism people will at once learn to work for society *without any standard of right;* and indeed the abolition of capitalism *does not immediately* create the economic premises for such a change" (p. 80). Where there are still remnants of the bourgeoisie around and where the bourgeois mentality is still very much with us, deeply affecting many of the workers, professionals and intelligentsia, there would still be a need for a worker's state in the struggle, in the years immediately following the revolution, to achieve a socialist transformation of society. There would be a need of a proletarian state which (a) safeguarded the public ownership of the means of production, (b) safeguarded equality of labour, and (c) safeguarded equality in the distribution of products according to the principle 'To each according to his labour contribution.'

However, as the productive forces develop and the productive relations change accordingly, and the wealth of the society is ever greater, then, moving into a higher phase of communism, our principles of justice will also alter (p. 81). With the higher phases of communism the economy will be radically transformed. Workers will by now be well educated people with an all-round development; the antithesis between mental and manual labour will have been broken down; the society will have achieved great social wealth, with the arts and the sciences flourishing and with the vast majority of the people in the society, in which everyone is a worker, in possession of a highly developed socialist consciousness with the motivations toward co-operativeness, solidarity, pleasure in meaningful work and commitment to work for the commonwealth that go with that consciousness[39] (pp. 81-3). But the material basis for this consciousness must be laid in a less developed society by the expropriation of capitalist ownership and control of the means of production and the substitution for it of co-operative worker's control of the means of production. Capitalism, which once promoted the development of the productive forces, by

now retards their development. "The expropriation of the capitalists,"
Lenin asserts, "will inevitably result in the enormous development of
the productive forces of human society" (pp. 81–2). But he immediately
adds a cautionary note, which his critics have tended to ignore, "how
rapidly this development will proceed, how soon it will reach the
point of breaking away from the division of labour, of removing the
antithesis between mental and physical labour, of transforming labour
into 'the prime necessity of life' we do not and cannot know" (pp.
81–2).

As society moves towards classlessness, the state will more and more
wither away. We will, of course, have a community—a *Gemeinschaft*—
and some of the administrative functions of the state will continue in
the ways of organizing social life adopted by the community, but the
state, viewed as Marxists do as an instrument or vehicle of control by
the dominant class of other classes in the interests of the dominant
class, will wither away. When the state so withers away and the society
finally stands in full abundance the 'maxim of justice' for the higher
phase of communist society can have application. For the first time in
history, we can and should live according to the maxim: 'From each
according to his ability, to each according to his needs' (p. 82).

Lenin is talking about a society, as he puts it, in which "people
have become so accustomed to observing the fundamental rules of
social intercourse and when their labour is so productive that they
will voluntarily work according to their ability" (p. 82). People will
not worry whether or not one has worked a little longer than another
or whether one gets a little more than another. Everyone will be
abundantly cared for. In such a condition, if ever we get there, there
"will be . . . no need for a society to regulate the quantity of products
to be distributed to each: each will take freely 'according to his needs'"
(p. 82). (Is that to be beyond the circumstances of justice? But, even
if it is, should this still not serve as a guide for how social life should
be organized?)

Surely one can predictably expect a chorus of remarks to the effect
that that is 'pure utopianism,' 'a morality for saints,' 'it just isn't the
way human nature is,' 'a nice pipe dream,' 'secular pie in the sky by
and by' and worse.

Lenin responds to this as follows:

> From the bourgeois point of view, it is easy to declare that such a social
> order is "a pure utopia," and to sneer at the Socialists for promising
> everyone the right to receive from society, without any control of the
> labour of the individual citizen any quantity of truffles, automobiles,
> pianos, etc. Even now, most bourgeois "savants" confine themselves to
> sneering in this way, thereby displaying at once their ignorance and their
> mercenary defence of capitalism (p. 82).

Lenin's reaction is understandable, but it still looks like, viewed as a
measured response, it fails by being badly *ad hominem*. But let us

see. In saying this bourgeois response reflects ignorance, Lenin makes this important point. Socialists do not *promise* or *guarantee* "that the higher phase of communism will arrive" (p. 82). They foresee its arrival because they foresee an ever greater productivity of labour and recognize, given the malleability of human nature, that rather different people will emerge from altered material conditions. Later Marxists would put the essential point in an even weaker way.[40] The thing is to recognize that such developments are a coherent empirical possibility and, given their evident desirability, they are worth struggling for and worth reading into one's plans for the future development of society. Any kind of reasonable approximation of them is surely an advance over what we have now.

There is a hope about the human prospect that goes with a conception of a higher phase of communism. It is not a question of guarantees or even, I should add, a claim about what *inevitably* will come to be. Arguments about the limits of growth make such a development more problematic than it was in Marx's time or even in Lenin's. (Lenin was writing *State and Revolution* in 1917.) But it is also too easy and rather too convenient from the bourgeois point of view, to hold firmly to pessimistic estimates about the limits of growth. *Perhaps a conservative [maximin]* strategy is best here for social policy? But it is also about as evident as anything can be that the full effect of that productive force that is science has not yet been utilized and that it certainly is not being utilized in a persistent and massive probe into how to use science maximally to meet human needs. It is not unreasonable to believe that with a socialist revolution that was world wide such energies would be unleashed and problems of undernourishment and deprivation plaguing the world could be met.

What is crucial to realize is Lenin's point that the Marxist is making no promises here. What he is saying is that over time the productive forces tend to develop and that with their development comes a development in the productive relations which in turn leads to an increasingly emancipatory development in non-economic social forms.[41] It is not as evident as Lenin believed that they will develop as far as Marx, Engels and Lenin foresaw, such that the higher forms of communism will surely become a reality with their extensive egalitarianism (*pace* Wood), in which the varying needs of everyone are fully met.[42] But, even if this state of affairs cannot be satisfied or even closely approximated—and that it cannot is something we do not know—it could still reasonably remain a heuristic to guide the direction of our social struggles and our conceptions of the design of a good society.

Moreover, whatever 'utopianism,' if any, there is there, it is compatible with a political realism, for while 'From each according to his ability to each according to his needs' will guide our *aspirations,* we can, with Lenin, also take, without any conflict or inconsistency, the following *Realpolitik* turn which is completely compatible with those communistic aspirations: "Until the 'higher' phase of communism arrives, the Socialists demand the strictest control, by society and by the state, of the measure of labour and the measure of consumption; but this control must start with the expropriation of the capitalists, with the establishment of workers' control over the capitalists, and must be carried out, not by a state of bureaucrats, but by a state of armed workers" (p. 83). It is the bourgeois theoreticians who worry repeatedly about the distant future. Socialists have a heuristic guide here, but they center their attention on the "essential and imperative questions of present policy" (p. 83). That has to do first with toppling capitalism and then with a start on the building of socialism (p. 83).

In the building of socialism, including the long-range goal of attaining, if possible, the higher phases of communism, it is crucial to recognize that in the earlier phases the remnants of old traditions will confront us at every step. We must also see things clearly in the light of developmental stages. The struggle for bourgeois democracy is a struggle for equal civil rights, equal political and legal rights, and the attainment of them in the bourgeois era was a great step forward from the feudal and pre-capitalist era, where they were not generally recognized. But this, as valuable as it is, is still only a formal equality and it does not bring equality in the economic sphere which is the most crucial sphere in our control of our lives and in our ability to attain and sustain our autonomy as human beings (p. 85).

Lenin follows Engels and Marx in claiming that the proletarian demand for equality is more extensive than the bourgeois demand: besides demanding such formal equalities, its essential and crucial demand for equality is a demand for the abolition of classes. As long as we live in class society we have not attained equality no matter how extensive or how secure our civil liberties. Even common ownership of the means of production—something we will gain in the first phases of socialism—will still only give us formal equality; we will attain real equality only when we attain a higher phase of communism. As Lenin puts it: "As soon as equality is obtained for all members of society in relation to the ownership of the means of production, that is, equality of labour and equality of wages, humanity will inevitably be confronted with the question of going beyond formal equality to real equality, i.e. to applying the rule, 'from each according to his ability, to each according to his needs'" (p. 85).

Again Lenin inserts a note of political realism. He adds by "what stages, by what practical measures humanity will proceed to this higher aim—we do not and cannot know" (p. 85). What is important is to make clear that such a *possibility* is indeed a real possibility: it is, that is, something which is on our historical agenda. Among a number of possible scenarios, it represents one coherent empirical possibility. Bourgeois cultural pessimism to the contrary notwithstanding (a pessimism which is very useful ideologically to capitalism), such a possibility is not an unreasonable one.[43]

With the development of capitalism in an ever more corporate and perhaps a more monopolistic direction, we get an even more complex and co-operative workforce, requiring greater and greater utilization of technology and an ever greater education of the proletariat. We have more and more people who are not capitalists who are capable of running society economically and politically. The capitalist is becoming increasingly superfluous (p. 85). We increasingly have the possibility that it could be the case that all citizens could readily be "transformed into the salaried employees of the state, which consists of the armed workers" (p. 86). (There are unfortunate connotations to this remark of Lenin's only if we forget that the state is to be democratically and collectively run by the workers.)

Such groups can run the state and can continue, indeed can accelerate, the development of the forces of production (p. 86). In such a situation it is possible to develop a set of economic and social relations where every able-bodied adult does roughly the same amount of work—each doing his proper share of work—and where each gets paid equally (p. 86). There will, in such a circumstance, be nowhere else for the capitalist or intellectual gentry with capitalist habits to go, for "the whole of society will have become a single office and a single factory with equality of labour and equality of pay" (p. 87). (Why must things be so centralized? Why, under socialism, could there not be more decentralization?) Still this 'factory discipline' is exclusively a matter of the transition. "But this 'factory' discipline, which the proletariat will extend to the whole of society after the defeat of the capitalists and the overthrow of the exploiters, is by no means our ideal, or our ultimate goal. It is but a necessary step for the purpose of thoroughly purging society of all the hideousness and foulness of capitalist exploitation, and for further progress" (p. 87).

Again we see Lenin, as Marx and Engels often are, quite willing to make moral judgments and not at all concerned at this point to keep his social theory *wertfrei* or to engage in value elimination.[44] Yet his moral judgments are still rooted in a *wertfrei* conception of how society functions and develops, and how human beings will act under different conditions.

However, with the vast majority of the members of the society having learned to administer the state themselves and having routed finally the capitalists and their allies and resocialized workers addicted to bourgeois habits—all things that could reasonably transpire—the state becomes less and less necessary and in that historical context the state will begin to wither away (p. 87).

VIII

I have described Marx's essential views in *The Critique of the Gotha Programme* about equality and justice or, if 'equality' and 'justice' are the wrong words here, his rationale, in different modes of production, for distributing in one way rather than another and for treating people in one way rather than another. We have also seen how the reading of Marx's view here, which seems to me the least strained, is also the reading that Engels and Lenin give to it. Assuming now that this is Marx's view about justice, I want to see how justified it is, how well it stands up to competitors and whether it is or is not a radically incomplete view which in an important way needs supplementation.

Consider the following three principles (putative principles) of social justice:

1. From each according to his choice, given his assets, to each according to his contribution (*The Capitalist Principle*).
2. From each according to his ability, to each according to his contribution (*The Lower Phase of Communism Principle*).
3. From each according to his ability, to each according to his need (*The Higher Phase of Communism Principle*).

Edward and Onora Nell point out in their "On Justice Under Socialism" that Principles (1) and (2) have advantages over Principle (3) in that, as principles resting on contribution, rather than on need, they, in a way Principle (3) does not, or at least does not as obviously, provide both "a general principle of distribution and indicate the pattern of incentives to which workers will respond."[45] Principle (1), whatever other objections we may reasonably have to it, can, on a reasonable reading, provide us with a principle of distribution which can have a general application: "it covers the distribution of earned and unearned income, and it applies in situations both of scarcity and abundance."[46] It appears, by contrast, that (3) the principle (putative principle) of justice for a higher phase of communism, however noble the sentiment it expresses, is quite unworkable. It simply will not do the job a principle of justice is designed to do. The Nells point out that even if all people conscientiously contribute according to their abilities, we still have no guarantees that *all* needs can be met, but a principle of distributive justice that does not tell us how to distribute when all needs *cannot* be met is, to put it conservatively, seriously incomplete and defective. It simply leaves us without guidance in the typical circumstances of justice, namely in conditions of moderate scarcity. And, if there were ever to be a situation where there is [no] scarcity, and everyone could just take what they need, then we could be in situations where we have no need for a principle of justice. The principle—as a principle of justice—is also defective because in circumstances where all contribute according to their abilities there may, in a society of considerable wealth, be a material surplus, even after all needs are met, but Principle (3) does not tell us how to distribute in such a circumstance and this again shows that it is an incomplete and inadequate principle of justice. Finally, it should also be noted that Principle (3) provides no adequate *incentive* structure for people to act, i.e. to contribute, according to their abilities. No reason, or at least no sufficiently stable motivating reason, is given in Principle (3) to motivate workers to contribute according to their abilities. But this makes Principle (3) defective as a principle which will guide action in society. But this is precisely what we expect of a principle of justice.

In reflection on Principle (3) "we seem to have reached the paradoxical conclusion that the principle of distribution requiring that worker's needs be met is of no use in situations of need, since it does not assign priorities among needs. . . . "[47] It is further argued, by some critics of Marx, that "a principle demanding that each contribute accordingly to his ability is unable to explain what incentives will lead him to do so."[48] Unfortunately, the principle will not give us a principle of allocation of benefits and burdens that will cover not only situations of sufficiency but situations of scarcity and abundance as well.[49] What is probably the most crucial defect here is that there are many situations, including situations of relative abundance, where the aggregate social product is such that all needs cannot be met. The principle of justice for the higher phase of communism will not tell us how to distribute in such a circumstance, but it is, perhaps most paradigmatically, for just these very circumstances that we need a principle of justice. As David Hume or John Rawls might very well say of the Communist Principle (Principle 3), it only is applicable in those circumstances where we are beyond the circumstances of justice. It is an important moral principle but it is not, and cannot be, a principle of justice.

The Nells attempt to respond to such criticisms of Marx, partly by way of concessions and partly by way of arguing that when we are clear about the kind of society and the kind of human beings for which Marx's principle for a more advanced phase of communist society was designed, and when we supplement that principle in perfectly plausible ways, we will come to see that it is the appropriate principle of justice for such a society.[50] And recall that Rawls also believes that his own two principles of justice only hold under conditions of moderate scarcity.

The first thing we need to see is that the society Marx was talking about, where what I shall henceforth call The Communist Principle, i.e. Principle (3), applies, would be a society of considerable wealth and abundance and a society in which much of our work was no longer alienated labour but a humanly fulfilling activity.[51] The needs that the principle is to fulfill would not be merely subsistence needs but the various social needs as well, some of which would be felt, indeed called into existence, only after our active powers began to be developed and we became increasingly well-rounded human beings. It would be a situation in which there would be a far greater degree of human flourishing than there is at present.

One of these needs that would increasingly come into prominence, and would be felt more acutely and self-consciously, is the need to have meaningful and satisfying work. Marx speaks in the *Critique of the Gotha Programme* of labour in a higher phase of communist society as being "no longer merely a means of life but" as something that becomes "life's principal need." This has led to quips that Marx's vision of a good society under conditions of abundance was that of a gigantic workhouse filled with compulsive workers trying to fill ever higher quotas. But this parody ignores what Marx says about alienated work under capitalism, what he says about the realm of necessity and the realm of freedom, and takes a remarkably superficial view of what work is and can be. It also narrowly limits our view of things to bourgeois conditions and conditions very like bourgeois conditions in the early years of the transition.

Much work is now pure drudgery and not even remotely engaged in for its own sake. If it were not for the fact that so many must engage in it under our thoroughly alienating conditions, the very idea of it being engaged in for its own sake would be laughable. Life on the assembly line, at a checkout counter, directing traffic or checking gas meters is surely not one of life's principal needs. We should avoid a romantic, university professor's view of work: a view in which he draws too much on his own atypical experience. Much work in our societies is just a means to an end and would, barring whipping people on the job, only be done for compensation. It is done in short, solely, or almost solely, so that the person who does the work can get things he wants, needs or at least thinks he needs. It is not in itself, or only marginally, a meaningful activity.

Marx believed, as is well-known, and it is something the Nells believe as well, that much of the work in a future communist society could and would become meaningful. The alienating nature of work under capitalism was in large measure a result of capitalism's distinctive socio-economic structure, a structure that would be radically altered in communist society. The Nells put Marx's key points about alienated labour from his *Economic and Philosophical Manuscripts* (1844) very succinctly: "Under capitalism labourers experienced a three fold alienation from the *product* of their labour, which is for them merely a means to material reward; alienation from the process of labour, which is experienced as forced labour rather than as desirable activity; and alienation from *others,* since activities undertaken with these are undertaken as a means to achieving further ends, which are normally scarce and allocated competitively."[52] But in the higher phases of communist society, where the underlying rationale of production will not be capital accumulation and profit-making, but the fullest possible satisfaction of the needs of everyone, work will not have those features. Work will be co-operatively done and the product of this labour will be under the democratic and collective ownership and control of the workers themselves. Work, under those circumstances, will be very different, since what is done, who does it, what life chances people have to do different things, what schedules of work exist and what is done with what is produced, where the vital interests of more than a given individual is involved, will be decided collectively by the workers themselves in a democratic fashion. This being so, labour will not, or at least not so extensively, be experienced as forced labour. Moreover, as it will be done co-operatively for commonly agreed on ends, and at roughly equal pay; workers will not in their work be alienated from each other.

However, the crucial thing is to see that work—or rather some work—need not be the curse of Adam but can be immensely rewarding and satisfying. It is so now for some intellectuals, craftsmen, farmers and professionals in capitalist societies and much more of it, for a more varied group of people, can become meaningful and highly satisfying—something that is one of life's prime needs—as societies grow wealthier and change their production rationale to production directed to meeting as fully as possible all human needs. We must remember that needs in certain ways will expand as this process becomes more and more a reality. But recall that under such an organization of society workers are making collective, democratically structured and informed decisions on what to produce, how much, in what way and how it is to be distributed. The work that we engage in in such a circumstance will have a point; senseless work will not be engaged in and work will become more and more challenging and interesting and more and more it will be something that requires the worker's thought and deliberative decisions. (Rawls' Aristotelian principle will come more and more into play.) There will be more and more occasions for the exercising of talents, for taking responsibilities that result in beautiful or useful objects. Moreover, it is increasingly true that more and more people will work at what they want to work at and, in doing that, they will do something which is more and more something they genuinely need. All of this plainly contributes toward making work more meaningful. For such work in such a society it is clear that there is no problem of incentives. People, generally speaking, will work willingly and happily at the levels of their abilities.

Many feel that such talk about unalienating labour under the higher phases of communism fails to face a very plain and very crucial problem: to wit that not *all* the work can be need-fulfilling and satisfying even in such a communist society with its high level of technology. Moreover, we cannot live by works of art and scientific achievements alone. Some work of drudgery, work which cannot but be unappealing, simply must be done. The Communist Principle of Justice provides no incentive for doing it.

It is an empirical problem just how extensive that work would be. And it is plain enough that under abundance and high technology and with an extensively educated population and with workers' control of society it would be much less than it is now. But, unless it is just a failure of our imaginations, it still seems likely that there would continue to be quite a lot of it. (Think concretely of all the various jobs that have to be done in a complex civilization.) It seems likely that there will be "certain essential tasks, in such a society whose performance is not need-fulfilling for anybody."[53] The amount of this will be diminished as technology and social consciousness develop, but some of it, it seems very reasonable to believe, will remain. But with the Communist Principle of Justice in force what will be the motivation for doing these tasks when reward is severed from contribution?

What is correct to say—and the Nells say it—is that given an equitable allocation of the burdens of these necessary but non-need-fulfilling jobs, no one would be prevented from having work such that most of his work could be need-fulfilling. No one would have to be a full-time dishwasher. But we are still without an incentive for doing the dirty, boring but necessary work that even such a technologically advanced, worker-controlled society could not dispense with. And it is not clear on what principle or by what criteria we decide what is an equitable allocation of the necessary but non-need-fulfilling work.

The Nells maintain that we need to make planning decisions here. But on what basis, by what principle? We need to engage in these activities to meet subsistence needs, to make possible the fulfilling of many other needs including needs that people would have, and would continue to have, in a society which was both a society of abundance and a society without classes. But in a communist society we would seek to reduce non-need-fulfilling work as much as is compatible with meeting these conditions. (People may differ here and in trying to ascertain what is equitable there *may* be some difficult tradeoffs.) Where such work does not meet those conditions we do not engage in it. Moreover, there would be a general awareness that for everyone to be able to do what he finds need-fulfilling these tasks must be done. The doing of them, when they are allocated equitably by collectively agreed on principles and procedures, would very likely be less onerous than they are now or would otherwise be. It is not implausible to believe that people in such circumstances would willingly take up such work once they realized that it was for the common good and was being fairly allocated.

It is also crucial to realize that this would be in a society toward which people would reasonably feel some considerable loyalty, for it would be a society which had ended class structures and exploitation and a society whose productive energies were directed to meeting the needs of everyone alike as fully as possible. A sense of social solidarity and community would develop. And in such a society, with its extensive reciprocity, people's willingness to work would be greater. At least this is not an unreasonable Pascalian wager to make about people.

Rational people would also realize that the opportunities for everyone to do creative need-fulfilling work would be enhanced by their doing efficiently the necessary work of drudgery so there would be a motivation to work at those tasks effectively. We would indeed, even in doing these things, acquire some skills we would not want for their own sakes but which are necessary for the carrying out, in an efficient way these burdensome tasks. After all, to will the end is to will the necessary means to the end. Where "the members of society take part in planning to maintain and expand the opportunities for everyone's non-alienated activity, they must understand the necessity of allocating the onerous tasks, and so the training for them."[54]

The problem of motivation to work under an advanced communist society should also be seen in historical and economic terms. The Nells put the matter thus:

> The link between work and rewards serves a historical purpose, namely to encourage the development of the productive forces. But as the productive forces continue to develop, the demand for additional rewards will tend to decline, while the difficulty of stimulating still further growth in productivity may increase. This at least, seems to be implied by the principles of conventional economics—diminishing marginal utility and diminishing marginal productivity. Even if one rejects most of the conventional wisdom of economics, a good case can be made for the diminishing efficacy of material incentives as prosperity increases. For as labor productivity rises, private consumption needs will be met, and the most urgent needs remaining will be those requiring collective consumption—and, indeed some of these needs will be generated by the process of growth and technical progress. These last needs, if left unmet, may hinder further attempts to raise the productive power of labor. So the system of material incentives could in principle come to a point where the weakened encouragements to extra productivity offered as private reward for contribution might be offset by the accumulated hindrances generated by the failures to meet collective needs and by the waste involved in competition. At this point, it becomes appropriate to break the link between work and reward.[55]

However, it is not enough for such a developed society simply to break the link between work and reward, but, for a significant domain of work, it is also necessary to show that work is its own reward—that it is intrinsically valuable as well as extrinsically valuable. But this is what, under the proper circumstances, much work can and should be. The short of it is that "Because man needs fulfilling activity—work that he chooses and wants—men who get it contribute according to their ability."[56] Yet, no matter how we cut it, there will remain, as we have noted, the routine, menial, unfulfilling but still necessary jobs. Such a society will be committed to mechanizing and automating as many as they possibly can of these jobs.[57] In such a society, the operative slogan for such work should be 'Machines to replace people.' But those tasks of drudgery that remain—those which are really necessary and for which the society, for the time being at least, can find no replacement—the society will rationally plan for, and in this planning, allocate them in as fair and as non-burdensome a way as possible. Fair here comes, most centrally, to the counting of each person's interests equally.

Since such a society is committed to the greatest equal satisfaction of need for every person in that society, it will allocate these burdens in a way such that the doing of them will become no one's full-time job such that no one will be kept by these burdens from having as his principal work, work that is need-fulfilling. Besides a demand for equality, that is, as Engels put it, a demand for the abolition of classes, there will also be a demand for an equal sharing of the burdens of these tasks. Where possible and feasible—and subject to the usual qualifications of age and health and the like—these burdens will be distributed equally among all the members of the society. Here a primitive conception of fairness is at work—a sense of fairness which is deeply embedded in our thinking and which animates Rawls' work and Dworkin's work—which is distinct from the Communist Principle but which is also in its spirit. The conviction about fairness is what pushes us to want to start at least from a baseline of equal (the same) benefits and burdens for us all. We need reasons (reasons we will frequently have) for departing from it. It is here, and in our recognition that we must start from an equal consideration of the interests of everyone, where our primitive sense of justice—a very basic considered conviction—tells us we should start. This is just a very basic conviction of ours about what is fair and there is perhaps no getting back of it and showing that it is something to which 'pure practical reason' commits us.[58]

Yet, whatever we want to say about the above, it remains true that the Communist Principle does not tell us how to distribute in conditions of scarcity, how to distribute the surplus product in situations of great abundance, when all needs are met, and how to distribute in classless societies of great abundance where it still is not the case that all needs can be met or all interests answered to.

As Marx makes perfectly evident, the Communist Principle was not meant to be used in conditions of scarcity but only in conditions of extensive abundance. In a socialist or early phase communist society, where some scarcity obtains, one reasons, Marx claims (as we have seen), according to the maxim 'From each according to his ability to each according to his labour contribution.' Need can only come in a wealthier more fully socialized society.

For someone who accepted the Communist Principle as such a guiding ideal, and accepted Marx's analysis, he could and, I believe, should, accept the principles of justice—the principles of distribution— of some form of what I have called radical egalitarianism.[59] The underlying rationale for them is that, in conditions of abundance, we should aim to distribute the benefits and burdens of our societies roughly equally, so that the needs and interests of each individual can be maximally satisfied. Each person is to have as many as possible of his needs satisfied and to have them as fully as possible satisfied, subject only to the limitation that everyone else be, in that respect, treated exactly alike. Where we cannot satisfy a given need of both Peter and Paul, we should try to ascertain whose need is the greater and then satisfy that or failing that we should choose by a fair roll of the dice. It is not that people who come out on the losing end here are being sacrificed—treated as means only—for in deciding what to do, Peter's and Paul's needs get equal consideration; but, if their needs are actually inspected—each one's needs counting equally—and it is also clear that they both cannot be satisfied, then, whichever need is the greater or the more urgent, that need is the need to be met. That it is Peter's need or Paul's is never relevant.

The Communist Principle should be supplemented by some such radical egalitarian principle, or set of principles, but it *may* be that the Communist Principle itself should not be regarded as a principle of justice. It is true that it does not tell us how to distribute when the needs of different people conflict and they cannot all be satisfied, but, it is also true that with its stress on from *each* according to his ability to *each* according to his needs, it is stressing that *every single person* should (where possible) have a certain sort of equal treatment and should, *ceteris paribus,* equally shoulder certain responsibilities. This tells us, as against, for example, *purely* maximizing doctrines, to aim at giving *everyone* the fullest possible need satisfaction, compatible with a like need satisfaction for all, and to expect of everyone the fullest contribution to his society that he can reasonably make. This is a deep underlying ideal of how to aim at distributing things in the world and captures our underlying ideal of what is through and through fair and thus just.

Notes

1. Karl Marx, *Kritik des Gothaer Programmes, Karl Marx–Friedrich Engels Werke* Band 19, Berlin, Dietz Verlag 1962, pp. 15–32. Citations are given in the text and are to the English translation, Karl Marx, *Critique of the Gotha Programme,* edited by C. P. Dutt, New York, International Publishers 1938. The original was published in 1875.

2. The Tucker-Wood thesis is articulated, developed and assessed in the following places: Robert Tucker, *The Marxian Revolutionary Idea,* New York, NY, Norton 1969, Chapter 2 and Robert Tucker, *Philosophy and Myth in Karl Marx,* Cambridge, England, Cambridge University Press 1961, pp. 11–27; Allen W. Wood, "The Marxian Critique of Justice," *Philosophy and Public Affairs* 1 (1972-3); Allen W. Wood, "Marx on Right and Justice," vol. 8 *Philosophy and Public Affairs,* (1978-9); Allen W. Wood, "Marx and Equality" in *Issues in Marxist Philosophy* IV; John Mepham and David-Hillel Ruben (eds.), Sussex,

England; Harvester Press 1981, pp. 195–221; and Allen W. Wood, *Karl Marx,* London, England, Routledge and Kegan Paul 1981, Chapters IX and X. For criticisms of the Tucker-Wood thesis see Nancy Holmstrom, "Exploitation," *Canadian Journal of Philosophy* 7 (1977); Gary Young, "Justice and Capitalist Production: Marx and Bourgeois Ideology," *Canadian Journal of Philosophy* 8 (1978); Ziyad I. Husami, "Marx on Distributive Justice," Philosophy and Public Affairs 8 (1978); George C. Brenkert, "Freedom and Private Property in Marx," *Philosophy and Public Affairs* 8 (1979); Derek Allen, "Marx and Engels on the Distributive Justice of Capitalism" in Kai Nielsen and Steven C. Patten (eds.), *Marx and Morality,* Guelph, ON, Canadian Association for Publishing in Philosophy 1981; Gary Young, "Doing Marx Justice" in *Marx and Morality;* and G. A. Cohen, "Review of Allen Wood's *Karl Marx*" in *Mind* (1982).

3. How this is so is nicely explicated and defended by Andrew Collier, "Scientific Socialism and the Question of Socialist Values" in *Marx and Morality.* I have discussed and developed this view in my "Coming to Grips with Marxist Anti-Moralism" (forthcoming).

4. William Shaw, "Marxism and Moral Objectivity" in *Marx and Morality;* Kai Nielsen, "If Historical Materialism Is True Does Morality Totter?," *Philosophy of the Social Sciences* (forthcoming); and Kai Nielsen, "Historical Materialism, Ideology and Ethics," *Studies in Soviet Thought* (1984).

5. Allen Wood, "The Marxian Critique of Justice," *Philosophy and Public Affairs* 1 (2) (Spring 1972).

6. This in spite of what he said about not producing recipes for the cookshops of the future. Presumably, what is vital here is the level of generality.

7. I say this in the face of what some of his detractors have said about his utopianism.

8. Stanley Moore appropriately raises the question of whether this need be so in socialist societies. Stanley Moore, *Marx on the Choice Between Socialism and Communism,* Cambridge, MA, Harvard University Press 1980.

9. Why need it in these early phases of communism (what later came to be called the socialist phase) be *entirely* according to labour contribution where there is illness, a large number of children and the like? Why would there not be 'corrections' similar to the corrections we get in welfare-state capitalism? To say that there could and should surely means to be in the spirit of communism.

10. Jon Elster, "Exploitation, Freedom and Justice" in *Marxism, Nomos* XXVI; J. Roland Pennock and John W. Chapman (eds.), New York, NY, New York University Press 1983, pp. 277–364; and Edward and Onora Nell, "On Justice Under Socialism," *Ethics in Perspective,* Karsten Struhl and Paula Rothenberg Struhl (eds.), New York, NY, Random House 1975, pp. 436–446.

11. For the underlying conceptual rationale for this see Collier op. cit.

12. Unlike Lenin, he does not speak of *the* higher phase of communist society. I owe this point to R. X. Ware.

13. Collier with his thesis of value elimination in the social sciences, something he takes to be Marx's actual practice, brings out an important theoretical underpinning of this. Collier, op. cit. See also Russell Keat, *The Politics of Social Theory,* Oxford, England, Basil Blackwell Ltd. 1981 and my "Coming to Grips with Marxist Anti-Moralism."

14. Hilliard Aronovitch, "Marxian Morality," *Canadian Journal of Philosophy* X (3) (September 1980), pp. 357–376; Derek Allen "Does Marx Have an Ethic

of Self-Realization?, Reply to Aronovitch," pp. 377–386; Hilliard Aronovitch, "More on Marxian Morality: Reply to Professor Allen," pp. 387–393, both in the same volume as Aronovitch's "Marxian Morality."

15. For an accurate and detailed picture of Marx's conception of a good society see Bertell Ollman, "Marx's Vision of Communism: A Reconstruction" in Seweryn Bialer and Sophia Sluzan (eds.), *Radical Visions of the Future*, Boulder, CO, Westview Press 1977. Note how this is combined in Ollman's work with a form of Marxist anti-moralism. See Ollman, *Alienation*, second edition, Cambridge, England, Cambridge University Press 1976, Chapter 4. See also Istvan Meszaros, *Marx's Theory of Alienation*, London, England, Merlin Press 1970, pp. 162–194.

16. Allen Wood, *Karl Marx*, pp. 141–156. See here, for the kind of questioning I think should be made of this thesis, G. A. Cohen's review of Wood's *Karl Marx* in *Mind* (1982); Gary Young, "Doing Marx Justice," *Marx and Morality*, pp. 251–268. For how far a Marxist anti-moralist could go with making judgments about one society being better than another see David S. Levin, "The Moral Relativism of Marxism," *The Philosophical Forum* XV (3) (Spring 1984), pp. 249–279. For a carefully structured and nuanced account which argues that Marx has an implicit theory of justice, see John Elster, op. cit., pp. 290–291. "Marx," Elster remarks, "may have thought he had no theory of justice, but his actual analyses only make sense if we impute such a theory to him," p. 290.

17. Elster, op. cit.

18. Joshua Cohen and Joel Rogers, *On Democracy*, Middlesex, England, Penguin Books 1983; Samuel Bowles et al., *Beyond the Waste Land*, Garden City, NY, Anchor Books 1984; Herbert Gintes, "Communication and Politics: Marxism and the 'Problem' of Liberal Democracy," *Socialist Review* 10 (2/3) (March-June 1980), pp. 232–289; Andrew Levine, *Liberal Democracy*, New York, NY, Columbia University Press 1981; and Andrew Levine, *Arguing for Socialism*, London, England, Routledge and Kegan Paul 1984.

19. In this section my account stands in sharp contrast with Allen Wood's account of Marx here and Engels' as well. See, most particularly, his "Marx and Equality." I shall in the future produce a critical discussion of Wood's account.

20. Not all contemporary Marxists have followed Marx and Engels here. See Mihailo Markovic, *The Contemporary Marx*, Nottingham, England, Spokesman Books 1974, Chapter 7; and Kai Nielsen *Equality and Liberty*, Totowa, NJ, Rowman and Allanheld 1985, pp. 57–60.

21. Friedrich Engels, *Herrn Eugen Dührings Umwälzung der Wissenchaft (Anti-Dühring)*, *Karl Marx–Friedrich Engels Werke*, Band 20 Berlin, Dietz Verlag 1972, pp. 5–303. English translation by Emile Burns, New York, NY, International Publishers 1939. Citations will be made from the English translation and the citations will be given in the text. On Engels see Kai Nielsen, "Engels on Morality and Moral Theorizing," *Studies in Soviet Thought* 26 (1983); George G. Brenkert, "Marx, Engels and the Relativity of Morals," *Studies in Soviet Thought* 17 (1977), pp. 201–224. See Terrell Carver, "Marx, Engels and Dialectics," *Political Studies* XXVIII (1900), pp. 353–363. See also his *Engels*, New York, NY, Hill and Wang 1981.

22. Kai Nielsen, "Formulating Egalitarianism, Animadversions on Berlin," *Philosophia* 13 (3-4) (October 1983), pp. 299–315.

23. Ronald Dworkin reveals something of the complexities in his "What Is Equality," *Philosophy and Public Affairs*, (Summer 1981 and Fall 1981) and

in his "In Defense of Equality," *Social Philosophy and Policy,* (1) (Autumn 1983).

24. I attempt to do just that in my *Equality and Liberty: A Defense of Radical Egalitarianism.*

25. See Frederick Engels' correspondence concerning the Gotha Programme (1875) as an appendix to Karl Marx, *Critique of the Gotha Programme,* New York, NY, International Publishers 1938, pp. 31–2.

26. I have argued for that in my *Equality and Liberty* and I have also argued here that the idea of classlessness does not completely capture it (pp. 57–60).

27. C. B. Macpherson has shown that if we have an adequate historical understanding of its import that it should be no cause for alarm or for a belief that Marx was defending or acquiescing in what we would now call totalitarianism or even in an authoritarian state. C. B. Macpherson, *The Real World of Democracy,* Oxford, England, Clarendon Press 1966.

28. Mikhail Bakunin, "Statism and Anarchy" and "God and the State" both reprinted in Sam Dalgoff (ed.) *Bakunin on Anarchy,* London, England, George Allen and Unwin Ltd., 1973, pp. 323–350 and 225–242. For an authoritative discussion of the relation of anarchism to Marxism see Paul Thomas, *Karl Marx and the Anarchists,* London, England, Routledge and Kegan Paul 1980.

29. It would be important to try to think through what this would come to.

30. I have argued for the claim that Marx and Marxists are not at all committed to the claim that moral utterances of their very nature or because of something about moral epistemology *must* be ideological. There is nothing about their logical status or semantical structure that requires that, though they do very pervasively have an ideological function in class societies. But this does not mean that this is the only function they can have such that all moral judgments, including those of Marx and Engels themselves must be ideological. Cf. Kai Nielsen "Marx and Moral Ideology," (forthcoming), "Historical Materialism and Ethics," *Laval Review of Philosophy of Theology* (forthcoming), "Marxism and Relativity in Ethics," *Philosophical Inquiry* VI (3/4) (1984), pp. 202–225.

31. See the references in the second note. See also Alan Gilbert, "An Ambiguity in Marx's and Engels' Account of Justice and Equality," *The American Political Science Review* 76 (June 1982).

32. For an extensive elaboration and defense of this see the essays cited in note 30.

33. The references I am using are to the English translations of these works by Lenin given in appendices to the *Critique of the Gotha Programme,* New York, NY, International Publishers 1938, pp. 47–88. Page references will be given in the text.

34. For a contrasting view see Stanley Moore, op. cit.

35. Unlike Marx, who, as we have seen, speaks of *a* higher phase, Lenin speaks of *the* higher phase of communism. Lenin, op. cit., p. 59.

36. Collier, op. cit.

37. Elster's emmendation is an important qualification here. Elster, op. cit., p. 298.

38. This remark, if it is to be taken seriously, must be taken as a hyperbole. After all we can hardly let infants, children, the disabled and the aged starve. Still, assuming a plausible reading, the moral of the maxim remains intact.

39. It is here where the charge of utopianism is often made. Is it bourgeois cynicism to persist in seeing utopianism here? Is to see these things as *possibilities* to depart from any ability to look at the world without evasion? Cf. Isaac Deutscher, "On Socialist Man," *Marxism in Our Time,* San Francisco, CA, Ramparts Press 1971.

40. Bertell Ollman, "Marx's Vision of Communism: A Reconstruction," in *Radical Vision of the Future,* Seweryn Bialer and Sophia Sluzer (eds.), Boulder, CO, Westview Press, 1977.

41. For the theory behind this see G. A. Cohen, *Karl Marx's Theory of History: A Defence,* Oxford, England, Clarendon Press 1978; William H. Shaw, *Marx's Theory of History,* Stanford, CA, Stanford University Press 1976; Allen W. Wood, *Karl Marx,* pp. 61–122; and Kai Nielsen, "On Taking Historical Materialism Seriously," *Dialogue* XXII (1983), pp. 319–338.

42. Charles Taylor points to some of the problems here in his "The Politics of the Steady State," *New Universities Quarterly* 32 (1978).

43. For a particularly probing form of that pessimism see Alasdair MacIntyre, *After Virtue,* Notre Dame, IN, University of Notre Dame Press 1981. See for a response, my "Cultural Pessimism and the Setting Aside of Marxism," *Analyse & Kritik,* no. 1 (1985) and my "Critique of Virtue: Animadversions on a Virtue-Based Ethic" in Earl E. Shelp (ed.), *Virtue and Medicine,* Dordrecht, Holland, D. Reidel Publishing Company 1984, pp. 133–150.

44. If one sticks, as Collier does, to the thesis of value-elimination in the *Social Sciences* then one should also recognize that there are items in Marx's corpus that are not social science but are bits of normative politicizing. But it is also true, as Collier stresses, that these are hardly central and distinctive aspects of Marx's canon.

45. Edward Nell and Onora Nell, "On Justice Under Socialism," p. 439. In conjunction with this article Jon Elster's "Exploitation, Freedom and Injustice" should also be read.

46. Edward Nell and Onora Nell, op. cit., p. 439.

47. Ibid.

48. Ibid.

49. Ibid., p. 438.

50. Ibid., pp. 440–446.

51. Ibid., pp. 440–441.

52. Ibid., p. 441.

53. Ibid., p. 443.

54. Ibid., p. 444. That there seems little evidence of such motivation in the Soviet Union says more (a) about its being a society emerging from a society that was largely a peasant society and (b) about its being a statist society in which there is not genuine worker control of the means of production. For an elucidation of the concept of a statist society see Svetozar Stojanovic, *Between Ideals and Reality,* New York, NY, Oxford University Press 1973, trans. Gerson S. Sher, Chapter 3.

55. Edward and Onora Nell, op. cit., pp. 445–6.

56. Ibid., p. 446.

57. Ibid.

58. See here my "On Not Needing to Justify Equality" (forthcoming); "On Liberty and Equality: A Case for Radical Egalitarianism," *Windsor Yearbook of Access to Justice* (1985) and *Equality and Liberty,* Totowa, NJ, Rowman and Allenheld 1985, pp. 13–44, 281–314.

59. Cf. Kai Nielsen, *Equality and Liberty.*

5

A Marxist Conception of Ideology

I

There are myriads of conceptions of ideology and it is perhaps fair enough to say that the concept of ideology is essentially contested.[1] Even within Marxism, and indeed within Marx's own usage, there are distinct characterizations of ideology such that it makes it misleading to speak of the concept of ideology.[2] I shall not be concerned with the history of this "concept" or with textual exegesis of Marx or the Marxist tradition. My aim shall be to state, explicate, and critically examine what I take to be a tolerably Marxist conception of ideology, which I shall argue is a key one in understanding society and in engaging in systematic social critique. I shall be far less concerned with the legitimacy of its Marxist pedigree than with its adequacy as a conceptualization of ideology.

An ideology, I shall contend, is a system of ideas, theories, beliefs, attitudes, norms, and social practices that (a) is characteristic of a class society or of a class or other primary social group in a class society and that (b) serves principally the interests of a class, typically a class in that society, or other primary social group while typically at least, putting itself forward as answering to the interests of the whole of the society. (I add "primary social group" to capture phenomena like that of the racist Afrikaner ideology.) The people who have been socialized

This essay was originally published in Anthony Parel, ed., *Ideology, Philosophy and Politics* (Waterloo, Ontario: Wilfrid Laurier University Press, 1983, for the Calgary Institute for the Humanities), pp. 139–161. Reprinted by permission of Wilfrid Laurier University Press.

into a particular ideology, in certain important ways, see their own position within their social environment in terms of this system (cluster) of ideas, beliefs, and values and they explain, evaluate, and justify the way they live their lives in terms of this system. Sometimes socialization into a particular ideology embraces the vast majority of the people comprising the various classes within the society. At other times, when class conflict is overt, widespread, and it is perceived on all sides that there are antagonistic class interests, socialization into an ideology will be principally the distinctive socialization of members of a particular class into the ideology of that class.

It is typically, and perhaps always, the case that an ideology serves principally the interests of a particular class. But it is not always the case that an ideology is mystificatory or in any way illegitimate.[3] However, it is generally the case, where the ideology is effective, that for people socialized into the ideology it mystifies, or at least distorts, their understanding of their society and indeed their understanding of the world they live in; people are so constituted by ideologies that an ideology, usually, but not invariably, distorts, for people socialized into the ideology, their self-images and conceptions of how they ought to live and relate to each other. It isn't that people first have their own self-images and then ideology distorts them but that in their very socialization they are in considerable measure constituted by an ideology. That is, the way they act, react, and view themselves is strongly conditioned by the ideology. The ideology, however, does this in ways that tend to serve the interests of a given class. It is this feature of ideology that licenses the move from "It's an ideology," or "It's ideological," to "It's in some way illegitimate," just as in the nineteenth century "He is a Swede" would have licensed "Then he must be a Lutheran." (Remember in this context that an ideology is something the other chap has.)

There are ideological beliefs, ideas, concepts, categories, propositions, forms of consciousness, theories, systems, attitudes, norms, and practices. It has been asked "What is the mark of the mental?" Similarly, hoping not to fall into essentialist errors, I shall ask "What is the mark of the ideological?" The answer, it seems to me, is that what is ideological serves class interests and has a distinctive role to play in class struggle. (I don't claim, however, that this is a sufficient condition for something's being ideological. Indeed, I think the search here, as in many other places, for necessary and sufficient conditions is a strategic error.)

I shall first contrast this Marxist conception of ideology with some non-Marxist conceptions. I shall exhibit central aspects of each, and in doing this it will become evident that the non-Marxist conceptions are contained within the Marxist one. What is distinctive about the Marxist conception is in what it adds, though this does mean that what is denoted by "ideology" is narrower in the Marxist conception. This, I shall argue, is to its advantage. With that contrast before us, I shall then raise a series of questions about the Marxist characterization of ideology.

II

There is a latitudinarian or, as some have called it, a global employment of "ideology" in which an ideology is said to be any "set of closely related beliefs or ideas, or even attitudes characteristic of a group or community," or any "cluster of closely interconnected ideas, beliefs, and attitudes which function both to interpret experience and as guides to action."[4] This is what some social anthropologists would call a belief-system, and so characterized it has none of the pejorative or polemical force of the more typical employments of many Marxist conceptions of "ideology."

I shall look at two ways in which this general latitudinarian conception of ideology can be fleshed out. The first stresses that in articulating an ideology we are setting out a general outlook which incorporates certain conceptions about what society is like, certain conceptions about how to live and how to order society, and certain conceptions about how to see one's life in society. So, on such a conception, we, in having an ideology, have a general outlook that incorporates certain values and aims at either an alteration of human life and society or at a sanctification and justification of the established order in such a way as to promote or at least protect group solidarity.[5] A second way of fleshing out this general conception of ideology is given by Bernard Williams. Williams remarks:

> In its broadest sense, I take the term "ideology" to stand for a system of political and social beliefs that does two things. First, it embodies some set of values or ideals, and, consequently, some principles of action: though such principles will be of necessity very general, and in some cases mainly negative, being concerned more with limitations on political action, for instance, rather than with an overall aim of it. Secondly, an ideology connects with its values and principles of action some set of very general theoretical beliefs which give the values and principles some sort of backing or justification. The generality of these beliefs must, moreover, be of a special kind, if we are to speak of "an ideology:" they must, I think, be general beliefs about man, society, and the state, and not merely about some aspect of man in society. For instance, a belief in Free Trade or federalism, even though supported by general economic or political reasons, could not by itself constitute an ideology. The distinguishing mark of an ideology is that its general beliefs concern man and society as such, and hence concern things that are presupposed in any political or social situation whatsoever.[6]

One of the most evident things is that Williams' formulation of the latitudinarian view of the mark of the ideological is different from my view. I am claiming that for something to be an ideology it must serve class interests or primary social-group interests while for Williams it must contain general beliefs concerning man and society as such. (I expect that both of use have necessary conditions or at least quasi-necessary conditions but that neither has a sufficient condition.)

The term "ideology" unlike the term "term" is a term of art so that we can hardly speak of a correct or incorrect definition or of some set of necessary and sufficient conditions for something being ideological or an ideology. We can, of course, stipulate something here, but the stipulations would have to be judged according to some pragmatic terms and it is not by any means clear what in such a context the proper "pragmatic considerations" would come to. I expect that my characterization of the mark of the ideological will strike many people as too narrow while Williams' will strike others as too broad. It by stipulation makes an "ideological world-view" pleonastic and a "non-ideological world-view" a contradiction. This can be harmless enough, though still rather unhelpful, if the normal pejorative force of "ideological" and "ideology" is consciously blocked and not implicitly carried over into the subsequent analysis of ideology. But the Williams way does miss what is very central in Marxist critiques of ideologies, namely how they are verbal weapons in class conflict, how they are polemical notions which serve class interests.[7] When we speak of "the ideological spokesman of the petty bourgeoisie" or when we speak, as Marx did, of the "official representatives of French democracy as being steeped in republican ideology" we are employing "ideological" and "ideology" as critical, polemical concepts pointing to distinctive interests and to distinctive class positions. One is not, in some class-neutral manner, referring simply to a world-view. Similarly, in criticizing the historical idealism of the Young Hegelians in *The German Ideology,* Marx and Engels sought to establish that in spite of their critical intentions they were the staunchest conservatives in an oblique way reinforcing the *status quo.*

Class dominance is reinforced in many ways, sometimes in ways which are very obvious indeed, and sometimes in ways which are hidden and require probing ideological unmasking. Marx had the greatest admiration for Ricardo. He regarded him, in a way he did not regard Malthus, as a genuine man of science, but he also stressed that he, even in his strictest scientific work, produced ideology serving bourgeois class interests by making it appear that certain economic relations had a permanently valid character.[8] What is important here is not what Ricardo's intentions were but the message that his work, genuinely scientific work, conveyed. Critique of ideology reveals intellectual structures and social practices playing key roles in class struggles.

It is indeed true that even if there were to be a society not divided into classes or with pronounced stratification, there would still be in that society a world-view incorporating certain values. It is a mark of something being a culture or a society that it has certain distinguishing general beliefs concerning man and society. An ideology will have these features too, but it might be that a society could come into being in which there were no intellectual structures or social practices which served the interests of a particular class or group. This may well be because there would be no classes or stratified social groups. That is to say, it would be a classless society. But we also have a perfectly good term, namely "the world-view of that society" that we can employ instead while saving "ideology" for intellectual structures and perhaps, as well, for social practices and institutions which serve class interests. It would seem that it would be better to follow the latter course and preserve the employment of "ideology" for something distinct, capturing a phenomenon much in need of capturing, and giving us conceptual space for the very possibility of a non-ideological world-view or *Weltanschauung* that did not distort our understanding of social reality. We are not forced, if we take this path, to say with Althusser that ideology is eternal.[9] It may be, but we have not made it true by a conventionalist sulk.

III

I want to lay out rather more explicitly the similarities and differences between those non-Marxist conceptions and my Marxist conception of ideology. I think the following "mapping device" catches the central similarities and differences.

A Latitudinarian Conception of Ideology
    An ideology
    1. embodies a set (cluster) of norms, values, or ideals characteristic of a community or communities or of a distinct sub-culture of a community or of several communities;
    2. contains principles of action;
    3. contains general theoretical beliefs about man and society that function to interpret experience and that play a legitimating role for those principles of action;
    4. aims at either an alteration of human life and society or at a sanctification and justification of the established order in such a way as to promote or at least protect group solidarity;
    5. links these norms to questions concerning the distribution of power in society.

A Marxist Conception of Ideology
    An ideology
    1* embodies a set (cluster) of norms, values, or ideas characteristic of a community or communities that reflects a certain class or primary social-group perspective and that (principally) serves the interests of the class or primary social group;

2* contains principles of action that reflect a certain class or primary social-group perspective and that serve (principally) the interests of that class or primary social group;

3* contains general theoretical beliefs about man and society that play a legitimating role for those principles of action and for the public self-images extant in that society;[10]

4* aims at, in the interest of a contending class or primary social group, an alteration of human life and of society or at a sanctification and justification, in the interests of the dominant class, classes, or primary social group, of those parts of the established order that are at least perceived to embody the interests of the dominant class, classes, or primary social group;

5* frequently mystifies (distorts) the social outlook of the dominated class, and not infrequently of the dominating class as well, by falsely representing itself as answering to the interests of the whole of the society;[11]

6* typically (but not invariably) distorts, for the people socialized into the ideology, their self-understanding and their understanding of the world they live in in a way which serves the interests of a determinate class or primary social group;

7* preserves group solidarity in accordance with dominant-class outlooks by socializing the members of the dominated class into that outlook in such a way that they (typically, mistakenly) see that general outlook and the associated set of norms and social practices of that outlook as answering to the interests of the whole society;

8* functions so that sometimes the socialization into an outlook will be either class specific or, at other times, it will be society-wide so that there will be across the whole of the society a tolerably common outlook;

9* will be generally, but still mistakenly, perceived, where there is an extensive dominant-class hegemony, to be morally legitimate and as generally answering to the interests of the society as a whole (It is a legitimating device in the society);[12]

10* typically, but not invariably, is morally illegitimate and is only rationally justifiable in accordance with the interests of the class, classes, or primary social group whose interests it serves;

11* has a distinctive role in class struggle.[13]

It should be apparent from the above that the Marxist need not deny anything given in the above non-Marxist conception of ideology (conceptions taken from Plamenatz, Gellner, and Williams). The difference is in what is stressed and in what the Marxist adds. He would stress the importance of conceiving of ideology in more determinate terms, and he would also stress the standard distorting nature of ideological conceptions. The Marxist adds reference to class: class conflict, class interests, class perspective, class mystification, class hegemony, class society and the like.[14] It is essential for his analysis that class, class interests, and conceptions of mystification and distorted social outlook be brought into the picture. There is a contrast drawn between class interests and a mystified sense of the interests of society as a whole. It is essential to the Marxist not only to be able to talk of world-views with distinctive conceptions of man and society functioning sometimes to preserve group solidarity and sometimes to promote an alteration, even a radical alteration, of social life, but also to speak of distorted world-views that obscure social relations and do not answer adequately to the needs of human beings. Ideologies are not only world-views, but typically distorted world-views in class society, and they are for the most part world-views which either serve the interests of a determinate class or rather more rarely of several classes or of some primary social group.

There are plainly a number of questions that could and should be raised about such a Marxist conception. It assumes the reality of classes and some form of class analysis, and there are people who would consider that problematic. What exactly classes are and what Marx meant by "classes" is not altogether clear. As is well known, Marx never completed the chapter devoted to class in *Capital*. It is also anything but clear whether the class divisions of our time are not in some non-trivial senses different from the class divisions of Marx's time, though this is perfectly compatible with the persistence of classes in the fundamental sense in which Marx spoke, namely, of primary social groups which differ fundamentally in their relationship to the means of production and by means of whose conflict society changes in accordance with developments in the forces of production.[15] "Society," as Allen Wood has put it, "is a structure, made up of roles or positions which differ determinately in the kind and degree of control their occupants have over the process of social production, the kinds of claims they have on social labour or its fruits, or the kinds of claims other members of society have on them."[16] The relations of production of society—the totality of which is the economic structure of society— divide people into economic roles and out of these economic roles social classes emerge. Masses of people come to exist whose roles leave them in a common situation with common interests, which stand opposed to other masses of people in other situations with other common interests. In our society this is instantiated by the fact that there are workers who must sell their labour power and capitalists who buy it and, directly or indirectly, control it and use it in production. In this way deep and irreconcilable class antagonisms between capitalists and the proletariat arise and are sustained.

All this, of course, can be and has been challenged. I am inclined to think that something like this is approximately true, but this is not the occasion to argue that point. If you think that the reality of classes, class conflict, or antagonistic class interests has not been established, emulate Husserl, bracket them for the nonce, and consider the coherence and utility of this Marxist model of ideology on the assumption that there are such antagonistic classes. Treat it counterfactually. We can argue about the reality of class and class conflict on some other occasion.

However, I would add that if one uses stratification analyses rather than class analyses very similar claims could be made, though, of course, in a different vocabulary, to the ones made in the Marxist model. Even if one were so misguided as to be a methodological individualist similar points could be made about ideology though in a more baroque language.[17]

IV

Another pronounced and distinctive feature of this Marxist conception of ideology and indeed of most Marxist conceptions is that there is a stress on how ideologies typically mystify and distort our understanding of our social situation. (See 5*, 6*, 7*, 9*.)

It is important to see how this distortion works. Where it is most beguiling it does not characteristically work by making false statements let alone by dishing out lies. Ideologists, of course, sometimes provide us with outright lies as happens with some manufactured ideological claims, e.g., Hitler's claim that Polish soldiers crossed the German border and attacked Germany, or the American claim that Duarte is a force standing against the right in El Salvador. But what is pervasive and harder to detect, and perhaps more pernicious and typical, is how ideology works by presenting and inculcating a false or slanted perspective that arranges the facts in a misleading way, or fails to mention certain facts, or places them in an inconspicuous context.[18]

Both the arrangement and the omissions function to further the interests of the class or primary social group whose ideology it is. In a capitalist ideology the facts are arranged in such a way that capitalist interests are furthered or at least protected and proletarian interests are harmed. Facts, plain facts, are, for example, pointed to about inflation, and workers are told they must moderate their wage demands to help whip inflation. Moderating their demands is in the public interest. It is for the good of everyone alike. What is not drawn to their attention is that this moderation on their part, while it may help slow inflation, will also, and more certainly, come to a transfer of some wealth from worker to capitalist, negating, or partially negating, gains made by workers in earlier struggles with capitalists under more favourable conditions. It is also not noted how such a "keeping of the social contract," as Callaghan used to call it, helps stabilize capitalism. No attention at all is paid to whether such a stabilization is in the interests of workers or indeed of the vast majority of the people in the society. About things like moderating wage demands in periods of inflation or accepting price and wage controls one cluster of facts is trotted out for ideological consumption and arranged in such a way as to protect the established order. Inconvenient facts are kept well out of sight.

A perhaps more interesting but somewhat more tendentious illustration of how the distorting mirror of ideology works by the arrangement of the facts and by the strategic omission of facts can be illustrated from the current (1981) interplay of American foreign policy and economic policy.[19] The Reagan administration is intensifying the cold war. Facts about Soviet involvement in Afghanistan, Soviet troop levels in Europe, Soviet military capability, and instability in Poland are appealed to. There may be in this some exaggeration and lying, but it is also the case that facts are invoked. Renewed and vigorous defense spending is stressed to protect "the free world" and pressure is directed to reluctant allies to start spending too. This is all allegedly for our mutual defense. But little careful attention is paid as to whether a dispassionate and comprehensive examination would reveal whether we really are so threatened. And in the mass-media—the television networks, the standard newspapers throughout North America, and the large circulation tabloids—the connection between this and the domestic economy is not stressed. Reagan's pseudo-libertarian talk to the contrary notwithstanding, there is a call for a big increase, through defense spending, in the state sector of the economy. The rich in a capitalist-state society need to be coaxed into investing in American industry. But it is here where military spending is useful, for it will provide a guaranteed market for high technology production—but only in an atmosphere of war hysteria will such waste production not provoke domestic discontent. But that production is deemed necessary, so the cold war with its war hysteria needs to be cranked up again. However, stress on this military production will increasingly weaken the United States position in world trade, particularly vis-à-vis western Europe and Japan. To offset that, the Americans must pressure western Europe and Japan into developing a military industry and into cutting their flourishing non-waste production. This requires, economically requires, increased international tension and arms production, and this in turn requires, in the domestic populations, hawkish cold-war attitudes and a fear of communist encroachment.

A simple ideological view of the matter is that the breakdown in detente, or the partial breakdown in detente, is due to Soviet aggression in Afghanistan and elsewhere. A less ideological view of the matter does not deny that the Soviet Union has so and so many troops in Afghanistan, but views this fact in a wider network of facts, together with less simplistic theories of political sociology, to come up with a less ideological understanding of the situation. It is important here, using coherence models of justification, to get a wider perspective with a more thorough sifting of the facts.

The crucial thing to see is that the mystification or distortion does not come principally, or sometimes even at all, through lies but through the inculcation of a perspective—through the arrangement and highlighting of certain propositions and through the omission or placement of others, and generally through the logical tone of voice in which things are discussed.

It isn't just a question of a comprehensive perspective—there can be total ideologies. What ideologies do is give false perspectives. In this respect they function analogously to the manner of functioning of a paranoid's account of why everyone is out to get him. His account could be false even though most, if not all, of the first-order statements made by the paranoid about this situation were true. A did cut in front of him as he was turning; B was very angry with him; C does avoid him; G was curt to him; and so on. It is the way he arranges these facts and the interpretation that he puts on them that produces the falseness, i.e., a radically skewed perspective. The person under the sway of an ideology has come to accept a certain arrangement and a certain reading of the facts and has been led to focus too narrowly on a certain set of facts while not relating, even what sometimes are quite plain and uncontroversial facts, to a wider set of background matters.

Evaluations—judgments of significance and consequent normative commitments—go with the acceptance of an ideology. With a more comprehensive and less ideological viewing of the matter, a very different understanding and appreciation, and a consequent weighing of the significance of the facts would occur. It is not a question of reading the values off the facts, but it is a question of considered convictions shifting with the way the pattern of facts are grasped and with related judgments concerning the plausibility of various interpretations and with judgments about how well these interpretations match with more comprehensive and nuanced interpretations ordered in a comprehensive overview.[20]

It is important to recognize that views, including world-pictures, can be more or less ideological; representations can be more or less perspicuous and more or less falsifying. Perspectives are not like statements which are either true or false *sans phrase*. What has been misleadingly called "ideological consciousness" is in reality the ideological mystification that people experience when they have a too-narrow and a too-skewed selection of the facts placed in a distorting perspective.

I think that to make clear exactly what is involved could best be exhibited by working in detail with some real examples of ideological thinking. That can hardly be done here, although I gestured in that direction with my two examples. But it is quite possible that some will think they were (particularly the second one) more ideological themselves than relevatory of how ideology works. Their *parti pris* nature reveals that the would-be unmasker has a mask blocking his own vision. I do not think for a moment that that is so, but if I am, as I hope I am not, self-deceived here, and if I am wearing ideological blinkers myself, my examples will still, just as well, illustrate my point, for they will show how, with them, I am unwittingly engaged in ideological thinking myself by selectively placing facts in a distorting perspective and by seeking to further my case by a tendentious and overly emotive series of representations.

V

An ideology, as I have remarked, is typically something the other chap has. On the latitudinarian conception one could very properly speak of one's own ideology, but where the ideology is a mystifying device mystifying class interests as universal moral truths, it is not something, in most circumstances, that one would wittingly accept. To be aware that one's thinking is ideological would be to take steps to try to correct it.

It is also the case that for both the latitudinarian and my Marxist conception of ideology, an ideology has a legitimating role in society. The latitudinarian either records it and makes no normative comment on the legitimacy of this legitimizing role or argues that in some instances the legitimizing role is genuine and there can be justified rationally and morally acceptable ideologies. There is conceptual space in such a conception for justified ideologies. I allow, as well, conceptual space for legitimate legitimizing ideologies. I do not rule out their possibility *a priori* by conceptual fiat.[21] But the space is very circumscribed. Generally I argue that ideologies distort and present *ersatz* rationally and morally legitimizing claims. Viewed from the moral point of view with any reasonable objectivity, ideologies are almost always both morally and rationally illegitimate. They would not be accepted by people under conditions of undistorted communication.[22] The ideology in question is not benignly distorting but morally illegitimate (a) where there is, as in the Fascist Italy that Gramsci wrote about or in our present capitalist societies, an extensive dominant-class hegemony, intruding, by way of the consciousness industry, into almost every area of our lives and (b) where the vast majority of the people are duped (socialized if you will) into believing that the institutional arrangements they live under generally answer to the interests of everyone alike as well as any possible alternative arrangements could in their historical circumstances, when in reality they answer principally to the interests of the dominant class.[23] That, I think, is our own condition. But whether I am right or not in this judgment, it is plain how an ideology could, and typically would, be morally illegitimate.

More simply still—unless, like Plato and the Grand Inquisitor, we believe in the moral necessity or moral efficacy of the "noble lie"—

that something distorts or mystifies is a *prima facie* reason for rejecting it and not accepting the norms dependent on it. Similarly, that something serves the interest of a small dominant class and is harmful to the interests of the vast majority of people is also a good reason for rejecting it. A system of ideas which engenders mistaken self-images and a distorted understanding of our condition is, at least, *prima facie* illegitimate: it is incapable of being defended morally.

It surely will be responded that to put it this way is very un-Marxist because for Marx morality is ideology.[24] There could be nothing called "the moral point of view" which could, in a Marxist conception of things, be legitimately appealed to in declaring a social order morally illegitimate. There are in reality only moral ideologies mystifying our consciousness and making us believe that there is something other than individual or class interests that we can rationally appeal to in deciding to do one thing rather than another.

It is true that both Marx and Engels frequently speak contemptuously of morality and moralizing and have flatly said that morality is ideology.[25] I think they should be taken not to be making what some would now call a meta-ethical conceptual remark, or a nihilistic critique of the very idea of an objective ethic, or any sort of semantical claim about what morality must be, or any epistemological claim about how we could know what is right or wrong. Instead, they should be taken as making a claim in the sociology of morals about how morality (moralizing) typically functions (what its social function is) in class societies.[26] They are making a remark about the social role or function of morality and not a philosophical (conceptual) comment about what morality essentially is. They are not engaged in Hume's, Kant's, Moore's, Hägerström's or Mackie's task of trying to say what moral ideas really are but are trying to show what social function they have in various class societies. And there, Marx and Engels say, with considerable plausibility, that morality (that is, particular moralities), like law and like religion, does ideological work. In the class struggle, morality typically has a mystifying role. In one way or another, it works to get people to accept the established order or, where it is a revolutionary ideology, to accept a new postulated revolutionary social order.[27] It typically serves ruling class interests although sometimes it can also be an ideological weapon of a rising class in its struggle with the dominant class. But this should be understood as a remark in the sociology of morals and not as a remark about the nature of morals.

It is very tempting for a moral philosopher to read into Marx some kind of philosophical moral doctrine—a claim about the epistemology or ontology of morals. Perhaps, we are inclined to think, he has an error theory like Westermarck's or Mackie's, or perhaps he really is assuming some kind of non-cognitivism, nihilism, or naturalism.[28] But there is no good warrant for that in Marx's text, or for that matter in Engels's either. Marx and Engels, as would befit their interests, show the ideological work moral notions typically do, but they also quite unabashedly make moral judgments of a diverse kind in their theoretical work, their polemical work, and in private correspondence. They do this, in all these domains, without the slightest hesitation, or embarrassment, or sense that they themselves are saying something ideological or subjective or in any way questionable. But even if they had—even if they did think that all morality must be ideological twaddle—there is no good reason for others, including Marxists, to follow them here.[29]

VI

It is tempting to say that if all talk about man and society must be ideological then nothing can be ideological, for if there cannot in any sense be a science, or theory, or account of society which is non-ideological, if we cannot even conceptualize what would count as non-ideological social thought, then we cannot even identify any system of social thought as ideological, and "ideological" could not qualify thought or, at least, thought about society.[30]

Either the adequacy of non-vacuous contrast arguments or the present application of such an argument might be questioned. Theories or images of conceptual imprisonment or of conceptual relativism, often linked with cultural pessimism, abound in a variety of forms in our society.[31] There are all sorts of powerful intellectual strands—Wittgenstein, Winch, and Rorty, on the one hand, a sociology-of-knowledge tradition, and a hermeneutical tradition, on the other—which tend to push us in that direction. There are respectable intellectual reasons for taking some such arguments very seriously indeed, but it is also true that they afford us a natural ideology, in some instances even a consoling ideology, for world-weary intellectuals during the period of the decline of capitalism.

Wittgenstein once said that talk of reason is not infrequently talk which is used as a club to beat down people who see the world in very different ways than do the "guardians of reason." Talk of ideology may have a similar function. If we operate within one conceptual system (one categorial framework) we can call something ideological with a certain determinateness, but, "outside of a categorial framework" or across such frameworks, there is no Archimedean point, there is no wide, reflective, equilibrium point, where, bursting out of the hermeneutical circle, we can say that something is ideological *sans phrase*. The contrast between the ideological and non-ideological is always systems-relative.[32] There is no objective way of saying of a whole system of thought or of a whole social system or way of life, that it is ideological, or, indeed, if we think about what we are saying, non-ideological. The appellation "ideological" or "non-ideological" has no proper application here. indeed, the very conception of what is objective and what is not is conceptualized in a way which is internal to the framework. There is no, it might not unnaturally be claimed, framework-independent and indeed domain-of-discourse-independent conception of objectivity.[33] If we claim that a whole system of thought is ideological because it is not objective, we are using "objective" polemically (ideologically?) as Wittgenstein says people often use talk of reason. We can, so the objection goes, take Marx's system and then, in terms of it, characterize something as ideological. But we cannot, without vicious circularity, test it for ideologicality itself.[34]

I think there is a myriad of uncontrolled metaphors and a questionable meshing together of disparate elements in the above remarks that together have the effect of making the whole situation seem worse than it is. In trying to sort some of this out, let me return to my non-vacuous contrast. If some social thought, Marx's or someone else's, could not count as being non-ideological or ideology-free, or relatively ideology-free, then the very term "ideological" becomes a Holmesless Watson. "Ideological" in such a circumstance could not qualify "social thought."

It is no use saying that the contrast could only come with natural science which is non-ideological while anything dealing with the human sciences or society is ideological. Such a contrast would not provide the relevant comparison. To get the relevant contrast, we need some social thought which is non-ideological, say historical materialism, to contrast, as Marx does in *The German Ideology*, with some other social thought, say historical idealism, which is ideological.[35]

We might, returning to the point that things could be more or less ideological, put the non-vacuous contrast point in a weaker way which some might think is closer to how things actually are. All theories, and indeed even all thinking, some might say, about man and society have some ideological elements, but some thinking and some theories are more ideological or ideology-prone than others. Perhaps Althusser is right and ideology is eternal—man, as he said, being an ideological animal.[36] But some systems and some thinking are more ideological than others. Indeed, the differences can be quite striking and that is where we get our valid contrast. We do not, if this stress is right, need to look for the realm—at best an empty class—of the non-ideological. We do not need to draw a sharp line between ideology and science. Instead we need to recognize that there is a continuum.[37] Science—genuine science—can have ideological elements, occasionally rather extensive ideological elements (Smith and Ricardo), though sometimes the ideological distortion is so deep and the theories are of such a character that they hardly have a scientific character at all (Malthus or Spencer). And sometimes something thoroughly scientific (say the labour theory of value) can also be ideological—can serve the interests of a particular class—with very little or perhaps no distortion of social reality. (Recall that being distortive or mystificatory was not taken as a *defining* property of ideology.) So, without claiming that any social theory, including Marxism, is utterly *ideologie-frei,* we can contrast ideologies with less class serving, less distorting, more objective, more extensively truth-bearing systems of thought. These systems can in turn be used in identifying and criticizing ideology so that all thought is not viewed as so relative or conceptually imprisoning that the very idea of an ideology drops out or, what comes to the same thing, everything becomes ideological. The claim is that this last bit of talk doesn't even make sense. If all talk about man and society is ideological, nothing can be.

VII

This variant on responses to the liar paradox is one way out of such a critique of ideological critique. However, there is another response that I want briefly to explore. The Marxist conception of ideology I sought to characterize has as *leitmotiv* the notion that an ideology serves class interests, is an intellectual weapon in the class struggle, and typically, but not invariably, distorts our understanging of our social situation in such a way that the interests of the class whose ideology it is are served. In any extended defense of such an account an appeal would have to be made to the concept of interests and some tolerably objective characterization of what human interests are would have to be given. It would also have to be the case that there would be given some objective and ramified characterization of classes and, in the doing of that, of historical materialism, forces of production, relations of production, and how the classes interrelate in the modes of production. Explicating that would in turn require a characterization of the relations of production and superstructures, and a specification of just what superstructures are and the roles they play in our lives.[38] This gives us the structure of a holistic social theory, a theory riddled with difficulties and destined to be replaced in time by a more adequate social theory, but still a social theory far more adequate in explanatory power than historical idealism. . . . There is perhaps no non-circular proof of that, but if we do work from the inside with different social theories and set them in comparison with each other we will come to recognize that not all systems stand on equal footing and that not all are equally distorting.[39] They may all distort, but they do not all equally distort. We can specify something of what human interests are and what are the interests of people within a determinate class. Talk of class and class-interests has explanatory power. Since these things are true, we should be very cautious about concluding that a Marxist account of ideology gives us no basis, or only a very relativistic basis, for a specification of ideology. With that specification, we have a foundation to appeal to in proceeding to the critique of ideology. To be justified in taking those notions to be themselves ideological and relativistic, we need a rationale much stronger than the bare recognition that there are in the world different forms-of-life with different and often at least seemingly incommensurable language-games with their own conceptions of adequacy and their own conceptions of where justification must come to an end. Some such systems could still encompass others and enable us to understand and assess others. That none will satisfy the craving for certainty should only remind us of what we have known for a long time—since at least Peirce's assault on Cartesianism—namely, that fallibilism is the name of the game. But fallibilism is not relativism, conceptual or otherwise, a relativism forcing us into saying that we can only pit one ideology against another and can never criticize ideology by appealing to a theory which can make a justified claim to being a reasonable approximation to truth.[40]

Notes

1. Arne Naess, *Democracy, Ideology and Objectivity* (Oslo: Oslo University Press, 1956); and Hans Barth, *Truth and Ideology* (Berkeley: University of California Press, 1976). Concerning the conception "essentially contested" see W. B. Gallie, *Philosophy and the Historical Understanding* (London: Chatto and Windus, 1964), ch. 8; Alasdair MacIntyre, "The Essential Contestability of Some Social Concepts," *Ethics* 84/1, (October, 1973); and William Connolly, *The Terms of Political Discourse* (London: D. C. Heath, 1974), ch. 1.

2. Raymond Williams, *Marxism and Literature* (Oxford: Oxford University Press, 1977), 55–7; and Allen Wood, *Karl Marx* (London: Routledge and Kegan Paul, 1981), 117–20.

3. Joe McCarney, *The Real World of Ideology* (Sussex, England: Harvester Press, 1980). McCarney cogently argues this point and also gives us good grounds for believing that not only Lenin, Lukács, and Gramsci believe this, but, more surprisingly, Marx and Engels as well.

4. John Plamenatz, *Ideology* (London: Pall Mall Press, 1970), 5. Joe McCarney shows how very inadequate Plamenatz's treatment is as a general introduction to the topic. See McCarney, *Real World,* 153. Similar things are pointed out about Popper's work here. Ibid., p. 158. R. G. Peffer makes similar distinctions to the distinctions I am making here. See R. G. Peffer, "Morality and the Marxist Concept of Ideology," *Canadian Journal of Philosophy* Supplementary Vol. 7 (1981).

5. Ernest Gellner, *The Devil in Modern Philosophy* (London: Routledge and Kegan Paul, 1974), 113–50.

6. Bernard Williams, "Democracy and Ideology" in M. Rejai ed., *Democracy: The Contemporary Theories* (New York, Atherton Press, 1967), 162–63.

7. McCarney clearly explicates this crucial element in Marx's work and in the Marxist tradition. There is a way in which Bernard Williams could invert the claim I am making here. The latitudinarian conception of ideology could find room for the Marxist conception as a sub-class of ideology which promotes class interests but also, as a sub-class, it has all the features of the latitudinarian conception as well. The latitudinarian could then claim that his is the more general characterization: the claim that captures what it is for something to be an ideology. The part about which conception captures what essentially an ideology is aside, it is true that such an inversion could be made. In one way, perhaps, everything can be said just as perspicuously in either terminology.

While there is force in that remark, it still seems to me that my way of putting it is preferable for at least the following reasons: it clearly does not broaden the conception of ideology so extensively that almost everything— almost all of the human sciences or social thought—becomes ideological by implicit definition; it points out clearly how an ideology, while still remaining a general outlook, is a tool in class struggles and reflects class interests; it locates our conception of ideology clearly in the actual practice of ideology-critique of Marxists and Anarchists. With my conceptualization, we have a distinct role for ideology while with the latitudinarian conception it becomes practically equivalent to "world-view" or "belief-system." (R. X. Ware made me see the need for this footnote.)

8. What is important to recognize is that it does not follow that if something is science it cannot also be ideology. There is (or can be) science which isn't ideological, there is science which is also ideological (Smith, Ricardo): there is *ersatz* science which is ideological (Malthus?, Spencer?): and there is ideology which is non-scientific, i.e., doesn't even purport to be scientific. For explications and defenses of these notions see Joe McCarney, *Real World;* and John Stevenson, "Marx's Theory of Ideology," *Radical Philosopher's News Journal* 9 (Fall, 1977), 14–34.

9. L. Althusser, "Ideology and Ideological State Apparatuses" in his *Lenin and Philosophy* (New York: Monthly Review Press, 1971). See also Jacques Ranciere, "On the Theory of Ideology," *Radical Philosophy* 1 (Spring, 1974). Joe McCarney devastatingly criticizes Althusser's account. See McCarney, *Real World,* chs. 3, 4. Althusser, to his credit, has abandoned his earlier, still very influential views. See L. Althusser, *Essays in Self-Criticism* (London: NLB, 1973), 119–25.

10. John McMurtry, *The Structure of Marx's World View* (Princeton, New Jersey: Princeton University Press, 1978), 123–56.

11. Bertell Ollman, *Alienation* (Cambridge, England: Cambridge University Press, 1971). See his chapter on ideology.

12. Jurgen Habermas, *Legitimation Critis* (Boston: Beacon Press, 1973); and his "What Does a Crisis Mean Today? Legitimation Problems in Late Capitalism," *Social Research* 40 (1973). See also Thomas McCarthy, *The Critical Theory of Jurgen Habermas* (Cambridge, Mass.: The MIT Press, 1978), ch. 5.

13. Joe McCarney, *Real World.*

14. Ibid.

15. G. A. Cohen, *Karl Marx's Theory of History* (Princeton, New Jersey: Princeton University Press, 1978).

16. Allen Wood, *Karl Marx* (London: Routledge and Kegan Paul, 1981), 84. See also G. A. Cohen, "Being, Consciousness and Roles: On the Foundations of Historical Materialism," in C. Abramsky ed., *Essays in Honour of E. H. Carr* (London: Macmillan Press, 1974), 82–97.

17. For the reasons why one should not be a methodological individualist see Steven Lukes, *Essays in Social Theory* (London: Macmillan, 1977), 177–86; Richard Miller, "Methodological Individualism and Social Explanation," *Philosophy of Science* 45 (1978), 387–414; and especially Alan Garfinkel's brilliant *Forms of Explanation* (New Haven: Yale University Press, 1981).

18. That a good bit of outright fabrication takes place is documented in Noam Chomsky's and Edward S. Harman's impressive *The Political Economy of Human Rights,* 1 and 2 (Montreal: Black Rose Press, 1979). For a more theoretical underpinning relating ideology to politics and the human sciences

see Noam Chomsky, *Language and Responsibility* (Sussex: The Harvester Press, 1978), Part I.

19. Noam Chomsky, "The Cold War Is a Device by Which Superpowers Control Their Own Domains," *Manchester Guardian Weekly* 124/25 (June 21, 1981), 8–9 and Lester Thurow, "How Reagan Can Wreck the Economy," *The New York Review of Books,* 27/8 (May 14, 1981), 3–8.

20. Andrew Collier, "Scientific Socialism and the Question of Socialist Values," *Canadian Journal of Philosophy,* Supplementary Vol. 7 (1981).

21. Joe McCarney makes a good case for that in his *The Real World of Ideology.*

22. Jurgen Habermas, *Communications and the Evaluation of Society* (Boston: Beacon Press, 1979) and Thomas McCarthy, *Critical Theory,* ch. 4.

23. Hans Magnus Enzensberger, *Raids and Reconstructions: Essays in Politics, Crime and Culture* (London: Pluto Press, 1976), 7–53.

24. Anthony Skillen, "Marxism and Morality," *Radical Philosophy* 8 (Summer, 1974); Andrew Collier; "Truth and Practice," *Radical Philosophy* 5 (Summer, 1973), and "On the Production of Moral Ideology," *Radical Philosophy* 9 (Winter, 1974). See as well Anthony Skillen, *Ruling Illusions: Philosophy and the Social Order,* (Sussex: The Harvester Press, 1977).

25. Allen Wood, *Marx,* 141–56.

26. William Shaw, "Marxism and Moral Objectivity," *Canadian Journal of Philosophy* Supplementary Vol. 7 (1981).

27. Kai Nielsen, "Morality, Marxism and the Ideological Functions of Morality," *The Occasional Review* 8/9 (Autumn, 1978). See also the citations in note 24.

28. For a succinct statement of this account see John Mackie's, "A Refutation of Morals," *Australian Journal of Psychology and Philosophy* 24 (1946). Mackie has elaborated his views and related them to Hume's in his *Ethics: Inventing Right and Wrong* (London: Penguin, 1971); and in his *Hume's Moral Theory* (London: Routledge and Kegan Paul, 1980).

29. See William Shaw, "Marxism and Moral Objectivity," *Canadian Journal of Philosophy,* Supplementary Vol. 7 (1981).

30. See the discussion of "ideological explanations" by J. L. Mackie, Renford Bambrough, and Martin Hollis in Stephan Korner, ed., *Explanation* (Oxford: Basil Blackwell, 1975), 185–216.

31. What is involved here is concisely expressed by Martin Hollis in Korner, *Explanation,* 205–214.

32. Ibid.

33. Ibid., and my "Rationality and Relativism," *Philosophy of the Social Sciences,* 4/4 (December, 1974); "Rationality and Universality," *The Monist* 59/3, (July, 1976); and my "Conceptual Relativism," *Grazer Philosophische Studien* 3 (1977).

34. Alasdair MacIntyre, *Marxism and Christianity* (London: Gerald Duckworth, 1969); and again in his *Against the Self Images of the Age* (London: Gerald Duckworth, 1971).

35. Allen Wood, *Marx,* 117–19.

36. See citations in note 9 as well as Alex Callincos, *Althusser's Marxism* (London: Pluto Press, 1976), 55–88, and Gregor McLennon, Victor Molina, and Roy Peters, "Althusser's Theory of Ideology," *On Ideology, Centre For Contemporary Cultural Studies* (London: Hutchinson, 1978), 77–105.

37. See the citations in note 8.

38. This work is beginning to be done in a rigorously analytical manner. See Geoffrey Hellman, "Historical Materialism" in John Mephan and David-Hillel-Rubin (eds.), *Issues in Marxist Philosophy,* Vol. 2 (Sussex, England: The Harvester Press, 1979), 143–66; William Shaw, *Marx's Theory of History* (Stanford: Stanford University Press, 1978); G. A. Cohen, *Karl Marx's Theory of History* (Princeton: Princeton University Press, 1978); and Allen Wood, *Marx.* Some of the necessary corrections occur in henry Laycock, "Critical Notice of G. A. Cohen and William H. Shaw's "Marx's Theory of History," *Canadian Journal of Philosophy* 10/2 (June, 1980), 335–56; and in Richard Miller's "Productive Forces and the Forces of Change," *The Philosophica Review,* 90/1 (January, 1981), 91–117.

39. For the underlying methodology see John Rawls, "The Independence of Moral Theory," *Proceedings and Addresses of the American Philosophical Association* 47 (1974/75); Norman Daniels, "Wide Reflective Equilibrium and Theory Acceptance in Ethics," *The Journal of Philosophy,* 76/5 (May, 1979); Norman Daniels, "Reflective Equilibrium and Archimedean Points," *Canadian Journal of Philosophy,* 10/1 (March, 1980); Jane English "Ethics and Science," *Proceedings of the XVI Congress of Philosophy;* and William Shaw, "Intuition and Moral Philosophy," *American Philosophical Quarterly* 17/2 (April, 1980); Kai Nielsen, "Considered Judgments Again," *Human Studies,* 5 (1982); and Kai Nielsen, "On Needing a Moral Theory: Rationality, Considered Judgments and the Boundary of Morality," *Metaphilosophy* 13/2 (April, 1982).

40. I would like to thank Elisabeth Nielsen and R. X. Ware for their helpful comments on an earlier version of this essay and Rodger Beehler and Jonathan Bordo for conversations about the underlying conception of ideology articulated here.

6

Marxism and Morality

Marx's attitude toward morality was complex and ambivalent, and by and large the Marxist tradition has followed him here, at least as far as the ambivalence is concerned and sometimes with the sense of complexity as well. Marx repeatedly, throughout his life, passionately, and with both indignation and scorn condemned capitalism as a dehumanizing social system that brutalized human beings and undermined their autonomy. He hammered away at this while still firmly recognizing that in certain historical epochs capitalism was an absolutely indispensable engine of human progress, although he also believed that by his own time capitalism's usefulness had ended and stood in the way of human progress. That is, he took capitalism to be not only an exploitative and dehumanizing social system but a system that had so built up the productive forces that no reasonable case could now be made for claiming that capitalist production was still a necessary evil on the way to productive progress. By now he took capitalism to be a system that it was irrational and inhumane to sustain. Capitalism, he believed, alienates, robs, needlessly exploits, and makes miserable countless human beings, while in a way that is no longer necessary for the enhancement of culture or science, a few live in positions of privilege and control. Possibilities for free development and leisure are not possible under such a system for the vast majority of people. Moreover, and contrastingly, for at least some of the capitalist class, this system makes possible a life of idleness and commodious living that comes off the backs of the laboring classes, classes not infrequently driven by the harsh economic realities of their lives to such a one-

117

sided development that they are close to becoming mere appendages to machines. The exploitation of the laboring classes is sometimes so steep that they are reduced to stupor and misery. Their lot is that of a dulled, dehumanized existence.

Marx was filled not only with indignation but with hatred of a social system that would allow such conditions to prevail when they can no longer be called necessary evils—that is, necessary to so develop the productive forces as to make a decent life available for all. He raged at maintaining a set of institutions with their misery-producing and dehumanizing practices; on the other hand, many of us, not at all following Marx here, just avoid facing these facts, and so we neither rage against these institutions nor despair over their very existence and stubborn persistence. However, Marx, the great denouncer—and here is where paradox enters—was also contemptuously dismissive of moralizing, moral philosophy, 'ethical socialism,' and attempts to find a moral basis for socialism or a foundation in moral theory for socialism. "Communism," he said, "breaks the staff of all morality." Morality is ideology. It is an obfuscating cluster of institutions that obscures from the working class what is in its own interests and confuses workers with prattle about right and wrong. Morality is one of the ideological instruments, Marx claimed, that help dull for workers the native edge of their resolution to revolt against inhuman conditions. Morality undermines the kind of resolution that even a tolerably clear under-standing of their class interests would trigger—a resolution that would lead workers to act decisively against capitalism and to struggle, in whatever way their particular situation makes possible, to begin the processes of constructing socialism.

Even when moralism is more benignly disposed (as in 'ethical socialism'), it still leads workers down the garden path by substituting abstract moralistic talk for concrete social analysis of how the capitalist system works, what will break it, and how we are to go about the construction of socialism. Moral-talk, Marx argued, confuses workers and makes it more difficult for them to attain a revolutionary con-sciousness. So it is tempting, although of course paradoxical, to describe Marx and many others in the Marxist tradition as, at one and the same time, moralists and anti-moralists.

II

Particularly with respect to discussion about justice and exploitation, there has come into being in the past decade a minor growth industry devoted to sorting out what is at least a tension (to put it minimally) between Marx's anti-moralism and what appears to be, and plainly is in his work up to 1843, his moral critique of capitalism.[1] Some faced with this have resourcefully defended a Marxist anti-moralism (for example, Allen Wood, Andrew Collier, Anthony Skillen, and Richard

Miller). Others (for example, G. A. Cohen, Norman Geras, Gary Young, and Jon Elster) have carefully and sustainedly argued that Marx, including the mature Marx, did make, among other things, a moral critique of capitalism and other social systems, and he defended democratic forms of socialism (if that isn't pleonastic) as preferable social systems to capitalism from a moral point of view. The claim is that it is better for the vast majority of human beings to live in a genuinely socialist society than in a capitalist society, even the best of capitalist societies. Marx, these scholars argued, plainly thought that socialist societies would be more just than capitalist societies; and that capitalism is less just than socialism; and that capitalist societies, even the best capitalist societies, are positively unjust societies. They are not only not truly human societies; they are thoroughly unjust societies with little respect for human rights. They are societies where people are exploited: treated as means only.

I think the case made here by Norman Geras, Gary Young, G. A. Cohen, and Jon Elster was well taken when they argued that although Marx (whose abiding concerns were not about the theoretical articulation of moral issues) was sometimes confused on these issues, he nevertheless did think capitalism was unjust and degrading. Further, he thought that ethically speaking, although not only ethically speaking, socialism was plainly to be preferred to capitalism. That Marxiological position is, I believe, the right stance to take, although, as I shall make plain in a moment, it is not part of my brief to argue that Marxiological point here. However, Norman Geras, in particular, made a good textual and interpretive case for it while reasonably responding to the not inconsiderable and at least prima facie telling texts brought forth by Marxist anti-moralists against that reading of Marx. G. A. Cohen and Jon Elster, with a different stress, made impressive speculative elaborations of where Marxists (going here beyond anything Marx said) could consistently go with such issues. Geras's account, in contrast with Cohen's and Elster's, had the added virtue of still showing, while clearly placing the ways in which Marxist anti-moralism is both credible and important, how what is important in Marxist anti-moralism can be accounted for without abandoning the view that Marx made, and rightly made, a moral critique of capitalism.

III

I do not want here, as I have just remarked, to enter that exegetical thicket. I think we can, at least reasonably and perhaps safely as well, take Norman Geras's exegetical position as the Marxiological rest point here, at least until some forceful arguments are deployed against it. I am, however, much more concerned with the soundness of such a Marxist account of justice on its own, quite apart from anything Marx or Engels may or may not have said about the justice and moral preferability of socialism. My interest here is in whether we can, in a manner consistent with the body of theory central to Marxism, make a good case for the claim that the capitalist system is an unjust system, even in its best forms, and that genuine forms of socialism are, among other ways of being preferable, morally preferable.

There will be those who will say that given the central canonical parts of Marxist social theory and practice (parts we have plainly inherited from Marx), we cannot coherently make moral critiques of capitalism and that, whatever Marx may have thought about morality, we should, if we wish to be consistent Marxists, reject the moral point of view as a rational basis for criticizing institutions.[2] These arguments have been powerfully made, and I shall be concerned to consider them here. But I also want to consider the arguments of those who would say, viewed both as a morality of emancipation and as a morality of rights, that Marxist morality, even if it is a coherent possibility, is far from being an adequate cluster of moral beliefs and conceptions.[3] I shall in the face of such an objection try to articulate a Marxist conception of morality—I remain here agnostic about whether it should also be viewed as a Marxist moral theory or a moral philosophy—that makes at least a gesture at adequacy. That is to say, I shall try to give a view of morality that has some reasonable plausibility; that is capable of refinement into a nuanced view; that would be a plausible candidate for a sound view; but that would still match well with the canonical core of Marxism, including its account of ideology and historical materialism, such that, if that account is right, it would *not* be correct to say of such moral conceptions that they are ideological twaddle.

IV

First I need to say something about the core conceptions of Marxism, which, as much as these Marxists might differ in other respects, will be found in some tolerably determinate form in all the classical Marxists and in militants and theoreticians working out of that tradition. Different theoreticians, of course, gave different emphases to various of these elements and gave them different readings. There are differences between Karl Marx and V. I. Lenin and between V. I. Lenin and Antonio Gramsci and between Antonio Gramsci and Mao Zedong; and all these theoreticians of socialist revolution had various ideas, more or less eccentric to themselves, that I have not included in the core. But all the classical Marxists accepted some form of dialectical method. They had a conception of the unity of theory and practice; a conception of human nature (that is, a conception of the needs and capacities of human beings and a conception of the importance of this in human life); a conception of the distinctive importance of economics interpreted around the labor theory of value and the historical functions of economics; a conception of historical materialism, of ideology and its critique, of class, class struggle; a conception of the necessity for revolution; a conception of the transition from capitalism to socialism; a conception of the future communist society; a belief that certain historical factors, among them class struggle, will lead to a communist society's occurrence; and a belief in the desirability of its occurrence.

These conceptions, I should repeat, are subject to very different readings and to very different emphases. Still, the classical Marxists— Karl Marx, Friedrich Engels, V. I. Lenin, Leon Trotsky, Rosa Luxemburg, Georgy Plekanov, Georg Luckács, Antonio Gramsci, Mao Zedong—all accepted these conceptions. However, the existence of this canonical core to the contrary notwithstanding, Marxism is a developing body of theory and practice and is not fixed in stone. Some of these core elements may in time drop out and new elements may enter. Analytical Marxists (for example, G. A. Cohen, Richard Miller, Marx Wartofsky, Robert Paul Wolff, John Roemer, and Jon Elster) have tended to be suspicious of talk of dialectics beyond the banalities that we should steadfastly look for connections, take a wider view, pay attention to historical developments, and have a diachronic as well as a synchronic point of view. Moreover (and perhaps more deeply as far as moving the core is concerned), some actually have rejected the labor theory of value, and a few have even come to be deeply skeptical about the truth, as distinct from the coherence, of historical materialism. Similar shifts can be seen among other Marxists, for example, in structuralist Marxism. The conceptions 'orthodox Marxism' and 'revisionism' should be purged from the consciousness of contemporary Marxists as an unfortunate residue of a theological past. Such conceptions are not worthy of Marxists who in some reasonable sense have the image of themselves as scientific socialists, a conception that surely we need— suitably de-mythologized—if in defending socialism we are to work out of the Marxist tradition.[4]

However, what makes us Marxists is that we take these core conceptions very seriously indeed and that our thinking at least takes its departure from these core conceptions. To this I would add that if too many of these core conceptions were jettisoned, one could no longer coherently and in good conscience think of oneself as a Marxist, although, and rightly so, 'too many' cannot be defined with precision. Marxism, to use old-fashioned terminology, is an open-textured concept.

What I want to do here, in taking this canonical core as given, is see what account of morality will best match with this; what will make the most sense out of what we, considering ourselves not only as spectators but also as agents with hopes for the world and designs for the realization of these hopes, can reasonably say about morality and its role in the stream of life; and what will also, without telling either Marxist or moralistic fairytales, have the most emancipatory potential in our class struggles. I shall stick here with what we, where we take seriously the core of Marxism and think carefully about morality, can

say about morality, and I will pay little attention to what Marx and
Engels, or for that matter later Marxists, have actually said about
morality. My reason for this is that although often suggestive, their
remarks about morality are fragmentary, possibly contradictory, and
certainly not well worked out or informed by long and careful thinking
about morality and moral theory. (We have on the Marxist side neither
an Arnold Hauser of the history of moral philosophy nor a Marxist
critic of Henry Sidgwick as we have Marxist critics of John Keynes.)
I do not, however, intend this as a criticism of the classical Marxists
for it seems to me perfectly appropriate to say they had better things
to do. Still, it is also important to recognize that it is the case that
they did not clearly think through their views here and that those, as
we have seen, who have tried to reconstruct Marx's or Engels's views
of morality on the basis of these fragments have come up with radically
conflicting accounts.[5] Be that as it may, I shall not in this chapter try
to play that reconstructionist game, but working from what I have
characterized as the canonical core of Marxist theory, I shall try to
articulate a reasonable account of the function of morality in our lives
and to consider what, if any, emancipatory potential it could have.
(One view that has to be squarely faced is whether morality is an
inherently conservative shoring up, either crudely or in nuanced,
intricate ways, of a given class formation—typically the dominant class
formation—of a given epoch.)

V

I first want to turn to the question of morality and ideology. The
concept of ideology and the critique of ideology play a large and
important part in Marxist theory, and Marx did famously say that morality
is ideology. I shall argue that philosophers in particular, but others as
well, are prone to misunderstand the claim that morality is ideology,
thereby in effect, if not explicitly, taking it as an epistemological claim
or a claim about the logical status of moral notions. Such a claim gives
to understand that moral ideas, all moral ideas, are nothing but class-
based social demands without, simply because of what moral ideas
must be, any rational basis. Their being ideological makes them just
so many irrational class prejudices distorting our understanding of what
our real situation is and obscuring from us our life chances as members
of a determinate class in a determinate historical circumstance.

I think such beliefs rest, for philosophers anyway, on some beguiling
confusions. Once they are cleared up it will be evident that nothing
like this follows from what I shall argue is an insightful remark on
Marx's part that morality is ideology. We must first come to see, and
take to heart, that Marx's remark about morality being ideology is a
remark in the sociology of morals and not in moral epistemology or
meta-ethics. For Mackie-like reasons 'believing in morals' may be

irrational, but there is nothing in the canonical core of Marxist theory, including Marx's account of ideology, that requires either its affirmation or denial. That is, there is nothing in the Marxist canonical core that requires us to say that 'believing in morals' must be an illusion because there can be no objective prescriptivity built into the fabric of the world and moral ideas are simply objectivized emotions, projections of emotional states onto completely fictitious, hardly comprehensible 'objective properties.' Neither this nor anything like it is rooted in Marxist theory.

These remarks, taken at face value, are dark sayings. They require elucidation, explanation, and defense. I shall start by giving a reading of what Marxists mean by 'ideology.' In social anthropology, to talk about a society's ideology is to talk about a society's belief-system. Marxists by contrast mean something much more specific when they speak of ideology. An ideology, put oversimply as a first approximation, is a system of social beliefs, typically illusory beliefs, that reflects in a disguised way the interests of a determinate class. Building on that, and trying to flesh the concept out a bit, some Marxists have characterized an ideology as a system of social beliefs and attitudes that for those held captive by the ideology distorts their understanding of the world and their positions and possibilities in it; ideology gives rise to social forces, characteristic of class societies, that pervasively tend not to bring these social ideas into accord with how things actually are. The impression is given to those under the sway of the ideology that there is such a fit when in reality there is not. Moreover, where the ideology, either directly or indirectly, prescribes that something is to be done or that something is to be sustained, as ideologies standardly do, the impression is given to those taken in by the ideology that what is prescribed supposedly impartially answers to the interests of everyone alike when in reality, although in a disguised way, it is not prescribed impartially; it actually answers to the interests of a particular class, typically the dominant class.

This is a standard Marxist characterization of ideology, and for certain purposes it is a useful one. It does indeed bring out important and standard features of ideologies, but, for reasons I shall give in a moment, I prefer instead to characterize an ideology as a system of ideas, theories, beliefs, attitudes, norms, and social practices that is characteristic of a class society or of a class or other primary social group in a class society and that serves principally the interests of a class (typically a class in that society) or other primary social group, while (typically at least) putting itself forward as impartially answering to the interests of everyone alike in the society.[6]

The reasons for my adopting this somewhat less typical definition are several. First, with the inclusion of social practices, we have a less exclusively intellectualistic understanding of ideology. My characterization highlights the fact that ideology (in spite of the terminological suggestion) does not always work through explicit ideation. Second, the initially curious-sounding and awkward phrase 'primary social group' is added to enable us to capture phenomena such as a racist Afrikaner ideology without needing to commit ourselves to the tendentious claim that Afrikaners constitute a class. Third, my conceptualization of ideology brings out more explicitly the centrality of class interests in ideology and with it the importance of class conflict. Finally, and vitally, in contrast with the other extended characterization I gave of ideology (and indeed with most characterizations), my conceptualization does not make distortion a *conceptually necessary* feature of ideologies. Most, perhaps all, ideologies distort. That, in many contexts, is for the class whose interests the ideology serves one of its most important functions, but logically speaking the mark of the ideological is that it serves or answers to class interests, not that it distorts or mystifies (although it typically does that as well).

Such a characterization, by contrast with the more standard characterization, does not set Marx and Lenin at odds with each other about what an ideology is and leaves (as Lenin would have it) conceptual space for the possibility of a socialist ideology that would answer to working-class interests without mystifying the working class or anyone else or distorting social reality. Moreover, such a conception of ideology does not set either science and ideology or morality and ideology at odds with each other as conceptually conflicting categories. Where ideology answers to class interests, as it must, but does not distort, if in fact that ever obtains, something could at one and the same time be genuine science and still be ideological (in the sense of answering to the interests of a determinate class), as presumably Marx's *Capital* was. If, for example, *Capital* in a systematic and clarificatory way managed to tell things as they are, it could have at one and the same time been both good science and good ideology. Likewise, something could answer to class interests and still, at least as far as conceptual possibilities are concerned, be genuinely moral in the sense of impartially prescribing that something be done without, in such a prescription, distorting our understanding of ourselves, our society, or our class position and prospects. Answering to class interests is what makes a belief ideological, but, like the scientific belief, the moral belief could answer to class interests without, cognitively speaking, being any the worse for that. It could answer to class interests while at the same time being impartially prescribable as a way of achieving a more general human emancipation. These features seem to me good reasons for preferring my somewhat atypical characterization of ideology. It enables us to say everything the more standard account of ideology does while avoiding its misleading and mystifying features.

VI

There is a further feature of ideology that must be noted in this attempt to give an illuminating and clear reading to the claim that morality is ideology. To do so will involve a discussion of the relation of ideology and superstructure. Morality—all moral beliefs, attitudes, practices, or principles—on any Marxist account must be a part of the superstructure. But then, it is tempting to believe, moral beliefs, attitudes, practices, and principles *must* also be ideological for everything that is in the superstructure must also be ideology. But that claim is a mistaken claim about Marx's ideas.[7] Being superstructural is a necessary, but not a sufficient, condition for being ideological. While all ideological beliefs are superstructural, not all superstructural beliefs are ideological. Consistently with historical materialism, we can distinguish among the various moral beliefs and between ideological moral beliefs that are distorting and ideological moral beliefs that are not.

More generally, if in the superstructure we could not distinguish between ideological and non-ideological beliefs, if it were not the case that it is false to claim that all forms of consciousness, including all forms of self-consciousness, are ideological, Marx would have put himself at risk, given the distortion proneness of ideological beliefs, of being hoisted by his own petard. But principles of interpretive charity would not allow us to attribute to Marx such vulnerability, if we can find a reasonable reading of what Marx was saying in this domain that would avoid that. The foregoing interpretation does just that. Ideological beliefs, and the like, as we have seen, are beliefs that answer to class interests. But among such beliefs, our various publicly articulated forms of self-consciousness are the primary subject matter of ideology. We must have a class society to have an ideology at all, but in such societies, the public conceptions, the socially sanctioned images of ourselves are most paradigmatically ideological. Public conceptions almost invariably distort our understanding of ourselves and also almost invariably answer to ruling-class interests. Public conceptions typically are the social rationalizations of a ruling class—rationalizations that members of that class may or may not partake of themselves—but that are rationalizations deeply embedded in the society in which that ruling class dominates. Public conceptions are the publicly approved self-images in the society in question.

There are, of course, other self-images in the society; most of them are not terribly distant from the publicly approved self-images, although, upon occasion, some are quite distant. Some, which are beliefs that also answer to the interests of the ruling class, are both moral beliefs and ideological beliefs, but there is nothing in Marx that either contends or entails that all self-images, all forms of self-consciousness, including all morally freighted self-images, must be ideological. They are all, given his classificatory system, superstructural, but they need not all be ideological. There is no reason to assume that Marx thought that his own forms of self-consciousness, his own self-images, his own moral beliefs, and those of his other closest and most trusted associates, including Engels, were ideological. Marx never showed the slightest worry that that might be so. Yet, if, à la Karl Mannheim, ideology were some crippling epistemological or conceptual incapacity, Marx, if he were the least bit self-reflective or tough-minded, would not have been so confident of his own moral judgments, his own firm considered convictions, or of those of Engels. But Marx characteristically showed no doubts at all here. (Perhaps he should have, but that is a different matter.)

Again we should work with a principle of interpretive charity. Doing so is not just a matter of saving the day for Marx; it is what we generally should do in such situations. It is crucial to appreciate that not all ideas or ideals, including moral ideas and ideals, *must* involve such a collective rationalization and mystification of social relations as *typically* goes with having an ideology. And that recognition, if you will, is perfectly 'orthodox Marxism.' There is nothing in the core to gainsay it.

It cannot be the case that *all* our beliefs about persons and society *must* be ideological because we must all be suffering from some grave epistemological confusion or blindness. This is not even a coherent possibility for if this were so, then nothing that could be conceptualized could even count as an unmystified idea; we would really have no idea of what an unmystified idea could be or would be like if we were ever to have one. But if that were so, then the very notion of an 'ideological belief' would be unintelligible, for then we could not even recognize that certain belief-systems mystify social reality. A 'mystified idea' would make no non-vacuous contrast with a 'non-mystified' or 'unmystified idea,' for we would have no idea of what the latter is like. But then we can have no idea of what the former is like either. Only if we can draw a conceptual distinction between 'a mystified idea' and an 'unmystified idea'—could recognize which is which—could we go on to develop a sociology of morals that would show how pervasively ideological most moral thinking actually is.

It is crucial not to turn ideology or being ideological into an epistemological issue about how we can know or into a claim about what can be true or false. Instead, ideologies are our public conceptions of ourselves that in one way or another serve class interests in class societies. Ideologies should not be taken as referring to *all* our beliefs, all our self-images, or, necessarily, all our philosophical or moral conceptions. 'Ideology' is not a term that refers to an all-inclusive range of cognitive or affective phenomena. Rather, ideology is paradigmatically the official currency of self-consciousness in class societies. This explains why the extant moralities—the moralities of the various tribes and classes—will all be ideological. And this is what Marxists should be understood to mean when they say that morality is ideological and when they remain, and rightly so, suspicious of moralities and moralizing.

VII

That not all moral and evaluative beliefs are ideological can be seen from inspecting some beliefs pervasively held not only in our societies and societies like ours but in all societies. It is generally agreed by conservatives, liberals, socialists, and whatnot that where avoidable, without creating something still worse, poverty, degradation, exploitation (the treatment of people merely as means), the crippling of human personality, the causing of human suffering, and the refusal to ameliorate it are all bad things, evils to be avoided. (Even the Nazis, paradoxically and dismayingly, believed things like this. They created monstrous, almost unimaginable suffering, but they thought it necessary to avoid something they regarded bizarrely—to grope for the right term—as still worse.) Similarly, it is agreed on all sides that happiness is good, that health is good, that autonomy is good, that self-respect is good. Different philosophers and other theorists put *somewhat* different readings, emphases, and placements on these beliefs, but there is agreement all around, in and out of wide, narrow, or what have you, reflective equilibrium, that these things are good, although there is very little agreement as to *why* these things are good or why the things mentioned previously are evils. But there is deep cross-cultural agreement *that* these are evils and that the other things I mentioned are good.

If we inspect these beliefs, not necessarily as they are placed, stressed, or read in certain moral theories or social theories but just as beliefs that are relatively insulated from theories and overall conceptions, they can be held in such a way that they are not supportive of any particular class interests. They, without further amplification and placement, neither favor the interests of the dominant class nor the interests of the challenging exploited class. Furthermore, just taken in themselves (as they can be at least in thought), these beliefs need not mystify social reality, need not express false consciousness or false beliefs, and need not rest on rationalizations. Moreover, they are beliefs that would not be extinguished if we came to know, and to firmly fix in our reflective self-consciousness, what caused us to come to hold them and the consequences of holding them. They need not be beliefs that are expressive of dominant-class or any class interests. They could all be beliefs that would be reasonable to hold in a classless society, although for some of them, such as poverty is bad, there would be no need to assert them in a classless society. But they still would be accepted there as correct moral judgments. When people in such a developed classless society heard about how in times past there was poverty, they would still judge it a bad thing and judge to be a good thing that a classless society had brought an end to poverty. These moral truisms, as I have called them, would not wither away with the ending of capitalism, the complete disappearance of the last vestiges of capitalist mentality, the withering away of the state, and the achievement of communism.

For all of these reasons, we can see that there is nothing about moral beliefs that makes them by definition ideological, although in our class societies most of them are in fact ideological. But moral beliefs are not per se ideological because of what moral understanding must be or because of anything about the logic of moral reasoning or about the logical status of moral utterances.

VIII

Why then did Marx make such a great fuss about morality being ideological? Not, I reply, because of epistemology, but because of the sort of social and psychological uses (uses with a perfectly good functionalist rationale in class societies) to which he saw morality—now moral ideology—being put, and for which he had good theoretical reasons to expect morality to be put in class societies.

It, following this up, is to Marx's sociology of morals that I now turn my attention. With it he wanted to show how morality typically functions in class societies and why it so functions. He wanted to show what effect rules, moral practices, and institutions have on our lives in class societies and how moralizing actually, standardly, and pervasively works in such societies. He argued that here morality, like law and religion, does ideological work and has a conservative system-supporting role through an extensive and beguiling mystification. Ideology, while purporting to be the exact opposite, is one of the techniques of domination of the ruling class. Ideology helps in various ways to reconcile people to their fate in the established order by convincing them, among other things, that any hope they have for dramatic, substantive change is a wild and possibly dangerous utopia.

In such ways morality plays a legitimizing role, sometimes by an outright sanctifying of the order and, at other times, more subtly, by giving to understand that something very like the extant morality is, everything considered, the best choice among evils in a world that after all is and must remain far from perfect. Morality is used, as Freud also recognized, to reconcile us to 'our fate.' But while Freud, deep cultural pessimist that he was, thought it really was our fate, Marx, during periods in which revolution was an objective possibility, thought we were only being reconciled to what ruling-class ideologies made us come falsely to believe was our fate. Morality teaches us, in this context, and many contexts like it, resignation and acceptance of our lot in a tough world that we did not make. The extant moralities have as a very central function to gull us into an acceptance of the social order, including our class position in that order, into which we were born. These moralities get us to accept our station and its duties. Here morality is indeed moral ideology.

Marx, because of what moral ideology is, not only described it, gave illustrations of it, and explained it; he also roundly condemned it with great indignation. Belief in morals, or at least a not inconsiderable part of it, in societies such as our own, leads most people, without being aware of what is happening to them, into moral ideology. They are duped into believing that what in reality are ruling-class interests are in the interests of society as a whole. Partiality and privilege are mystified so that they seem impartial, fair across classes, and endowed with a holy odor: respect for the moral law. Of course, for moral ideology to work it must not be seen as moral ideology, as a class thing. It is by such mystification that ruling-class hegemony is legitimated. We have, where this is working well, ideological moral control rather than the much more costly and much less efficient direct control by the police and the army.[8] And this, of course, is useful to the dominant class for it is cheaper, easier, and more stable. The dominant class is in a bad way indeed when it must rely on the police and the army.

Talk of legitimization in this discussion of moral ideology is in a sociological sense only. Marx in such remarks about the social functions of morality was talking about just that and not about what morality essentially is or about whether any moral claim in any circumstance could be rationally warranted. There is no question of its being the case that moral *ideology* could really justify anything, but the flip side is that ideological analysis or the critique of ideology, just taken by itself, cannot show that no genuine justificatory question could possibly arise concerning what was or was not a legitimate social order. Put another way, ideology critique, in displaying the social functions of moral ideology, will show that 'believing in morals' is often a pernicious moral swindle, but what this critique cannot do is to show that genuine belief in morals is impossible because morality rests on a mistake. Ideology critique cannot do the Mackie thing.[9] (Indeed, only if there could be some genuine non-ideological moral notions could we coherently or in a non-mystifying way even speak of 'a pernicious moral swindle.' The very possibility of there being distorting, ideological moral discourse is parasitical on its being possible for there to be moral discourse which is genuine and non-distorting.)

A sociology of morals that is Marxist shows the distorting function of much moralizing in class societies in the interest of the ruling classes, but, properly understood, also shows that such a functional account of morality is one thing; moral epistemology or a critical examination of the claims of morality is another. A critical account of the claims of morality might conceivably show that while most moral claims are ideological twaddle and in a disguised way serve class interests, there still are some genuine moral claims that are rationally warranted. The sociological issue and the epistemological issue should not be collapsed or confused.

Marx's condemnation of morality and his utter distrust and contempt for moralizing were directed at moral ideology. His confidence, as I have remarked, in his own moral judgments and in those of some close associates shows, in spite of what he sometimes thought about morality, that he had confidence in our human moral capacity, a capacity that he, in practice at least, recognized could be clearheadedly exercised in certain optimal circumstances. There is nothing about morality, just taken by itself, that makes it something illusory. Once these distinctions are drawn and noted, as I have noted them, the tension between Marxist anti-moralism and Marxist moral commitments simply evaporates.

IX

We are not, if we keep in mind the Marxist canonical core, at the end of the road yet. It has not infrequently been thought that historical materialism conflicts with morality and thereby requires, at worst, Marxist immoralism and, at best, some form of relativism. I shall argue that, on the contrary, historical materialism supports a contextualism that in turn is compatible with a robust objectivism in ethics, although it is incompatible with what Engels rightly ridiculed as a belief in eternal principles of morality—that is, principles alleged to be correctly applicable in any situation such that there would be certain, non-trivial, substantive moral principles that would hold no matter what.[10] If these 'eternal principles' are thought to have any determinate substance, they will not sit well with historical materialism. But this is not at all to reject a contextualist objectivism.

In seeking to clarify what is involved here I will go at this indirectly by first briefly and schematically saying something about what historical materialism is. I will then move directly to my point. Historical materialism is meant to be a scientific theory of epochal social change. As Marx put it in capsule form in his classical summarizing statement in his 1859 Preface to *A Contribution to the Critique of Political Economy,* the economic structure of society, constituted by its set of relations of production, is the real foundation of society. That is to say, the economic structure is the basis on which there "rises a legal and political superstructure to which correspond definite forms of social consciousness." But even this economic structure, as part of the whole mode of production, is what it is during a given epoch because it corresponds to a certain development of the productive forces, another element of the mode of production. In this way, to cite Marx from the Preface, "the mode of production of material life conditions the social, political and intellectual life process in general."[11] The crucial thing to see, in looking at human history *as a whole,* is that the productive forces tend to develop throughout human history, and as they develop they will periodically clash with the production relations in a society when these production relations impede the growth of the productive forces. This in turn tends to cause conflict in the society, including, most centrally, class struggle.[12] The different socio-economic organizations of production, which at various times have characterized human history, rise or fall as they enable or impede the expansion of society's productive capacity. The growth of the productive forces explains the general course of human history.

If this, or something bearing some family resemblance to it, is true or approximately true, what does this mean for ethics?[13] To see what bearing it has also will be to see why historical materialism rejects the claim that there are substantive eternal moral principles *and* accepts a contextualistic objectivism. It has often been thought that if historical materialism is true, then this precludes the very possibility of there being a transhistorical or transmode-of-production-justifiable set of moral principles in the sense that there is any such set of principles to which all people should adhere regardless of class position or socio-economic formation.[14] If historical materialism is true, Engels might well have been right in denying that there are any eternal moral principles with any substantive bite that always apply no matter who or where we are. But that there are no such eternal moral principles does not establish relativism, subjectivism, or nihilism, for it is at least equally compatible with historical materialism to accept a contextualism for moral principles—a contextualism that, as I argued in Chapter 1, gives us a certain distinctive objectivity.

To see a little more what this would come to, we should note that the preceding denial of eternal moral principles is perfectly compatible with being able to say objectively that at such and such a time with such and such a mode of production such and such moral principles are correct; that at another time with another mode of production such and such moral principles are correct; and that at still another time with yet another mode of production a still different set of moral principles is correct. These judgments about what is or is not correct at each of these times, as far as historical materialism is concerned, can be perfectly objective.[15] These judgments are general and can be made about these different societies with these different modes of production by people in societies other than those in which these principles are applicable. Moreover, these judgments can, in principle at least, be understood as correct by any reflective person with normal sympathies and with a good knowledge of the relevant facts.

The general form of self-consciousness, the dominant public self-images, will, where a mode of production is stably in place, fit with that mode of production. This, as we have seen, is the name of the game for ideology. But, as we have also seen when we discussed ideology, Marx was not claiming, as he could not to make sense of his own theory, that all consciousness is ideological so that at all times and at all places there is for everyone a massive and pervasive conceptual imprisonment. Most people's moral understanding will be an ideological one. They will mistakenly take principles functional for their society to be eternal moral truths, but that such ideological understanding is widespread does not rule out the possibility of there being a rational critique of ideology or of there being contextual, but still objectively contextual, moral principles on the model I gave previously. These contextual principles are logically on a par with the contextual but arguably objective judgment that while in normal societies under modern conditions with approximately equal numbers of males and females monogamy is the best form of marriage (given that we want any form of marriage at all), in an otherwise similar society devastated by war in which 90 percent of the male population had been killed while the female population was left relatively intact, that very same institution of monogamy should not be followed in those circumstances.

The de facto mode-of-production dependency of the extant moralities—the moralities that sociologically speaking will flourish and remain stable during a given epoch—do not rule out, as it did not for Engels, a belief in the human capacity rationally to assess moral codes and to have a belief in moral progress. As the productive forces develop, they open up more and more possibilities for well-being, for human flourishing, and, specifically, for more people having greater control over their lives and thus for more autonomy for more people. Feudal society opened up more such possibilities than ancient slave-owning society possessed; capitalist society opened up more such possibilities than feudal society possessed; and socialist societies will open up still more such possibilities for more people than do capitalist societies. The lives of more people become objectively better as we go through these epochal transformations.

Historical materialism itself generates this way of viewing things morally, a way of viewing things that in an important sense is contextualistic but still thoroughly non-relativist. Historical materialism points to a Marxist sanctioning, in the way I explained previously, of transhistorical moral judgments about human progress and of moral assessments, including assessments of the justice of whole social formations. However, this should not be misunderstood. Marxists are not historical idealists; they are not saying that we can change the world in any fundamental way just by moralizing at it, no matter how soundly, although this is not to deny that moral critique can sometimes have some relevant causal input. Superstructures can, and do, have some causal effect on the base.[16] Still, moral argument, no matter how sound, is not the cause of major social changes. Moreover, in addition to rejecting any historical idealism, Marxists do not think there is a set of substantive principles, beyond moral truisms that are hardly adequate to guide action, that we can simply appeal to anywhere and at any time. In that they are in agreement with John Rawls.[17] However, they do think that there is such a thing as moral progress so that it can be justifiably claimed that socialist societies are more just than capitalist societies and that the emergence of socialism is better than the continued existence of capitalism.

Marx thought that capitalism robs workers and that in circumstances, such as he took his own to be and would surely take ours to be, the world with this mode of production, which requires such exploitation, is still a world that has in place as a historical possibility feasible alternative modes of production that would not require such exploitation. This means that such exploitation should—morally should—not be accepted in such a circumstance as a grim necessity.[18] Indeed, given a historically feasible, alternative, socialist mode of production, in a society with that mode of production, there could be no such exploitation because of the very nature of that mode of production. For the working class to accept such exploitation, where such alternatives are feasible, is, if not irrational, at least unfortunate and morally defeatist.

Such a pattern of belief explains Marx's passionate denunciation of the injustice of the capitalist system. It is a mistake to characterize Marx's denunciation as anything other than a moral denunciation of the gross injustice of the capitalist system both under conditions such as he knew it and under contemporary conditions. (The latter claim is a safe extrapolation from Marx's beliefs.) Without the slightest hesitation or suggestion that he was just engaging in ideological rhetoric or hyperbole, Marx asserted, as I remarked at the outset, that capitalism alienates, robs, needlessly exploits, and makes miserable countless human beings in circumstances in which it is no longer necessary for the advancement of culture or science or the sustaining of the material culture necessary for human well-being to maximally flourish. Capitalism generally dehumanizes great masses of people while a few live in positions or privilege and control. The great masses of people have little in the way of possibilities for leisure or (far more importantly) for control over their own lives. Such a social system with its distinctive division of labor makes a life of commodious, even idle, living possible for the capitalist class and some of its hangers on, while workers are characteristically driven to a stunted, one-sided development.

Defenders of capitalism do not deny that these things are wrong. Rather, defenders (a) deny that these things actually happen under capitalism; (b) deny (somewhat more plausibly) that they need to happen with a proper development of capitalism; or (c) (more subtly) admit that there are such evils and that some must remain under capitalism, but say that some are necessary evils that we must accept in order to avoid still greater evils. But, and this is the key point here, to take any of these turns is not to deny that if capitalist society is as Marx described it and if socialism could come to be what he thought it could come to be, then, given where we stand now in history, capitalism is a very unjust system indeed. Defenders of capitalism cannot reasonably deny this claim. To argue with Marx they must meet Marx on *factual grounds* about how things were, how they are now, and what they could reasonably come to be.[19] If Marx is even approximately right about those assessments of the facts of the matter, capitalist societies (or at least most capitalist societies) are not minimally unjust—they are grossly so. Welfare statist reforms, if thorough, could ameliorate this to some extent, but they could not overcome it. While Sweden is indeed a better place in which to live than is the United States, injustice just goes with capitalism, any capitalism at all.

Notes

1. Allen W. Wood, "The Marxian Critique of Justice," *Philosophy and Public Affairs* 1 (1972–73):224–282; Allen W. Wood, "Marx on Right and Justice," *Philosophy and Public Affairs* 8 (1978–79):267–295; Ziyad Husami, "Marx on Distributive Justice," *Philosophy and Public Affairs* 8 (1978–79):27–64; Allen E. Buchanan, *Marx and Justice* (Totowa, N.J.: Rowman and Littlefield, 1982), Supplementary vol. 7 (1981); Richard Norman, *The Moral Philosophers* (Oxford: Clarendon Press, 1983), pp. 173–201; Allen W. Wood, *Karl Marx* (London: Routledge & Kegan Paul, 1982), pp. 125–156; Allen W. Wood, "Marx's Immoralism," in Bernard Chavance (ed.), *Marx en Perspective* (Paris: Editions de l'Ecole des Haute Etudes en Sciences Sociales, 1985), pp. 681–698; Allen W. Wood, "Justice and Class Interests," *Philosophica* 33, no. 1 (1984):9–32; Richard W. Miller, *Analyzing Marx* (Princeton, N.J.: Princeton University Press, 1985), pp. 15–97; Steven Lukes, *Marxism and Morality* (Oxford: Clarendon Press, 1985); Jon Elster, *Making Sense of Marx* (Cambridge: Cambridge University Press, 1985), pp. 196–233. For an important review article with a good grasp and an illuminating categorization of the literature and one that provides a defense of Marxist moralism, see Norman Geras, "On Marx and Justice," *New Left Review* 150 (March/April 1985):47–89. He also provided a useful bibliography.

2. Wood, "Marx's Immoralism" and his "Justice and Class Interests"; and Miller, *Analyzing Marx*, pp. 15–97.

3. Lukes, *Marxism and Morality*; Eugene Kamenka, "Review of *Marxism and Morality*," *New York Times Book Review*, February 2, 1986, p. 20; and Elster, *Making Sense of Marx*, pp. 196–233.

4. Andrew Collier gave an important, de-mythologized, and non-religiose characterization of scientific socialism in his "Scientific Socialism and the Question of Social Values," *Canadian Journal of Philosophy*, Supplementary vol. 7 (1981):121–153.

5. For radically conflicting accounts of Marx's views on justice see Wood, *Karl Marx*, pp. 125–156; G. A. Cohen, "Review of Wood's *Karl Marx*," *Mind* 92, no. 367 (July 1983):440–445; and G. A. Cohen, "Freedom, Justice and Capitalism," *New Left Review* (March/April 1981):3–16. For some parallel conflicts see Miller, *Analyzing Marx*, pp. 15–96; and Alan Gilbert, "Marx's

Moral Realism: Eudaimonism and Moral Progress," in Terence Ball and James Farr (eds.), *After Marx* (Cambridge: Cambridge University Press, 1984), pp. 154–183.

6. Joe McCarney, *The Real World of Ideology* (Brighton, England: Harvester Press, 1980). See, as well, his "Recent Interpretations of Ideology," *Economy and Society* 14, no. 1 (1985):77–93; and Chapter 5.

7. This has been well argued, along with the appropriate documentation to the texts of Marx and Engels, by John McMurty, *The Structure of Marx's World-View* (Princeton, N.J.: Princeton University Press, 1978), pp. 123–156.

8. Anthony Skillen, *Ruling Illusions: Philosophy and the Social Order* (Brighton, England: Harvester Press, 1977).

9. J. L. Mackie, "A Refutation of Morals," *Australasian Journal of Philosophy* (1946):77–90; for a more developed and nuanced statement of what is still essentially the same view see his *Ethics—Inventing Right and Wrong* (Harmondsworth, England: Penguin Books, 1977).

10. Frederick Engels, *Anti-Dühring,* Emile Burns (trans.) (New York: International Publishers, 1939), Chapter 9–11. See also Chapter 3.

11. Karl Marx, "Preface" to *A Contribution to the Critique of Political Economy* in *The Marx-Engels Reader,* 2nd ed., Robert C. Tucker (ed.) (New York: Norton, 1978), p. 4. Karl Marx, *The Critique of the Gotha Programme,* C. P. Dutt (ed. and trans.) (New York: International Publishers, 1938). See also Chapter 4 herein.

12. Kai Nielsen, "On Taking Historical Materialism Seriously," *Dialogue* 22 (1983):319–338.

13. Miller, *Analyzing Marx,* pp. 171–270; and Andrew Levine, *Arguing for Socialism* (London: Routledge & Kegan Paul, 1984), pp. 155–225.

14. Wood, "Marx's Immoralism"; and his "Justice and Class Interests."

15. William H. Shaw, "Marxism and Moral Objectivity," *Canadian Journal of Philosophy,* Supplementary volume 7 (1981):19–44; and Chapter 7 herein.

16. See Wood's discussion of historical idealism in his *Karl Marx.*

17. John Rawls, "Justice as Fairness: Political Not Metaphysical," *Philosophy and Public Affairs* 14, no. 3 (Summer 1985):223–251.

18. There can be other forms of exploitation as well. See Levine, *Arguing for Socialism,* pp. 65–76.

19. Andrew Collier, "Scientific Socialism," pp. 121–154; his "Positive Values," *The Aristotelian Society,* Supplementary volume 58 (1983):37–54; and Kai Nielsen, "Coming to Grips with Marxist Anti-Moralism," *The Philosophical Forum* 19, no. 1 (Fall 1987):1–22.

7

If Historical Materialism Is True, Does Morality Totter?

I

Friedrich Engels in his graveside speech at Karl Marx's funeral in 1883 depicted Marx in a dual role as a revolutionist and as a man of science. Both of these roles were of fundamental importance for Marx, both are distinct though still interwoven in a complex way, and in both Marx made fundamental contributions. Speaking of him as a revolutionist, Engels remarks: "For Marx was before all else a revolutionist. His real mission in life was to contribute, in one way or another, to the overthrow of capitalist society and of the state institutions which it had brought into being, to contribute to the liberation of the modern proletariat, which he was the first to make conscious of its own position and its needs, conscious of the conditions of its emancipation."[1]

But Engels also sees Marx as a man of science, though as someone who also saw science as "a historically dynamic revolutionary force."[2] He speaks of Marx's "historical science." And he thinks of him, in science, as making a Copernican turn in two related spheres that have come to be called *historical materialism* and the *labour theory of value*. Engels describes the former thus: "Just as Darwin discovered the law of development of organic nature, so Marx discovered the law of development of human history. . . . "[3] That 'law' rests, or so a

---

This essay was originally published in *Philosophy of Social Sciences* 15 (1985): 389–407. Reprinted by permission.

plausible gloss on Engels' claim goes, on the historical fact that throughout history there has been a tendency for human beings to develop their productive forces (their means of production and their productive faculties).[4] These developing productive forces (*Produktivkräfte*) determine (condition) the production relations of a society, the totality of which constitutes its economic structure, and this economic structure in turn determines *the general character* of the state, its legal institutions, its religions and the dominant political, religious, philosophical and moral conceptions and practices. At time t^1 the general character of the state, its legal institutions and the ruling ideas about government, religion, morality and philosophy have the general character they do because they match with, correspond to, the economic structure at that time. As Engels put it himself in his speech at Marx's graveside, "The degree of economic development attained by a given people or during a given epoch form the foundation upon which the state institutions, the legal conceptions, arts, and even ideas on religion, of the people concerned have been evolved. . . . "[5] Fundamental social change occurs either because the forces or production develop over time or there develop, over time, conflicts internal to the mode of production. While at a given time the forces of production and the relations of production may be perfectly suited for each other, at a later time, after these forces of production have evolved, they will no longer be in such a match and indeed in time the relations of production—the economic structure—will fetter the forces of production, i.e., prevent them from functioning optimally. At that time society begins to be destabilized and we enter the period of social revolution.

II

If this picture is accepted or some rational reconstruction bearing some family resemblance to it is accepted, it is perhaps natural to believe that morality must simply be ideology and nothing else. There can be no question of justifying any moral conceptions, socialist or otherwise; there can be no 'their morality and ours' and no justification of a socialist morality or any other morality. There cannot possibly be a justified moral theory or normative political theory; and to speak, as E. P. Thompson does, of a disciplined socialist moral critique, or, as some others have, of communist principles of justice or, as Douglas Kellner does, of Marx's moral critique of capitalism, must be a confusion.[6] There can be moral ideology—something which sometimes may be a useful instrument in class warfare—but no genuine morality or moral critique. A consistent Marxist is a Marxist anti-moralist.[7] If historical materialism is true, and if Marx's conception of ideology is a coherent one, there can be no moral truth or moral objectivity.

William Shaw, in his "Marxism and Moral Objectivity," powerfully and clearly contests these claims, specifically challenging the claim that the very idea of moral objectivity is incompatible with the truth of historical materialism.[8] His article is careful and informed. I shall begin my discussion of these issues by examining some crucial portions of it.

Shaw starts by pointing out that within Marxist theory there is a *sociology of morals* and that it is integrally linked with historical materialism.

> Historical materialism tenders a sociological theory of morality. According to it, different types of society are characterized by different and distinctive moral codes, values, and norms, and these moral systems change as the societies with which they are linked evolve. Morality is not something immutable and eternal; rather, it is part of "the general process of social, political and intellectual life"—part of the social consciousness—which is conditioned by the general mode of production of material life. It is no accident, but rather a functional requirement, that different forms of moral consciousness accompany different modes of production. Moreover, since all existing societies have been class societies, their moralities have been class moralities in the sense that they sustain and reflect the material relations that constitute the basis of the different forms of class rule. Although the moral outlook of subordinate classes may diverge from that of the ruling class, the perspective of the dominant class tends to prevail throughout society.[9]

It is, I believe, unproblematic that Marx and Engels had such a conception of the sociology of morals. What is not unproblematic is the details of such a conception, the details of its supporting argument or its plausibility. That is tied up with the assessment of historical materialism itself, something which Shaw does not undertake in "Marxism and Moral Objectivity," though he does in his *Marx's Theory of History*.[10] Rather, he is concerned instead "with the question of whether the historical materialist view of morality is compatible with Marxists claiming validity for their own value judgments."[11]

Shaw agrees with Andrew Collier and Anthony Skillen that Marx did not see himself "as offering a distinctively ethical critique of capitalism or as furnishing primarily a moral case for socialism."[12] It is, however, true enough, as Douglas Kellner remarks, that Marx was one of the great denouncers.[13] Marx surely did not refrain from making moral judgements himself, indeed typically very strong moral judgments; his works are peppered with them, but it does not follow from this that his account of capitalism or his critique of capitalism in his mature works—say from *The German Ideology* on—depends on those moral judgements. Shaw claims, along with Collier and Richard Miller and indeed many others, that they do not; and that claim, to put it minimally, is at least reasonable.[14] Yet it is also true, Marxist [anti-]moralism notwithstanding, that any reading of *Capital* which fails to see Marx's moral commitment is blind. The book seethes with rage at a socio-economic system that, having ceased to enjoy any historical justification, continues to escalate the "misery, agony of toil, slavery, ignorance, brutality, (and) mental degradation" suffered by the bulk of the population.[15] In circumstances where the capitalist system runs on after it has lost its historical rationale, Marx turns his bitter sarcasm and contempt at that system. He sees it as a system which "mutilate(s) the labourer into a fragment of a man, degrades him to the level of an appendage of a machine, destroys every remnant of charm in his work and turns it into a hated toil."[16]

I think that it is beyond serious dispute that both Marx and Engels thought, to put it minimally, that "capitalism produced real evils" and that "socialism was morally preferable."[17] But it does not at all follow from this, nor is it in fact even remotely true, to say, as Karl Popper did, in his *The Open Society and Its Enemies,* that "*Capital* is, in fact, largely a treatise on social ethics."[18] To hate and condemn capitalism is one thing; to turn one's critique of it into a moral critique is another. In a world dominated by bourgeois ideology Marx wanted his critique of capitalism to be a lasting and an effective one; he wanted it to be a real tool to place in the hands of the working class and their allies in their struggle for emancipation, and, he believed, and not without reason, that, for it to be such a book, it must be through and through scientific. Indeed Marx did say famously in his *Theses on Feuerbach,* "The philosophers have only interpreted the world, in various ways; the point, however, is to change it."[19] But this is not to say, or to give to understand, that one is to change it without understanding it or that understanding it is unimportant. Marx did not think much of philosophy's capacity to understand anything of substance. In that respect he was like the positivists, but he did think that science gave us such an understanding. And indeed, as science develops, there develops in us, in ever greater degrees, such an enhanced understanding. (Remember that science develops as a productive force and along with the other productive forces.) Marx took his historical economic science to be a theory of society which provided us with such an understanding— an understanding which he thought was useful to the proletariat in their ongoing class struggle with the bourgeoisie. It is a useful tool, that is, in their struggle to destroy the Capitalist System. But that it was used for that end does not make it *non-wertfrei.*

Marx, as we have seen, has moral views and makes moral judgements, but they are not part of the machinery of Marxist social science. It might, of course, be the case that, though Marx made these judgements and had these moral views, he, and Engels as well, like Edward Westermarck and John Mackie, thought they were subjective. But neither Marx nor Engels ever said that or clearly implied that. And much that they did say and do runs contrary to that. They were perfectly willing, in all sorts of contexts, both practical and theoretical, to make all sorts of moral judgements without the slightest diffidence. Moreover, as Shaw points out, Engels did say boldly in his *Anti-Dühring* that it "cannot be doubted" that "there has on the whole been progress in morality, as in all other branches of human knowledge. . . . "[20] He is claiming that there has (1) been moral progress and (2) he is perfectly willing to speak of 'moral knowledge.' And Marx, we should recall, went over this book and indicated his agreement with it. Indeed he wrote one chapter of it.

Both Marx and Engels could very well be mistaken here about morality and Westermarck and Mackie might be closer to the mark.[21] Still, such responses, on the part of Marx and Engels, do give us very strong evidence that they were not themselves subjectivists or, what now would be called noncognitivists. They had confidence in their moral claims—in that plain sense they believed in morals—but they took no meta-ethical positions or any foundational positions in ethics. They neither proceeded like Stevenson or Mackie nor like Rawls or Gewirth. They took no *philosophical* interest at all in morality and it is not at all evident that they should have: that their accounts of society or their revolutionary practice would have improved if they had taken such an interest in morals.

To this it might be responded that, if they had consistently thought through what their doctrines of historical materialism and ideology committed them to, they would have been sceptics after all. Their worked-out intellectual structures, i.e., their accounts of historical materialism and ideology, are incompatible with their belief in moral knowledge or even their 'belief in morals.' So it is incumbent on us to try to ascertain whether historical materialism and moral objectivity are compatible conceptions. Our first move should be a little more specifically to find out what it is to be a historical materialist.

III

Shaw argues, as do G. A. Cohen, Allen Wood and John McMurtry, for a "social-scientific interpretation of historical materialism"—an interpretation that in general would follow the schematic view that we presented at the outset. They think that it is a mistake to see Marx's theory of history or his analysis of capitalism "as normative theories or as dependent upon certain ethical premises."[22] Shaw, however, rightly enough points out that "it does not follow from the scientific nature of Marx's work that his adherents are prohibited from ethical discourse."[23] Yet, it still understandably might be felt that moral utterances (any moral utterance you like) can hardly be objective given what Marx says about historical materialism, superstructure and ideology. Must not morality, given Marx's overall typology, be part of the superstructure and, as such, must it not be ideological? And, if it is ideological, it can hardly be objective or truth-bearing. Shaw will resist this conclusion and will argue, on the contrary, that "the theory of historical materialism and the Marxist analysis of capitalism lead one to affirm certain moral commitments, rather than to abandon value judgments altogether."[24] Still, the difficulty is to see how this could be, given the truth of historical materialism.

Shaw shows, without too much difficulty, that a Marxist need not endorse any version of *ethical* relativism, namely the doctrine that an action or practice X is morally right in society S if and only if X is permitted (approved) by the conventions of S or by the dominant class in S. Historical materialism is a thesis about what generates and sustains moral beliefs in society and the related Marxist doctrine of ideology explains how moral beliefs function in a society. (In that way it is a sociology of morals.) It is probably the case that these doctrines do not commit one to any assertions that so-and-so is right and such-and-such is wrong. But most certainly they do not commit one to saying that because a moral belief is deemed right by the conventions of the society or by the ruling or dominant class in the society that moral belief is therefore right in that society or indeed in any society. At most, it would require the historical materialist to say that if it is so believed to be right by the ruling class of that society, it will generally be believed to be right in that society. But that anthropological observation, that bit of the sociology of morals, is perfectly compatible with denying that it is therefore right in that society, or with a scepticism about whether we could even determine what is right or wrong period. Historical materialism is as compatible with ethical scepticism and ethical nihilism as it is with normative ethical relativism.

Moreover, if a Marxist committed himself to ethical relativism, he would have to say that, if society S were a capitalist society and action X were a revolutionary act designed to overthrow capitalism, he, the Marxist, would have to say that it is wrong to do X in society S, for X is not approved by the conventions of S or by its ruling class unless (perhaps) he could show that the production relations in S no longer suit the productive forces. But no Marxist need say that. He could, and in my view should, stick to the innocuous and trivial thesis in descriptive ethics that such acts would be generally *believed* to be wrong in society S and he could use historical materialism and its correlated theory of ideology to explain why it was so believed to be wrong in society S. But this is to assert nothing at all about what is right or wrong, let alone to assert that, if it is generally *believed* to be wrong in society S, it is wrong in society S. To assert anything like this ethical relativist thesis is entirely contrary to the spirit of Marxism and is not required by historical materialism. Historical materialism sees the dominant moralities in a society as cultural 'legitimizing' and stabilizing devices in that society. They are devices "functionally required by a given mode of production."[25] But to make such a claim is not to make or imply anything about what is or is not right or claim that what is functionally required by a given mode of production ought to obtain.

IV

It is more difficult to ascertain whether historical materialism requires meta-ethical relativism. It is not an insignificant question to ask, If historical materialism is true, must one, to be consistent and coherent in one's views about values, be a meta-ethical relativist? Meta-ethical relativism is the thesis that there are no objectively sound procedures for justifying one moral code or one set of moral judgements. Two moral codes may be equally 'sound' and two moral claims may be equally 'justified' or 'reasonable.' There is no way of establishing what is 'the true moral code' or 'set of moral beliefs.'[26]

Shaw considers whether historical materialism commits one to meta-ethical relativism and concludes that it does not. He points out, rightly I believe, at the beginning of his discussion of that issue, that "meta-ethical relativism is not entailed by normative ethical relativism nor does it commit one to any particular criterion of right and wrong. Rather, meta-ethical relativism rules out (or else severely restricts) the objective certification of moral principles." If meta-ethical relativism is true, it is also trivially true that there can be no objectively sound method of establishing which moral judgements are true or which moral claims are warrantable. If such a state of affairs obtains, there is no method that all rational, properly informed and conceptually sophisticated people must accept for fixing moral belief and there are no general moral principles that all such human beings must just accept if they are to be through and through reasonable. In short, there neither are nor can there be any Archimedean points in morality.

Should we say that historical materialism requires meta-ethical relativism? Shaw discusses three reasons for claiming that historical materialism commits one to meta-ethical relativism and attempts to show that none of them provides us with the basis for a sound argument for such a claim. The reasons are: (1) the extensive diversity of moral standards, (2) their relative appropriateness to a historically determinate mode of production and (3) the causal genesis of moral beliefs.

Shaw believes that Marxism must be committed, with its historical materialism, to a belief in the cultural and historical diversity of moral standards. But, he points out, acceptance of this is not sufficient in itself to establish meta-ethical relativism, for the fact that there are a number of different moral standards does not establish that they are all equally sound. Diversity of procedure and method does not establish that all methods are equally sound.

However, the historical materialist will not only assert a diversity of moral standards and methods, he will also assert that the various moral standards, methods and codes are "for their respective societies at their respective historical levels functionally appropriate, historically necessary or socio-economically unavoidable."[27] But, if this is a genuine social-scientific thesis, it would be a mistake "to see it as stating an ethical thesis at all."[28] And this should indicate something to us about how deep the *wertfrei-thesis* concerning social sciences has dug. On such a reading what we are talking about is simply, as a scientific thesis, an empirical thesis, about the genesis and functional role of moral conceptions in different societies. It, by itself, asserts nothing about what is right and wrong or good and bad or what ought or ought not to be done. It asserts, as we have just said, that the "various moral codes among societies are, for their respective societies at their respective historical levels, functionally appropriate, historically necessary, or socio-economically unavoidable."[29] But this is not to say—though the conceptions are easily confused—"that moral standards are *vindicated* if and only if they are functionally appropriate or necessary."[30] That 'meta-ethical thesis' with such an employment of 'vindicated' is not a normatively neutral meta-ethical thesis, but, if actually meta-ethical at all, it is a meta-ethical thesis with a plain normative import. Indeed, since the normative term 'vindicated' occurs in use rather than in mention, and the whole statement makes a first-order moral claim, it is a mistake, I believe, to call it a meta-ethical statement. But historical materialism, as a scientific, empirical theory, could not be asserting any such normative things. Historical materialism shows us how such superstructural phenomena work: how a distinctive superstructure supports such a base. It says nothing about whether such a moral code is or is not vindicated. It only makes a comment about what in a certain historical circumstance is functionally appropriate. There is no good reason, Shaw claims, to believe that historical materialism commits us to such a meta-ethical relativism (if meta-ethical relativism it be) with genuine normative implications, or, for that matter, Shaw believes, to any other version of meta-ethical relativism.

Shaw's argument here does not seem to me to be convincing. He is right about vindication. But trouble begins when we reflect on some other things that Shaw here appears at least to be claiming. It sounds as if Shaw is giving us to understand that meta-ethical relativism here must be read as stating, or at least implying, a *normative* thesis and as such, it is at least arguably something which could not be a part of the corpus of science. But that is absurd and Shaw, in personal correspondence, has made it perfectly clear that that is not what he intended. His thesis—he does not call it a meta-ethical thesis—should be taken instead to be a thesis in the sociology of morals that plainly can be a part of historical materialism. If it is so integrated with historical materialism and if that thesis is itself true, there could—or so it appears—be no ground for asserting a transhistorical or transmode of production justifiable or warrantable set of moral principles or even a single such moral principle. In that way such an empirical thesis, for that is what it would have to be to be a thesis in the sociology of morals, supports a moral claim without entailing it. This thesis is ambiguous in this respect and its logical status is unclear, for it does assert that there can be no objective transcultural method of ethics which can establish itself as the correct or even as the most plausible method of ethics and this appears at least to be incompatible with a belief in moral objectivity.

Historical materialists might be thought to have gone around this meta-ethical or ethical bend, or whatever you want to call it, if they are taken to be claiming that the more historically advanced perspectives, perspectives generated ultimately by the continued development of the productive forces, are, as the more historically advanced perspectives, also the more adequate perspectives—more adequate in at least the plainly relevant sense that the stable adoption of those perspectives will lead to a fuller realization of wants and needs across the whole population. Over time, as the productive relations develop, this comes to a progressive advance in superstructural phenomena including moral phenomena. What we need to recognize here is that contextualism does not commit one to relativism, meta-ethical or otherwise, and it is only contextualism that historical materialism is committed to. But that is perfectly compatible with an objectivist conception of ethics.

However, we must be careful to distinguish, as Max Weber taught us to distinguish, a growing differentiation and complexity, on the one hand, from *moral* development or *moral* progress, on the other.[31] As Weber has powerfully argued, these are distinct notions. That later forces of production are more complex or more efficient or produce more does not automatically mean that all later relations of production, with their corresponding moral forms, are superior, morally speaking, or in other ways humanly speaking, to the previous moral forms. It is not clear that we have criteria for moral progress or that we would, or even could have, if historical materialism is true. It is not clear that we can simply or at all read moral development off from noting the development of the productive forces. That in a given society the forces of production are more efficient than in a previous society is not in itself sufficient to establish that that society, everything considered, is a better society than the previous productively less efficient society. However, while that is true, it is also true, as we noted in the previous paragraph, that these more technically developed modes of production enable more human beings to more fully and more equitably satisfy their wants and needs and that gives us good reason to believe they are also ethically superior.

V

Be that as it may, let us now turn to Shaw's discussion of the third *prima facie* reason why historical materialism is thought to require meta-ethical relativism. That has to do with its causal account of the origin and strength of moral beliefs. Historical materialism gives us to understand that people come to have the moral beliefs they have because of the distinctive production relations of the societies in which they live. Shaw makes the expected response to such a claim:

An elementary distinction can be drawn between the causes of a person (class, society) holding a certain belief and the evidence for that belief or, alternatively, between the reasons for which one believes and the reasons which justify belief. A fundamental tenet of Marxist class analysis is that one's class position, one's particular location in a specific type of economic structure, strongly conditions one's outlook, moral and otherwise. But it is a simple truth of logical analysis that the origin of a belief is not relevant to its evaluation as true or false. Thus, there is nothing inconsistent in a Marxist maintaining (say) both that the value judgments of the proletariat are socially determined and that they tend to be more veridical than the judgments of other classes.[32]

One might, à la Habermas, Hanson or Miller, be a little more cautious than Shaw about what one claims about the genetic fallacy.[33] Still, Shaw is surely right in stressing that we should distinguish questions concerning how we come to have the beliefs we have from questions concerning what, if anything, justifies them or what rationale these beliefs have. That economic structures strongly condition what moral outlook we come to have, such that we would not have them but for the fact that these economic conditions prevail, does not show that they do not have some independent justification or indeed even some justification *sans phrase*. The fact that they so arose does not, at least in many circumstances, in itself provide any justification at all for them (*pace* Lukács), but it also does not *eo ipse* invalidate them either. It does not show that they could not be justified. What is more troubling is that, since moral ideals are part of the superstructure and thus—or so it would seem—ideological, they do not seem to admit, on such an account, of any justification.

Shaw shows, I believe, that from the fact that (*a*) there is in various societies and at different times a diversity of moral standards, (*b*) that these standards have a distinct historically limited functional appropriateness and (*c*) that they are what they are because of the economic structure of the society, it is not *entailed* that these beliefs are subjective or are without any objective validity. It is at least logically possible for these three things to obtain and for moral beliefs to have an objective validity. But what Shaw does not show is that there is any good reason to think that, if such conditions obtain, moral beliefs are or are likely to be objective. They could be objective, but it is not unnatural to believe that if the above conditions obtain they are hardly likely to be objective.

This 'relativistic worry' is exacerbated when we remember that historical materialism carries with it an account about base and superstructure and an account of ideology and its functions. The base determines, or at least strongly conditions, the superstructure, and if something is part of the superstructure, it is also—or so at least it would seem—ideological. Moral ideas—all moral ideas—are superstructural and thus ideological. But an ideology, on Marxist accounts, is something that characteristically mystifies consciousness, distorts our understanding of social reality, reflects distinctive class interests and typically functions to further or at least protect the class interests of the dominant class in that society.

It is clear enough that Marx and Engels see most moral beliefs and all systems of ethics extant in the various class societies over time and cultural space as being ideological in just this way. They see morality (that is, the moralities of the various class societies), along with law, as ideology. Moreover, given historical materialism and its base/superstructure division, it is difficult to see how morality could, on that account, be anything other than ideology. It seems at least impossible, given Marx's conception of historical materialism, with its integral doctrine of ideology, for morality to be anything other than ideology and, if it is ideology, it cannot, given Marx's characterization of ideology, be a system of objectively validated beliefs or even a set of attitudes which have an objective rationale.

VI

Let us see if there are resources within Marxist theory to resolve these difficulties, if indeed they are genuine difficulties. Shaw argues in Section V of his "Marxism and Moral Objectivity" that, if we attend reasonably closely to Marx's conception of ideology, we can "distinguish within *the moral realm*—at least in principle—between ideological and nonideological beliefs."[34] If Marx's social theory, his empirical-analytical theory, is approximately correct, that is, if it is a reasonable approximation of the empirical facts, then socialism is preferable to capitalism because a socialist society will have more liberty and will be without the poverty and oppression that a capitalist society has. That is indeed a moral judgement, but it is not a moral judgement which could be sustained if the empirical pictures given of capitalism and socialism by Marxist theory were not approximately true. One litmus paper test, or rather a partial litmus paper test, for whether a belief is ideological is whether, when a person becomes aware of the real reasons for or causes of his holding that belief, he would continue to hold it. An ideological belief on the Marxist account characteristically is a belief which a rational person could not continue to hold once he was aware of the reasons for or causes of his believing it. There are many beliefs we have, where we have not correctly identified either the reasons for or the causes of our having those beliefs, which are beliefs which we would still continue to hold even when we had come correctly to identify the causes of or the reasons for holding them. These beliefs, then, given that they would still be held under such circumstances, are not ideological, socially mystified beliefs. But where, for normally rational people, the belief rests on ignorance of the real reasons (causes) for holding it, and that belief would *not* survive a dispelling of this ignorance, then, if that belief is also a societal belief and answers to class interests, we have good reason for believing that that societal belief is an ideological one. But there are moral beliefs which, by that perfectly reasonable test, are not ideological. This would, if Marxist empirical theory is approximately correct, be true of the Marxist moral judgement expressed above, i.e., that socialism is morally preferable to capitalism, and it is equally true of such judgements as "Suffering *per se* is bad" and "Oppression and denial of liberty *per se* is evil" or "Respect for human rights is good." However, it would not be true, if Marxist empirical social theory is correct, of the moral belief that there is a fundamental absolute right to private property in the means of production. If the causal genesis of this belief were exposed and its rationale examined in the light of the facts, in a world where a Marxist empirical representation of the facts was approximately true, that belief would be extinguished just as the moral belief that it is wrong for unmarried people to cohabit would not survive an accurate understanding of the facts. Thus we have some moral beliefs that do not pass the ideological litmus paper test, but we have good reasons for believing that the unproblematic moral beliefs mentioned above, e.g., 'suffering *per se* is bad,' can and do pass that litmus paper test and we thus have no good reason for believing them to express false consciousness or to involve a distorted conception of social reality or any social mystification. In what way, to translate this into the concrete, do the truistic moral beliefs that pain is bad and pleasure is good or that health is good and illness is bad express any social mystification?

It might be responded that still on Marx's account all such beliefs are part of the superstructure and thus they *must* be ideological. Perhaps in the light of the above examples, and many others that could easily be elaborated, we should say that being superstructural is a *necessary* but not a *sufficient* condition for being ideological. While all ideological beliefs are superstructural, not all superstructural beliefs are ideological.

To the question as to whether this involves an alteration of Marxist theory, the answer should be that *if* it does, then an alteration is in order. Moreover, if it does involve such an alteration, by making that alteration, nothing of substance would be lost that gave Marxist theory power and plausibility in the first place. At most we would have a lacunae in our typology or categorization. We would not know how to classify some moral beliefs in terms of Marxist theory, though the great bulk of them could, and would, continue to be classified, in a nonarbitrary manner, as ideological.

Someone might respond that while not all moral beliefs are rationalizations expressive of false consciousness, they still are all ideological because, whether they are expressive of false consciousness or not, they are beliefs that serve the interests of one or another of the contending classes—typically the dominant class—while putting themselves forward as serving the interests of the whole of society. But it is far from evident that this is always true of all moral ideas. That pleasure is good, that health is good and that suffering and denial of freedom are bad are not in many contexts expressive or supportive of the interests of any one class. Of course, they can be, and frequently are, part of an overall moral or social theory which is itself ideological. As Nietzsche observed, a stress on freedom is sometimes a part of a slave morality and the great stress on freedom—the stress on individual liberty—in both libertarian and liberal moral theories arguably has a definite ideological function in supporting the capitalist order. Certainly a Marxist would think so. Similar arguments can and have been made about the ideological function of hedonism and utilitarianism. But while the moral beliefs mentioned above have a life in some of those moral theories, they also have a moral life outside them and outside of any definite moral theory. While in some contexts such moral beliefs may very well function ideologically, there is no good reason to believe that they are *per se* ideological and that anyone who has such moral beliefs must hold them or apply them in such a way that they must serve the interests of one of the contending classes and harm the interests of another while purporting to be universally valid moral ideas. Would it not plainly, indeed truistically, be the case that in a classless society pain still would be bad and pleasure good? What class interests *must* such a belief serve and why must it mystify anyone's consciousness or distort his understanding of social reality?

Ideologies, on a Marxist understanding, standardly mystify our understanding of social reality and serve the interests of one of the contending classes while purporting to have universal validity. But, I think, it is plain from what we have said above that not all moral ideas do that. At the very least there is no *a priori* reason why they must. And it does not seem to me to be the case that a Marxist sociology of morals shows that they *all* do or that the reasonable expectation should be that they all do.

There remains, on the Marxist conceptual scheme, the problem of just where to place those moral beliefs which are nonideological. Shaw remarks that though social consciousness selects social existence, it is not, on Marx's own account, necessarily ideological.[35] Yet that remains something of a dark saying. Perhaps something of what he has in mind is captured more perspicuously in some distinctive remarks about ideology made by John McMurtry in his *The Structure of Marx's World-View*.[36]

McMurtry, while making many of the points about ideology we have made above, makes some additional ones that would help to make more perspicuous the difference between ideological moral beliefs and moral ideology on the one hand, and nonideological moral beliefs on the other. McMurtry begins by stressing that in talking of ideology in *The German Ideology* Marx and Engels start by linking an ideology to "men's conceptions of themselves," that is, to "men's various artic-ulated forms of social self-consciousness—from religious to economic, from moral and aesthetic to legal-political."[37] So characterized, it is important to recognize—and indeed it is not something which is generally recognized—that, on Marx's account, it is not the case that "all ideas or beliefs as such" are going to count as "ideological" "but only special superstructural conceptions of human matters or affairs from one or another perspective. . . . "[38] McMurtry also stresses how Marx's conception of ideology is linked to "our everyday concept of rationalization. . . . "[39] But he goes on to point out that we must also see an ideology as a *collective* theory. The "articulation and referent of such rationalization is social rather than 'private.' . . . "[40] Ideologies are "public conceptions that men have about themselves. . . . "[41] It is important to recognize, McMurtry claims, that, for Marx, for beliefs to count as 'ideological,' they must be social mystifications and thus, to get a nonvacuous contrast, they must contrast with beliefs that are not social mystifications. Moreover, these ideologies, these public con-ceptions of ourselves, are not to be taken as referring to an "all-inclusive range of cognitive phenomena."[42]

Many commentators have so globally conceived of Marx's concept of ideology or they have thought it covered all cognitive phenomena other than science and so have found themselves forced to conclude that for Marx all moral ideas or beliefs *must* be ideological. But that, McMurtry argues, is to give 'ideology' a wider referent than it actually has on Marx's own use. This does not mean that ideology is not a very pervasive sociohistorical phenomena in all societies that we so far have known. We need to recognize, as McMurtry well puts it, "ideology's existence as the body of public self-consciousness to which most or all other forms of cognition—including private—are likely to conform in one way or another, because man is a 'social animal.' "[43] So understood, Marx, in arguing that ideologies are determined by the economic structure, *should not be read, though sometimes his manner of speech invites this reading, as making the very tendentious epistemological claim that all our ideas and beliefs are determined by the modes of production of our society.* It is not man's consciousness as such which is so determined but the public self-conceptions extant in society. It is those that are ideological, not all his thoughts and beliefs.

Given this conception, individuals, and perhaps even groups, can have ideas or self-conceptions which are not in the public mode or subject, so plainly and directly, or perhaps not even at all, to state or class control. These ideas are not on Marx's account ideological. Thus there is conceptual or epistemological space for critical and challenging moral conceptions which are not, in the manner I have characterized above, in the public mode and are not a part of the official currency of public discourse in the society in question. This means that there can be various challenges to the system coming from individuals or

groups who have beliefs, including moral beliefs, which are not ideological. There is at least conceptual space on a Marxist account for a
critical moral stance—a (in part) morally based critique of moral
ideology in an overall situation of class domination. It is not *a priori*
impossible that moral ideas could have a liberating role in class struggle.
This means that Marx's social system has found conceptual space for
a form of ideology critique practised by Marx and Engels and by socialist
anarchists such as Michael Bakunin and Peter Kropotkin.

Such moral beliefs could have such a nonideological status. They
might still, of course, without being objective, be nonideological though
still thoroughly eccentric and arbitrary beliefs. However, if they were
also principles which were impartial, considered (where this is relevant)
the interests of everyone alike, would be endorsed behind the veil of
ignorance and would be principles that people would also remain
committed to once the veil was lifted and with a good understanding
of the genesis of their beliefs and in the face of a good knowledge
of the relevant facts under vivid recall, then, if the moral beliefs in
question were of that sort, we would have some, not inconsiderable,
reason for regarding them as having some objectivity, as well as being
nonideological.[44] What is involved here is that assent to a principle
will only be objective if assent to it will *not* be withdrawn when the
causal history behind that assent is known. This is an important and
tolerably practical test for objectivity, though I do not say that by itself
it is sufficient to give us objectivity.

VII

The recognition that it is at least possible that there are or could be
some moral ideas or beliefs, or *perhaps* even moral systems, which are
not ideological or ideologies should not be taken to be at all incompatible
with Marx's sociology or morals or to at all detract from its force or
importance. Marx and Engels, and indeed most Marxists following them,
have seen, and not without reason, most morality as ideology. If we
look at the general run of moral advocacy, advice or preaching in our
society, it is ideological and nicely fitting into the Marxist conception.
Even in 'high culture' a lot of moralizing, perhaps practically all of
it, has that function. It is, that is, ideology. Marx also argued that
utilitarian, Kantian and various idealistic ethical theories were ideologies
and contemporary Marxists have tried to pin that label on libertarian,
contractarian, Christian and existentialist accounts of morality. The
sociology of morals account, Marxist style, has tried to show, that is,
how various popular moral conceptions, theological and philosophical
normative ethical theories and indeed even meta-ethical theories, such
as Hare's, Foot's and Hampshire's, are ideological or have their various
unwitting ideological biases. They have tried to show how such moralities, both popular and theoretical, have, sometimes wittingly, but

far more typically unwittingly, rationalized a view of how to act or live one's life which serves dominant class interests in various and, in the case of the philosophical accounts, often unobvious and disgsuised ways.[45] (It is not that these moral philosophers are being accused of deliberate malpractice. But the claim is that self-deception is deeply at work here.)

For such Marxist accounts to be viable, Marx's account of historical materialism and ideology, or at least his account of ideology and class, must be approximately true. These various Marxist conceptions here must be probed and elucidated and their application to moralities and to moral theories must be examined on a case by case basis. I think it is reasonably evident that Marx was too short with the utilitarians and Feuerbach and some Marxists have been too short with Rawls. But, as George Brenkert and Richard Miller have shown in the utilitarian case, a Marxist account could be articulated which would show utilitarianism to be deeply ideological and not an account that a Marxist should take over and use as the 'ethical foundation' of Marxism, even if, what is surely not at all evident, there is any need for such a foundational account.[46]

<h1 style="text-align:center">VIII</h1>

Let us, to bring this to a close, review what is most troublesome about historical materialism and ethics. We should start by reminding ourselves that it does not make sense to say we ought to do something unless we can do it. If a people could not at a particular time do other than what in fact they do, then it hardly makes sense to say either that they ought to do that thing or that they ought to do something else instead. Yet the sociology of morals historical materialism tenders, says, in effect, that the dominant moral views of an epoch will be determined or at least strongly conditioned by the mode of production of that epoch. The moral views that are the pervasive ones in a society, where that society is in a condition that for a reasonably determinate time is stable, will be the moral views that are functionally appropriate for the reigning mode of production of that epoch. This means that the dominant moral views will have predictably determinate features that are quite distinct from any considerations concerning their validity and distinct from considerations turning on questions concerning what would be chosen by fully informed, reflective individuals under conditions of undistorted communication. It would seem to be the case that for most people in any class society during any period of considerable social stability there would, as a matter of fact, be little question of their choosing and rationally assessing the moral views they have. The moral views they have are the moral views that are functionally appropriate to the reigning modes of production in their society.

This appears at least to undermine the very possibility of morality, for belief in morals appears at least to be a violation of the 'ought implies can' maxim. A response to this, which taken by itself is indeed a weak one, will still have force when taken in conjunction with some other considerations. That response is this: that most people will have their ethical views so settled for them does not entail that all will. It does not entail that there cannot be such a thing as critical moral reflection. And, as we have seen, neither Marx nor Engels thought that it did.

Still, it will in turn be responded, in making moral judgments about what a society should be like, if the moral views in the society are as determinate as historical materialism gives to understand, then we can hardly reasonably make moral assessments about how that society at a given time ought or ought not to be.

In *a way* that is fair enough but it needs clarification and when that is carried through we can come to see how historical materialism does not require morality to totter. If, on the one hand, to say that we cannot reasonably make moral assessments about how a society at a given time ought or ought not to be, means that we cannot reasonably assert, where for a time no change is possible, that a society ought to have moral practices and institutions which it cannot have, then that reply is well taken. If, on the other hand, it is taken to mean that no one in the society can see how the modes of production could in time change and indeed ought to change, because with that change a better life for people could obtain, though at that time such a change is not on, then the claim that we can make, and should make, no moral assessments of society or can or should have no moral vision of what society should become, if historical materialism is true, is plainly false. The reach of some people can go beyond their grasp. They can have a coherent moral vision of how things ought to be even if at that time that state of affairs is not achievable.

Historical materialism does not create a form of conceptual imprisonment in which such moral visions are impossible. Whether they are an irresponsible, harmful utopianism depends entirely on what is done with them. We will not change the world by becoming clearer about what morality requires of us or what the design of a good society would look like. But where some of us, as we can, can have some enhanced understanding of what a better society would be like, this can help us better focus the direction of our struggle. Far from rendering this nugatory historical materialism can help us tie these struggles to the world.[47]

Notes

1. Fredrick Engels, "Speech at the Graveside of Karl Marx" (1883), in Robert C. Tucker (ed.), *The Marx-Engels Reader,* 2nd ed., New York 1978, p. 682.

2. Ibid.

3. Ibid., p. 681.

4. This type of argument is developed in detail and with care in G. A. Cohen, *Karl Marx's Theory of History: A Defense,* Oxford 1978; and in W. H. Shaw, *Marx's Theory of History,* Stanford 1978. For a perceptive critique of Cohen and a significant statement of an alternative model see Richard Miller, "Productive Forces and Forces of Change," *The Philosophical Review,* 90, 1981, 91–117.

5. Tucker (ed.), *The Marx-Engels Reader,* p. 681.

6. E. P. Thompson, *The Poverty of Theory,* New York 1978, pp. 171–81; and Douglas Kellner, "Marxism, Morality and Ideology," in Kai Nielsen and Steven Patten (eds.), *Marx and Morality,* Guelph 1981, pp. 93–126.

7. Anthony Skillen, *Ruling Illusions: Philosophy and the Social Order,* Brighton 1977; Skillen, "Workers' Interest and the Proletarian Ethic: Conflicting Strains in Marxian Anti-Moralism," in Nielsen and Patten (eds.), *Marx and Morality,* pp. 155–70; Andrew Collier, "Truth and Practice," *Radical Philosophy,* 5, 1973, 9–16; and Collier, "Scientific Socialism and the Question of Socialist Values," in Nielsen and Patten (eds.), *Marx and Morality,* pp. 121–54.

8. William Shaw, "Marxism and Moral Objectivity," in Nielsen and Patten (eds.), *Marx and Morality,* pp. 19–44.

9. Ibid.

10. See citation in note 4. I have also tried to say something about this in my "Taking Historical Materialism Seriously," *Dialogue,* 22, 1983, 319–38.

11. Shaw, "Marxism and Moral Objectivity," p. 20.

12. Ibid.

13. Kellner, "Marxism, Morality and Ideology," p. 96.

14. Shaw, "Marxism and Moral Objectivity"; Collier, "Scientific Socialism and the Question of Socialist Values"; and Richard Miller, "Marx and Morality," in J. Roland Pennock and John W. Chapman (eds.), *Nomos,* 26, New York 1983, pp. 3–32.

15. Shaw, "Marxism and Moral Objectivity," p. 21.

16. Ibid.

17. Ibid.

18. Karl Popper, *The Open Society and Its Enemies,* vol. 2, Princeton 1950, 1966, p. 199.

19. Tucker (ed.), *The Marx-Engels Reader,* p. 145.

20. Engels, *Anti-Dühring,* tr. Emile Burns, New York 1939, p. 105.

21. Shaw, "Marxism and Moral Objectivity," pp. 42–44.

22. Ibid., p. 22; John McMurtry, *The Structure of Marx's World-View,* Princeton 1978; and Allen Wood, *Karl Marx,* London 1981.

23. Shaw, "Marxism and Moral Objectivity," p. 22.

24. Ibid.

25. Ibid., pp. 27–29.

26. Ibid., pp. 24–26; and George E. Panichas, "Marx's Moral Skepticism," in Nielsen and Patten (eds.), *Marx and Morality,* pp. 45–66.

27. Shaw, "Marxism and Moral Objectivity," p. 27.

28. Ibid.

29. Ibid.

30. Ibid.

31. Max Weber, *On the Methodology of the Social Sciences,* tr. and ed. by E. A. Shils and H. A. Finch, Glencoe 1949.

32. Shaw, "Marxism and Moral Objectivity," p. 28.

33. Jürgen Habermas, *Knowledge and Human Interests,* tr. Jeremy J. Shapiro, Boston 1971; and Richard Miller, "Marx and Aristotle," in Nielsen and Patten (eds.), *Marx and Morality,* pp. 323–52.

34. Shaw, "Marxism and Moral Objectivity," p. 37.

35. Ibid., pp. 36–40.

36. McMurtry, *The Structure of Marx's World-View,* pp. 123–44.

37. Ibid., p. 124.

38. Ibid.

39. Ibid., p. 125.

40. Ibid.

41. Ibid.

42. Ibid., p. 126.

43. Ibid., p. 127.

44. Shaw, "Marxism and Moral Objectivity," pp. 36–40.

45. See citation in note 8 and see as well Robert Eccleshall, "Ideology as Common Sense," *Radical Philosophy,* 25, 1980, 2–8; David Murray, "Utopia or Phantasy?," *Radical Philosophy,* 22, 1979, 21–26; Kai Nielsen, "Morality, Marxism and the Ideological Function of Morality," *Occasional Review,* 8–9, 1978, 165–82; Richard Norman, "Moral Philosophy Without Morality," *Radical Philosophy,* 6, 1973, 1–8; and Trevor Pateman, "Liberals, Fanatics and Moral Philosophy: Aspects of R. M. Hare's *Freedom and Reason,*" *Radical Philosophy,* 10, 1975, 26–27.

46. G. G. Brenkert, "Marx's Critique of Utilitarianism," in Nielsen and Patten (eds.), *Marx and Morality,* pp. 193–220; and Richard Miller, "Marx and Aristotle," in Nielsen and Patten (eds.), *Marx and Morality,* pp. 323–52.

47. I would like to thank Ronald Bayer, Arthur Caplan, Jerry Cohen, Frank Cunningham, Thomas Murray, Peter Rossel, Bruce Jennings, William Shaw and Robert Ware for their helpful comments on earlier versions of this paper.

8

Marx on Justice:
The Tucker-Wood Thesis Revisited

Robert Tucker and Allen Wood, in developing their influential and iconoclastic views of Marx and Marxism on justice, stressed that many people, including doubtlessly "numerous followers of Marx," have assumed plausibly enough "that distributive justice is the value underlying" Marx's harsh judgment "against existing society."[1] As Tucker put it, many have taken Marx's "indictment of capitalism" to be rooted in a "concern for justice in the sense of a fair distribution of material goods."[2] "It seems," Tucker added, "to lurk behind his analysis of capitalism as a system of production founded on wage labor."[3]

Let me sketch roughly a rather typical view of the matter. It might be called without exaggeration 'the received naive view.' If we think about the system of wage labor, the generation of surplus value, and exploitation, it is impossible, if one reflects at all, not to conclude that workers are treated unjustly under capitalism. Surplus value, we should recall, comes from the additional working time over and above the time during which the worker produces beyond the amount whose monetary equivalent he or she receives as the day's wages. Suppose I am hired by the day at a fixed hourly wage and that by noon I have produced for the capitalist the monetary equivalent of my entire day's wage. I have, that is, produced in goods and services something that is worth what I get in a day's wage. Yet I go on working until five P.M. My work from noon to five is surplus working time. Under the capitalist system my labor power is a commodity. My labor power, being a commodity, the value of my work—what my day's wage should be to be fair—is determined by how long it takes me to produce something for the capitalist that is equivalent in monetary value to what it would take to maintain me in the socially determined necessities of life for a day. That would be an equivalent traded for an equivalent in a fair way. My employer gets the use of my labor power on a given day, which is equal in monetary value, labor power being a commodity, to what is necessary to maintain me in good working order for that day.

If that is how things stand, equivalents will be traded for equivalents in a fair way. But that is not how things stand, for by our labor contract, the capitalist gets my labor power not just until noon but for the whole day. With me working away during that surplus labor time, he (or she) is able to extract surplus value from me, get, that is, for his own use and enrichment the value of what I produce beyond any equivalent he gives me. This extraction of surplus value, it is natural to say, is exploitation and, as such, is unfair. The capitalist robs me of something I produce with my labor power for which I have not been paid, for I receive no equivalent to what I have produced during the day. I am robbed of something that, at least in part, granting that the capitalist provides the machinery, the work space, and the like, is rightly mine. (Even here, it should be remembered that the capitalist's ownership of machinery and land is based, in part at least, on *past* exploitation. This, it is sometimes believed, is grossly unfair and unjust and reveals that the capitalist system is an exploitative one and thus an unjust system of production and distribution.)

Tucker and Wood agreed that this is a natural response to a superficial reading of Marx and that it all has a certain surface plausibility, but, they argued, that appearances to the contrary notwithstanding, it is not Marx's view, for Marx and Engels asserted, as Tucker put it, "quite emphatically that no injustice whatever is involved in wage labor."[4] Relying heavily on the same passage from Volume 1 of *Capital* as did Wood, Tucker maintained that the subsistence wage, what in my case in contracting for work I needed to keep myself going for a day, is precisely what my labor power for the day is worth under capitalism.[5] Tucker remarked:

> The worker is receiving full value for this service despite the fact that the employer extracts surplus value at his expense. To quote Marx: "It is true that the daily maintenance of the labor power costs only half a day's labor, and that nevertheless the labor power can work for an entire working day, with the result that the value which its use creates during a working day is twice the value of a day's labor power. So much the better for the purchaser, but it is no wise an injustice (*Unrecht*) to the seller." It is no wise an injustice because the subsistence wage is precisely what the commodity labor power, sold by the worker to the employer, is worth according to the laws of commodity production. But is there

no higher standard of justice than that implicit in these laws? Is there no abstract idea of justice in relation to which wage labor, though perfectly just on capitalist principles, could be adjudged as unjust *per se*? Marx and Engels are absolutely unequivocal in their negative answer to this question. "Social justice or injustice," writes Engels, "is decided by one science alone—the science which deals with the material facts of production and exchange, the science of political economy." "Right," says Marx in his *Critique of the Gotha Program,* "can never be higher than the economic structure of society and its cultural development conditioned thereby."

The latter work, consisting of marginal notes that Marx penned in 1875 on a draft program for a united German workers' party and published posthumously, contains a furious diatribe against the whole idea that fair distribution is a socialist goal. Marx points out sarcastically that socialists cannot agree on any criterion of distributive justice: "And have not the socialist sectarians the most varied notions about 'fair' distribution?" He speaks of "ideological nonsense about 'right' and other trash so common among the democrats and French socialists." He dismisses the notions of "undiminished proceeds of labor," "equal right" and "fair distribution" as "obsolete verbal rubbish" which it would be a "crime" to adopt as a party program. It is here that Marx quotes, for the only time, the old French socialist slogan, "From each according to his ability, to each according to his needs." But in the very next breath he declares that "it was in general incorrect to make a fuss about so-called *distribution* and to put the principal stress upon it." To present socialism as turning principally on distribution was characteristic of "vulgar socialism," Marx says, and he concludes by asking: "Why go back again?" It should be clear in the light of all this that a fair distribution of the proceeds of labor is not the moral goal for Marx. The ideal of distributive justice is a complete stranger in the mental universe of Marxism.[6]

As Tucker put it later in his *Philosophy and Myth in Karl Marx,* "The issue for Marx was not justice but man's loss of himself under enslavement to an *unmenschliche Macht* and his recovery of himself by the total vanquishment of that force."[7]

II

I shall query these claims of Tucker and Wood. In the end, I wish to claim that something closer to the natural, untutored response more accurately reflects Marx's views. But Tucker's and Woods's views were powerfully and carefully stated with a good bit of textual basis in both Marx and Engels. To make a start we must recognize there is a not inconsiderable sorting out to be done. Moreover, it is important not to forget in so doing that there are no canonical texts that can give us Marx's account of justice. We have to deal not only with the fact that Marx's texts were often in rough drafts and occasional texts, but we have also to deal with his profoundly Swiftian satire and mocking irony. It is very difficult to ascertain with any confidence what Marx's views here actually were.

It was Wood's contention that if we gain a correct understanding of historical materialism and the labor theory of value (surely parts canonical to Marxism if anything is), we will come to understand why Marx could not have claimed that the appropriation of surplus value and thus exploitation are unjust. David Ricardo and some Ricardian socialists, Wood argued, believed that if the capitalist had paid the worker for the full value of his (or her) work that no surplus value would have resulted. Surplus value, on Ricardo's account, is a result, and an unavoidable one, of the capitalist process. Without it there would be no profit or capitalist accumulation. So it is the capitalist who must, Ricardo tells us, in effect cheat the worker and treat him unjustly. The capitalist cannot, if capitalism is to survive, pay the worker for the full value of his work.

Wood maintained that Marx would reject this. The foregoing description contains a mistaken account of the origin of surplus value, and Marx would reject the Ricardian view that the existence of surplus value shows that there has been an unequal exchange between worker and capitalist.[8] No injustice is done to the worker by extracting surplus value from him. There is, in the capitalist economic system, no unequal exchange simply because that happens. We should remember, according to Wood, that for Marx "labor is the substance and imminent measure of value, but has no value itself."[9]

We need, in trying to understand what is going on here, to clarify what is being talked about when we speak of the 'value of labor.' *First,* there is the value present in the commodity *created* by the labor. In this first sense, 'the value of labor' connotes the value present in the commodity created by labor minus the value of the means of production consumed in producing it.[10] But the capitalist does not purchase this when he strikes a wage deal with the worker. The capitalist does not buy the finished commodities from the worker minus the amount of the capitalist's means of production that is consumed in the worker's creating those commodities. The commodity that the capitalist buys is not what the worker's labor creates; rather, the capitalist buys the worker's *labor power (Arbeitskraft).* It is this *power* that is sold as a commodity for wages. Then the capitalist merely makes use of the commodity he has bought in a contract struck, a purchase made, antecedent to the labor process, just as I typically would make use of a pasta machine I had purchased, only after I have purchased it. Once the worker has sold his labor power and his work commences, then his labor power, for the duration of the contract, as Marx put it, "has ceased to belong to him; hence it is no longer a thing he can sell." Moreover, the value of labor power, like the value of any other commodity, depends "on the quantity of labor necessary for its production."[11] The value of a worker's labor power "depends on the quantity of labor necessary to keep the worker alive and working, or to replace him if he should die or quit."[12]

However, taken in this way, this account is incomplete and misleading, for Marx also talked about *socially necessary* labor time. What is necessary to keep the worker alive and working is historically and culturally variable. It is not always bare subsistence, and it will generally go up as productive forces develop and the concrete production relations change.[13] Unless there is some cheating within the terms of the system itself, something that sometimes, but not usually, happens, the wage worker usually is paid the full value of his labor power. That is to say, he is paid "what is socially necessary for the reproduction of his life-activity as a worker."[14] According to the strictest rules of commodity exchange, equivalents have been exchanged for equivalents, and so we have a just transaction. Wood pointed out significantly:

> Surplus value, to be sure, is appropriated by the capitalist without an equivalent. But there is nothing in the exchange requiring him to pay any equivalent for it. The exchange of wages for labor power is the only exchange between capitalist and worker. It is a just exchange, and it is consummated long before the question arises of selling the commodity produced and realizing its surplus value. The capitalist has bought a commodity (labor power) and paid its full value; by using, exploiting, this commodity, he now creates a greater value than he began with. This surplus belongs to him; it never belongs to anyone else, and he owes nobody a penny for it. "This circumstance," says Marx, "is peculiar good fortune for the buyer (of labor power), but no injustice at all to the seller." The appropriation of surplus value by capital, therefore, involves no unequal or unjust exchange.[15]

Labor or, more exactly, labor power is the sole creator of value. The capitalist's means of production do not grow in value unless they are consumed by labor.[16] The surplus value comes about, on Marx's account, through the worker's labor power alone. This being so, many have thought it is only fair that the entire increase ought to go to the worker once the means of production he consumes in so laboring is paid for. There may be no unequal exchange between worker and capitalist, but, such people have argued, in reaping the fruits of the worker's unpaid labor the capitalist is still exploiting him and, the standard view has it, taking from him what is justly his. Again we return to the received view against which the Tucker-Wood thesis is centrally set.

This very common view, Wood argued, rests on a mistaken and ideologically distorted conception of property. In effect, it assumes the idyllic *mutualite* of purely individual private property. This view talks as if the capitalist system were a system of individual commodity production. But if such a system ever really existed, surplus value, and hence exploitation, could not exist, and the whole problem would not arise. To claim injustice arises from such exploitation assumes that all legitimate ownership is in *individual* private property. This assumes, utterly unrealistically, that each person's property rights are based on his or her own labor and thus that every human being has a right to appropriate the full value created by his or her own labor and anyone who deprives the person in question of what this labor has created does that person an injustice.[17] Marx claimed that this is a mystification and that it exists only in some crude bourgeois *ideologies* where property rights are so conceptualized. It is, that is, part of the bourgeois ideology, not part of the bourgeois social reality.

The reality of capitalist production and capitalist production relations is quite otherwise. There people engage in cooperative labor in which they use the means of production together; moreover, in such a system there is a working class that uses the means of production and a capitalist class that owns it and controls it, with the result that there is a separation of labor from the means of production. Moreover, while there are individuals who can own the means of production, it is not individual property they own but a means of production *used* cooperatively although not controlled cooperatively. We have, where capitalist property relations obtain, a society divided into a class that owns and controls productive property—for example, the means of production— and a class that does not and indeed typically only owns its own labor power. In such a society, it is not the case, as the argument from exploitation to injustice requires, that every person's right to private property is based on his or her own labor. A capitalist system would not be a capitalist system if surplus value could not be extracted. And it can only be extracted from the labor power of workers, people who sell their labor power as a commodity in a commodity market. Moreover, a commodity, which is what labor power is, would not be a commodity unless it could be purchased to be used and unless it is typically useful to its purchaser. "If the entire value of the commodity produced by the wage laborer were expended in wages and means of production, the capitalist would have received no use from the labor power he purchased and he would have done better simply to convert the value of his means of production into commodities he could consume."[18] Indeed, if he received no surplus value, he would have no incentive to develop the forces of production. Capitalist property is not simply a system of individual property rights of individual producers; it is a system of rights that conforms to capitalist relations of production. The capitalist system—the capitalist mode of production—is not a system of individual commodity production. Productive property rights become, as Marx put it in *Capital,* "the right on the part of the capitalist to appropriate alien unpaid labor or its product, and on the part of the worker the impossibility of appropriating his own product."[19] Given such a system of property rights, no entitlement of the worker has been overridden in extracting surplus value, no right of his has been violated, and thus no injustice could have been done to him. "The justice of the transactions in capitalist production relations rest on the fact that they arise out of capitalist production relations, that they are adequate to, and correspond to, the capitalist mode of production as a whole."[20]

To complain in this general way about the injustice of the system of capitalist property rights is simply to complain that capitalism is capitalism. Capitalism is only possible if labor power is used as a commodity to produce surplus value and expand capital. If "workers performed no unpaid labor and were not exploited, the capitalist mode of production would not be possible. Under a capitalist mode of production, the appropriation of surplus value is not only just, but any attempt to deprive capital of it would be a positive injustice."[21] In Marx's language, economic relations are not ruled by juridical concepts; rather, juridical relations arise out of economic ones.[22] Capitalism could not possibly function without profits. "Capitalism exploitation," as Wood put it,

> belongs to the essence of capitalism, and as the capitalist most of production progresses to later and later stages of its development, this exploitation must in Marx's view grow worse and worse as a result of the laws of this development itself. It cannot be removed by the passage or enforcement of laws regulating distribution, or by any moral or political reforms which capitalist institutions could bring about.[23]

III

However, pace Wood, isn't it because of the very system's exploitative and dehumanizing features that we want to say *of the entire system itself* that it is unjust? It is the whole system that is rotten. In reading Wood's account of Marx, it is natural to respond, "Yes, given that system of property rights, given that system of relations of production, we can see that if they are accepted and acknowledged as legitimate, as it is certainly in ruling class interests to do, then, given the acceptance of those standards and that system, we cannot consistently say that an injustice is done to the workers. But we also want to say, when we reflect on the facts of exploitation, that this whole system of property rights, with its corresponding relations of production, is unjust and ought to be overthrown." Marx himself referred to that system of property rights as something that, for the workers of his time, and by extrapolation for workers now, is a "social curse."[24] Why cannot such judgments of the wrongness of the system—indeed the injustice of the system—be legitimately made, and what reason have we to think that Marx would have regarded them as necessarily ideological or in any other way mistaken?

Wood's response in effect was that, if it is Marx exegesis that is at issue, we have to reply that it is just a fact that Marx (rightly or wrongly) regarded such a position as an 'ideological shuffle.' He regarded such justice-talk as "outdated verbal trivia."[25] Wood put it very un-equivocally:

> It is simply not the case that Marx's condemnation of capitalism rests
> on some conception of justice (whether explicit or implciit), and those
> who attempt to reconstruct a 'Marxian idea of justice' from Marx's manifold
> charges against capitalism are at best only translating Marx's critique of
> capitalism, or some aspect of it, into what Marx himself would have
> consistently regarded as a false ideological or 'mystified' form.[26]

In the pages just prior to that unequivocal statement, Wood provided
Marx with something of a rationale for his unequivocal rejection of
the legitimacy of justice-talk. I want in several ways to probe this.
Perhaps here Wood imputed more to Marx than an examination of his
texts will bear.

The positions in Marx that Wood appealed to in trying to stress
that such employments of justice-talk are ideological are these. If we
say that capitalism itself is unjust or that capitalist exploitation is
unjust, we are giving to understand that capitalism's system of distribution is unfair, perhaps even grossly unfair. The worker is not receiving
the share of the collective product of society he or she *deserves*. But
when we look for some criterion for what it is that the worker, or
indeed anyone else, deserves, we are at a loss. We are reduced to the
subjectivism of appealing to our *sense* of justice or to what our
considered convictions—our intuitions if you will—inform us would
be the ideal set of juridical or moral principles, rules and practices
that should govern society. The moral agent, in effect, is "treating the
social whole as if he in his sublime rationality, could measure this
whole against some ideal of right or justice completely external to it,
and could then, standing on some Archimedean point, adjust social
reality to this ideal."[27]

Even if we concede that such a socialist moralist need not, and
indeed should not, claim to be able to so adjust social reality but only
to provide a criterion for guiding social change, when it can and will
come about, the core of Wood's challenge on Marx's behalf remains,
How can the socialist revolutionary or, for that matter anyone else,
particularly given the facts about imposed consciousness, be so confident
that his or her sense of what is rational—even when, and indeed
particularly when, it is riding in tandem with his or her sense of
justice—provides such criteria for assessment? Isn't to accept anything
like this in effect to adopt an unscientific, intuitionistic individualism
that is hardly appropriate for a socialist? Can we reasonably expect to
recover so much by what is in effect an appeal to our intuitions, to
what, on careful reflection, just *seems* to us as individuals right and
just?

Moreover, even if some appeal to some historically and culturally
specific consensus will take us around that bend (something that is

challengeable itself), such an appeal to considerations turning on distribution is a mistake.[28] Marx stressed that distribution is not "something which exists alongside production, indifferent to it, and subject to whatever modifications individuals in their collective moral and political wisdom should choose to make in it."[29] We need to recognize that a mode of distribution is a functional part of a mode of production and that the former is determined by the overall character of the latter. We cannot in any way fundamentally change the distribution without changing the production relations. But in arguing as we have about justice, we are concerning ourselves with distribution relations alone, which means we are concerning ourselves with something that is a very derivative matter.

If this was Marx's view, this criticism does not cut very deep, for anyone even remotely intelligent in the socialist tradition who sought to articulate socialist principles of justice would articulate a combined set of productive-distributive principles. Such a person, in challenging the justice of capitalism as a whole, would challenge the system of production relations and the system of distribution that flows from it. This same person, in claiming that this exploitative system is unjust, would claim that a system with such productive-distributive principles and practices is unjust.[30] The criticism is directed to the system as a whole, although a vivid and reasonably important way of making this criticism is by showing what distribution relations flow from that productive system. However, Marx's previous challenge, if indeed it was really Marx's, that no one is in a sufficiently Archimedean position to make such a judgment is still in place, but the claim that the critic is only concerned with distribution is not. The challenge is to the justice of the system as a whole, including, very fundamentally, its modes of production. This challenge says that a whole mode of production is unjust and that an alternative mode of production would be fairer. That, particularly during a period when a revolution is possible, can (or so it would seem) be very much to the point. It could (a) be justified and (b) be a somewhat useful element in a revolutionary class struggle. (It surely would be unwise or at least un-Marxist to claim more for such a challenge.)

Wood, however, would resist this. Marx, Wood had it, believed that such judgments of the justice of whole social systems are both futile and counterproductive from the point of view of revolutionary practice. Moreover, they have no rational basis. If the forces of production are not sufficiently developed to be in conflict with the relations of production, moral-talk will have little effect in changing anything. If the forces of production are in sufficient movement such that the production relations are now fettering the productive forces, and the working class has gained sufficient class consciousness to see that its interests are being systematically frustrated by the capitalist masters and indeed by the very nature of capitalist system itself, such moral-talk is supererogatory. When that situation does not obtain, and such a fundamental change is not in the offing, calls to revolutionary activity on the basis of cries of injustice are, on Marx's view, irrational, irresponsible, and futile.[31] *The German Ideology* asserted, "Communism is for us not a *state of affairs* to be brought about, an ideal to which reality must somehow adjust itself. We call communism the actual movement which is transcending (*aufhebt*) the present state of affairs. The conditions of this movement result from presuppositions already existing."[32] What is vital to realize, and take to heart, is that we are not going to change society through moral theorizing and appeals.[33]

IV

Again, it does not seem to me that the foregoing is an effective criticism of the claim that socialists can and should critique capitalism by claiming that it is unjust. Certainly to make such a critique does not imply (a) that it is the only relevant critique; (b) that it is the most important sort of critique; (c) that calls for revolution should be made, independently of other practical considerations, simply when these gross injustices obtain; or (d) that much of a moral critique can plausibly be done without a good understanding of the mechanisms at work in capitalism and the underlying forces for change in the historical epoch in which the critique is made. There need and indeed should be no belief that moral critique, particularly by itself, will change the world or typically trigger social change. And there need be no insane or quixotic use of moral critique to call for revolution where revolution is not in the offing, where the structural contradictions of capitalism do not manifest themselves.

There only need be a recognition in debates about the viability and the necessity of socialism, debates that will go on within bourgeois societies whether we like it or not, that such moral arguments, including arguments about the injustice of capitalism generally, can reasonably play a modest role in those debates. And, in acknowledging the legitimacy of such a role for arguments about justice and claims concerning the injustice of capitalism, there need and indeed should not be the slightest retraction of the claim of historical materialism that the actual juridical structure of society is a dependent moment of the prevailing productive mode.

Such a socialist critic can and should, quite in accord with Marx, stress that it is also the case (a) that superstructures react on bases and that bases need superstructures (there is reciprocal causal inter-action) and (b) that there is class conflict in society and that at times the superstructural conceptions favoring the interests of the dominated class (working class ideology if you will) can affect production rela-tions.[34] Moral beliefs can sometimes have some emancipatory use in such class struggles.

Marx did indeed believe that capitalism is a system of slavery. As Wood well put it, Marx thought of capitalism as "a slavery the more insidious because the relations of domination and servitude are *experienced* as such without being *understood* as such."[35] On Wood's understanding of Marx, and on Tucker's as well, "although this servitude is a source of misery, degradation, and discontent to the worker it is not a form of *injustice*."[36] It is, on their view, a form of ideological mystification to think that it is. It is not injustice on their understanding of Marx's view because the "servitude of the wage laborer to capital is an essential and indispensable part of the capitalist mode of production, which neither the passage of liberal legislation nor the sincere resolve by bourgeois society to respect the 'human rights of all its members' can do anything to remove."[37] If we have a firm grasp of the labor theory of value and historical materialism, we will recognize, bitter although this recognition will be, that this servitude is sometimes of considerable instrumental value and, as such, not an "unqualified wrong, an evil to be abolished at all cost with an attitude of *fiat, justitia, pereat mundi*."[38] There is the harsh and bitter historical lesson that "the servitude of capitalism . . . and even the direct slavery involved in capitalist colonies have been necessary conditions for the development of modern productive forces."[39] This particular claim seems to me probably too strong a claim. To contend that capitalist forces could not have developed without slavery in the colonies needs some proving. Still, Marx's general point, stressed here by Wood, is well taken—namely, that to condemn the servitude involved in capitalism unqualifiedly would be to condemn all the productive advances of modern society, and that would be tantamount to condemning socialism, too, for socialism is impossible without such productive advances, and to will the end, as we know from Kant, is to will the necessary means to the end.[40] In this connection Wood remarked, "Condemning a relation of servitude when it results from historical limitations on productive forces is for Marx about as rational as condemning medical science because there are some diseases it cannot cure."[41]

However, the socialist who wishes to condemn capitalism as an unjust system because it systematically treats some human beings, in their conditions of servitude, as means only, could still recognize that sometimes such evils and such injustices are necessary. Not infrequently in morality, we have to choose the lesser evil. Such socialists could grant, as John Rawls would not, that sometimes, in grim circumstances, utility outweighs justice and that we then must accept injustice as morally necessary. This seems to me both a realistic and, if one thinks about it carefully, a morally sensitive reaction. But this does not mean that we have to throw up our hands in the face of arguments about the justice or the lack thereof of whole social systems or regard all such talk as the ideological twaddle of confused ideologues. These remarks can be, and I think should be, made quite consistently from within Marx's point of view.

Wood also contended that a Marxist who intends to follow in Marx's footsteps cannot argue that "capitalism could be condemned as unjust by applying to it standards of justice and rights which would be appropriate to some post-capitalist mode of production."[42] This cannot be done because such a response would be an emotional or ideological reaction without any rational grounding. Given that such post-capitalist standards of justice, Wood remarked, "would not be rationally applicable to capitalism at all, any such condemnation would be mistaken, confused and without foundation."[43] The person who thinks he or she can do such a thing is operating "from the vision of the post-capitalist society as a kind of eternal juridical structure against which the present state of affairs is to be measured and found wanting."[44] Marx, Wood claimed, repudiated any vision of this kind.[45]

During periods of socialist transition, as Marx's *The Critique of the Gotha Programme* made clear, there will be various phases of development with different standards of right. When a fully classless society of extensive abundance is attained, we will be beyond conflicts of interest and the circumstances of justice that Hume and Rawls spoke of, and we will have no need for principles and theories of justice.[46] Marx believed, as Wood put it, "that the end of class society will mean the end of the social need for the state mechanism and the juridical institutions within which concepts like 'right' and 'justice' have their place."[47] In a fully developed communist society, there will be no need for principles of justice or even for the concept of justice. People, without being unjust, will be beyond the circumstances of justice and will have no need for this conception or its principles. We will, in such a circumstance, have no more need for justice than humanists have for God.

V

Perhaps this was Marx's view. Certainly he at times talked like this, although it is not at all clear to me that 'to each according to his needs' is either not meant to be taken as a principle of justice or is meant, like the state, to wither away.[48] But whatever Marx's own view was here, I see no reason why someone with even a thorough Marxist orientation must or even should follow Marx here. It is quite possible, indeed perhaps probable, given our resources and our world population, that we will never be so beyond scarcity that there will not be some conflicts of interests for which we would require principles of adjudication and that some of these principles would or at least should plainly be principles of justice.[49] There would, in such a society, be no class conflicts because there would be no classes, but there would still be some conflicts of interest such that we would not be altogether beyond the circumstances of justice. Moreover, to hold that there can be post-capitalist principles of justice for assessing such conflicts, we need not assume that we will either have or need some kind of eternal juridical structure. Even if the appropriate concept of justice is a juridical one, it need not follow that it is eternal.[50] A Marxist could accept a developmental but non-relativistic account of principles of justice in which the post-capitalist ones would, or at least could, be higher than the capitalist ones without assuming at all that we even have any coherent picture of eternal principles of justice.

Furthermore, a Marxist need not accept the restriction that all principles of justice must be juridical and coercive and thus require the existence of the state and legal institutions. There can, as in primitive stateless societies such as the Tiv and the Nuer, be conceptions of justice as a right balance between sometimes conflicting interests without justice being treated as a juridical concept. Similarly, the standard of justice in a post-capitalist society need not be a juridical one; at the very least, it has not been shown that such a standard must be juridical.

Wood asserted, in one of the few places where he differed in detail from Tucker, that Marx did not think of 'justice' as connoting a rightful balance between conflicting interests, but as "the rational measure of social acts and institutions from the *juridical* point of view."[51] But Wood gave no textual basis in Marx that would justify the claim that *all* ascriptions of justice or even all coherent ascriptions of justice are juridical, so that 'legal justice' for Marx was pleonastic. But 'legal justice' is not pleonastic for us, and, whatever it actually was for Marx, I see nothing essential to his account or, for that matter, anything canonical to Marxism that commits us to so reading it. That is to say, such a conception could be abandoned and the central structures of his account would be quite uneffected.[52]

My arguments in the last several paragraphs have been designed to show that if Wood had got Marx right, then Marx on several points we have discussed was mistaken, or at least his arguments were anything but conclusive.[53] But my remarks were not designed to show that Wood had got Marx wrong, although they were designed to show that in some places Wood's arguments were inconclusive and that he over-generalized from his evidential base. However, in some places my reading of Marx squares with Wood's, and in other places I just don't know what to say. But what I principally want to stress is this: Even if Wood had got Marx roughly right here or indeed even exactly right, there is still not enough in Wood's account to show that a Marxist who accepted the labor theory of value, the dialectical method, historical materialism, Marx's theory of ideology, and his account of the state and class—in short for a Marxist who accepted the essentials of Marxism—that he or she need reject what might very well be an untutored conviction and what might have turned such a person toward socialism in the first place—namely, his or her conviction that capitalism is a rotten, unjust social system. If Wood's Marx on justice was indeed genuine Marx, a Marxist could, and I believe should, part company with Marx here. But in parting company with Marx here, a Marxist still need not reject anything that is essential to Marxism or reject what is distinctive and important in Marx's own contributions.

If my replies to Wood have been on the mark, we could even accept most of Wood's reconstruction of Marx and still believe that it does not show that someone working within Marx's general framework could not continue to believe that capitalism is an exploitative, enslaving, through and through unjust system.[54] That this is a rather too mild criticism, given what on Marx's political sociology would be the social curse of capitalism, does not make the term inapplicable. If Hans is a swindler, he is also dishonest.

What does still stick in the craw is Wood's claim, on Marx's behalf, that the belief that capitalism is unjust must be without a *rational* basis, although here it is important to recognize that Wood imputed this view to Marx without an adequate textual basis. Perhaps Wood's very claim reveals more about Wood's own historicist assumptions and moral positivism than it does about Marx. Nevertheless, it would be nice to know what it would be like to have a rational grounding for such a belief. Perhaps it would be sufficient to appeal to our considered judgments in what Norman Daniels called, developing a conception from Rawls, *wide* reflective equilibrium?[55]

VI

The foregoing criticisms of Wood have been piecemeal and rather internal. I now want to turn to some more full-bodied criticisms of the claim made by Wood and Tucker that Marx stressed that the capitalist system is exploitative, dehumanizing, alienating, and enslaving while still, quite consistently, claiming that it is not unjust. They contended that Marx believed that it is perfectly in place to claim that exploitation is just in a capitalist society.

Ziyad Husami and Gary Young vigorously opposed the Tucker-Wood reading of Marx; Wood replied and Derek Allen defended Wood in an even more extended way.[56] Because the issue is well joined, I shall try to sort out what is at issue and try to go some way toward ascertaining who is telling it like it is.

The reading of Marx that Husami was out to refute is that because in Marx the "standards of right and justice appropriate to a given society are those which in fact fulfill a function in social production," and because Marx also believed—and indeed his theory required him to believe—"that the exploitation of wage labor by capital is essential to the capitalist mode of production," then he further had to believe "that there is nothing unjust about the transactions through which capital exploits labor, and that the workers' rights are not violated by capital's appropriation of their surplus value or by the capitalist system of distribution generally."[57] Centrally at issue is whether it must be the case that exploitation is unjust.[58] Wood's central claim, as we have seen, was that close attention to Marx's texts would show that "he does not regard capitalism as distributively unjust or as violating the rights of workers."[59]

There was no disagreement at all between Husami and Young, on the one hand, and Tucker, Wood, and Allen, on the other, that Marx firmly believed that capitalism exploits and "that one essential feature of all economic exploitation for Marx is *coercion.*"[60] They further agreed that Marx believed that capitalists coerce through their control over the means of production. It is their common view that "Marx's frequent insinuations that capital not only robs but also cheats or defrauds the worker are due to Marx's belief that capital's coercion is disguised by the *ficto juris* of the voluntary contract between individual capitalists and workers."[61] They differed about whether this shows that Marx believed that capitalism is unjust. Against the Tucker-Wood thesis, Husami argued that although Marx's explicit statements about this were few and far between, the most plausible reading of many texts is one that concludes that Marx did think that capitalism is unjust.[62] That is, pace Tucker and Wood, and indeed Richard Miller as well, our first impressions, our naive impressions, if you will, are the correct ones.[63]

Husami drew our attention to the evident fact, which Tucker and Wood do *not* overlook, that in passage after passage Marx pointed to the concentration of wealth under capitalism into a few hands; to the misery of the proletariat; to its condition of servitude, alienation, and dehumanization; to how wage labor forced the proletarian class "into creating wealth for others and misery for itself"; to how the proletariat "has to bear all the burdens of society without enjoying its advantages"; to how the capitalist has an ever-increasing control over social development (a control that he or she employs principally for capitalist-class interests and at the expense of the proletariat); and to how the media and the control of intellectual life (the consciousness industry) are principally in the hands of the capitalist class. In passage after passage, Marx would not let us forget that there are in the capitalist world extreme inequalities of wealth, power, education, access to meaningful work, and conditions of security and health. A reading of Marx and Engels yields readily enough, as Husami put it,

> the picture of a society with extreme inequalities of wealth. This wealth is produced by one class and enjoyed by another which is indifferent to the poverty, suffering and misery of the producers. One class monopolizes material and intellectual advantages such as access to education and culture at the expense of another class which is coerced into shouldering all the burdens of society. The capitalists do not amass their wealth and

its attendant material and cultural enjoyments from their own labor but by exploiting the labor power of the workers.[64]

If this description is accepted in its essentials as an accurate rendering of Marx, something all parties to the dispute accepted, it is very natural to respond that in this very description we have a clear and vivid picture of social injustice. If what is pictured there isn't social injustice, what is? If there are any paradigm cases, aren't those paradigm cases?

Given the foregoing social description, there are many other grounds on which we should condemn capitalism as well, but it surely licenses our saying, most emphatically, that if these things are true of capitalism, capitalist society is an unjust society. This was Husami's reading of Marx's view as well as that of Gary Young, G. A. Cohen, and Jon Elster. Husami thought that Marx viewed capitalist society as an unjust society, but Husami was aware that Tucker and Wood would resist this and indeed Wood did. They will remark (a) that Marx did not explicitly say capitalism is unjust—indeed, he said on one occasion that capitalist transactions are typically just—and (b) that we cannot rightly infer that Marx, given his account of society, regarded capitalism as unjust.[65] Exploitative, dehumanizing, enslaving, and radically inegalitarian, yes; but unjust, unfair, or in violation of rights, no.

At this point, it is perfectly natural to react by exclaiming, "This must be a tempest in a teapot." If Tucker and Wood accept the previous social descriptions as genuine Marx, then they must conclude that as the term 'justice' is plainly and unequivocally used in everyday life, Marx and Engels were condemning capitalism as unjust. All that Tucker and Wood could show is that if their own readings are correct, in a specialized, quasi-technical use of the term 'justice,' or more accurately, '*Gerechtigkeit*,' that Marx and Engels did not, in that *special sense*, claim that capitalism is unjust. Quite to the contrary, Marx and Engels, again in this very special sense, gave to understand that capitalism is just or at least not unjust.[66]

But no serious substantive issues actually divide the contestants because given Tucker and Wood's acceptance of the foregoing descriptions as accurate renderings of Marx's beliefs, they must agree with Husami and Young that capitalism is indeed, in the plain untechnical sense of the term, an unjust social system. After all, that is the genuinely important consideration about which we need to get clear. If I say, "Tomatoes are a good vegetable to mix with corn," and you deny this on the grounds that tomatoes are a fruit but grant that tomatoes do go well with corn, nothing important or relevant to the issue at hand divides us.

Given a common acceptance that the foregoing description is an accurate description of Marx's views of capitalism, it looks like nothing of substantive importance vis-à-vis the injustice of capitalism can divide Tucker, Wood, and Allen, on the one hand, and Husami, Young, and Cohen, on the other. They agreed on the following issue. Marx described capitalism in a certain way, and if that description is for the most part accurate, then Marx, in the ordinary sense of that term, must have regarded capitalism as plainly unjust. They only differed about whether it is true, as Wood and Tucker believed, that Marx (perhaps following Hegel) used the term 'Gerechtigkeit,' which we would render in English as 'justice,' in a specialized way such that he would not speak of capitalism as unjust, but, again in that specialized way, as 'just' or at least as 'not unjust.' But if this way of putting the matter is accepted, that trivializes the Tucker-Wood thesis; renders if normatively and substantially innocuous; and does nothing to show that Marx was a critic of morality who did not appraise capitalism in terms of justice or even of morality.[67]

Wood was perfectly aware that it is natural to level this charge at him, and he responded to it even in his first article. He first characterized the issue thus:

> We might be tempted at this point to think that whether capitalism should be called "unjust" or not is merely a verbal issue. Marx did, after all, condemn capitalism, and he condemned it at least in part because it was a system of exploitation, involving the appropriation of the worker's unpaid labor by capital. If Marx chose to call these evils of capitalism not "injustices" but something else, they still sound to most of us like injustices, and it seems that we should be free to apply this term to them if we like. The difference between Marx and ourselves at the point we might suppose, is only that his application of the term "justice" is somewhat narrower than ours.[68]

He then responded:

> It is extremely important to see why such an attitude would be mistaken. When Marx limits the concept of justice in the way he does, he is not by any means making a terminological stipulation. He is basing his claim on the actual role played in social life by the concept of justice, and the institutional context in which this term has its proper function. His disagreement with those who hold that capitalism is unjust is a substantive one, founded on his conception of society and having important practical consequences.[69]

It remains unclear to me how either in his first article, in his reply to Husami, or in his Karl Marx, Wood demonstrated that after all there is a substantive issue here. He didn't show that the term 'justice' hasn't a plain use in our stream of life where such ascriptions of justice would naturally be made, given an acceptance of Marx's description of capitalism. Wood admitted that this is a natural way to talk, but he argued powerfully that that is not the way Marx conceptualized justice and that it is not the way someone who accepts historical materialism and believes in the reality and human importance of class interests and class struggle should talk.[70] Still, such ordinary talk of

justice seems perfectly reasonable in the light of Marx's social descriptions of life in capitalist society and his conceptions of feasible
alternatives. Indeed, it would seem reasonable to believe that historical
materialism could be read in such a way so as to not conflict with
such natural remarks about justice.

Only, or so it seems at least, if we make on Wood's behalf a 'sociology
of morals' point and insist that *all* talk of justice is entirely ideological
and mystificatory could we coherently maintain that there is an important
issue of substance between him and the person who claims that Marx
condemned capitalism for being unjust. That is indeed just what Wood
claimed. But in doing so he transformed the issue, and we would also,
I believe, have to claim, as Wood did not, that Marx regarded as
ideological his own talk of the exploitative, enslaving, and dehumanizing
nature of capitalism as well as his powerful claims that it is a system
destructive of any true community or truly human life.[71] Wood believed,
as his article in response to Husami made reasonably evident and as
did his *Karl Marx,* that Marx regarded all distinctively moral notions
as ideological. But, oddly and indeed quixotically, Wood did not regard
talk of exploitation, dehumanization, and enslavement as talk of distinctively moral notions. Here again we seem at least to have a purely
verbal issue, with Wood pointlessly making what are in effect verbal
stipulations about the range of 'the moral.'[72]

It also seems to me that the trivializing reading I gave previously
to the Tucker-Wood thesis remains in place and that they have not
been able to show, in any substantively significant way, how Marx or
Engels could deny, given their social science and their descriptions of
capitalism, that capitalism is thoroughly unjust, if, it is true, on their
account, that we can reasonably make any normative judgments at all.
Given Marx's understanding of the facts, we can only resist the claim
that capitalism is an unjust system (given our ordinary use of 'unjust'),
if we claim, on the one hand, that all moral reasoning, all moral
standards, and indeed all normative judgments are ideological and thus
not rationally based or, on the other hand, if we take the line (which
was taken by Richard Miller in his *Analyzing Marx*) that Marx believed
that the central moral claims vitally relevant to the moral appraisal of
capitalism versus socialism are so rationally indeterminate that we
cannot make a cogent claim for saying that capitalism is an unjust
social system or that, morally speaking, socialism is superior to capitalism.[73]

If the former claim is so—that all moral-talk is ideological—then
the line must be that except when Marx and Engels were engaging
in propagandistic rhetoric, they made no normative or evaluative claims
at all. All their moral or other evaluative utterances were just so much
emotive effusion with no cognitive standing. But this turns into propaganda, or at least into a non-rational expression of attitude, more in
Capital and elsewhere than it would be plausible to believe Marx

would accept or anyone with a good understanding of his texts would accept. Moreover, it trivializes Marx's critique and condemnation of capitalism. We would have to say that Marx and Engels were just emoting when they made normative remarks and that they knew they were just doing that. Alternatively, Wood might shift to Miller's position and claim that the key evaluative claims here (whether or not we regard them as moral claims) are all rationally indeterminate. But then, again, if those claims could be sustained, we would have undermined Marx's condemnation of capitalism.

Neither of these is a direction Wood would like to take, but it seems to me that he must take one or the other to avoid my argument about the issue being a trivial verbal one. But then to escape trivia he would have to embrace implausibility, both in the reading of the texts and in claims about what in the real world is the case. It is just not very plausible to claim that *all* moral beliefs must be ideological beliefs that undermine or at least work against our understanding of social reality or that all such moral assessments are so radically indeterminate.[74]

VII

However, let us now assume what I have just questioned—namely, that there is a substantive issue, as Wood believed, dividing Tucker and Wood, on the one hand, and Husami and Young, on the other. If for the sake of argument we accept that assumption, then let us see if Husami or Young can undermine the Tucker-Wood arguments that in spite of their distinctive condemnation of capitalism, Marx and Engels regarded capitalism as just, or at least as not unjust.

Husami began by claiming that Wood and Tucker largely conducted their case on the strength of one passage in *Capital,* which he believed they misread. All the parties to the dispute have fastened on this passage, and they have accused each other of misreading it. Interestingly enough, they also all warned against lifting passages like this out of their immediate textual and theoretical contexts. They all thought, not unsurprisingly, that they in their own analysis had not done that, but believed their adversaries had.[75] The key passage in question is from the first volume of *Capital.*

> The seller of labour power, like the seller of any other commodity, realizes the exchange value, and parts with its use value. He cannot take the one without giving the other. The use-value of labour-power, or, in other words, labor, belongs just as little to its seller, as the value of oil after it has been sold belongs to the dealer that has sold it. The owner of the money has paid the value of a day's labour-power; his, therefore, is the use of it for a day, a day's labour belongs to him. The circumstances, that on the one hand the daily sustenance of labour-power costs only half a day's labour, while on the other hand the very same labour-power can work during the whole day, that consequently the value which its

use during one day creates, is double what he pays for that use, this circumstance is, without doubt, a piece of good luck for the buyer, but by no means an injury to the seller.[76]

The standard English translation cited here renders the German '*Unrecht*' as 'injury.' Wood rendered it, more accurately, as 'injustice.'

Husami did not challenge Wood's translation; instead, Husami claimed that both Tucker and Wood failed to take proper note of the context of this passage. They failed to note that Marx was satirizing capitalism. Marx spoke immediately afterward of the trick of the capitalist and of his laughter. The capitalist has ideologically bamboozled the worker and appropriated surplus value from him (or her). The capitalist's trick has worked, and money has been converted into capital.[77] The trick played on the worker is that of exploiting his labor power.

Husami went on to remark that "Marx elsewhere uses identical and far more explicit language when he characterizes exploitation as 'robbery,' 'usurpation,' 'embezzlement,' 'plunder,' 'booty,' 'theft,' 'snatching,' and 'swindling.'"[78] Husami cited a passage from the *Grundrisse* where Marx spoke of "the theft [*Diebsthal*] of labour time [that is, of surplus value or surplus labour] on which the present wealth is based."[79] Husami then made what he considered his clinching point about the contested passage cited previously. Tucker and Wood failed, he claimed, to note the trick in extracting surplus value and how Marx regarded that trick. Missing this, they were led falsely to assert that Marx gave us to understand in that passage that the worker, although exploited, is not cheated, robbed, or treated unjustly. Husami said that the context of the passage clearly shows, as do many other passages as well, that Marx believed that in exploiting the worker the capitalist robs him. Husami then went on to make the solid conceptual-cum-moral point that "if the capitalist robs the worker, then he appropriates what is not rightfully his own or he appropriates what rightfully belongs to the worker."[80] Thus, "there is no meaningful sense in which the capitalist can simultaneously rob the worker and treat him justly."[81]

In his response, Wood stuck with his reading and tried to give grounds for rejecting Husami's reading. Wood agreed that "Marx finds it ironic that capital's appropriation of surplus value is just."[82] But Wood interpreted the irony differently, and indeed plausibly, in accord with his own claim that Marx regarded all ascriptions of justice and injustice as mode-of-production dependent and thus—for anyone who properly understands them as bits of moral ideology—as claims that are apologetically worthless. They are claims that can have no transhistorical or transmode-of-production validity and no critical force. Marx's irony, Wood claimed, was in the recognition that "the defenders of capitalism have been hoodwinked by ideological nonsense about right and justice."[83] But Wood thought (pace Husami) that when Marx said that capital's appropriation of surplus value is "by no means an injustice" to the worker that Marx was "speaking in his own person";

that he was not being ironical; and that he meant exactly what he said. Wood argued, correctly I believe, that while Marx indeed was in a satirizing dialogue with the vulgar economists, by the time he came to the paragraph from which the quotation is taken, he was giving his "*own* theory of the origin of surplus value, his own account of why the capitalist's 'trick' succeeds."[84] The capitalist, as a practical businessperson, proceeds actually (although unwittingly) in accordance with Marx's account. This is not, of course, to say that in his (or her) ideological thinking he or she has a picture of surplus value. There is *knowing how* and *knowing that*. The practical businessperson has the former. We must distinguish the picture he has of his activity from his purposive business activity. It is in the former where the businessperson is a victim of ideology. Perhaps, most crucially here, there is Wood's parting remark that if we do not take this passage straightforwardly as an endorsement of Marx's own explanation of surplus value, it is difficult to see what his theory of surplus value could be.

I think that Wood is right in his claim about how to read this passage.[85] The context makes reasonably clear that Marx was *not* being ironical in claiming that it is "by no means in injustice to the seller," although it is difficult to be sure. Moreover, this does look like a straightforward statement of how the labor theory of value applies here.

However, things do not always go Wood's way. Wood did not respond to Husami's key argument about Marx's use of 'trick' in the passage that followed the one previously cited. Wood did not give us reasons for believing that set alongside other parallel remarks by Marx this does not, as it appears to do, give us grounds for believing that Marx thought that such a production mode, with such production relations, robs the worker of something that in a more just sytem would be rightfully his or hers and that therefore this capitalist mode of production perpetrated an injustice against the worker.[86] That is the key point that Wood needs to meet, and he did not meet it in his response to Husami's direct criticism on this point or indeed, as far as I can see, elsewhere.

VIII

Husami went on to develop an alternative account of Marx on justice, but before I turn to that, and as a way of helping to give it added force, I want to remark on another reading of that crucial passage from Marx's *Capital* made by Gary Young.[87] Young first remarked that it appears to be the case that we must choose between (a) asserting that for Marx extraction of surplus value is unjust and (b) asserting "that Marx's condemnation of capitalist exploitation has nothing whatever to do with justice or injustice." It looks as if we must either say Marx was blatantly inconsistent or that we must abandon one of these claims. Concerning this Young remarked significantly:

The key to this apparent contradiction lies in the fact that when he says that capitalists rob workers, Marx is evaluating the direct production process with its extraction of surplus value. In passages such as the one just quoted, however, he is speaking of what is just or unjust to persons in their roles as buyers and sellers, as parties to exchange transactions. The exchange between each capitalist and worker, taken by itself, is just. . . . The capitalist purchases labor power "at its full price, so that equivalent is exchanged for equivalent." Yet nonetheless, and contrary to Tucker's interpretation, the process of direct production involves theft, because "there is not a single atom of" surplus value "that does not owe its existence to unpaid labor" of workers.[88]

Generally, in considering whether in Marx there actually is a critique of *capitalist production* as unjust, as distinct from his critique of the falseness and the ideological distortion of bourgeois pictures of capitalist production, we should recognize that issues about the justice of capitalist production should be divided as follows: (a) Is the process of circulation and especially the wage exchange internal to capitalism just, and (b) is the extraction of surplus value from the workers in direct production just?[89] In the passage from *Capital* that we have been discussing, Marx said that in the wage exchange there is no injustice. But how then are we to understand Marx's remarks, in the next paragraph, that the "trick has at last succeeded: money has been converted into capital"? We do so by seeing how a capitalist relation of production comes into place so that surplus value can be extracted.[90] But this involves the exploitation of workers, and now what is at issue is whether it is correct to assert that the production system is just, not whether the system of circulation is just.

With this vital distinction in mind we should turn to Husami's own account of Marx on justice. Husami maintained that "in his mature works" Marx developed "at length his empirical theory of the distribution of wealth and income under capitalism."[91] Husami's picture drew on a distinction like the one we have just seen Young make, only Husami stressed that the two aspects of justice are closely related. He further maintained that they cannot be adequately understood in isolation one from the other. Husami put his point as follows:

Every mode of production involves a corresponding mode of distribution. Actually every mode of production involves two basic types of distribution: (1) the distribution of the means of production (or of productive wealth) and (2) the distribution of the annual product of society (or of the annual income) among the population. Marx holds that the distribution of wealth and of income are related by the dialectical category of reciprocal action (*Wechselwirkung*) or bilateral causation. Given a certain distribution of productive wealth in, for example, class society, there results a certain distribution of income among the various classes. And, reciprocally, the distribution of income reacts upon and reinforces the prevailing distribution of wealth. It should be emphasized that the distribution of

income cannot be considered separately from the distribution of wealth—
except "in the shallowest conception."[92]

Husami believed that in *The Critique of the Gotha Programme* we
have the "*locus classicus of Marx's* treatment of distributive justice,"
a conception Wood fiercely criticized.[93] In speaking of distributive
justice Husami referred to the distribution of the annual product among
the population, and he concentrated particularly on the distribution
of income between workers and capitalists. "Distributive justice is
concerned with the moral evaluation of particularly distributions."[94]
The standards of distributive justice "define *inter alia* how wealth and
income ought to be distributed in measuring the moral desirability of
actual distributions."[95] He thought that in *The Critique of the Gotha
Programme* Marx advanced a theory that specified such standards. In
talking about what could constitute a just distribution of the products
of labor, Marx articulated two principles of *distributive justice:* "distribution according to labor contribution and distribution according to
need."[96] They are not principles sub specie aeternitatis, not 'eternal
principles of justice'; they are principles "to be realized in post-
capitalist society" that are taken as "suitable for adoption by a proletarian
party."[97] Moreover, we can say, Husami contended (as did Young) that
whole social formations are higher or lower, more fully human and
more just societies, depending on which principles of justice their
modes of production make applicable to the lives of human beings
generally in such social formations.[98]
    Husami argued, as I have just remarked, that these maxims are
taken by Marx to be principles of justice for a post-capitalist society.
The question whether we can, on Marx's grounds, ask if the capitalist
system is just or unjust may well come, in part, to asking whether we
can justifiably and intelligently evaluate capitalist distributions of wealth
and income "in terms of these distributive standards," that is, the
standards of *The Critique of the Gotha Programme.* However, we have
here to contend with the Tucker-Wood thesis and, more generally, with
the considerations of a Marxian sociology of morals, which on some
readings sides with the Tucker-Wood thesis in suggesting that morality,
including thinking about the rationality of moral claims or moral
reasoning, is specific to its social context. If this is so, we cannot, as
Husami claimed Marx believed, legitimately "evaluate capitalist practices by post-capitalist or proletarian standards."[99]
    We need, in probing this, first to ask whether or not Marx could
consistently make such transepochal evaluations in accordance with
the conceptions of ideology and the sociology of morals contained in
his historical materialism. Could he consistently, and did he in fact,
either explicitly or implicitly use what (begging some questions for
the moment) we will call the standards of justice articulated in *The
Critique of the Gotha Programme,* or any other post-capitalist standards,
to evaluate the justice of capitalism? Husami argued that (a) Marx did

and (b) in doing so he was not being inconsistent. I shall follow out
the central portions of his arguments here and attempt to show that
Wood has not succeeded in undermining them.

In *The Critique of the Gotha Programme,* Marx discussed in some
detail the workings and qualifications of what Husami took to be Marx's
principle of distributive justice for the first phase of communist society,
the pattern of distribution being, *"To each according to his labor
contribution."*[100] Husami pointed out that on Marx's account not all
of the total social product is to be so distributed. Deductions must
be made for future generations; for keeping up productive capacity;
for insurance against emergencies and disasters; for social consumption
such as the meeting of social needs (for example, health and education);
and for caring for those unable to work, the very young, the old, and
the infirm. But after such deductions are made, the remainder of the
social product is to be allocated on the basis of labor contribution.

Husami took Marx to be saying that these socialist principles of
justice, for all their defects, mark an advance "over the capitalist
distribution of wealth and income."[101] By abolishing private ownership
and control of the means of production, and by stressing social ownership
and control in a world in which everyone is a worker and no class
differences are recognized, "socialism establishes the principle of equal
right by removing asymmetrical power relations or irregularities associated with social classes and their attendant privileges."[102] There
will indeed be differential income rewards associated with different
labor contributions, but they will not solidify into new class differ-
entiations or even into social strata because (a) this differential income
cannot be passed on from generation to generation and (b) because
deductions for *social* needs precede individual income distribution.
These social needs for education, health care, and culture will grow
as the new society develops, thereby making it the case that there will
not be sufficient left of the total product to make for great differentials
in individual income for individual consumption. There will not be a
basis here for the existence of inequalities, including the reemergence
of inequalities in social and political power. All these features mark
a clear advance over capitalist principles of justice.

Another ground for claiming that socialist principles of justice are
an advance over capitalist ones lies in the simple fact that socialism
will "end class exploitation."[103] There will no longer be any way of
extracting surplus value. The deductions are made by "the associated
producers in the interests of the associated producers for the common
satisfaction of their needs."[104]

With a different rationale for production—production for needs rather
than production for capital accumulation—we will come to have
distributive principles that serve to meet the needs of the associated
producers rather than principles of justice designed as a system of
entitlements to protect capitalist productive property rights. This dif-

ferent productive system will afford us the basis for a different distributive system. There will be no appropriation of the products of anyone's labor by a non-working class for its own benefit. This cannot happen under socialism, and thus there can be no such exploitation under socialism. This again marks an advance toward a more just social order than we have under capitalism. Husami claimed that such considerations show that in *The Critique of the Gotha Programme* Marx accepted the legitimacy of morally assessing capitalist society. Marx showed the defects of capitalism and indicated the direction in which a society must go in order to become a more just society.

This leading principle of justice for the first phase of communism (sometimes called the socialist phase) still leaves much to be desired, and as the social wealth of the society progresses, this phase will be replaced, in a second higher phase of communism, with a different and still more adequate leading principle of distributive justice. The defects of the principles of socialist justice for the first phase of communist society are (a) that "human beings are treated one-sidedly as workers" and "their individuality is ignored"; (b) that for utilitarian reasons, but for *otherwise* morally irrelevant reasons, different individuals are still differentially rewarded, not because their needs are different but because of their unequal productive contributions, rooted in their unequal physical and mental endowments; and (c) that there is still material inequality and a failure to take into consideration in social distribution under the first phase the fact that equal labor contributors, as well as unequal ones, will still not infrequently have different needs.

There are, in short, defects in this society that will lead us, when the productive forces are sufficiently developed, to try forming a still more just society where everyone's needs, different as they are, will (as far as possible) be equally met, where those who are more gifted and more energetic by nature will no longer be favored over those who are not, as is the case in a lower phase of communism. The lower phase treats natural entitlements to relative social advantages as morally acceptable in a society that still has scarcities and still bears the birthmarks of its emergence from the capitalist womb. A new kind of human being and a radically different society cannot come about in a day. But Marx, as much as Jean-Jacques Rousseau, recognized that we must have a new kind of human being if such a just society is to ever come into existence and be sustained.

The distributive principle of justice of such a developed communist society reads: 'From each according to their ability, to each according to their needs.' It makes "the satisfaction of a person's needs—hence the full development of individuality—its guiding principle."[105] This is an advance over the distributive arrangements of the earlier phase of communist society. Now the individuality of workers, in a world in which everyone is a worker, can, for the first time in history, be fully taken into consideration. The whole person (*totaler Mensch*) is taken into consideration with all of his or her distinctive needs; his or her ultimate need for self-realization (*Selbstverwirklichung*) will be fully met in the distributive arrangements of society.

To be able to implement the (alleged) distributive principle, 'From each according to his ability, to each according to his needs' requires, Marx was perfectly aware, a very considerable material abundance. In such a society of abundance, there will remain, and properly so Marx argued, in a way liberals such as Isaiah Berlin and Ralf Dahrendorf should applaud, different people taking different things because they have different needs, and there will be no attempt at all to mold them into a gray sameness.[106] Marx rejected the inequality "which creates privilege and accepts only that inequality which allows for the development of individuality."[107] Furthermore, Marx would not accept any "arithmetic equality of rewards" because under such a system "some people would receive less than they need for the free, all-round development of individuality" that Marx advocated.[108] Marx's preoccupation with *equal* concern for the lives of *all* humans, and for their free and full development, led him to reject a strict equality of reward. The thing to recognize, on such a conception, is that everyone's life matters and everyone's life matters equally.

We can see from looking at the program of *The Critique of the Gotha Programme* that, pace Wood, Marx set out socialist principles of justice for evaluating capitalist institutions and indeed for evaluating the whole capitalist system. There is a non-equivalence and injustice in the distribution of income and wealth between workers and owners all along the line in capitalist societies. In the first place, Husami argued, workers do not even get the value of their labor power. Even if we could assume that they did, there is, under capitalism, the injustice of a system in which there is a "despoliation or exploitation of labor power."[109] Moreover, there is a non-equivalence in capitalism between contribution and reward. It is in such things that capitalist injustice consists. A socialist model of society, by contrast, gives us a model of society, achievable with the appropriate development of the productive forces, in which such injustices do not obtain. This give us grounds for assessing the capitalist system.

Wood did not accept any of this. He thought Husami had "seriously misread the entire section of *The Critique of the Gotha Programme* from which he draws his cherished proletarian principles of justice."[110] Husami, Wood claimed, missed Marx's recognition that demands for justice, where they are intelligible, are tied to particular modes of production. We can say, given a particular mode of production, what is or is not just relative to that mode of production. But we cannot coherently say of the whole mode of production itself whether it is just or unjust.[111] Wood significantly cited the following passage from *The Critique of the Gotha Programme:*

Do not the bourgeois assert that the present distribution is just? And isn't it in fact the only just distribution on the basis of the present mode of production? Are economic relations (*okonomische Verhaltnisse*) ruled by juridical concepts (*Rechtverhaltnisse*) or do not, on the contrary, juridical relations (*Rechtsverhaltnisse*) arise out of economic ones?[112]

He then interpreted that passage as follows:

I take it that the second and third questions are to be answered affirmatively. The bourgeois do assert that the present distribution is just, and it is in fact the only just distribution on the basis of the present mode of production. Lest we think that the justice or injustice of a system of distribution might be judged on some other basis, the implied answer to the further rhetorical question reminds us that juridical concepts do not rule economic relations but, on the contrary, juridical relations (the actual justice or injustice of transactions between agents of production) do arise out of economic ones. All this accords perfectly with Marx's account of the justice of transaction as presented in *Capital*.[113]

Wood speculated that Husami, faced with this argument, might try to respond that here "Marx is not talking about what is really just or unjust but about what is 'considered just' on the basis of the present mode of production or about the 'dominant conceptions' of justice."[114] But this, if it were true of Marx, Wood argued, would muddy his critique of the moralizing socialists—for example, the Lassalleans— who drew up the Gotha Programme. Where, Wood asked, if that is what Marx was claiming, would he disagree with them? They did not deny that the present distribution is commonly *considered* to be just. What the Lassalleans did say was that whether or not it is considered just, the distribution must *really* be just according to a *correct conception of justice*. But then, Wood argued, it looks as if Marx were in reality agreeing with the Gotha Programme in its demand for a just distribution. Marx disagreed, on this reading, with the details of it, but agreed with its *utopian* aims and manner of conceptualizing the situation. What Husami didn't see, Wood claimed, is that Marx was functioning in this context as a *critic of morality,* much in the general manner of Friedrich Nietzsche, and not as an articulator of a socialist normative ethic or socialist principles of justice. Marx was not setting out a morality at all, not even an iconoclastic one. He was, Wood would have it, rejecting the Lassallean claim that there are rational principles of just distribution for determining the justice of whole societies.[115] We cannot coherently assert or deny that capitalism is just or that socialism is just or that any whole social orientation or way of life is just or unjust. Husami, Wood claimed, made Marx sound *not* like a trenchant critic of the Gotha Programme, but like someone who was trying to do much the same thing, only hopefully a little better.

However, not everything is so neatly open and shut. Husami could reply—and I believe should reply—that in the light of how Marx developed his own account of historical materialism, the passage Wood cited from *The Critique of the Gotha Programme* is, taken as it is out of context, seriously misleading and Wood's use of it reflects that. Of course, a historical materialist is going to say that juridical concepts arise out of and are determined by or at least strongly conditioned by economic relations. And of course Marx, as a historical materialist, would deny that economic relations are ruled by juridical ones, but he would also realize that bases need superstructures; that juridical relations can and do influence economic relations; and that although the economic relations are primary, there is a dialectical category of reciprocal action (*Wechselwirkung*) or bilateral causation between base and superstructure. So there is no reason to think that Marx would believe that principles of justice are causally inefficacious. Only if we have reason to believe that *all* the principles of distributive justice are ideological and distort our understanding of ourselves and our society, have we reason to reject what appears to be the case—namely, that here Marx was (a) articulating (as Lenin took him to be articulating) principles of justice that could and would be acted on in the various phases of communist society and (b) indicating to us ways in which a capitalist society would have to be transformed—indeed, transformed right out of capitalism—in order to become a thoroughly just society.[116]

It need not and should not be the case that questions of distribution be considered independently of questions of production. Husami actually fastened on questions of distribution in his discussion, but it is clear from his reading of Marx here that Husami thought that these two questions are closely intertwined. Marx himself made it very clear in *The Critique of the Gotha Programme,* in passages immediately following his discussion of the principles of justice, or, so as to not beg any questions, the putative principles of justice, that he thought these questions are closely intertwined, although he did stress, and indeed I believe rightly, that the structure of the "distribution of the conditions of production" is the more central consideration.[117]

Perhaps we can establish on the basis of other passages that Marx believed, as Wood claimed, that (a) *all* morality is moral ideology and as such (on one standard, although I believe mistaken, Marxist reading of 'ideology') distorts our self-understanding of ourselves as well as our understanding of social reality and (b) that consequently all commitment to principles of justice, no matter what their form and content and no matter with what background beliefs they are associated, are 'ideological shuffles.' Certainly much of our common morality is indeed moral ideology and for the reasons that Wood persuasively drew to our attention.[118] It is also at least arguably the case that this holds as well for much that moral philosophers say. Ideological thinking and reaction are very pervasive features of our lives. But that does not show that it all is or that moral conceptions are, as Wood believed, necessarily ideological.

It is important to realize that there is no claim in *The Critique of the Gotha Programme* that *all* morality is moral ideology. Wood simply read that into the text, although there are indeed earlier texts of Marx that do give that impression. (Here it is very important to give them a careful reading.) Until the ideological-through-and-through reading is established, if indeed it can be established, and all this ideology is shown to be invariably distortive, I do not see why we cannot and indeed should not read those passages as Husami read them—namely, as articulations of principles of justice.[119]

Marx's critique of the Lassallean view of justice was directed at the Lassalleans' treatment of distribution *independently* of production, at their lack of stress on class struggle, and at their naive assumptions about the extent of the efficacy of moralizing. But all of this could be accepted without rejecting the idea, which the text seems at least to bear out, that those principles of just distribution that Husami isolated from *The Critique of the Gotha Programme* were regarded by Marx as morally appropriate and reasonable principles of justice appropriate to different phases of communism and that a capitalist society, in comparison to a society governed by such principles of justice, could be considered a thoroughly unjust society.

Wood believed, contrary to Husami, that in *The Critique of the Gotha Programme* Marx introduced the principles 'To each according to his labor time' and 'From each according to his ability, to each according to his needs' in "the context of *predicting* what distribution will be like once the workers have taken control."[120] Wood contended there is no textual evidence for either Husami's claim that these principles are (a) presented as principles suitable for adoption by a proletarian party or (b) "intended as 'proletarian' principles of justice against which Marx is measuring capitalist distribution and (implicitly) declaring it to be unjust."[121] We have already discussed (b) and, if we do answer (b) as Wood did, it would indeed be difficult to believe Marx could have intended (a). However, if we answer (b) as Husami did and as I am inclined to, (a) (pace Wood) becomes plausible as one of Marx's intentions in setting out these distributional principles in *The Critique of the Gotha Programme*. So a lot rides on (b).

Without returning to my earlier arguments about (b), I would like to note here the implausibility of Wood's claim that Marx was *only* predicting what the future will be like. He was indeed making such a prediction, but the context also makes clear that 'from each according to his ability, to each according to his needs' is also a ringing declaration of what Marx took to be a central principle that should govern the relations among human beings in a fully communist society. It is surely not *only* a prediction, although it is indeed that.

It is true that Marx, as well as Engels in his *Anti-Dühring*, attacked what he took to be a radical egalitarianism that would urge a *strict equality* in which everyone would be literally treated identically.[122] It

is doubtful if any egalitarian, radical or otherwise, ever held such a
view, but if egalitarians did, their views would surely be mistaken in
light of reasons Marx brought to the fore—namely, that such 'strictly
egalitarian' principles do not treat people as individuals with differing
needs. Such principles would, if instantiated, undermine a quite legitimate individuality that has nothing to do with bourgeois individualism. The stress on 'to each according to his needs' is an important
advance over earlier conceptions of justice. This stress acknowledges
and gives conceptual and moral space for autonomy, individuality, and
equality—all key ideals of progressive thinking.

Wood returned to the question of *moral ideology*. He took it that
Marx's basic criticism of Section 3 of the Gotha Programme "is that
demands phrased in terms of right and justice should not be included
in a working class program at all."[123] The passage I think Wood was
referring to does give *some* support to his reading. This passage, which
follows immediately after the famous paragraph concluding with the
dictum, 'From each according to his ability, to each according to his
needs' and supposedly shows that justice-talk and rights-talk are so
much ideological twaddle, reads as follows:

> I have dealt more at length with the "undiminished proceeds of labour,"
> on the one hand, and with "equal right" and "fair distribution" on the
> other, in order to show what a crime it is to attempt, on the one hand,
> to force on our Party again, as dogmas, ideas which in a certain period
> had some meaning but have now become obsolete verbal rubbish, while
> again perverting, on the other, the realistic outlook, which it cost so
> much effort to instill into the Party but which has now taken root in it,
> by means of ideological nonsense about right and other trash so common
> among the democrats and French Socialists.[124]

Wood's reading certainly is a possible reading. Marx was indeed
contemptuous of the moralizing of the 'true socialists' and regarded
it as dangerous nonsense that might confuse the proletariat. But I am
still inclined to think that Husami's reading is closer to the truth here.
I would take it, by setting the paragraph in the light of the whole
discussion of Section 3 of *The Critique of the Gotha Programme,* that
Marx was *not* saying that 'to each according to his labor time' and 'to
each according to his needs' are "ideological nonsense about rights."[125]
Rather, the ideological nonsense about rights is evident, albeit unwittingly, in the talk about rights and fair distribution found in propositions
1 and 3 of the Gotha Programme—propositions that Marx criticized
and then contrasted with his own principles. It is the Lassallean's
sloppy and confused moral-talk that it would be a crime for the party
to adopt. Marx need not and would not naturally be read as also
asserting this about his own principles. (Note, by the way, the confident,
straightforward moral judgment about Lassallean moral-talk being a
crime. Marx felt perfectly free to make that judgment without a trace

of hesitation, embarrassment, or irony. How then could he have believed that *all* moral-talk is ideological or simply ideological?)

In addition to his remarks about how sloppy the Lassallean talk about justice was, Marx's previous analysis reveals the moral arguments of the Lassallean to be atavistic as well. The Lassalleans were in effect trying to get a revolutionary party—a party engaged in a class struggle to revolutionize the existing relations of production—to adopt essentially Rousseauean conceptions of morality applicable to older forms of society, but hardly applicable to the new post-capitalist society struggling to come into being. Such ideas "in a certain period had some meaning but have now become obsolete mental rubbish."[126] But that they at one time had meaning (significance) suggests at least that in that context they had some point or validity. But if this is true, exactly the same thing could be true of Marx's maxims, maxims Husami believed to be proletarian principles of justice. Moreover, these two communist principles clearly apply to different phases of communist society, and just as the Rousseauean principles had some point, significance, and validity at an earlier time and for a society differently situated, so, for such communist or socialist societies, such proletarian principles could serve as legitimate norms. At least the passage mentioning 'ideological nonsense' does not show that these two communist principles are not so viewed, and if they indeed were not so viewed by Marx, as seems at least plausible, it would make Wood's argument here utterly mystifying.

It should also be remarked that the stress on the importance for the party of a "realistic outlook" should not be taken to mean that Marx was advocating what later bourgeois theoreticians characterized as a *wertfrei* end-of-ideology outlook, which, in its *posture* of normative neutrality, will neither avow nor defend any normative claims.[127] The realistic outlook that Marx referred to is an outlook well grounded in a proper economic understanding of the situation and with a good understanding of historical materialism, class antagonisms, and the dialectical method. Such a sociologically realistic position need not be a position, as Wood suggested it is, that has no principles of justice and denies there can be proletarian ones. It is indeed true, as Marx remarked earlier in *The Critique of the Gotha Programme,* that "socialist sectarians" have "the most varied notions about 'fair' distribution."[128] But it doesn't follow from this that Marxists, at least some of whom are surely not regarded by Marx as socialist sectarians, must have such varied notions. Egalitarian conceptions of justice, as Marx put it, are "constantly stigmatized by a bourgeois limitation."[129] But Marx's argument was that we should transcend such *bourgeois* conceptions of right. Yet this should not be understood to mean that he was advocating that we transcend thinking in terms of moral notions altogether, including conceptions of justice.

Wood remarked that "Marx emphasizes that there will be different (progressively higher) systems of distribution in post-capitalist society in order to drive home the point that no demands based on specific principles of distribution can really represent long term goals of the working class."[130] Surely Marx, as the last two paragraphs of his discussion of Section 3 of the Gotha Programme make plain, believed that it is a mistake to turn our attention to distribution without recognizing that "any distribution whatever of the means of consumption is only a consequence of the distribution of the conditions of production themselves."[131] Indeed, not to see that is not only a mistake; it is also an ideologically distorting mistake. But this does not mean that he did not think that the distributive principles he had just articulated were not, as principles closely related to questions about production, the correct ones for two different phases of a future communist society. Marx was, and I think quite properly, too much of a Hegelian, and particularly a Hegelian about morality, to talk of eternal principles or principles sub specie aeternitatis.[132] But this does not mean that he thought that the working class would not need principles of justice in the future communist society and that he did not think 'To each according to his needs' did not apply as far down the road as he could envision.[133] It seems to me that it is Wood, not Husami, who misread Part I of *The Critique of the Gotha Programme*. Marx articulated there some "cherished proletarian principles of justice" that he did not view as ideological nonsense.[134]

After discussing the role of 'To each according to his labor time' in earlier phases of communism, and after pointing out both its limitations, which reflected its bourgeois origins, and its appropriateness for a "communist society" that has not "*developed* on its own foundations but, on the contrary, just . . . [emerged] from capitalist society" and "thus in every respect, economically, morally and intellectually, is still stamped with birthmarks of the old society," Marx, several passages later, remarked, "But these defects are inevitable in the first phase of communist society as it is when it has just emerged after prolonged birth pangs from capitalist society. Right can never be higher than the economic structure of society and its cultural development conditioned thereby."[135]

The last sentence in this quotation reveals Marx's historical materialist foundations, and Wood was entirely right in stressing that we must take to heart such claims if we would understand Marx on justice. But we must also, to understand Marx properly, avoid a *historicist* reading of him.[136] If that last sentence were quoted in isolation, it would surely suggest such a reading. But its context makes it clear that this is not how it is to be taken. Marx was *not* telling us that our moral *under-standing,* our *understanding* of right and wrong, can never transcend the relations of production we are immersed in; rather, he was telling us that the principles of right that will be dominant in a given society will be those of the dominant relations of production of the society in which such principles are articulated. He was making the sociology of morals point that those distinctly moral notions—which also happen to be ideological notions—are ones that will call the tune in mass culture and will be utilized by the consciousness industry.[137] But this is not to say anything about what an individual's moral understanding must be. It is not to say anything about what Marx's or Engel's own moral understanding must have been. It is not to claim that anyone's moral understanding, no matter what self-understanding he or she has, must be so ideologically distorted. That morality is ideology *prone* does not mean that morality is *necessarily* ideological. Marx could not have been giving a thoroughly historicist reading of moral understanding, for then he, who was himself immersed in the economic structure of capitalist society, could not have coherently claimed that he understood the "defects" that are "inevitable in the first phase of communist society" in relation to right and justice, nor could he have understood the alternative principles to be appealed to in a higher phase of communism.

Finally, given that the bourgeois view of right is *not* the historical materialist conception that 'right can never be higher than the economic structure of society, and its cultural developed conditioned thereby,' Marx, if he really was such a historicist, could not have understood that either. But he felt no embarrassment about his ability to articulate these things and to make judgments about them. He did not write as if he were trying to hint at or show the unsayable. Thus, it cannot be the case that Marx intended a relativist, historicist reading of that claim. We must not confuse Karl Marx with Karl Mannheim.

Notes

1. Robert Tucker, *The Marxian Revolutionary Idea* (New York: Norton, 1969), p. 18; Robert Tucker, *Philosophy and the Myth of Karl Marx* (Cambridge: Cambridge University Press, 1961), pp. 11–27; Allen W. Wood, "The Marxian Critique of Justice," *Philosophy and Public Affairs* 1 (1972-73):224–282; and Allen W. Wood, "Marx on Right and Justice," *Philosophy and Public Affairs* 8 (1978-79):267–295. Tucker did not turn to a reexamination of his views, but Wood did in his *Karl Marx* (London: Routledge & Kegan Paul, 1982), pp. 125–156; his "Marx's Immoralism," in Bernard Chavance (ed.), *Marx en Perspective* (Paris: Editions de l'Ecole des Haute Etudes en Sciences Sociales, 1985), pp. 681–698; and in his "Justice and Class Interests," *Philosophica* 33, no. 1 (1984):9–32.
2. Tucker, *Philosophy and Myth in Karl Marx,* p. 18.
3. Ibid.
4. Ibid.
5. Karl Marx, *Capital,* vol. 1 (Moscow: Progress Publishers, 1961), p. 194.
6. Tucker, *Philosophy and Myth in Karl Marx,* pp. 18–19.
7. Ibid., p. 223.
8. Wood, "The Marxian Critique of Justice," p. 261.
9. Marx, *Capital,* vol. 1, p. 537.
10. Wood, "The Marxian Critique of Justice," p. 261.

11. Ibid., both quotes on p. 262.

12. Ibid.

13. Ibid.

14. Ibid.

15. Ibid., pp. 262–263. Note the key passage from Marx, *Capital,* vol. 1, pp. 194, 583.

16. Wood, "The Marxian Critique of Justice," p. 263.

17. Ibid., pp. 263–264.

18. Ibid., p. 265.

19. Marx, *Capital,* vol. 1, p. 265.

20. Wood, "The Marxian Critique of Justice," p. 265.

21. Ibid.

22. Karl Marx, *The Critique of the Gotha Programme,* in *The Marx-Engels Reader,* 2nd ed., Robert C. Tucker (ed.) (New York: Norton, 1978), p. 528.

23. Wood, "The Marxian Critique of Justice," p. 268.

24. *The Marx-Engels Reader,* p. 527.

25. Marx, *Selected Works,* volume 2 (Moscow: Progress Publishers, 1969), p. 23.

26. Wood, "The Marxian Critique of Justice," p. 272.

27. Ibid.

28. Ibid., p. 268.

29. Ibid.

30. Jon Elster, *Making Sense of Marx* (Cambridge: Cambridge University Press, 1985), pp. 196–233; G. A. Cohen, "Review of Wood's *Karl Marx,*" *Mind* 92, no. 367 (July 1983):442–445; Gary Young, "Justice and Capitalist Production: Marx and Bourgeois Ideology," *Canadian Journal of Philosophy* 8 (1978):421–454; and Gary Young, "Doing Marx Justice," *Canadian Journal of Philosphy,* Supplementary vol. 7 (1981):251–268.

31. Karl Marx, *Grundrisse,* D. McLellan (ed.) (London: Harper & Row, 1971), p. 69. Also see Richard Miller's critique of Wood's account in Richard Miller, *Analyzing Marx* (Princeton, N.J.: Princeton University Press, 1985), pp. 61–95.

32. Karl Marx, *Writings of the Young Marx on Philosophy and Society* (Garden City, N.Y.: Doubleday, 1967), p. 426.

33. Richard Miller criticized this account for being too functionalist. Historical materialism is not a mechanical determinism, although it may be a determinism. There is no reason to believe that causal relations just go from base to superstructure. Is it plausible to believe, even granted a fairly orthodox Cohenist reading of historical materialism, that moral critique will never have *any* effect concerning what happens in the world? I do not think that it is, and I do not think that it is at all an implication of Cohen's views.

34. Joe McCarney, *The Real World of Ideology* (Brighton, England: Harvester Press, 1980).

35. Wood, "Marx on Right and Justice," p. 278.

36. Ibid.

37. Ibid.

38. Ibid.

39. Ibid., pp. 276–278.

40. Ibid., p. 279.

41. Ibid.

42. Ibid., p. 276.

43. Ibid., p. 270.

44. Ibid.

45. Ibid.

46. Elster, *Making Sense of Marx*, argued that such a claim comes close to being self-contradictory.

47. Wood, "The Marxian Critique of Justice," p. 271.

48. Elster, *Making Sense of Marx*.

49. Charles Taylor, "The Politics of the Steady State," *New Universities Quarterly* 32 (1979):45–68.

50. I do not mean to suggest that the appropriate concept of justice here is a juridical one. Ziyad I. Husami, in his "Marx on Distributive Justice," *Philosophy and Public Affairs* 8 (1978-79):27–64, had powerful arguments against Wood's views here.

51. Wood, "The Marxian Critique of Justice," p. 275.

52. See here Husami's arguments for not sticking with an exclusively juridical understanding of justice in "Marx on Distributive Justice."

53. See Elster on justice here in *Making Sense of Marx;* and Cohen, "Review of Wood's *Karl Marx*."

54. At the very end of Wood's response to Husami there seemed to be some recognition of this possibility. See Wood, "Marx on Right and Justice."

55. For a discussion of wide reflective equilibrium see John Rawls, "The Independence of Moral Theory," *Proceedings and Addresses of the American Philosophical Association* 47b (1974-75):5–22; Norman Daniels, "Wide Reflective Equilibrium and Theory Acceptance in Ethics," *The Journal of Philosophy* 76 (1979):256–282; Norman Daniels, "Reflective Equilibrium and Archimedean Points," *Canadian Journal of Philosophy* 10, no. 1 (March 1980):83–103; Kai Nielsen, *Equality and Liberty: A Defense of Radical Egalitarianism* (Totowa, N.J.: Rowman and Allanheld, 1985), Chapter 2; and Kai Nielsen, "Searching for an Emancipatory Perspective: Wide Reflective Equilibrium and the Hermeneutical Circle," in Evan Simpson (ed.), *Anti-Foundationalism and Practical Reasoning* (Edmonton, Alberta: Academic Printing and Publishing, 1987), pp. 143–163.

56. Husami, "Marx on Distributive Justice"; Young, "Justice and Capitalist Production"; Young, "Doing Marx Justice"; Wood, "Marx on Right and Justice"; Wood, *Karl Marx;* and Derek Allen, "Marx and Engels on the Distributive Justice of Capitalism," *Canadian Journal of Philosophy,* Supplementary vol. 7 (1981):221–250.

57. Wood, "The Marxian Critique of Justice," p. 269.

58. Ibid., p. 273.

59. Ibid., p. 272.

60. Ibid., p. 279. For a dissenting view on exploitation see G. A. Cohen, "The Labor Theory of Value and the Concept of Exploitation," in Marshall Cohen et al. (eds.), *Marx, Justice and History* (Princeton, N.J.: Princeton University Press, 1979), pp. 135–157.

61. Wood, "The Marxian Critique of Justice," p. 280. But see Allen here on the idea of its being rhetorical in "Marx and Engels on the Distributive Justice of Capitalism."

62. Husami, "Marx on Distributive Justice."

63. Miller, *Analyzing Marx,* pp. 15–97.

64. Husami, "Marx on Distributive Justice," p. 29.

65. See Wood and his citation from Marx in his "Justice and Class Interests," pp. 9–10. Still, there is Cohen's puzzle about how Marx could say that, given other things he said.

66. Miller, *Analyzing Marx,* pp. 60–95. See also Steven Lukes's chapter on justice in his *Marx and Morality* (London: Routledge & Kegan Paul, 1985).

67. That Marx was a critic of morality is perfectly unproblematic. But the claim that he made no moral judgments himself or that he rejected all morality as irrational is another matter.

68. Wood, "A Marxian Critique of Justice," p. 267.

69. Ibid.

70. Wood, "Marx's Immoralism," pp. 681–698; and his "Justice and Class Interests," pp. 9–32.

71. George Brenkert, *Marx's Ethics of Freedom* (London: Routledge & Kegan Paul, 1983); and Norman Geras, "On Marx and Justice," *New Left Review* 150 (March/April 1985):47–89. For sceptical remarks about such talk see John Anderson's essays on Marx in his *Studies in Empirical Philosophical* (Sydney: Angus & Robertson, 1962), pp. 292–327.

72. Wood, it should be noted, did make a spirited defense of himself in the last part of his "Marx on Right and Justice." But it has been just this part of his account that seemed the most unconvincing to most of the people with whom I have discussed it.

73. Miller, *Analyzing Marx,* pp. 15–97.

74. Kai Nielsen, "Marx and Moral Ideology," *African Philosophical Inquiry* 1, no. 1 (January 1987):71–86.

75. Husami, "Marx on Distributive Justice," p. 19; and Wood, "A Marxian Critique of Justice." Both Wood and Allen gave other instances, but it is far from clear whether they improved their case substantially.

76. Marx, *Capital,* vol. 1, pp. 193–194.

77. Ibid., p. 194.

78. Husami, "Marx on Distributive Justice," p. 30. See also G. A. Cohen, "Freedom, Justice and Capitalism," *New Left Review* 5, no. 126 (1981):3–16.

79. Karl Marx, *Grundrisse* (Harmondsworth, England: Penguin Books, 1973), p. 705.

80. This point was also made by Cohen in "Freedom, Justice and Capitalism"; and in his review of Wood's *Karl Marx.*

81. Husami, "Marx on Distributive Justice," p. 30. Again, Cohen, "Freedom, Justice and Capitalism."

82. Husami, ibid., p. 31.

83. Ibid. See Wood, "Marx on Right and Justice," pp. 273–274.

84. Wood, ibid., p. 274.

85. See also Allen, "Marx and Engels on the Distributive Justice of Capitalism."

86. Cohen, "Review of Wood's *Karl Marx,*" pp. 442–445. But for complications see Elster's and Lukes's response to that argument of Cohen. Elster, *Making Sense of Marx;* and Lukes, *Marx and Morality.*

87. Marx, *Capital,* vol. 1, pp. 193–194. See Gary Young, "Justice and Capitalist Production," pp. 421–454.

88. Young, ibid., p. 434.

89. Ibid., p. 431.

90. Marx, *Capital,* vol. 1, p. 194.

91. Husami, "Marx on Distributive Justice," p. 31. Young referred here especially to the introduction to the *Grundrisse* and to *Capital,* vol. 3, Chapter 51. See also G. A. Cohen's final long substantial footnote (footnote 7) of his "Freedom, Justice and Capitalism."

92. Husami, "Marx on Distributive Justice," p. 31. See Marx, *Grundrisse* (1971 ed.), p. 96.

93. Wood believed, mistakenly I think, that Husami radically misread *The Critique of the Gotha Programme.* See Wood, "Marx on Right and Justice." For extended further remarks on how Wood believed *The Critique of the Gotha Programme* should be read, see his "Marx on Equality," in John Mepham and David Hillel-Ruben (eds.) *Issues in Marxist Philosophy,* vol. 4 (Brighton, England: Harvester Press, 1982). I have criticized Wood's account in my "Marx, Morality and Egalitarianism," *Ratio* 28, no. 1 (1986):56–69.

94. Husami, "Marx on Distributive Justice," p. 31.

95. Ibid.

96. Ibid.

97. Ibid.

98. See also Elster, *Making Sense of Marx;* and his "Exploitation, Freedom and Justice," in J. R. Pennock and J. W. Chapman (eds.), *Marxism* (New York: New York University Press, 1982), pp. 277–304.

99. Husami, "Marx on Distributive Justice," p. 32. Note that this claim is independent of the claim that all moral propositions are ideological.

100. Ibid., p. 42.

101. Ibid., p. 41.

102. Ibid., p. 43.

103. There are, however, other forms of exploitation. See Andrew Levine, *Arguing for Socialism* (London: Routledge & Kegan Paul, 1984), pp. 65–77, 85–98.

104. Husami, "Marx on Distributive Justice," p. 43.

105. Ibid., p. 45.

106. Nielsen, *Equality and Liberty.*

107. Husami, "Marx on Distributive Justice," p. 46.

108. Ibid.

109. Ibid., p. 47.

110. Wood, "Marx on Right and Justice," p. 292. See also pp. 274–275, 291–292.

111. William McBride, "The Concept of Justice in Marx, Engels and Others," *Ethics* 85 (1974-75):321–343.

112. Karl Marx, *Marx-Engels Werke,* vol. 19 (Berlin: Dietz Verlag, 1959), p. 18. Wood, "Marx on Right and Justice," pp. 274–275.

113. Wood, ibid.

114. Ibid., p. ˙275.

115. Wood, "Marx's Immoralism."

116. V. I. Lenin, *Selected Works,* vol. 2 (Moscow: Progress Publishers, 1970), pp. 283–376. For documentation of this see Chapter 4.

117. *The Marx-Engels Reader,* pp. 531–532.

118. Wood, "Marx's Immoralism"; and "Justice and Class Interests."

119. Nielsen, "Marx and Moral Ideology."

120. Wood, "Marx on Right and Justice," p. 291.

121. Ibid.

122. Frederick Engels, *Anti-Dühring,* Emile Burns (trans.) (New York: International Publishers, 1939), Chapters 9–11, Chapter 3.

123. Wood, "Marx on Right and Justice," p. 292.

124. *The Marx-Engels Reader,* p. 531.

125. Ibid., pp. 528–532.

126. Ibid., p. 531. This also fits in well with Engels's line of reasoning about morality in *Anti-Dühring.*

127. Wood, it should be said, did not take Marx to be a normatively neutral social scientist. See Wood, "Marx's Immoralism."

128. *The Marx-Engels Reader,* p. 528.

129. Ibid., p. 530.

130. Wood, "Marx on Right and Justice," p. 292.

131. *The Marx-Engels Reader,* p. 531.

132. Wood, "Marx's Immoralism."

133. See here Wood's and as well Allen Buchanan's remarks about being beyond the circumstances of justice. See Wood, "The Marxian Critique of Justice," pp. 274–282; Allen Buchanan, "The Marxian Critique of Justice and Rights," *Canadian Journal of Philosophy,* Supplementary vol. 7 (1981):269–306.

134. This is also how Engels and Lenin understood them. For documentation of this see Chapter 4 herein.

135. *The Marx-Engels Reader,* pp. 528, 531.

136. Alan Gilbert, "Marx's Moral Realism: Eudaimonism and Moral Progress," in Terence Ball and James Farr (eds.), *After Marx* (Cambridge: Cambridge University Press, 1984), pp. 154–183.

137. Nielsen, "Marx and Moral Ideology."

9

On Marx Not Being an Egalitarian

In the Anglo-American philosophical world in recent years there has been a flood of articles and several books roughly in the analytical mode explicating, interpreting, and not infrequently defending Marx and some forms of Marxism. This analytical Marxism, as I shall call it, has had powerful, and indeed importantly differing, statements in the work of G. A. Cohen, Robert Paul Wolff, Jon Elster, Allen Wood, and Richard Miller.[1] I want to fasten here on some facets of the work of Allen Wood and Richard Miller, which, if these facets are in the main correct, will make us think about both morality and moral philosophy in radically new ways.[2] Wood and Miller perceptively saw Marx as remaining of the party of humanity, while he was driven by that very humanitarianism to an attempt to not only subvert moralism but also to subvert morality itself and its, for we moderns, characteristically egalitarian commitments. Wood and Miller viewed Marx, and Engels as well, as critics of morality who rejected egalitarianism (and appeals to equality generally), moralism, and the very moral point of view itself. Wood and Miller argued this thesis in a nuanced way with subtlety and philosophical sophistication and with a thorough familiarity with the work of Marx and Engels.

All that notwithstanding, I shall argue that Wood and Miller were mistaken. Marx and Engels were indeed critics of morality, denouncers of moralism, and suspicious (to my mind rightly) of moral philosophy, but they did not seek to subvert morality; they did not reject morality; and they did not reject the moral point of view or equality. (They could, of course, have done this last thing without doing any of these other things.) It is neither the case (or so I shall argue), on the one hand, that Marx and Engels did these things or, on the other, that those who take Marx seriously should do those things or indeed that anyone should.[3] I shall in the process argue that Marx and Engels did not reject an egalitarian morality. Indeed, I shall make the rather more traditional, contrasting claim that Marx and Engels, as heirs to the Enlightenment, were committed to a belief in equality. I shall begin with a discussion of Miller's views and then turn to a somewhat briefer discussion of Wood's views where they do not overlap with Miller's.

Richard Miller in his *Analyzing Marx* concluded that Marx believed that "morality is not an appropriate basis for political action and social choice" (M, 96). Marx realized that the motivations that sustain them in their socialism in the first place and the motivations that continue to sustain them in their socialism are not infrequently moral. Indeed, many people "support workers' struggles and socialist goals . . . on the grounds that capitalism is unjust." Yet it is also the case, at least on Miller's reading, that Marx rejected "justice and allied standards as an irrational basis for socialism" (M, 94). What we need instead is an understanding of how the capitalist system works, of alternatives, of politics, and a commitment to shrewd and determined political action. But—and this is paradoxical given the foregoing claim—in that very political struggle Miller saw Marx as believing that if "socialism is to be created, people must be led to take on burdens out of a concern for others" (M, 94). Moreover, "these others may not be confined to the circle of family and intimate friends" (M, 94).

According to Miller, when Marx spoke of the Paris Commune, it was patently evident that the Communards who risked their necks had no good reason to believe that their families and close friends would profit by their actions. These actions were not analogous to figuring out some clever way of having an automobile crash so that your death will look accidental and your family can collect a bundle. Marx urged that in the class struggles to bring on social change that people do in fact come to have "a concern for others that motivates the taking up of burdens" (M, 94). Similar motivations must obtain during the process of the consolidation of socialism. Even when we get to communism where the rule, "From each according to ability, to each according to needs" is in order, that very rule presupposes not only circumstances of full abundance but certain human motivations. It assumes that people will care about each other and that communists, for the most part, will not be free riders. If that does not obtain, the rule cannot work. Human nature is not infinitely malleable, but it is malleable, and as the springs of social wealth flow ever more freely with the development of the forces of production, the consolidation of socialism, and the slow emergence of communism, the level of mutual concern will rise, and people will increasingly find their self-respect not merely in individual activities but also in various forms of striving for a common good.

This, at least, on the surface, looks like a Marx claiming a moral base for communism. But that is not the message Miller wished to convey. Marx, Miller claimed, in spite of the foregoing, rejected the adoption of the moral point of view. Still, he was not skeptical about being able under optimal circumstances to identify a common good. We are not, under all circumstances, Hobbesists who seek to maximize self-interest and to be free riders wherever we prudently can (M, 95). Here we do have a sharp conflict with contemporary conservative thinkers such as David Gauthier, Milton Friedman, and Robert Nozick. These conservatives do think we have, at least if we are rational, roughly Hobbesist motivations. And indeed in our society, particularly among a lot of those who think they are being tough-minded, there is a common belief that this is just the way people are wired.

Marx, by contrast, thought that this attitude is more ideological than tough-minded and says more about human nature in certain circumstances than about human nature *sans phrase*. One of the things to ask, of course, is whether this is too rosy a picture of human nature, which is surely a possibility, but it is also not inconceivable that the other view is too jaded a view of human nature and is in reality pseudo-realistic.

Still the preceding argument does not help us to see how Marx is to be taken as rejecting the moral point of view. Indeed, the argument would lead us to conclude (pace Miller) that he was affirming it. Be that as it may, assuming for the moment such a rejection, the preceding remarks about concern for one another and the importance of having non-egoistic motivations reduce the paradox of speaking, as Miller did, of Marx abandoning morality. The foregoing explains Miller's closing sentences of his section in *Analyzing Marx* on morality where he remarked, "Decent people do not abandon morality if they believe that the alternative is narrow self-interest, caprice or bloodthirsty *Realpolitik*" (M, 96). Miller argued that here Marx made a special philosophical contribution. He described "an outlook for politics that is decent without being moral" (M, 96–97). Without these explanations for motivations in political struggle, it sounds self-contradictory to speak of decent people abandoning morality or, to speak, as Miller did, 'of an outlook for politics that is decent without being moral' or of a 'human rejection of morality.' It may still sound paradoxical, as it certainly does to me, but it is not as paradoxical as it would otherwise be.

We should also remember in this connection that Miller spoke of Marx mounting an "attack on the moral point of view as the basis for *social* choice" (M, 52, emphasis mine). Miller did not say that Marx was launching an attack on the appropriateness of moral relations in the face-to-face relations among individuals—for example, about how I should relate to my students in giving them grades or relate to them in class. Rather, the question of abandoning morality comes up in a political context where we are considering how institutions are to be judged. Miller is talking about a "replacement for the moral point of view in politics." Miller's claim is that reflective and humane people who have a Marxist outlook on how social structures function will come or at least should come to appreciate that the moral point of view is inappropriate in those domains (M, 7, see also 10). Marx provided us, Miller contended, instead with a reasoned critique of morality. He provided us, that is, with arguments designed to show that appealing to morality in political contexts tends to impede working-class emancipation, which is the basis for human emancipation.

II

We have started at the end of Miller's analysis of Marx on morality. Now that we see where he wanted to go and have, at least partially, obviated the paradox and what may even be the offense of this anti-morality stance, let us now return to the beginning and see how Miller built up his case. In *Analyzing Marx,* the first page of the first chapter on morality, entitled "Against Morality," contained his version of the perplexity that almost everyone feels when they start thinking about Marx and morality:

> In a very broad sense, Marx is a moralist, and sometimes a stern one: he offers a rationale for conduct that sometimes requires self-sacrifice in the interests of others. That the conduct he calls for will sometimes involve "self-sacrificing heroism" is epitomized in his praise of the "heaven storming" men and women who defended the Paris Commune. His concern that conduct be reasonable and well-informed is clear when he distinguishes the scientific basis for present-day workers' struggles from the "fantastic," even "reactionary" misconceptions supporting workers' struggles in the past.
>
> At the same time, Marx often explicitly attacks morality and fundamental moral notions. He accepts the charge that "Communism . . . abolishes . . . all morality, instead of constituting [it] on a new basis." The materialist theory of ideology is supposed to have "shattered the basis of all morality, whether the morality of asceticism or of enjoyment." Talk of "equal right" and "fair distribution" is, he says, "a crime," forcing "on our Party . . . obsolete verbal rubbish . . . ideological nonsense about right and other trash so common among the democrats and French Socialists" (M, 15).

Marx, or at least Miller's Marx, as we have seen, abandoned morality, rejected morality. Yet, as Miller remarked initially, it "is not clear in just what ways Marx's outlook differs from morality" (M, 16). Miller, however, thought that in complete faithfulness to Marx's texts we can all the same extract from Marx "plausible arguments for a radical departure from the moral point of view, at least as philosophers have conceived it" (M, 16). It is this claim that I am going to challenge.

In characterizing the moral point of view, which Miller took Marx to be rejecting, Marx was speaking of what Miller called "morality, in the narrower sense," in which it is "distinct from self-interest, class interest, national interest or purely aesthetic concerns." Here Miller conceived of morality in a sense similar to how morality was conceived by Immanuel Kant, J. S. Mill, and Henry Sidgwick or by contemporary philosophers such as Kurt Baier, John Rawls, or Geoffrey Warnock and not in the extremely broad senses advocated by R. M. Hare, H. D. Monro, or J. L. Mackie.[4]

Morality, as Miller characterized it—and this characterization seems to me distinctively modern—has three basic characteristics: *equality, general norms,* and *universality.* In speaking of *equality* Miller had in mind a conception where "to be shown equal concern or respect or afforded equal status is to come under the net of equality" (M, 17). A necessary condition for taking the moral point of view is to reason in accordance with that conception of equality. (Note this makes an Aristocratic morality or a Nietzschean elitist morality self-contradictory. That is, to put it minimially, very strange. Miller consistently referred to Nietzsche as an amoralist. I think Miller should have instead talked of a distinctively modernist conception of morality. Still, I also think nothing of any considerable substance turns on this.)

However, the exact, or inexact, nature of the standard of equality is a matter of controversy. Still, Miller would have it, morality requires "some standard of equality . . . to be the ultimate basis for resolving conflicts among different people's interests" (M, 17). The standard may be the minimal one that is not infrequently called 'moral equality'— a standard at least nominally accepted by radical egalitarians such as Richard Norman and Kai Nielsen, liberal egalitarians such as John Rawls and Ronald Dworkin, and conservatives such as Robert Nozick and F. H. Hayek—namely, that the life of everyone matters and matters equally.[5] The radical egalitarians and the liberal egalitarians would then go on to argue for more determinate conceptions of equality, conceptions that the conservatives would reject, but all modernist moralists, radicals, liberals, and conservatives alike, would at least nominally accept this minimal conception of moral equality.[6]

Miller then spoke of what he took to be the second necessary condition for taking the moral point of view—namely, general norms. To believe in general norms or that there are general norms is to believe that there are rules of conduct, to be applied "to the specific facts of the case at hand," that "are valid in all societies in which there is a point to resolving political disputes by moral appeal" (M, 17). Such norms have a point and are justified, Miller maintained, in those "societies in which cooperation benefits almost everyone" but where it is still also the case that "scarcity is liable to give rise to conflicts" (M, 17). Someone, taking the moral point of view, believes that the "right resolution of any major political issue would result from applying such valid general norms to the specific facts of the case at hand" (M, 17). But this rests very heavily on the very questionable assumption that cooperation, even in class societies, benefits everyone.

The third feature is *universality,* which Miller characterized as the claim that "anyone who rationally reflects on relevant facts and arguments will accept these rules"—the general norms and the very general standard of equality—"if he or she has the normal range of emotions" (M, 17).

In saying Marx was anti-moral, that Marx advanced a non-morality, was a critic of morality, abandoned morality, rejected morality, and the like, Miller meant that Marx argued "against all three principles as inappropriate to choosing what basic institutions to pursue" (M, 17). Miller was, however, willing to admit that "there is still a broad sense in which Marx does describe a moral point of view" (M, 17). By way of explanation, Miller stressed the importance that Marx attributed to concern for each other, to class solidarity across national boundaries, to revolutionary self-sacrifice, to distinctions between decency and indecency, and to "what ought to be done and what ought not to have a role in a Marxist outlook" (M, 17). Marx's arguments, which are primarily directed at choices among political and economic systems, "may leave standing most ordinary morality concerning actions toward individuals" (M, 17). But, particularly when we think of morality in a social and political context, we think of it as a point of view that impartially adjudicates the interests of everyone alike in the manner Miller described where there is a commitment to equality, to general norms, and to universalization. Particularly when someone rejects all three conditions, he or she is, Miller argued, clearly rejecting the moral point of view. Moreover, even if morality were considered much more concrete and not necessarily attached to some of these features, Marx still should be seen as attacking very deep-seated and pervasive modernist philosophical assumptions about what morality is (M, 18). However, once it is put that way the claim is not nearly so radical or so iconoclastic.

Where we reflectively adopt, as most of us do, morality so conceived with those three essential features, we do so for decent and humane reasons. Marx would persuade us, argued Miller, that if we get clear about what our social world is like, the very motivations that attract us to morality so impersonally and impartially conceived will lead us to reject morality when we are reasonably clear about the consequences for political decisions of sticking with the moral point of view (M, 18).

III

Let us try to get a purchase on this striking claim of Miller's. Very often Marx is thought of as an egalitarian, as is Engels. Miller, like

Allen Wood, viewed both Marx and Engels as critics of morality who rejected egalitarianism and a commitment to equality. To quell this paradox, Miller first displayed what he called the "grains of truth that Marx discerns in the demand for equality" (M, 19). Without this, as he realized, his interpretation "will seem perverse" (M, 19).

What, Miller argued, superficially looks like egalitarianism is Marx's advocacy of "social arrangements that would . . . make people much more equal in power and enjoyment than they are at present" (M, 19).[7] During an early transition period to socialism, a standard for equal right for each to receive according to his or her labor would be the key norm of such social arrangements. But the value of such a standard is that it would "enhance people's lives, not that it would conform to some ultimate standard of equality" (M, 14).

Right here at the beginning, I have to demur, for although it is indeed true that such a standard of equal right is appealed to in order to enhance people's lives, there is also in that very standard an appeal to *fairness*. By this I mean that there is a demand that as far as possible social structures be put in place that are designed to enhance the lives of *everyone,* where it is taken as a fundamental guiding principle that the life of each person counts and counts equally. Marx would no doubt say, in ways I take to be compatible with the preceding remarks, that proletarians come first, but he also thought that proletarian emancipation would make a general emancipation possible. There could be no truly human society for human beings without proletarian emancipation. Because proletarian emancipation provides the causal mechanisms for a more general liberation and because proletarians are exploited and oppressed, particular attention should be directed to them. But this would be true for *anyone* who is or becomes a proletarian (something that would take a determinate description). For by universalizability, anyone properly so described must be so treated.

This emancipation of the oppressed is, in the Marxian view, the vehicle for the eventual enhancement of the lives of everyone. Proletarians are not simply being picked out as proletarians. They are picked out and given special attention in virtue of what the proletarian class is, what the condition of proletarians are, and what the potential of that class is. Because of this underlying concern with the lives of everyone, it seems to me (pace Miller and Wood as well) that Marx accepted a standard of equality. This is a condition of life that is a fundamental desideratum. Marx was, of course, aware of the ideological uses of talk of equality and sought to counter them. But this does not mean that he did not make the deep, underlying assumption (with its attached commitments) to which I have just referred. If what I have said is on the mark, then I have undermined the claim that Marx was making anti-moral arguments against equality.

One can argue that way against Miller, and still agree with Miller's important point that under socialism and communism, most people are less dominated, more in possession of their lives, since they are better able to develop their capacities in light of their own assessments of their needs. Moreover, people's interactions will be governed to a greater extent than now by mutual well-wishing and concern. In Marx's view, these goods of freedom and reciprocity are what most people have really desired, when they have made "equality" their battle cry (M, 19).

I would only demur at saying that this is what they really desired and not equality as well and this for the fairness considerations stated just before that citation. What most people want is a gestalt of freedom, equality, and reciprocity. Most people not only want freedom; they want equal freedom for everyone (which I would call a central element of fairness). They not only want reciprocity, but they want it extended to everyone without anyone stinting or being stinted here. Here egalitarian justice (equality) rides with reciprocity as well as freedom. These are ultimate desiderata to be attained by human beings, and under normal circumstances these desiderata come as a package.

Equality can only rightly be taken to be a one-sided ideal if it is not considered part of a gestalt with these things! But egalitarians have never, as Miller implicitly recognized, taken equality to be the *sole* ultimate value.[8] However, if equality is left out in the articulation of ultimate ethical ideals (if it is not part of the firmament of ultimate values), and if this in turn is translated into social policy, there very well could be a pervasive unfairness in society that will be manifested in an extensive freedom for some privileged elite and oppression in various degrees of severity for many or lack of liberty for a despised minority while there is considerable liberty for the vast majority. If the former situation is thought to be hyperbolic for people in advanced industrial societies with bourgeois democratic traditions, consider first what the lives of the vast majority of people are, what they could be, and how little control most people actually have over their lives. However, if we only stress freedom and well-being and do not also stress that it is vital to consider the distribution of these things, then it might well be thought that there is nothing very wrong with such a society. To bring out in a perspicuous way how all is not well in such a society, it is essential to point out how equality is an essential element in the firmament of values.

IV

I have challenged Miller right at the start of his making a case for Marx's rejection of the norm of equality. If I am right, Miller cannot get his arguments off the ground for he missed a sense of egalitarian justice and a sense of fairness that are in the thought of Marx and Engels as well as in some liberal thought (in J. S. Mill and John Rawls[9]). Miller, in effect, failed to recognize that freedom, reciprocity, and equality can all be both intrinsic goods and instrumental goods. It is not that equality is of instrumental value *only* to freedom and reciprocity, which are in turn only intrinsically valuable. All three of these fundamental values are intrinsically valuable, but they are not infrequently instrumentally valuable as well.

However, let us now set those arguments aside and examine in some detail Miller's arguments against the various forms of equality he discussed where they are taken, as he put it, "as ultimate bases for decision in the face of inescapable conflicts in class-divided societies" (M, 20). (This, as my preceding arguments should have made clear, is not how I think equality or a commitment to egalitarianism should be construed. But I am letting that go for the sake of continuing the argument.)

He first considered, as an "ultimate demand for equality," *equal distribution*—namely, a standard that would require "that all possess an equal bundle of goods, resources or opportunities" (M, 19). Miller claimed that Marx and Engels rightly believed that such a "general demand for equal goods and powers" is a mistaken conception, inappropriate "as the main standard for judging social arrangements" (M, 20). Our main concern is, or at least should be, Miller maintained, with well-being and humane social relations, "not with equal distribution as such" (M, 20). Such a demand for equality could, in theory at least, lead to a crude barracks communism—a Spartan communism where equality is achieved "by dragging everyone down to a common, low level" (M, 20). What we want, or at least should want, instead, Miller claimed, is for the springs of social wealth to flow freely. We want, if we would reflect morally, human flourishing and human well-being and not a society where people envy one person having a little more than another. We want a society of mutual concern and respect and we want an end to exploitation; we do not need a society, Miller maintained, where the goodies of the world are equally distributed. We should not want a world where there is a pervasive concern about whether one person has a little more than another. That is, in effect, to place a premium on envy.

I think what is left out here is very like what I have just criticized. When we think about what Marx called a truly human society we realize that it cannot be such without it also being a just society. In such a society we are concerned not only with mutual concern, respect, and human flourishing, but—and here is where justice comes in—we also are concerned that these conditions hold for everyone and, where possible, equally. We do not want it, as in South Africa, at most for whites only or, as in more modernizing capitalist countries, predominantly for the capitalist class and its allies. (This includes most intelligentsia.) Marx and Engels wanted classlessness, and that entails wanting such conditions of well-being, mutual concern, respect, and non-exploitation to obtain for everyone as far as is possible. Such a sentiment is not, or at least need not be, rooted in envy, in the worry that someone may have a little more than you do. It is rooted rather in a sense of fairness and concern for humankind. What we see is a gestalt or a bevy of fundamental values all mutually interdependent. But if equality is not a part of that gestalt as an ultimate value, we have an incomplete moral scheme, and we could not have a fully classless society where relations of mutual concern for well-being and respect obtained as far as they were achievable.

Miller also attacked in the name of Marx the egalitarian conceptions of the classical anarchists (Pierre-Joseph Proudhon and Mikhail Bakunin) as utopian, which he took as something to be criticized. They aimed to attain in the world a "sufficient equality of resources and opportunities to guarantee full and equal independence for all" (M, 21). What must be obtained, as Miller read the anarchists, is a society of independent producers, none of whom is in a condition of economic (or political) subordination such that he or she must work for others in order to live. But this anarchist conception is atavistic because such a situation is possible only in a society of independent commodity producers. But such a society, if indeed it ever did or even could exist, would lose, among other things, all the productive capacity of cooperative social labor. Moreover, such a society would be so unstable that it could not sustain itself as "a politically decentralized society of independent producers, sufficiently equal in resources that no one economically dominates others" (M, 21). Miller put Marx's critique here powerfully and showed clearly, I believe, how commitments to equal distribution cannot reasonably be construed in this anarchist way, and, in effect, if they are to be maintained, they must be qualified in the light of these remarks by Miller.

> In Marx's view, this ideal is utopian. Sufficient equality of productive resources is ephemeral, at best, in a modern setting of physically interdependent production. The network of production, if carried out by independent units, must be regulated by market mechanisms. Even if the distribution of productive resources is initially equal, luck, if nothing else, will soon create some inequalities. Market mechanisms will magnify the first inequalities, as the rich get richer through economies of scale, thicker cushions against calamity, greater access to credit, and greater capacity to innovate. The eventual result is financial ruin and dispossession of the many and their subordination to the few who come to control the means of production (M, 21).

I think this would shipwreck some of Ronald Dworkin's conceptions of equality as extensively as it would Bakunin's. Be this as it may, Miller's argument surely shows the folly of any attempt at an equal distribution of productive forces. Indeed, it is a crazy kind of individualism as incompatible with capitalism as it is with the socialist conceptions held in common by Marx and Bakunin. If we want the

social conditions essential in modern conditions for the human flourishing of all, then productive property, or at least the crucial bits of
productive property, must be socially owned in a society of cooperative
producers. It cannot be divided up to be individually owned like a
cake might be divided or indeed like many consumer durables can
be divided. Equality in the holding of productive property cannot
come in this way if we want to be even remotely reasonable, although
equality of this kind does show itself in the ultimate control of this
productive property, which under socialism is socially owned. Marx's
conceptions are unequivocally democratic here. Control of productive
property should be firmly in the worker's hands with, through democratic
mechanisms, each worker having, in any final disposition, an equal
say in what is to be done. But this is very different from equally
distributing productive property. Rather, in some indirect and practically
feasible way, equal distribution of *control* of productive property is
the desideratum. (Here effective democratic mechanisms are essential.)
But this clearly requires a restriction on equal distribution of resources.
What we have instead, on the part of an egalitarian, is a claim for the
rightness, under conditions of abundance, of an equal distribution of
those benefits and burdens that coherently, rationally, and indeed rightly
can be individually distributed.

What this would come to would, of course, have to take a careful
reading, a reading that I shall not try to give here, although it seems
to me that one needs to be given and that there are no insuperable
difficulties in doing so. (This, of course, is a promissory note.) There
should, of course, be no evading the fact that we must give such an
egalitarian claim a convincing and perspicuous reading to coherently,
rationally, and rightly make such a claim. It must be a reading, if
egalitarianism is to be maintained that, on the one hand, does not so
limit the domain of equal distribution that it becomes trivial and, on
the other hand, keeps some determinate content in such appeals. We
want, if we are egalitarians and sane, neither equal distribution of
productive property nor (pace Nozick) equal distribution of husbands
and wives.[10]

V

Sometimes egalitarianism and a commitment to equality are cashed in
in terms of equal rights. Miller criticized that account as well, thinking
he had justifiably set distributive equality aside. He thought that "rights-
based equality encounters its own distinctive problems" and that Marx
rejected it and rightly did so (M, 22).[11] Miller thought these problems
should be particularly evident in class-divided societies such as our
own. In such a world there are the conflicting interests of different
groups. In such a situation there are too many rights. Equally basic
rights come into conflict, thereby producing disagreements that are

irresolvable on a rights-based account because there is no super-right
to govern the resolution of such conflicts.

We could, of course, resolve such conflicts by "treating rights as
means for enhancing people's lives not as ultimate standards" (M, 22).
But then we would have departed from a rights-based theory, and we
would no longer be taking an appeal to equal rights as the, or even
an ultimate, standard. To illustrate: The "equal right of all to be left
alone by government and the equal right of all to effective participation
in government are independent and important aspects of rights-based
political equality" (M, 23). In our class-divided societies these two
rights inevitably come into conflict (M, 23). As Miller put it, "Without
collective ownership dominated by a worker's state (with the interference
that entails), economic power becomes concentrated in the hands of
a few, who dominate effective participation in government as a result.
Yet the demand for non-interference is not in general misguided or
purely ideological. Individuality and independence are real needs" (M,
23). If we stay within a rights-based context with an appeal to the
equal rights of people, we have no way of resolving such conflicts.
We feel attracted to both non-subordination and non-interference. What
we should do, Miller argued, is treat both rights as devices for attaining
and securing human well-being and see which stress in particular
situations would best protect that. But this plainly is not to treat an
appeal to rights as ultimate.

The thing, of course, that a rights-based theorist would try by way
of response would be to claim that there is a right or a non-conflicting
set of rights that is sufficiently preeminent "to resolve conflicts without
encountering a contrary equally basic right" (M, 23). Marx in turn
responded that no satisfactory candidate has been brought forth.

Miller, agreeing here with Marx, tried an update on this. He sought
to show that contemporary rights-based accounts such as Rawls's or
Nozick's have not solved Marx's problem (M, 24–26). Rawls's account,
in Miller's judgment, is the really serious contender for such a super-
right. "In Rawls's view, we have an ultimate, equal right to be governed
by principles that we would choose in fair deliberations over rules for
assessing basic institutions" (M, 24).[12] Miller argued that Rawls's account
is too skewed "toward one dimension of rights" to resolve such conflicts
of rights in a non-question begging way (M, 24). There are "honest,
non-violent people with capitalist inclinations," potential Horatio Alger
types. Under the alleged Rawlsian super-right, such Horatio Alger types
"will be denied the opportunity to use all the fruits of their self-
sacrifice to set up and develop factories and farms" (M, 25). The right
to non-interference is overridden; the Rawlsian is not operating under
the principle, 'To each the results of his or her honest toil and exchanges'
(M, 25). It is no answer to these potential Horatio Algers, Miller said
for the Rawlsian to remark "that they would have accepted the relevant
restrictions in fair deliberations" (M, 25). After all, the Horatio Alger

type did not actually consent to the Rawlsian restrictions. The Rawlsian contract is purely hypothetical. Moreover, as Miller put it, it is not the case "that the honest toil principle derives whatever moral force it has from the hypothetical fair deliberations" (M, 13).[13]

Miller did face an objection that comes trippingly on the tongue. Surely, it will be objected, "the right to be governed by rules that would emerge from fair deliberations has more moral weight than the right to the results of honest toil, at least as those principles affect people's lives in the real world" (M, 25). Miller responded to this in a way that seems telling but by no means devastating. He argued that we have no rights-based Archimedean point here. We have no scale to weigh those conflicting rights and come out with that conclusion or any conclusion. "No further standard of equal right seems fit to serve as the balance" (M, 26). Some people's reflective preferences, their considered convictions, their firm pro-attitudes, will favor "the results of fair deliberation" as being more in "accord with the judgment that people have a right to cooperate on fair terms when cooperation is inevitable and the stakes are high" (M, 26). But there are others who will have equally firm reflective preferences, considered convictions, pro-attitudes, toward it being the case that "people have a right to be left alone in their initiatives if they do not interfere with others" (M, 26). People disagree here, and according to Miller there is no general rights claim to which we could appeal that has a rational consensus or any other kind of consensus. This means that we cannot plausibly use a standard of equal rights as an ultimate moral standard in the way some egalitarians would wish.

Perhaps this is right. I share Miller's skepticism about the adequacy of rights-based theories, but I think that he moved too quickly. Suppose we argue, as some libertarian rights-based theorists have, "that there is really only one natural right, namely the equal right of all persons to the most extensive liberty compatible with a like liberty for other persons, and that all other natural rights are species or instances of the right to liberty."[14] Here 'liberty' is probably being construed in the 'negative liberty' sense, but the view *may* be strengthened where 'liberty' is construed in the 'positive liberty' sense as autonomy. But whichever reading we give 'liberty,' why cannot such a very general right be appealed to here as a rights-based standard to be utilized in determining, in connection with our appraisal of the facts in the case, the relative stringency of rights to cooperation and rights to non-interference as well as other possible conflicting rights claims? Why can't it be considered our super-right—the sole natural right, the right we appeal to in assessing the relative stringency of both other rights-claims and other moral or evaluative non-rights claims?

If the Marxist *factual* picture of the world is even near to the mark, it will generally *not* be the case that where we are honoring such a rights claim (such a super-right) that a more extensive liberty will obtain for everyone, or at least for more people than otherwise, if the right to non-interference is given pride of place over the right to fair cooperation. If we are in conditions of reasonable abundance, where the productive forces have been developed to the degree they have been developed in late capitalism and we start with the super-right, the, on that theory, sole natural right, namely, the equal right of all persons to the most extensive liberty compatible with a like liberty for other persons—then giving pride of place to rights of fair cooperation over the right to non-interference when they conflict is more in accord with that single natural right than the non-interference alternative. Where the right to fair cooperation has such pride of place, there will be more liberty around. Where that right trumps the right to non-interference, there will be more liberty for more persons. In any social arrangement where there is an appeal to rights, somebody's liberty will be restricted, but there will be less restriction of liberty where fair cooperation so trumps than with the alternative arrangement. This will obtain in a world in which the interests of each are given equal initial consideration.

Presumably Miller would reply that an appeal to such a natural right is arbitrary. It just overrides what is very important to us—namely, "to pursue whatever desires one has without interference" (M, 26). That conviction is indeed a very strong one, particularly in North America, and it is in part captured in the articulation of this sole libertarian natural right, this putative super-right. But something else is added as well in appealing to this super-right—namely, that our own right to extensive liberty must be compatible with a like liberty for *everyone*. This in addition catches a very fundamental, if you will, brute, or rudimentary sense of fairness. To not so reason and act is not to be fair, and to flaunt requirements of fairness is to reject reasoning in accordance with the moral point of view. There is no moral alternative to so reasoning. You can no more ask, *within morality,* "Why be fair when it is not in your individual interests to do so?" than you can ask, "Why be moral?" There are no *moral* alternatives here.[15]

Well then, someone might say, there are non-moral alternatives. An individual or even a determinate group doesn't have to take the moral point of view. To say that they do is to beg the question. But surely a rights-based theory, or indeed any moral theory, does not have to show how it can defeat the amoralist or immoralist—the person indifferent to morality—in order to defend a rights-based theory. Miller's argument, after all, is that rights-based theories rest on a mistake, for there are conflicts of rights that cannot, without a tendentious begging of the question, be resolved within their theories by appealing to some pecking order of rights.

Perhaps that is so, but it is also the case that we have been given some reasons for believing that after all there might be such a super-right capable of such social adjudication. At least we need some further argument from Miller to show that this is not so. We need a stronger argument than anything Miller has given us for concluding that all appeals to rights must be an ideological shuffle. That many are does not prove that all must be.

We must recall that Miller took it to be the case that it is definitive of the moral point of view that we have some kind of commitment to morality and that he took it that Marx was rejecting morality, as a standard for political and social assessment, and that Marx's rejection was done on rational and humane grounds. One of his grounds, as Miller read Marx, is to reject an appeal to equality. I have argued that *if* Miller's rational reconstruction of Marx is correct, then Marx was not justified in rejecting all forms of distributional equality, and his case was not even conclusive against equal rights.

I turn now to a third type of equality that Miller thought Marx rejected—namely, what Miller called an attitudinal equality "requiring that equal concern or respect be shown to all" and a related equality, linked to *impartiality,* "requiring that the general welfare be promoted, without bias toward the good of some" (M, 20). In effect, some of my previous remarks have touched on the topic of impartiality, but I wish now to explicate and then face head on Miller's critique of impartiality.

Suppose we argue for a characteristic utilitarian equality. What is vital in morality, if we take such a perspective, is that we assess things according to their contribution to the general welfare. Our ultimate standard is the general welfare, and the general welfare is to be determined without bias toward some people's well-being. But ought implies can, and, Miller argued, Marx maintained that such an "unbiased determination of the general welfare is impossible" (M, 31). In our societies there are deep and irresolvably conflicting class interests that just in one way or another must be fought out. There is no impartial perspective from which we can adjudicate them. Militant strikes that can improve the condition of the working class may very well "harm the vital interests of factory owners and may drive some into bankruptcy" (M, 30). If the aim, as it is for Marx, is the self-emancipation of the working class, there can be no equal concern here, and there can be no impartial concern for the interests of everyone alike. Such a concern with impartiality in effect plays into the hands of the status quo.

At this point Miller made a set of remarks that seem to me in the way they add up not to be beyond question. He first, in an innocuous enough way, remarked, as a defender of utilitarian equality could as well, that making a ranking "for the distinctive institutions of socialism and communism or arguing that they are superior to capitalist institutions is an activity that humanitarian emotions would sustain" (M, 30–31). But we must also have means, Miller continued, that are appropriate to our ends. However, equality, because of the depth of class conflict, will, if adhered to, stand in the way of humanitarian, egalitarian ends (M, 96). We have something here similar to the paradox of hedonism—

namely, to have a good chance at being happy one should not concentrate on making oneself happy. Analogously, to achieve humanitarian equality in a classless society (the only place where we can attain such equality) we must first struggle to achieve classlessness, and to do that we must *not,* in sharply class-divided societies, show an equal concern for all, but we must seek to further proletarian interests where they clash with capitalist interests or indeed with the interest of any other class. Only by doing that can we attain a more general emancipation. Still, pace Miller, I do not see how this is a rejection of utilitarian equality because as far as anything he has shown is concerned, this remains one of the fundamental ends to be attained. There is only, on Miller's account, the recognition that because of the class nature of our social world, such equality is not to be aimed at *directly.*

Such an attention to modalities no more shows that it is an inappropriate end than hedonism can be proved an inappropriate end by showing that we are not going to succeed in being happy by concentrating on being happy. The underlying aim, for such an egalitarian, is not just that the general welfare is to be determined without bias toward some people's well-being, but the egalitarian wants to see attained a state of affairs where, as far as possible, each person's well-being counts and counts equally in the design of society. We cannot, if there is anything at all to Marx's sociology, have this without classlessness, but if, say because of residual sexism, classlessness will not give us that, we should, egalitarians argue, push, pace Engels, beyond classlessness. Classlessness then would be a necessary but not a sufficient condition for human emancipation. What I do not see is how Miller has shown that such a utilitarian equality is either in conflict with Marx's perspective or an inappropriate moral ideal that humane and knowledgeable people in class societies should reject.

In defense of his denial that such impartial and egalitarian assessments of welfare are possible in class societies, Miller argued that in class societies such as our own conceptions of the good as well as actual judgments as to what is good are various and conflicting. We do not rank our preferences in one way; what makes one set of persons happy will not make another set of persons happy. Even if the majority, where it had good access to information, would have preferences of a socialist sort, that does not mean that there will not be a minority who would have different, equally rational preference schedules. To override the minority here would cause it—or so Miller claimed—acute deprivation. Such overriding can hardly be morally justified and certainly does not square with a commitment to utilitarian equality where the welfare of everyone has equal weight. Some people, perhaps many people, even when they reflect about it carefully with adequate information, will not be socialist persons or rush to be socialist persons. "Some care too deeply, for their own and for others' sake, that striving for personal betterment, free from direct interference, be allowed, even if lack of resources often makes the prospects dim" (M, 34). The institutions of Marx's classless society allow little scope for purely self-interested competition. But for some this "activity is an important positive good" (M, 34). There is no way, Miller argued, to show here that one set of preferences is more rational than another. Some rational human beings will go one way and some go another. Even if under conditions of maximally accurate information most people would be socialistically inclined, this does not show that the majority is right or that the majority is justified in overriding the minority here (M, 34–35).

According to Miller, Marx argued that there is no generally acceptable standard for ranking equally intense enjoyments, varying needs, or different interests. People socialized in different ways will differ here. And we have no yardstick for measuring or ascertaining the morally preferable preferences or the rational preferences. We cannot make the necessary social discriminations without social bias.

> No ranking of all important goods, including, say, leisure as against material income, the enjoyment of competitive striving as against the enjoyment of cooperation, and the chance to occupy the top of hierarchies as against the guarantee of a secure, moderately comfortable life, is faithful to the needs or the reflective desires of all—industrial workers, farmers, investment bankers, housewives, shopkeepers and professors alike (M, 32).

It, Miller claimed, is a myth—perhaps a liberal ideological distortion—to believe that if we had all the relevant data, then we would agree on a ranking. Such a consensus does not exist among people so variously formed and variously situated, and it is not reasonable to expect that one can come to exist in class-divided societies. J. S. Mill's solution, which consists in appealing to the preferences of those who have wide experience, in effect, shows a "bias toward the upper strata who are able to practice such connoisseurship" (M, 32). Mill's "procedure cannot do justice to the connection of the enjoyment of the individuals at any given time with the class relations in which they live" (M, 35).

Marx, I believe, was right to stress the depth and the class nature of the impact of social processes on our basic wants and needs (M, 33). (I do not, of course, say that is the only kind of social influence.) In this connection, Miller argued that if we appeal, à la Mill, to what the experienced person prefers—the person who has a great range of experiences and has the leisure to compare and reflect on those experiences—we do leave the working class and its preferences out and skew things in the direction of the wealthier strata of society.[16] In class struggles and in fighting for social change, we cannot gain such a superior vantage point from which we can, in a rather olympian manner, make moral evaluations. Jürgen Habermas and John Rawls led us down the garden path here. There is no such Archimedean point. We must instead just fight it out in terms of perceived class interests.

If that is all that Miller meant in claiming that Marx rejected egalitarianism and the moral point of view in political struggles, then Miller's claim is *perhaps* on the mark. However, it does seem to me that the Marxist can and should make the following kind of *gedanken* experiment—perhaps it is better to call it a Pascalian wager—namely, that if we come to have a classless society, with the clarity about ourselves and our social relations that this society would bring, then under such circumstances, the prediction goes, people would come to have egalitarian, utilitarian preference schedules. They would adopt attitudes that would favor that all people be shown an equal concern and respect and that the general welfare be promoted in such a way that the interests of everyone are considered equally. The *gedanken* experiment predicts that this is the way people's preference structures will go when they live in conditions of security and abundance and under conditions of undistorted discourse.[17] It seems to me that Mill, Rawls, and Habermas indicated ways in which we can simulate and approximate impartiality without jettisoning the empathetic understanding that will help us adjust for class biases and the like. When we conscientiously attempt to do this, we will come to have such egalitarian attitudes, and this will, I predict, become stronger, more pervasive, and more entrenched the closer we come to actually living in conditions of undistorted discourse under conditions of abundance.

This prediction grows out of some hunches and empirical assumptions that are quite fallible. It seems to me that there is something to the Humean-Smithian-Westermarckian conception of natural sympathies and to Westermarck's belief that, as our tribal myths get eroded, something that goes increasingly with modernity (Weber's progressive disenchantment of the world), the range of our sympathies, as a matter of fact, tend to be gradually extended.

I take it to be a fact that we do tend to care for one another and that our sympathies, with our increased understanding and our experience of the world, do get extended. I also take it as a fact that with all our differences, there are also similarities among us sufficient to make it rather compelling, or at least not unreasonable, for us to say and justifiably believe that where circumstances make it possible without continued oppression of the underclass, we all should be objects, viewed from the point of view of society's concern, of equal concern and respect. Where we come across a particularly depraved individual or a particularly nasty sort, we can hardly avoid acknowledging, if we are reflective and not too neurotic, that there but for the grace of God, go we, which, de-mythologized, comes to believing that there but for better fortune in social upbringing or genetic wiring go we. When we reflect along these lines, and when we have natural sympathies, we will go in an egalitarian way. If we are both Marxists and egalitarians, we will recognize that generally we must favor proletarians over capitalists. But this is principally an instrumental thing with perhaps, for some of us, a bit of justice in restitution thrown in. We want a world in which the proletarian and the capitalist can no longer be viewed as, or indeed be, either capitalist or proletarian, but will be viewed just as human beings in a producer's society where all adult, able-bodied persons prior to their retirement are in some broad sense producers. (I qualify in this way because, among other things, the service sector grows.) The class perspective is instrumental. It is the engine for attaining the classlessness that is necessary for attaining equality and its closely related ideals: autonomy and fraternity.

It might be objected that the stress I put on thought experiments in the last several paragraphs sits badly with the stress I have put all along on the importance of distinguishing between, on the one hand, the sociology of morals and, on the other, the epistemology of morals and moral philosophy more generally. Suppose it is true that people would come to choose and have the attitudes of caring impartiality that I, in hopeful moods, predict they would acquire in undistorted circumstances, why should this sociological fact or psycho-sociological fact (if indeed it is a fact) have any moral relevance? After all, it is just another fact in the world; it is just another item in the sociology of morals.

It is indeed, I respond, an item in the sociology of morals but not *just* any item in the sociology of morals, for, as the ideal observer and contractarian traditions have taught us, such thought experiments under such conditions help specify for us what it would be reasonable to choose or prefer in such ideal circumstances, and part of this would be to specify what we would choose without illusion. But this is a comment in social psychology, as well as a normative comment. We need, however, to be careful that we do not unwittingly cook the books here, thereby reflecting the way our attitudes and beliefs may be, behind our backs, ideologically skewed. We are all deeply at risk here. There is no standing free of our prior conditioning. But the power of this influence will vary from case to case and with the particulars of our conditioning. For some of us, our ideological imprisonment is very deep; others are more fortunate. However, that such ideological bedazzlement cannot be escaped, or largely escaped, by some people (say Marx himself) is not to be taken as a foregone conclusion. Moreover, there is nothing in the canonical parts of Marxism that requires such a pessimistic belief. What we would prefer under conditions of undistorted discourse would (tautologically) give us great clarity about ourselves and would *not* allow us, where we were choosing the design of a society or forging its change, to give pride of place to ourselves, our classmates, members of our tribe, race, and the like.

Equality with these elements is a gestalt that, when the concept of human flourishing is thrown in as well, will give us the central elements in the firmament of values, elements that Miller gave us no good grounds for believing the Marxist tradition should reject. (See here, counting for this, Miller's own remarks on page 36.) Miller reconstructed Marx as saying that our preferences "among social arrangements must be a preference among needs, and the bias cannot be removed in the Millian style" (M, 38). I have argued that Miller did not sustain that claim.

Miller in effect responded to this by arguing that utilitarian equality does not operate with the relative weak premise with which I am operating—namely, to 'give everyone's satisfaction some prima facie weight,' but with the stronger premise, 'Give everyone's interests prima facie equal weight.' As egalitarians we want morality to become, as we move to classlessness, so structured that we will want, in the way I have explicated, to weigh "the satisfaction of desires without bias toward desires of certain people" (M, 37). However, this standard should be qualified with a phrase such as 'prima facie' or 'ceteris paribus' because we run into situations where everyone's desires cannot be satisfied or everyone's needs cannot be met, and then we need to make hard, and sometimes tragic, choices. Fairness (justice) requires that we start out considering everyone's interests alike. But where two interests cannot both be satisfied in a given situation, we must look for morally relevant grounds for favoring one person's interests over another's. Hence, we should not say, 'Give everyone's interests equal weight' but 'Give everyone's interests prima facie equal weight.' But this gesture in the direction of realism is not a departure from equality, from equal concern and respect. For we must consider everyone's interests, give equal initial weight to each person's interests, and, at least in conditions of abundance, seek to satisfy the interests of everyone and satisfy them equally where we can. It provides us *lebensraum* where we cannot satisfy the interests of everyone, although of course the principle itself does not provide the criteria for deciding which interests are to be favored when not all interests can be met.

I think what is important to stress is that Marx, Engels, and indeed Lenin had as an ultimate aim universal human emancipation.[18] However, I think this needs to be given a careful reading. On the one hand, human emancipation does not mean *just* the emancipation of the immense majority, although it does have their emancipation as a central objective. And, on the other hand, human emancipation should not be read so literally that Marx is taken to be claiming that everyone in class societies would be helped by the coming of socialism or communism; this is plainly a flight from reality. About 1 percent of the current population of North America would not be helped, although everything considered, they need not be harmed as much as they are wont to believe. If Marx's empirical picture of the world is even roughly right, there is a far greater thwarting of interests under capitalism than under socialism. But there still are some whose interests would flourish under capitalism more than under socialism (M, 39).

Class interest are essential; the firm protection of proletarian class interests is a strategic instrumental modality that cannot be set aside by anyone who is actually interested in human emancipation. Where the forces of production are sufficient to make socialism a real possibility, we cannot deny that the interests of the proletariat are frequently in sharp conflict with those of the haute bourgeoisie. But still such class interests are instrumentalities to human liberation, whose ideal remains the liberation of every single human being, where in the classless society of the future we are simply regarded as human beings and not as personifications of economic categories: where, viewed now simply as individuals, the life of every human being matters and matters equally. It is a luxury we cannot afford in the midst of class struggle, but it is the end to which the class struggle is directed.

Thus, we are concerned in such a circumstance, where that circumstance is the ideal to be aimed at, with the satisfaction of human interests as such. Furthermore, and vitally, where, even in such a circumstance, not everyone's interests can be satisfied, we are to aim at the most extensive satisfaction of interest possible for as many people as possible, where the interests of everyone must prima facie be given equal consideration. We seek, in short, the greatest possible satisfaction of interests for as many people as possible where everyone's interests have an equal initial weight—that is, each is to count for one and none to count for more than one. (This is a core egalitarian notion.) Alternatively, put in terms of wants, the underlying ideal to be realized in a classless society is this: Everyone is to have as much as possible of whatever it is that she or he wants, and would continue to want with adequate information, reflectively taken to heart, that is compatible with as many people as possible having their wants satisfied in exactly that manner.[19]

I do not want to be misunderstood here. I am not turning Marx into a utopian socialist. Miller quite properly showed Marx to be a revolutionary socialist who clearly saw the necessity of class conflict, which would lead in most circumstances from disguised civil war to open revolution where the proletariat would overthrow the bourgeoisie and begin laying the foundation for a new society—the foundations for what Brecht called the new kindliness. This, as Miller nicely put it, is "not the statement of someone who believes that all resistance to socialism rests on misinformation" (M, 40). Neither Miller's Marx nor my Marx was an economistic Marx or a kind of latter-day Bersteinian. And indeed I do not think Marxists should take such a reformist turn. In such revolutionary struggles "the state in transition from capitalist to classless society 'can be nothing but the revolutionary dictatorship of proletariat'" (M, 40). The state, in the circumstance of consolidating a revolution, must be concerned, as Marx put it, with "intimidating the mass of the bourgeoisie" (M, 40). It is clear from this that Marx believed that the interests of the bourgeoisie "would be offended, deeply and on balance by socialism" (M, 40).

All this is vital to keep steadfastly before our minds, but, as I have been at pains to argue, except in the most literally wooden way this does not mean that Marx was not a believer in universal emancipation in the way I have explicated. His aim was to see a world in which the interests of as many people as possible would be satisfied. That a few capitalists continue to have intransigent interests, which are antithetical to the fulfillment of the interests of the vast mass of humankind, does not mean that the compossible interests of everyone are not to be satisfied.

We can stress, as Miller rightly did, that Marx was a thoroughly political creature who would never acquiesce in economism or reformism; he was without question a thorough revolutionary. Along with that, we should emphasize Marx's sensitivity to the social determination of needs without coming to the conclusion that Marx was rejecting equality and the moral point of view. Some sorting out will help here. It is correct to say that Marx rejected the moral point of view in politics, if what is meant by this is that Marx, as a historical materialist, rejected the historical idealist thesis that we could fundamentally change the world by making, no matter how convincingly, the moral case for the wrongness of a social system (say capitalism).[20] Marx most certainly did not believe that any class-divided social system could be fundamentally changed by such a moral critique. However, there is also a more telling and sophisticated way in which Marx rejected morality in politics. He realized that in the midst of class struggle there are clashes of class interests that cannot be rationally resolved and where sometimes the fair thing to do is not obvious and perhaps even, in some instances, is indeterminate. It will hurt proletarian emancipation to insist that the revolutionary or the worker struggling for her (or his) liberation must always, or even typically, avoid taking any militant action, until she has some tolerably clear idea in the context of her struggle of what fairness comes to or of what morality requires. That is a sure recipe for inaction. It is a mistake to maintain that she must *in that way* always seek to be fair and impartial, to consider the interests of everyone, capitalist and worker alike. Such well-meant moralizing will stand in the way of proletarian emancipation and thus of universal human emancipation. In the name of that very universal emancipation, the workers and their militant allies, cannot, Miller argued, afford to take the moral point of view and must in certain respects reject morality.

All of this to the contrary notwithstanding, there is an equally important way in which Marx was not rejecting the moral point of view, but was guided by that very point of view in specifying the higher stages of communism and in showing why it is desirable. And that conception, far from involving a rejection of equality, is firmly committed to it in a number of important ways, although I also think Marx was right in rejecting morality in the two rather less central ways

I have just specified. But the ways he rejected morality do not show that in the deeper sense I have been concerned to specify that Marx did not stick with morality and indeed an egalitarian morality at that.

VI

Richard Miller was not alone among the important interpreters of Marx on morality in arguing that Marx and Engels were not egalitarians. Allen Wood, most extensively in his "Marx and Equality," also took that line.[21] There is a considerable overlap with Miller, and I will not step in the same river twice. But because I want to read Marx and Engels as egalitarians, and because I think such a reading is important to a Marxist conception of morality, it is incumbent on me to look at Wood's distinct arguments. (His article also had the virtue of helping us get clearer about what is at issue in arguing for or against egalitarianism.)

The first paragraph of Wood's article would lead one to believe that he was going to articulate a position bearing a close family resemblance to the egalitarian Marx I have defended.

A capitalist society for Marx is essentially a class society, a society whose fundamental dynamics are determined by the oppression of one class by another. And of course Marx was always an uncompromising foe of oppression in any form. The fundamental mission of the proletariat as Marx sees it is to abolish class oppression, by abolishing class differences which make it possible. The division of society into classes, however, and especially the oppression of one class by another, always involves striking social inequalities, of wealth and opportunity, of power and prestige, of freedom and self-actualization, of fulfillment and happiness. A classless society, by contrast, would seem to be above all a society of equals, where all share equally in the burdens and benefits of social life. Fighters against oppression in many forms have often viewed their fight as a fight for social equality. They have framed their demands in terms of ideals or principles of equality, whether it be equality of formal legal rights or of their *de facto* recognition by society, or equal opportunity for education and achievement, or an equal share of wealth or well-being (W, 195).

However, like Miller, Wood regarded it as a mistake to believe that Marx was an egalitarian, "a fighter for equality and a believer in classless society because he is a believer in a society of equals" (W, 195). Wood first pointed out that there are "no explicit and unequivocal endorsements of the notion of equality in Marx's writings," and he found "in the writings of both [Marx and Engels] . . . explicit disavowals of egalitarianism and criticisms of it" (W, 195). On the basis of Marx's texts the correct conclusion to draw, according to Wood, is that Marx was an opponent of the ideal of equality, despite the fact that "he is also and not any the less an opponent of all forms of social privilege and oppression" (W, 196).

In discussing Wood's argument that Marx was no defender of equality, I will try to show against Wood that to make the most sense out of Marx in these domains it is important to see him as accepting equality as a *goal*. Wood pointed out helpfully that we can regard equality as a goal or equality as a right and that in many discussions of equality, including some defenses of egalitarianism, these conceptions, unfortunately, get confused. He then remarked:

> Toward equality as a goal, I believe Marx's attitude is one of indifference. We find in his writings no specific criticisms of the attempt to achieve equality in people's status, wealth or well-being. Yet I think it can be shown that Marx does not frame his own conception of a classless society in terms of any goal of equality. Further, I think it is at best highly doubtful that Marx regards social equality as something good or desirable for its own sake (W, 196).

This claim seems very tendentious. It is clear enough that Marx and Engels were against the oppression and servitude of class society and that they wanted this social curse, as one of them put it, lifted from all humankind. They believed that to achieve this we need a classless society that eventually will be a worldwide phenomenon. Moreover, it is not enough that the vast majority achieve that condition of life, but that, as far as possible, *everyone* does so. Marx and Engels wanted a world in which no one would be oppressed or dehumanized or live in conditions of misery. They wanted a world in which people, that is everyone capable of it, could control their own lives, that is be autonomous, and in which human flourishing, including human well-being, would be general. But to have such ideals is to be committed to equality as a goal. That other matters, such as autonomy and well-being, figure centrally does not mean that social equality is not regarded as something good or desirable in itself (something wanted in itself as Georg von Wright would put it), although it does mean that it is not the *sole* intrinsic good. But the recognition that fairness requires, where classlessness is achieved, autonomy for *everyone,* as far as that is possible, and not just widespread autonomy, shows that fairness is thought to have an intrinsic value. Because fairness amounts, in some aspects, to treating people equally in certain ways, equality also has an intrinsic value insofar as it is implied in fairness.

It is important not to forget that things can have both intrinsic value and instrumental value.[22] This is true of the gestalt of values—fairness, equality, autonomy, fraternity, and well-being. Egalitarians have wanted that gestalt.[23] They have not treated equality as the *sole* intrinsic value but as a member of this cluster of fundamental values where, if all people are securely to have any of them, they must come together as a package. It seems to me evident that Marx and Engels, as heirs of

Enlightenment, took the achievement of these ideals to be an ultimate desideratum.[24]

This is also a bourgeois ideal shared with Marxists by progressive bourgeois thinkers. What Marx and Engels did was to show (a) that this ideal is unattainable in class societies; (b) that to try directly to attain it in class societies is a mistake; (c) that a necessary condition for its achievement is the attainment of classlessness; and (d) that the primary thing now is to struggle to destroy capitalism, for only with its destruction can we attain classlessness, and only with classlessness can we attain that cluster of values that, as I see it, define egalitarianism. But these matters I have just mentioned are all instrumental modalities whose value lies precisely in that they can finally produce a world in which the gestalt or cluster of values can possibly be achievable by humankind. But to see things in this way and to have these values is to treat equality as a goal.

Engels did say in a famous passage in his *Anti-Dühring*, which Wood quoted and then commented on, that "the real content of the proletarian demand for equality is the demand for the *abolition of classes*."[25] I consider this a partial specification of what Engels took to be a correct articulation of equality.[26] Wood said this is a natural reading but a mistaken one all the same. The demand for the abolition of classes, Wood argued, is

> not a demand for equality: the notion of equality is not used to formulate this demand. Instead, it is a demand formulated in terms of the Marxian concept of class. Engels' view is that the demand for equality is a confused and outmoded demand, because it is a demand framed in terms of concepts which have been superseded by the more scientific and realistic ones of Marxian social theory. Before this theory existed, and especially during the time when the bourgeoisie was the most progressive social class, the concept of equality may have been the best one available for the purpose of attacking oppressive social relations (especially feudal ones). But now there is no longer any place in the proletarian movement for the notion of equality or for demands framed in terms of it (W, 201).

It seems to me that there is both truth and falsehood in Wood's claim here. There is truth, and not just scientist bias, in the recognition that the concept of class is a more determinate notion, more clearly linked with a determinate social reality, and better integrated into Marx's overall theoretical machinery than is purely moral-talk of equality. This is surely the reason in many contexts for substituting talk of class for talk of equality. It is also true that the notion of equality is not used in the formulation of the demand for classlessness. Rather, as Engels put it, the notion of classlessness is "the true rational content" of demands for equality. But then demands for equality are not dropped, but because they can mean so many things, they are given a more precise formulation in demands for classlessness. But this does not mean, pace Wood, that egalitarianism is rejected or the demand for equality dropped. It is not like the move from talk of God to talk of an unconscious projection of a father figure.

We should also demur at the last passage I quoted from Wood. Marx and Engels did not write, even in their most scientifically demanding work, in a normatively neutral vocabulary. They spoke of the misery of the workers, of ways in which they are oppressed, of inhuman working conditions, of workers' servitude and virtual enslavement. If these evaluative terms are quite in order, as Wood plausibly assumed Marx and Engels thought was the case, then unless we can show that such evaluative terms are out of place in a work of social critique, the use of such normative, appraising conceptions can be perfectly in place in their work, even though these are not scientific conceptions. (Wood did not argue that proper social description and critique cannot use evaluative concepts.)

Talk of equality did occur in Marx and Engels, and it occurred in Lenin as well. They did not always talk about equality in a derisive or ironical manner as ideological. Wood himself cited Engels' description of communism as real equality. Why not consider this talk as legitimate as talk of inhuman conditions and oppression? After all, they are also clearly evaluative conceptions. Indeed, Marx and Engels wished to create and did create a scientific social theory in which they appealed to theoretically central concepts such as class and surplus value. But Marx and Engels also continued to use, quite unself-consciously, ordinary language of an evaluative sort as well with no suggestion that the concepts they expressed were confused or untoward. I see no reason why talk of equality should be excluded from their ranks. Moreover, talk of equality has the added advantage of being clearly linked in their specifications to talk of class. But if someone were to ask why classlessness matters so much, the answer from Marx and Engels would be in terms of the emancipation of the working class. With classlessness there would be an end to oppression, the achievement of autonomy, humane reciprocal human relations, and, generally, the enhancement of well-being for vastly more people then obtains under capitalism. Oppression, inhumane conditions, human misery, and the undermining of autonomy go with the existence of classes. A classless world *under conditions of abundance* would allow almost everyone a greater human flourishing without being destructive of the life of anyone, setting anyone into conditions of misery, or making anyone's well-being impossible. However, the haute bourgeoisie might, at least by some lights, have a lesser well-being. After all, it would no longer rule society and run things in its own interests, and members of the bourgeoisie would no longer be able to live in great splendor. Still, there is no need to reduce the former haute bourgeoisie to misery or servitude in the transition society or beyond, so that their well-being becomes impossible. Moreover, it must not be forgotten that this group is only a miniscule part of the society, although the bourgeoisie is the core of the capitalist class without which the latter could not sustain its class integrity and hegemony.

In such a classless world human autonomy would be much more extensive: equal liberty would no longer have institutional impediments as it has in class societies. Classlessness would enhance human well-being, increase autonomy, and make these things possible for everyone, barring certain physical or unalterable psychological impediments. With this very stress on classlessness, we also get a commitment to equality. The more extensive autonomy of classlessness necessarily requires a greater equality because autonomy is undermined where some people have power over others. To avoid this in those domains closely related to power (such as wealth), people must stand to each other in conditions of rough equality. The rationale for that is not envy, as conservatives believe, but the attainment and preservation of human autonomy for as many people as possible. In these ways classlessness carries with it a commitment to equality. Someone, unless he or she is confused, who thinks classlessness is important will also think social equality is important. Unless we want to attribute a very extensive confusion to Marx and Engels, we cannot say that they valued classlessness and did not value equality as a goal.

There *may* be status, sexual, and racial inequalities, in a way neither Marx nor Engels anticipated, that will remain after the abolition of class distinctions.[27] However, it may still be possible eventually to eliminate these inequalities. Classlessness, it is reasonable to expect, will create the conditions in which their elimination is more readily achievable. Engels may very well have been mistaken in believing that the elimination of classes will give us *all* the equality we might reasonably want. Still when he said that "the 'elimination of social and political inequality' is . . . a very questionable phrase *in place* of 'the abolition of class distinctions,'" it is the 'in place' that does the work (SW, 339–340, my emphasis). The former will only obtain if the latter obtains. A necessary condition for the elimination of social and political inequalities is the attainment of classlessness. What is so very valuable about the latter is that it makes possible the former along with autonomy and widespread human flourishing.

Wood, in discussing *The Critique of the Gotha Programme,* agreed that Marx explained how with the development of the productive forces and with the transition from socialism to communism the distribution principles of the society will change. But, Wood claimed, Marx was not saying that the distribution scheme of communism is superior to that of socialism and that the distribution system of socialism is superior to that of capitalism. Above all, Marx was not saying of the distribution system of communism that it is "an end in itself or . . . one of the long-term goals of the movement" (W, 203). Rather, Wood claimed, the "general purpose of the description of communist distribution is to reject the distributive orientation as a whole" (W, 203).

I think that Wood did not show this at all and that Marx (pace Wood) was concerned in *The Critique of the Gotha Programme* with the justice and, more generally, with the moral adequacy of different distributive schemes that go with different modes of production. What Wood actually showed instead was that Marx was not concerned with the justice of various distribution schemes *independently* of how they are organized in production. The mode of production fixes the general types of distributions that are possible. But one way of coming to see what is rotten about a whole mode of production is to see the distribution it results in. This is particularly relevant when other modes of production are historically feasible with better distributive schemes—that is, fairer distribution schemes that would make for a greater amount of well-being for more people. Marx was concerned with whole social formations and with demonstrating that some productive-distributive systems are better than others because the former make for a greater need satisfaction, which brings a fairer, because more equal, distribution. So there is a gain in equality here, and Marx, Engels, and Lenin took that to be an unequivocally good thing.[28]

One can say what I have just said and still agree with Marx that "right can never be higher than the economic structure of society and its cultural development conditioned thereby." Translated into the concrete, this last remark means that if you were a prescient moralist living at the height of the Middle Ages you would not, if you knew what you were about, try to apply any bourgeois conceptions of justice to the distributional arrangements of your society, although you would in certain circumstances point out to people that better ways of arranging things could be envisioned and that they could find an institutional embodiment as the wealth of the society increased. You would if you were very prescient have envisioned different distributional principles from those that could possibly apply in the world in which you were living. You could come to see that these distributional principles, which would become applicable in the world in which the productive forces were more developed, would be better, morally speaking more adequate, distribution principles than the ones that were possible during the time in which you lived. Similarly, Marx envisioned different distribution principles for communism than those that could possibly apply in a time when capitalist relations of production are firmly in the seat. (To be imprisoned by a mode of production that is for a time stably in place does not mean we are conceptually imprisoned, although given the way ideology works, there is a tendency for us to be so imprisoned.)

To try putting such principles in place, when the productive forces are not sufficiently developed, is bad utopianism. But we can envision several social formations, with their distinctive systems of production and distribution, which we can rank as higher and lower along several dimensions, including saying of these whole social formations that a world in which one was exemplified rather than another would be a more just world than the other and that *one* of the reasons that it would be a more just world is that it would have a greater equality of condition in it. It seems to me that Marx was reasoning in this way in *The Critique of the Gotha Programme* and Engels in his *Anti-Dühring*. They pictured a number of possible worlds, only one of which at a particular time can be actual. Concerning all of those possible worlds they were considering, Marx's and Engels's historical materialism led them to believe that, barring externalities such as thermo-nuclear wars, certain determinate ones will one day be actual. (They need not, and indeed should not, go beyond probability judgments here.[29])

Picturing these worlds now, one of which is already actual, Marxists believe they can say which are more truly human and, I believe, (pace Wood) more just. To say this they do not have to say that they should try in the world they are in, where a certain mode of production is stably entrenched, to apply the moral principles of a future society. But Marxists can say, without the slightest contradiction or intellectual or emotional jarring, that the future society will be a better moral order than the present society. *One* of the reasons why it will be a better society is that in that society there will be a more extensive equality of condition and because of that more liberty will be abroad where people can achieve greater autonomy and more self-realization.

If we were to make a Mannheimish sociology of knowledge point— a conceptual imprisonment point—and say that our very understanding is so very culturally skewed that we can make no such judgments of higher and lower, then we should reply that the deep, conceptual relativism implicit in such a sociology of knowledge vantage point may possibly be justified, but this is not Marx's viewpoint we are explicating, for he thought that we could make such judgments.[30] This should be taken to be a species of the contextualistic objectivism I characterized in my introduction and contrasted with various varieties of relativism, including conceptual relativism.

However, we should not let matters rest here, for I must confront Wood's reading of 'From each according to his ability, to each according to his needs.' Wood thought that this is neither a principle of justice for such a society nor an egalitarian slogan (W, 211).[31] He thought Marx chose it for such a society "precisely because it is *not* an egalitarian slogan" (W, 211). Wood attempted to justify his claim by saying that the slogan does not advocate treating people "equally from any point of view, but instead considers people idividually, each with a different set of needs and abilities" (W, 211). I agree that the principle does stress that each person is to be treated individually and that his or her particular needs are, where possible, to be satisfied. But I think it is *also* an egalitarian slogan. We are *all* to be treated equally in that way. The desideratum is that for each and everyone of us our needs are to be satisfied. We cannot rightly or fairly ignore *anyone* here. This is to give expression (in a partial way) of what it is to have a society of equals.

It is not (pace Wood) just that this is what *will* happen in this future society, but that it is *appropriate* for it to happen. It is something that, with wondrous productive abundance and the withering away of bourgeois conceptions, we can finally inscribe on our banners and make an actual social reality. Marx was not *just* making predictions; he was stressing that the needs of everyone *are to be* satisfied. In doing this he was setting out a central normative conception of the egalitarian.

Wood forgot what he had stressed a few pages earlier—namely, that Marx would have been more "deeply disturbed by unequal need satisfaction" than by unequal wealth. Seeing the point, well stressed by Wood, that if "people have unequal needs, then one cannot expect them to have both equal wealth and equal need satisfaction," we should then go on to say that because people have different needs, Marx would not consider "unequal wealth a defect *if* no one's needs," including needs for autonomy, "were left unsatisfied" (W, 206; italics mine). Where we have a productively advanced society, what then becomes humanly and morally appropriate is a commitment to the satisfaction of the needs of everyone, where we are equally concerned with the needs of everyone alike. This will mean that because people have different needs, they will not have exactly equal resources. This egalitarian claim, or at least what I take to be this egalitarian claim, gives us a more determinate reading of equality of condition—namely, that where possible the needs of everyone are to be satisfied as fully as possible.

What is crucial to stress is that for everyone, his or her 'needs are to be satisfied as fully as possible' and that we add, as well, the vital qualification, 'To each according to needs that are, as far as possible, compatible with a similar satisfaction of needs of everyone.' What we want is that all people's needs be satisfied and indeed satisfied as fully as possible as is compatible with everyone, if capable, having such a satisfaction of needs. It is where the satisfaction of a particular need of mine may be antithetical to a need satisfaction of yours that a *question* is rightly to be raised about the need's satisfaction. There are indeed difficulties here, but so arguing is in the spirit of Marx, and it is also surely radically egalitarian.

Wood contended, as I have already mentioned, "that Marx does not consider social equality as something good for its own sake" (W, 211). That is, he did not consider it something to be wanted in itself. I have already tried to show how Marx's stress on classlessness and its value involves an appeal to social equality as an intrinsic good and as an instrumental good. I think Wood is right in believing that there is not much stress in Marx on anything like a Rawlsian egalitarian acceptance of something approaching equal benefits and burdens, although even here I think 'From *each* according to his ability' stresses that we all without exception should shoulder our fair share of the work that needs to be done in society. Contribution according to our abilities is equally required of each of us, although because our abilities are different, we will in fact make unequal contributions. It is part of an egalitarian conception to stress that contribution according to ability is equally required and that none can freeload. This is part of what it is to establish equal conditions of life.

Wood rightly stressed that Marx "favours the abolition of classes because he thinks it will lead to other things he values, such as increased human freedom, well-being, community, and individual development of self-actualisation" (W, 212). This is all true but also importantly incomplete, for Marx wanted these things not only to be increased but he wanted them, as far as feasible, for everyone. That is where the equality and the related conception of egalitarian justice come in and form, as I argued, a gestalt of ideas with autonomy, freedom, self-realization, well-being, fraternity, and community. This is a fundamentally egalitarian conception that is very distant from the Spartan minimum of 'crude communism' (W, 212).

Wood saw Marx, in the domain of normative argument, fastening on working-class oppression. Indeed, Wood thought that Marx too exclusively stressed oppression, but as a Marxological point thought that Marx attributed no intrinsic value to any form of equality, including social equality, and only regarded equality as valuable when it is an effective instrument in fighting class oppression (W, 213–235).[32] I have tried to argue that this is not Marx, nor is it right, although I would not for a moment deny Marx's claim (supported by Wood) that "oppression . . . may thrive on *formal* equality" (W, 216; italics mine).[33]

Notes

1. G. A. Cohen, *Karl Marx's Theory of History: A Defence* (Oxford: Clarendon Press, 1978). Also Cohen's "Reply to Four Critics," *Analyse & Kritik* 5, no. 2 (1983):195–222; and "Reconsidering Historical Materialism," in J. Roland Pennock and John W. Chapman (eds.), *Marxism, Nomos,* vol. 26 (New York: New York University Press, 1983), pp. 227–251. Robert Paul Wolff, *Understanding Marx* (Princeton, N.J.: Princeton University Press, 1984). Four publications by Jon Elster: "Marxism, Functionalism and Game Theory," *Theory and Society* 11 (1982):463–483; *Explaining Technical Change* (Cambridge: Cambridge University Press, 1983); *Sour Grapes* (Cambridge: Cambridge University Press, 1983); and *Making Sense of Marx* (Cambridge: Cambridge University Press, 1985). Allen Wood, *Karl Marx* (London: Routledge & Kegan Paul, 1981). Richard W. Miller, *Analyzing Marx* (Princeton, N.J.: Princeton University Press, 1984). The texts of Miller and Wood I most frequently cite are Miller's *Analyzing Marx;* and Wood's "Marx and Equality," in John Mepham and David Hillel-Ruben (eds.), *Issues in Marxist Philosophy,* vol. 4 (Brighton, England: Harvester Press, 1982), pp. 195–221. They will be referred to in the body of the text as

(M) and (W) respectively. There is in the text occasional reference to *The Selected Works of Marx and Engels* (New York: International Publishers, 1968), identified as (SW). All other references will be given in the normal fashion in these endnotes.

2. I do not mean to suggest that their views are the same. In fact Miller, while acknowledging important similarities, produced an important critique of Wood's views on justice (see M, 78–96). There is, however, common ground in their views on what they took to be Marx's and Engels's critique of appeals to equality and in their characterizing Marx and Engels as critics of morality. (The latter could hardly be denied by anyone who knew anything about Marx and Engels.)

3. I take it that this is also the stance that Miller believed should be taken toward morality. Wood, by contrast, was more Marxological.

4. For a comprehensive elucidation of the views of Monro, Mackie, and Harman, which brings out their complex, often mutually supporting arguments for a sophisticated form of subjective ethical naturalism, see Russell Cornett, *Subjective Ethical Naturalism* (Ph.D. diss., University of Calgary, 1983).

5. For this conception of *moral* equality see Thomas Nagel, *Mortal Questions* (Cambridge: Cambridge University Press, 1979), pp. 106–127.

6. Kai Nielsen, *Equality and Liberty: A Defense of Radical Egalitarianism* (Totowa, N.J.: Rowman and Allenheld, 1985).

7. Richard Norman argued that such things have in fact been stressed by egalitarians. Richard Norman, "Does Equality Destroy Liberty?" in Keith Graham (ed.), *Contemporary Political Philosophy* (Cambridge: Cambridge University Press, 1982), pp. 83–109.

8. Ibid., pp. 99–108.

9. This was brought out convincingly for J. S. Mill by Fred R. Berger in his important interpretation of the moral and political thought of J. S. Mill in *Happiness, Justice and Freedom* (Berkeley: University of California Press, 1984), pp. 96–204. Berger also made clear that there is less distance between John Rawls and J. S. Mill than is usually thought. Indeed, Rawls himself failed to see the closeness of their views.

10. I have tried to make a start here in my *Equality and Liberty*.

11. See also Richard Miller, "Rights and Reality," *Philosophical Review* (July 1981):383–407; "Rights or Consequences," *Midwest Studies in Philosophy* (1982):151–174; and "Marx and Aristotle: A Kind of Consequentialism," *Canadian Journal of Philosophy*, Supplementary vol. 7 (1981).

12. See here, as well, an earlier article of Miller's on Rawls. Richard Miller, "Rawls and Marxism" in Norman Daniels (eds.), *Reading Rawls* (New York: Basic Books, 1973), pp. 206–230.

13. It seems to me that Miller's argumentation here was rather inconclusive. At the very least it needs to be extensively filled out. I shall not pursue the issue here, but there should, I believe, be a return to the argument, concerning which there has been considerable discussion, about whether there must be *actual* consent. Why isn't there considerable moral force, if we can really make it stick (that is, if we have good reason to believe that people in such circumstances would consent), in such a claim of hypothetical consent? Suppose, for example, that I know that I probably will take a bribe if the rich man makes it attractive, but I also recognize that if I were capable of acting in an impartial manner I would not. Isn't the recognition of what I would do if I were capable of acting impartially of a not inconsiderable moral support?

14. Thomas Hurka, "Rights and Capital Punishment," in Jan Narveson (ed.), *Moral Issues* (Toronto, Ontario: Oxford University Press, 1983), p. 121.

15. Kai Nielsen, "Why Should I Be Moral?," *Methodos* 15 (1963):276–306; "On Being Moral," *Philosophical Studies,* 16 (January/February 1965):45–66; and "Why Should I Be Moral Revisited?" *American Philosophical Quarterly* 21 (January 1984):81–92.

16. I think we should be more cautious here. Parallel to the considerations gestured at in footnote 13, we should also consider what people, including working-class people, would prefer if (to use Habermas's jargon) they were in an ideal speech situation. Moreover, and distinctly, working-class people have a range of experiences not readily available to people from the professional strata or to members of the capitalist class. It is an elitist myth to think that working-class people do not make comparisons and reflect on their experience.

17. Jürgen Habermas, *Communication and the Evolution of Society,* Thomas McCarthy (trans.) (Boston: Beacon Press, 1976), pp. 1–68.

18. I document this in Chapter 4.

19. Kai Nielsen, "On Liberty and Equality: A Case for Radical Egalitarianism," *The Windsor Yearbook of Access to Justice* 4 (1984):121–142; and "Justice and Ideology: Justice as Ideology," *Windsor Yearbook of Access to Justice* (1981):165–178.

20. Allen Wood clearly explicated the concept of being a historical idealist and contrasted it with being an historical materialist in his *Karl Marx,* pp. 88–90, and 117–122.

21. He argued the same point more briefly in ibid., Part 3. See also his "Marx and Morality," Arthur Caplan and Bruce Jennings (ed.), *Darwin, Marx and Freud: Their Influence on Moral Theory* (New York: Plenum Press, 1984), pp. 131–144.

22. W. K. Frankena, *Ethics,* 2nd ed. (Engelwood Cliffs, N.J.: Prentice-Hall, 1973), Chapter 5. For more extended discussions see C. I. Lewis, *An Analysis of Knowledge and Valuation* (LaSalle, Ill.: Open Court Publishing Company, 1946), Chapters 12–14; and Georg von Wright, *The Varieties of Goodness* (London: Routledge & Kegan Paul, 1963), pp. 1–39.

23. See Norman, "Does Equality Destroy Liberty?"; and Nielsen, *Equality and Liberty.*

24. For some documentation of this see Chapter 4.

25. Frederick Engels, *Anti-Dühring,* Emile Burns (trans.) (New York: International Publishers, 1939), pp. 117–118.

26. See Chapter 3.

27. Mihailo Markovic, *The Contemporary Marx* (Nottingham, England: Spokesman Books, 1974), pp. 130–137; and Nielsen, *Equality and Liberty,* pp. 57–60.

28. See Chapter 4.

29. Maximilien Rubel, *Rubel on Karl Marx: Five Essays,* Joseph O'Malley and Keith Algozin (eds. and trans.) (Cambridge: Cambridge University Press, 1981), pp. 58–66.

30. See the exchange between Martin Hollis and J. L. Mackie in Stephen Körner (ed.) *Explanation* (Oxford: Basil Blackwell, 1975), pp. 185–197, 205–216.

31. See also the two articles reprinted in M. Cohen et al. (eds.), *Marx, Justice and History* (Princeton, N.J.: Princeton University Press, 1980). These included his response to Ziyad Husami. In this context see also the criticism

by Gary Young, "Doing Marx Justice," *Canadian Journal of Philosophy,* Supplementary vol. 7 (1981); and G. A. Cohen, "Review of Wood's *Karl Marx*" *Mind* (1982):440–445.

32. Nielsen, *Equality and Liberty.*

33. I claim here, following what I have argued in my *Equality and Liberty* and elsewhere, that commitments to the ideals of liberty and equality are not only compatible—they require each other for their fullest flourishing. Some might respond in the following way to the utilization of such a conception in *Marxism and the Moral Point of View.* Marx's ideal of a good society, they could agree, is complex and multifaceted. It is indeed a complex gestalt of interlocking ends, including freedom, equality, and reciprocity. I am justified, they could claim, in stressing that. Moreover, there is plainly some interconnectedness among the component ends that make up the complex Marxian ideal. Still, they could go on to point out, there is a widespread belief in our culture that there are deep conflicts between freedom and equality such that we not infrequently cannot maximize both and must make trade-offs between them. Perhaps, in certain key circumstances, we will even have to sacrifice one for the other. I need extensive argument, which I do not give here, to show that liberty and equality are so mutually supportive. I do little more than gesture at an argument here. But, it might be further contended, it is sufficient for my argument in this chapter to make the weaker claim that equality is one among several ends that make up the complex Marxian ideal. This weaker claim is indeed sufficient for the historical claim made here that Marx was an egalitarian. But I also claim he was a consistent, autonomy-respecting egalitarian. If that is so and we want to defend this egalitarianism, as I do, as not only a view that Marx had but as a sound view, we need to be able to justify the further claim that liberty and equality are mutually supportive. My *Equality and Liberty* has as its essential burden to do that against conventional wisdom. For an essentially similar line of argument to my own in *Equality and Liberty,* see Richard Norman, *Free and Equal* (Oxford: Oxford University Press, 1987).

10

Class Interests, Justice and Marxism

I

What I attempt in this chapter is largely negative. I shall be a nay-sayer and a second-sayer rather than a yea-sayer and a first-sayer. I am not unambivalent about this for I realize it is an easier task to be a nay-sayer. Moreover, it is crucial to give a first-saying, positive account. But the issues here are complex and confusing if not confused. There needs to be a good bit of sorting out before we can profitably engage in yea-saying. In such a situation it is important, if we can, to set matters straight. Doing so will reveal, I believe, that a strong Marxist case can be made for the preferability, morally speaking, of socialism (whatever we might say about its statist distortions in some existing socialisms) over capitalism given the development of productive forces. This case also extends to the injustice of capitalism and the moral unacceptablity of the institution of private productive property. (I do not, of course, speak of personal property such as owning a house or a car.) However, I do not yet, philosophically speaking, see my way clearly enough here. What I shall argue instead, is that two very influential, powerfully argued accounts, which I shall label *Marxist immoralism* and *Marxist moralism* respectively, are both seriously in error. However, they have identified some things that are importantly true and they are enough to motivate us to look at familiar moral terrain in another way and to try developing a more adequate positive account that incorporates in a more comprehensive, even more dialectical, way the valid elements in Marxist immoralism and Marxist moralism.

My own nascent view, which I shall not argue for in this chapter, although I shall argue for it in the following two chapters, is closer to Marxist moralism in substantive conclusion, but *methodologically speaking* is more in the spirit of Marxist immoralism with its more historicist setting aside of a freely proclaiming moral rationalism. Despite my agreement with some Marxist moralists, I distance myself from their confident reliance on rights—indeed what G. A. Cohen called natural rights—and from their implicit reliance on moral intuitions unchastened and unweeded by the coherentist discipline of wide reflective equilibrium. Such a coherentism would, in principle at least, leave no intuitions (considered judgments) intact, independently of a consideration of how well they fit with other claims so as to make a consistent and coherent whole matching with everything we know or can reliably believe. Indeed, there are some very firmly embedded considered judgments that probably will in fact never be challenged, but they also fit in well in this coherentist package and are not in principle unchallengable. (We should take to heart here the attitude of Peirce's critical common-sensism.)

Marxists, theorists sympathetic to Marx, and Marxologists are divided about whether Marx thought and whether Marxists should think that capitalism or any whole social formation is just or unjust or about whether we can properly use such terms of appraisal for whole social formations.[1] Even analytical philosophers sympathetic to and thoroughly knowledgeable about Marx and Marxism and with a similar philosophical and social science orientation are sharply divided about this issue.[2] The contrast comes out both vividly and starkly if we compare the views of Allen Wood and G. A. Cohen. They are both analytical philosophers thoroughly immersed in the work of Marx, and they both have written distinguished critical interpretations of Marx.[3] All that notwithstanding, they are deeply divided about this issue. On the one hand, Wood would have it that for Marx concepts such as justice were ideological constructions that could have no critical content for appraising capitalism or any social formation (or indeed anything else) and that this was not just Marx's own possibly eccentric view about morality but was something integral to a thoroughly and consistently Marxist conception of things.[4] Cohen, on the other hand, took it that Marx condemned capitalism as unjust, in a suitably nonrelativist sense, and Cohen further claimed that such a moral critique should be a central element in contemporary Marxist theory. The centrality of this critique would enable philosophers to establish whether the capitalist system itself, and not just some capitalist systems, is in our historical epoch unjust and whether, by contrast, under socialism and eventually under communism justice can reasonably be expected to flourish along with a more general human flourishing.

I want to make a start at sorting this general issue out by inspecting their respective arguments to see where these leave us. I focus on Wood and Cohen because they are distinguished interpreters of Marx and perceptive, able philosophers with a similar philosophical orientation and, about most issues (although not this one) they have similar views on Marx. Given Wood's and Cohen's general similarity of approach, coupled with their sharp disagreement about this issue, they are instructive subjects for comparison.

II

I should like to make one disclaimer initially. I think Wood and Richard Miller, who had a broadly similar conception to that of Wood, were exactly right in arguing that such a rejection of justice or, more generally, a rejection of the moral point of view in assessing institutions or in deciding what is to be done as far as social issues are concerned, does not entail, justify, or excuse a bloodthirsty *realpolitik,* the lack of common human decency, or the sorts of excesses that have sometimes been committed in the name of socialism.[5]

In "Justice and Class Interests," Wood wanted to confront what I have called Marxist moralism.[6] In particular, he wanted to confront the kind of Marxist, sypathetic to justice, who (a) sets out to show, along Marxian lines, that a case can be made for the injustice of capitalism and the justice of a properly democratic socialism, one that conforms to Marx's conception of a socialist society; and (b) also will agree with Wood that Marx would not so appraise capitalism and socialism and indeed regarded moral conceptions as through and through ideological. So the position Wood wished principally to refute[7] (a position more concessive to Wood than to Cohen) is that of the person who will agree on the Marxological point that Marx did not regard capitalism as unjust, but who will then argue that this Marxological point does not count for much because Marx's "views about morality [were] sufficiently idiosyncratic and sufficiently far removed from the central insights of his social thought that they need not be taken seriously" (11).[8]

Wood set out to show that Marxist moralism rests on a mistake. To take Marx seriously, to accept some reasonable reading of the core canonical claims of Marx's social theory, would, Wood argued, lead one to reject the moral point of view as irretrievably ideological. One would then reject justice as a critical category for assessing institutions and see justice-talk, and moral-talk more generally as ideological instruments with (in most circumstances) a pervasively conservative social function. Moral norms are not good vehicles for "revolutionary demands and aspirations." Rather, moral norms are "expressions of a given social order, and specifically as expressive of the demands that order makes to insure its survival and smooth functioning" (10).

Such a view of the essentially conservative social function of morality is, Wood argued, grounded in Marx's historical materialism, his conception of ideology, his conception of class, class interests, and class conflict. It is not rooted in any eccentric and possibly philosophically naive meta-ethical or normative ethical conceptions that Marx may have had. It is not that Marx or Marxists, following Marx here, are committed to a kind of irrationalism or conceptual relativism with some theses of conceptual imprisonment. Marx and Engels were plainly children of the Enlightenment and most Marxists have followed them here. Marx and Engels believed, as Wood put it, that "rational deliberation about social institutions would be an important part of any free or truly human society" (11). They would agree with John Rawls that this is one of our highest-order interests. But what Marx and Engels also wanted to expose—and here they were not typical Enlightenment figures—was what they took to be the pervasive self-deception of most moral and political philosophers. This deception was based on the belief that what is most essential in "deliberating about how best to set up social arrangements is to develop and utilize principles of justice to distribute the burdens and benefits of social life" (11). Wood wanted to show that what most philosophers and political theorists consider an almost self-evidently natural and reasonable way to proceed is, from the point of view of a consistently worked out Marxist social theory, a retrograde step that embraces a utopianism that blinds us to the nature of social reality.

Wood agreed that Marx did object, in a manner perfectly consistent with his overall orientation, to the way control over the means of production was distributed in capitalist societies and to the way opportunities for education, leisure, health care, decent housing, security, and the like were distributed. Wood granted that given these concrete judgments of Marx, it seems plausible to attempt constructing a conception of justice that might be used to explain and justify those, and similar, specific assessments of capitalist distributions. Wood claimed, however, that despite this initial plausibility, when we take to heart what justice is and when we reflect on some central features of Marx's core theory, this initial plausibility will evaporate.

In his argument, Wood adverted to three elements: Marx's historical materialism, his conception of revolutionary practice based on it, and a non-Marxist conceptual point about what justice is. Let us turn to the last point first. Any principle of justice, to be called such, must be disinterested or impartial as regards the interests of those to whom the principle is supposed to apply. Any differential treatment of those to whom it is supposed to apply "must be justified on the basis of some impartial standard, such as the special desert of individuals or the greatest common good of all concerned" (14). If such differential treatment is not in some way so justified for the distributions, then we do not have a principle of justice. Any principle of justice, even the most elitist or aristocratic, must "be justified on the basis of disinterested or impartial considerations" (15). This is a necessary condition for something's being a principle of justice.

Next Wood adverted to the fact (which Richard Miller also stressed) that "Marx refused to evaluate social institutions from an impartial or disinterested standpoint, and regarded the whole enterprise of doing so as ensnared in ideological illusions" (15).[9] Wood next sought to establish that this was not just an eccentricity of Marx's but was integral to central elements in his theory. Rather than a disinterested appeal to the interests of everyone alike, one must appeal, if one is serious about defending socialist revolution and socialism generally, to the class interests of the proletariat and their allies. They are indeed, on Marx's reckoning, the vast majority, so we are appealing to what is in fact the interests of the vast majority, but, Wood claimed, Marx "never confuses this with the common interests of all society" (16). Indeed, Marx regarded any conception of the common good or of universal interests in class societies as an ideological myth.[10] There are, Marx unblinkingly recognized, large groups of people (the bourgeoisie and the landed aristocracy) "whose interests are going to be simply ignored or sacrificed by the revolution" (6). Marx was perfectly explicit and straightforward about this.[11] This attitude, Wood argued, is what is required if we are to make a consistent application of Marx's account of historical materialism and his theory of classes.

Marx—to get on with investigating Wood's claim here—saw history as divided into epochs, each with its distinct mode of production. Where there are classes in society, they stand in different positions vis-à-vis the mode of production, and they have different roles in the economic relations that are a part of this mode of production. These classes, with their distinctive socio-economic roles, do not all have the same effective control over the means, process, and fruits of production of the society in which they live. Throughout history, when we view human society as a whole, the forces of production tend to develop and indeed have developed, and this will invariably, as the productive forces develop, lead in determinate historical circumstances to situations where the relations of production come to make a bad fit with the forces of production. This in turn tends to sharpen class conflict.[12] But even when the forces and relations of production are for a time in matching harmony, it still remains the case, because with classes there are relations of domination and subordination, that with their very existence there are class interests that are antagonistic and irreducibly so in a society with such a class formation. Indeed, something like this will be true in any class society at all. As the productive powers (forces) develop and the extant relations of production become obsolete in the face of that development, the mechanism, according to historical materialism, by which the adjustment of social relations to productive powers is carried out is the class struggle, which culminates (where the changes are extensive) in a social revolution. This revolution will bring into being new relations of production more consonant with the new powers of production, which together will come to constitute a new and distinct mode of production.

On Marx's conception, there is no reality to the contention that there are society-wide interests that would constitute a common good that might, in a good Durkheimian fashion, bind society together. What we actually have instead are the conflicting class interests of the various antagonistic and contending classes, which for each class is based on a situation common to the members of each class.

In our society, to take the two main classes, there are the capitalists, who own and have control over the means of production and have a perfectly rational interest in maintaining that ownership and control, and the workers, who are excluded from control over the means of production and who have a perfectly rational interest in wresting it away from those who do have control over it. Where we are not just talking about the individual interests of the members of the class, but about the interests of the class as a whole (the long-term goals of a class movement), we are in effect talking about "the establishment and defense of a certain set of production relations in society" (18). In this way we identify class interests, and these class interests are the proximate driving force of history, the central triggers in epochal social change. The underlying, more fundamental causes are the developing productive forces, which when they come in conflict with the relations of production give rise to class struggle. Still, as Wood put it, it is through class struggle that we as historical agents relate effectively to history. Our historical role "depends on the relation of our actions to class interests and the struggle between them" (19).

III

This account of historical materialism and revolutionary class struggle prepares the ground for what Wood called *the class interest thesis,* which is an essential premise for what he called *the class interests argument.* The latter is an argument designed to show that Marxists cannot have a theory or an account of justice as a critically normative concept, nor can they coherently maintain that in some transhistorical, critical, and non-mode-of-production-relative sense capitalism is unjust and socialism just. Wood's *class interest thesis* is as follows:

> To understand ourselves as historical agents is to understand these interests [class interests] and the bearing of our actions on them. Whatever the aims or conscious intentions of our actions may be, Marx believes that our actions are historically effective only insofar as they involve the pursuit of class interests, and the historical meaning of our actions consists in their functional role in the struggle between such interests (19).

Wood's key point is that when we carefully and nonevasively think through the implications of the class interests thesis, we will come to see that we cannot be historically effective by moralizing. We cannot in any fundamental way change the world by making a case, no matter how sound, for the injustice of capitalism. But given our conception of the unity of theory and practice, it is one of our deepest interests to be historically effective. This means that in thinking politically about society we should not have much interest in considerations of justice and injustice. Wood tried to establish this by what he called "the class interests argument," which I will now critically examine.

Why does the acceptance of the class interests thesis dictate setting aside such an appeal to justice? If we accept the class interests thesis, which as historical materialists it seems we must, and if we wish to be historically effective, we will take to heart the fact "that whatever desires, values and goals we may have, our accomplishments as historical agents are basically going to consist in the way we further the interests of certain classes" (19). In struggling to be historically effective, we will look at the existing historical movements and come, particularly if we have the anomalous class position of most intellectuals, to side with a movement (as in taking the standpoint of labor), to identify with it (albeit sometimes critically), and to seek to realize its goals as our goals. If we wish to be historically effective, we will take such a standpoint rather than engage in the task of "setting our goals according to abstract values or standards and then trying to find some means for achieving them" (19). We will, of course, in a manner consonant with our vocation as intellectuals, do so critically, and this will (speaking now of intellectuals as a group) have its own, sometimes more, sometimes less, important political effects. But we must side with one or another of the contemporary classes if we have a sense of ourselves as historical agents and care about playing some role in the struggles of our time. This, of course, holds only if we are convinced of the approximate truth of historical materialism and Marx's conception of class struggle and if indeed these theses are approximately true.

So, at least given certain factual beliefs, to be effective historical agents we must take some class position, but the class interests thesis also asserts that in no case can these goals (the goals consonant with determinate class interests) be determined by disinterested or impartial considerations. What is involved in class struggle is always "the particular interests of one class struggling against other classes" (20). What we need firmly to recognize is that to identify ourselves with a class movement is therefore to abandon the pretense that our fundamental concern is with what is disinterestedly or impartially good. For "according to the class interests thesis, no effective historical action ever takes the form of pursing what is impartially or disinterestedly good" (20). What we are to do, in public life at least, is determined by our identification with a class movement. But, according to Wood, that

involves pursuing class interests as such and not for the sake of some
further end. A concern with "justice as one's fundamental goal and an
acceptance of the practical consequences of the class interests thesis
are therefore incompatible" (20). It is this argument that Wood called
the class interests argument.

IV

Once Wood set out the basic structure of his argument, he considered
objections, qualifications, and caveats. It is here—or shall so I argue—
where he made remarks that began to render his case against a justicizing
Marxism or a Marxist moralism vulnerable. Wood remarked (as had
Richard Miller) that "sometimes Marx appears to think that the class
interests thesis, perhaps together with the fact that society is torn by
deep class conflict, entails the very idea of a common interest, or of
what is impartially and disinterested good, is a mere chimera, that
there is no such thing" (21).[13] But now, Wood claimed, there is nothing
in the canonical core of Marxism, nothing in Marx's historical materialism
or conception of revolutionary practice, that would require that. Marx,
as Miller showed, pointed out that while in each class society there
is a motley of goods, of which there is generally a wide acceptance,
there is no general consensus about the specific items (or, at least, all
the specific items) or on the weighting of these sometimes conflicting
goods. The motley remains just a motley. There is plainly an overlap
in people's interests, but there is conflict as well, and there is no
consensus about how to resolve such conflicts. There is no hierarchically
ordered unified picture of the good life or even a unified picture of
the good life toward which there is consensus. Concerning this Wood
remarked, "The idea of what is impartially or disinterestedly good is
not the idea of an empirical agreement or overlap between people's
interests. Instead, it is the idea of something which is good from a
standpoint independent of any particular interests, though perhaps not
independent of all human interests whatever" (21).

Wood argued (as did Miller), although without reference to any
element of the canonical corpus of Marxism, that in our bourgeois
societies there are such sharp conflicts of interest and there is no
agreement about any generalized human interests that might constitute
a common good. But, Wood added, this does not show that there could
not be such an agreement, that careful deliberations, using wide
reflective equilibrium, could not reasonably be expected, if conditions
of undistorted discourse were to prevail, to establish such a consensus.
Moreover, it also does not show that Marxist theoreticians, if there is
something to Marxist empirical theory, with their sensitivities to the
way ideology functions and the like, would not be in a good position
to have some shrewd idea what those generalized interests are, if
indeed there are any.

Perhaps, contrary to what I have just said, a critically skeptical moral theory (say a theory such as J. L. Mackie's) could establish that we have no good reason to expect that such a consensus could be attained. Such a theory might even be able to show that there is something incoherent, or in some other way radically mistaken, in the very idea of such a standpoint. But while all these things are possible, neither of these claims, or anything bearing a reasonable family resemblance to them, is part of the core conceptions of Marxism, and there are no clear implicates of these conceptions that establish either them or their country or city cousins. As Wood well put it, it is not enough to show "that people's interests do in fact profoundly conflict"; we must also show that there are no deep underlying interests that would enable us to eke out a sound conception of what is impartially and disinterestedly good and that would provide a basis for a resolution of these conflicts.

However—and this is the really vital point here—Wood's class interests argument, intriguingly and significantly, does not rest on a belief that there is no "universal interest or a disinterested standpoint" (21). What his argument requires, instead, is what Wood called the weaker claim "that the practical recognition of the class interests thesis excludes self-conscious historical agents from taking justice (or what is impartially good) as their primary object of concern" (21). But now the narrative begins to have another look, a look that (pace Wood) is not so favorable to Marxist immoralism. This comes out in an argument of Wood's meant to establish just the opposite.

Wood contended that it may well be the case that "in pursuing the interests of a class" we will also be pursuing what is in fact just or disinterestedly good" (20). The class interests argument only claims that we cannot take moral reasons as the primary reasons for supporting the working class. Given the truth of the class interests thesis, such an historical agent with a sense of his or her vocation must value proletarian class interests ahead of what, if anything, is disinterestedly good (21). Where Marxist immoralism most decisively comes in, Wood claimed, is in the belief (resulting in a commitment) that if there is ever a conflict between proletarian class interests and what is disinterestedly good, the proletarian interests trump those moral interests. This reverses the usual belief that moral considerations override any such conflicting considerations.

The justicizing Marxist (the Marxist moralist) should reply that this is an unreal situation, a desert islandish, hypothetical situation. Given a realistic understanding of what proletarian class interests are, they cannot, as a matter of fact, conflict with what is disinterestedly good; therefore, a historical agent could not be faced with a situation where he or she must choose between struggling to realize proletarian class interests and supporting what is disinterestedly good. The Marxist, rightly or wrongly, conceives the matter in such a way that the class

interests of proletarians will also, as a matter of fact although surely
not as a matter of definition, be the interests of the vast majority of
humankind: proletarians and, as well, many other groups (farmers,
lumpen-proletarians, petty bourgeoisie, and most intellectuals and
professionals).

What is in the class interests of the proletariat will only go against
the interests of the capitalist class. But the latter's membership is only
a minuscule part of the total population (in our times, to put it
conservatively, hardly more than 5 percent of the population). Moveover,
proletarian interests would not go against all of the interests of capitalists
as individuals but only against those interests closely linked to en-
gagement in capitalist acts. The vital interests of capitalists that center
on what are usually called our civil liberties need not be affected in
most situations. Where they would be affected, say in the unsettled
aftermath of a bitter civil war, their free speech rights would indeed
by overridden. But, or so a Marxist is perfectly and consistently at
liberty to claim, they still (in the way Joel Feinberg has shown[14])
remain inalienable. What happens in such a particular situation is no
different than what happens in any bourgeois society when it is in a
state of war (or something similar) where all sorts of censorship
restrictions are routinely recognized as essential. Moreover, they are
recognized to be essential from the perspective of what is disinterestedly
good. (Leon Trotsky was surely right in pointing out in his *Their
Morals and Ours* the hypocrisy of bourgeois critics of the communists
on such issues.)

In morality, when push comes to shove, numbers count. If you are
standing by a lakeshore in rough weather and you are a strong swimmer
and you see two boats equidistant from you capsize, one to your right
and the other to your left, with three small children in the one to the
right and one child in the one to the left, ceteris paribus, you will,
and indeed should, first try to help the one on the right. Although
moral issues are not vote issues, it is also the case that numbers just
do count. Where interests of the same type and of the same order of
importance intractably conflict and both interests cannot be satisfied,
morality (the moral point of view) requires that we satisfy the greater
or more extensive interests where these can be ascertained. In the
case of my example the interests of three children trump the interests
of the single child. Similarly, in situations where proletarian interests
conflict with bourgeois interests of the same order, the proletarian
interests trump them and for at least the same reasons as the interests
of the three children override the interests of the single child. It is
crucial in making this evaluation to keep firmly in mind the fact that
the interests of the proletariat are also the interests of the vast majority
and that the interests of the capitalist are that of a very small minority
indeed.

I say 'at least for the same reasons' because there seem to me
additional reasons in the proletarian case that do not apply in my

simple example. An added item is relevant here. It is at least arguable in the proletarian/bourgeois case that the conflicting interests are not of equal importance and that it is also morally relevant that capitalists—and unavoidably so—exploit workers.[15] The worker's essential interests are to escape from dehumanizing conditions and to attain autonomy, or at least achieve greater autonomy.

Even *if* a worker is in a sufficiently wealthy capitalist society such that his or her health and security are not threatened, nonetheless his or her autonomy surely is—namely, the ability to control his or her own life, to be self-directed. This good—surely a very precious higher-order interest of human beings—is undermined, or at least hedged in and weakened, in capitalist societies because there is and can be no thorough workplace democracy. That is to say, a capitalist society cannot be a society where (a) the people in the workplace own and control their own means of production; (b) they collectively and democratically decide what to do; (c) they similarly decide under what conditions to do it (where this can be controlled and where there are feasible options); and (d) they have, in an overall democratic environment, a say in what is to be done with what they produce. In a socialist society a worker would have such autonomy, as would the former capitalist as well because the former capitalist would be a worker like others and would have the same possibilities for autonomy that the other workers would have. What the former capitalist would lose is some negative liberty; with the proscribing of capitalist acts, there would be an interference with his or her freedom to buy, sell, and invest and thus, in certain domains, an interference with the freedom to do what he or she wants. However, this is not the same as a limitation on a more comprehensive freedom, and it does not, as is the case for workers in capitalism, undermine his or her autonomy.

The undermining of autonomy, of self-direction, is far more important than an undermining of negative liberty. These two interests, while important, are not on a par. The proletarian interests are not only the interests of a far greater number of people; they are also more important than the interests of the bourgeoisie, which get sacrificed in socialism.

The defender of the class interests thesis, if he or she is well informed, knows this. Thus, in siding with socialism he or she does not have to choose between the pursuit of proletarian class interests and the pursuit of what is disinterestedly good, for if there is such a thing, it will best be achieved, if it can be achieved at all, by pursuing proletarian class interests. It is on the Marxist story—and this is part of its canonical core—the case that proletarian emancipation, which is a key to the creation of a classless society, will provide the conditions for a general human emancipation. The defender of the class interests thesis does not have to choose between pursuing class interests and pursuing what is disinterestedly good, for *by* pursuing class interests he or she thereby pursues what is disinterestedly good. If, contrary to what is involved in this claim, the disinterestedly good is an ideological illusion (something that Wood, as distinct from Miller, did not believe Marxists must assume), then there is nothing that can be coherently contrasted with proletarian interests. Thus, no choice is necessary. If, on the other hand, there is a coherent concept of the disinterestedly good, as we have assumed, then proletarian interests are the means by which we achieve a situation in which the disinterestedly good can prevail. In practical political action, by placing proletarian interests first, we achieve a differential treatment of interests that is impartially defendable from the vantage point of what is disinterestedly good both at the point of choice—where sometimes hard choices must be made and the lesser evil chosen—and in the future. There is no good reason for claiming that someone who accepts the class interests thesis, as I believe we should, must reject the moral point of view or the possibility of assessing capitalism and socialism in terms of justice.

V

The foregoing (pace Wood) does not stand in conflict with a practical, tactical stress on the class interests thesis—namely, that it is counterproductive and harmful to the socialist cause to be preoccupied, as Marxist humanism is, with trying to ascertain what the disinterested human good is or with what is a really fair distribution of things. Marx remarked of such utopian 'true socialists' that they "have lost all revolutionary passion and proclaim instead the universal love of humanity."[16] In the midst of revolutionary struggle, there is no time for such Feuerbachian proclaiming. It is hard enough to try figuring out what proletarian class interests are, let alone to try figuring out what is disinterestedly good or what is the really fair distribution of things. If successful, such a moralistic stress would breed a generation of revolutionary Hamlets, and that would impede a socialist transformation of society. The thing to do, if we can, is to work toward ascertaining what this interest is and then try to spread among the working class and their allies as widely as possible this understanding, which will constantly be refined by workers as they gain, in struggle, a better understanding of their situation. This, with a caveat I shall mention in a moment, seems to me the right tactical move for socialist intelligentsia.

But a firm acceptance of these tactics does not entail an abandonment of the belief that capitalism is unjust and that with the establishment of socialism we will have established a better society that is more comprehensively and extensively just than even the best capitalist societies. The belief that socialism is just is, moreover, fully compatible with the belief that by furthering the cause of proletarian class interests we thereby will in fact further the cause of justice. Such a belief is fully compatible with an acceptance of the class interests thesis and is not undermined by the class interests argument. If we ourselves are committed to acting as historical agents on the side of the working class and to acting with awareness and a sense of moral responsibility, we can and should say to the person similarly committed who worries about whether he or she can ever know what justice is or can ascertain what is disinterestedly good, "For the time being, do not put such questions at the center of your consciousness. Struggle instead for proletarian emancipation and come back to these deep questions about justice and the good after socialism has been established. Remember, however, that even if we do not have them in reflective equilibrium, we have some deeply embedded, fairly specific, considered moral judgments in these domains, and they count for something, even though they should clearly not be taken as self-evident truths (whatever that may mean) clear to the light of reason (whatever that may mean). These deeply embedded considered judgments should guard you against the feeling that you are acting in a morally arbitrary manner. But, for the time being, put such deep questions about justice and moral philosophy aside, and, being the intellectual you are, concentrate instead on critiquing ideology; ascertaining in our concrete historical situation what proletarian class interests actually are; and seeing how they can be made to prevail. Do your bit, and be part of a movement that seeks to bring into existence and sustain a social world that answers to these interests."

I said that I had a caveat to make to what I believe to be this largely correct tactical position. We in North America, Western Europe, and Japan, whether we like it or not, are (or so at least it appears) distant from a socialist revolution, and we do not have a proletariat that shows much militancy or even a recognition of itself as a class. Philosophers and social scientists are almost invariably situated in universities where debates about the justice, including the justice of whole social systems, go on. However, in a wider, vastly more influential world, there are also all sorts of plays, novels, television dramas, films, and the like that, sometimes with great subtlety and sensitive nuance and sometimes (indeed more frequently) just as crude propaganda, give their readers/viewers to understand that Marxist revolutionaries are a fanatical lot who have substituted historical necessity for morality and decency. Lenin and Trotsky were tarred with the phrase 'Bolshevik amoralists,' and similar things go on today. In the context of such debates, it is appropriate, even tactically appropriate, to make the claim (which can rationally and morally stand on its own) that socialism, indeed socialism in the Marxist mode, can be justified ethically speaking. Indeed, it can even be justified in terms of claims of justice and what is disinterestedly good. In the world of propaganda in which we are immersed that claim is worth making, in the very name of proletarian emancipation. But this remark about what should be done in our rather special environment need not carry over to what should be stressed to revolutionary cadres forming in South Africa, Central America, the Philippines, or in the shantytowns of Kenya or Peru.

VI

Wood would, I believe, still resist and maintain that the class interests thesis and the class interests argument dictate that the pursuit of justice is of secondary importance for a consistent Marxist, that Marxist socialists must get their "priorities straight and dampen their enthusiasm for justice" so that they can "get on with what really matters"—namely, furthering "the particular interests of the proletariat" (22). The consistent Marxist, Wood claimed, who has really taken to heart the class interest thesis cannot take the moral point of view because it requires not just that we "look to some degree favorably on what is disinterestedly or impartially good," but that we place "what is disinterestedly or impartially good ahead of any particular interest" (22).

The Marxist, for the reasons I have named, should accept the class interest thesis but can quite properly resist this counter-argument by elaborating the nature of the commitment that the class interests thesis requires. The class interest thesis indeed requires, he or she should argue, that class interests must be given center stage. We must put them first, but doing so also furthers the cause of justice. There is no good reason to believe that in any non-desert-island situation he or she will have to choose between proletarian interests and justice. To think otherwise is just Koestlerian dramaturgy. We do not need to be able to say in some very unlikely counter-factual situation what we should do if what might conceivably be the case were to happen and proletarian class interests and moral interests were pulled apart. To take a mundane analogy, we need not, in thinking about social policy, decide what we should do if the whole society at the same time needed blood transfusions or dialysis machines. We do need to think about things such as the effects of an increasingly large aging population, but we do not need to think about desert island situations. We do not need a morality for all possible worlds. Moral theory, even assuming we need one, should be constructed, as John Rawls stressed, for our world and worlds recognizably like ours and not for all logically possible worlds.[17]

It is important for me to reemphasize at this juncture that I agree with Wood that it is vital for a moral agent to attend to the historical effects of actions, and I would further contend that this requires a proletarian class affiliation, for someone who has a good grasp on the facts, is clearheaded, and is impartially caring. It requires, that is, siding with the working class, taking the standpoint of labor. I also agree with Wood that for such a person—indeed for any consistent Marxist—that it would be irrational and immoral to place any interests above proletarian class interests. But, pace Wood, I am claiming that the moral agent will never in fact have to pit class interests against morality. In fine, I agree with Wood that "what the class interests thesis tells us is that those who strive for justice in human history are, objectively speaking, always striving on behalf of the interests of some class or other, and that their striving must, from a historical point of view, be regarded in this light, whatever their private aims and intentions may be" (25). He was also right, I believe, in recognizing that we "cannot accept this thesis and still pretend to view our own aims and intentions in the same way we did before" (25). Indeed, as I have tried to make evident, I accept the class interests thesis, but this does not commit me to Marxist immoralism or to a rejection of the assessment of socialism or capitalism by the canons of justice. There is no sound reason for saying with Wood that "objectively speaking the pursuit of justice is *only* a vehicle or mask for the pursuit of class interests" (27, emphasis mine). It is perfectly possible, and indeed desirable, while adhering firmly to the class interests thesis and a Marxist conception of revolutionary practice, to engage in a moral critique of capitalism (pace Wood, 30–31).

VII

I have tried in previous sections, after bringing out its not inconsiderable force, to set aside Marxist immoralism. I now wish to consider and, after due consideration, to set aside at least some forms of Marxist moralism as well. I shall consider a very strange yet powerful form of it. It is a form that contends, much against the grain of what most Marxists think, that Marxists should argue for the injustice of the capitalist system and for the wrongness of the institution of private productive property on the basis that such institutions violate *natural rights.* It is, of course, this last claim that sits so strangely with a Marxist perspective.

This strange thesis came from G. A. Cohen, a Marxist with impeccable credentials, whose *Karl Marx's Theory of History: A Defense* is the most distinguished rational reconstruction and defense of historical materialism to have come along in many years.[18] Cohen, reasonably enough, urged Marxists not to be knee-jerk and Luddite in their rejection of natural rights. He enjoined them carefully to reconsider whether they are not in effect appealing to natural rights when, giving expression to what is surely one of their deepest convictions, they maintain that private productive property is to be abolished. They should consider as well whether bad theories about the nature of morality, and nothing more, stand in their way of acknowledging what Cohen took to be an operative feature of their thinking—namely, a belief in natural rights and some objective conception of justice.

Cohen's reasoning was, if nothing else, challenging; it jarred those of us who like to think of ourselves as working in the Marxist tradition out of our more accustomed ways of thinking about morality. Suppose it could be shown (as I think I have shown in my *Equality and Liberty*[19]) "that socializing the principal means of production would enhance freedom, because the extra freedom gained by the less well off would be greater than the amount lost by the rich" (11). However, Cohen remarked, even if this is so, it might still remain the case that it would be unjust to expropriate and socialize any private productive property (8). While it is a good thing to bring more freedom into the world, it is not right to do so if rights are violated in the process. Considerations of justice tend to override considerations of freedom "because justice is a matter of rights, and rights are especially potent weapons in moral debate" (11).

There are many defenders of capitalism who defend the right to private productive property on the ground that we have a natural right to acquire private property and that to deprive people of such legitimately acquired private property is to violate their natural rights. This, these defenders claim, is about as deep a form of injustice as you can get.

Many philosophers, among them almost all Marxists, will, as Cohen was well aware, reject any such an appeal and will believe with Bentham that talk of natural rights is nonsense on stilts. Cohen considered this attitude plain, unreflective dogmatism. There is nothing problematic at all, he believed, about a suitably sanitized conception of natural rights. "Natural rights," Cohen told us, "are rights which are not merely legal ones. We say that we have them on moral, not legal, grounds" (11). He thought there is no good reason to consider this notion nonsense or even particularly problematic. He did not think (pace John Locke and Robert Nozick) "there are natural rights to private property," but he did think "there are natural rights." He offered the following paradigm case, which he thought Marxists and other left-wingers (people who normally scoff at talk of natural rights) should be sympathetically inclined toward in spite of their distaste for natural rights–talk. Suppose a government, using constitutional means, forbids plainly peaceful protests against its nuclear defence policy by claiming that these protests will endanger national security. Suppose people outraged at such a patent maneuver—national security is hardly threatened—express their outrage by asserting, "People have a right peacefully to protest against any part of government policy." When they so respond, they are, said Cohen, whether they know it or not, appealing to natural rights because *ex hypothesi* what they claim would not be true at the level of legal rights. What they must be claiming, Cohen argued, when they claim their rights have been violated, must be a natural right because they "would be claiming to possess a right which is not merely a legal one" (12). But to claim a right that is not merely legal, or perhaps as in this case not a legal right at all, is just what Cohen meant by claiming a natural right. There is, he believed, nothing at all problematic here, nothing to get excited about that would lead to wild claims about natural rights being nonsense on stilts. As he summed it up, "The language of natural (or moral) rights is the language of justice, and whoever takes justice seriously must accept that there are natural rights" (12).

Marxists often deny they believe in natural rights or in justice because they, Cohen claimed, have a bad theory about their own moral beliefs. They have a deficient self-understanding here, and with these defects they misdescribe their own beliefs about justice and rights. Cohen put it thus:

> Now Marxists do not often talk about justice, and when they do they tend to deny its relevance, or they say that the idea of justice is an illusion. But I think that justice occupies a central place in revolutionary Marxist belief. Its presence is betrayed by particular judgments Marxists make, and by the strength of feeling with which they make them. Revolutionary Marxist belief often misdescribes itself, out of lack of clear awareness of its own nature, and Marxist disparagement of the idea of justice is a good example of that deficient self-understanding. I shall try to persuade you that Marxists, whatever they may say about themselves, do have strong beliefs about justice (12).

Cohen tried to show where in practice Marxists would typically make a strong judgment of justice at a point where social democrats typically engage in evasion.

Social democrats object to an unmixed capitalist market economy. They complain rightly that laissez faire capitalism sends the weak to the wall. We must, they argue, have welfare cushions to protect the weak: that is, the unemployable, those temporarily out of work, the underemployed, or those whose salaries are so low that they cannot maintain themselves in anything like a decent manner. According to this argument, a good society, indeed a just society, will be a *caring* society. But, Cohen claimed, the humaneness and reasonableness of these remarks notwithstanding, social democrats will have a hard time meeting the conservative counter that while an unregulated free market in any unmixed capitalist economy does indeed hurt a lot of people, still we cannot justly and rightly move to the mixed economy of the liberal welfare state. With its taxation powers to sustain welfare payments, the liberal welfare state will violate the rights of people to do what they will with what is their own—their private property—to which they have a natural right. Being theirs they can do with it what they will as long as they do not violate the rights of others. Indeed, under capitalism people do sometimes get hurt. After all, capitalism isn't the Salvation Army, but, if need be, it is better that people get hurt than that their rights be violated. Where rights and harms that do not violate rights conflict, rights trump. Capitalists should become charitable persons and give philanthropic aid, but they cannot be forced to do

so by the state, the church, or anyone because it would be a far greater
evil to override considerations of justice and violate people's rights
than to be uncharitable and not help people in need. The social
democrat, as Cohen saw it, will lose out to the conservative here.

According to Cohen, the revolutionary socialist (the Marxist), in
contrast to the social democrat, has a principled reply to the preceding
argument, but it requires an appeal to justice and to natural rights.
Instead of bemoaning the unfortunate effects on human well-being of
the absence of transfer payments of the welfare state, the Marxist should
reply "that the socializing state is not violating rights, or even overriding
them in the interest of something more important, but righting wrong:
it is rectifying violations of rights, violations inherent in the structure
of private property" (13). The very existence of the institution of
private productive property, the Marxist will argue, is unjust. As Cohen
put it in vividly contrasting the Marxist and socialist position with the
more evasive position of the social democrat, "The socialist objection
of justice to the market economy is that it allows private ownership
of the means of existence which no one has the right to own privately,
and therefore rests upon an unjust foundation" (13). Marxists should
set aside their traditional aversion to moral-talk and argue on a natural
rights basis here. Here we have, of course, a sharp contrast with Wood.

Cohen knew and granted that such rights-talk has a very un-Marxist
ring, but he urged Marxists and socialists to persist in such moralizing
talk in spite of the long-standing tradition that claims moral-talk is
ideological and that rejects Marxist moralism. "I am sure," he remarked,
"that revolutionaries believe this in their hearts, even those revolutionaries who deny that they believe it, because of ill-conceived philosophical commitments" (9). Well, I do indeed believe in my heart
(and in my head as well) that capitalism is unjust and that the private
ownership of productive property is morally unacceptable, but I am
also very uncertain, indeed deeply skeptical, as many socialist revolutionaries are, as to whether such natural rights–talk—*such* justice-
talk—has any non-rhetorical force. I wonder, that is, whether it is not
utterly caught up in the distortions of ideology.

Marx was not scathingly contemptuous of such talk of natural rights
and natural justice for nothing. Nozick told us that we have a natural
right to private property, including private productive property, and
that no one can override that right without violating our rights. Cohen,
by contrast, told us that we have no such natural right; that private
ownership of productive property is theft; and that morally speaking
the right to productive property belongs to all of us in common. He
believed this obtains whatever the law of a given society may say and
that as a moral right it is our natural right. This is just something we
somehow discover by moral reflection to be true just as Nozick thought
he had discovered the opposite to be true.

There are, however, all the old problems about natural rights standing
there before us unresolved as well as all the old problems with what

John Rawls called 'rational intuitionism.' These problems seem at least to apply to Cohen and Nozick alike with equal force. There are problems about how we would determine with any objectivity what is and isn't a natural right. We know historically and sociologically from the lists that have been proffered over cultural space and historical time by philosophers, politicians, theologians, and the like that very different and not infrequently incompatible things with different rationales have been claimed as human rights or as natural rights. Some claimants have been very abstemious, such as H.L.A. Hart at one time, about what, *if anything,* could count as a natural right, while others have been very latitudinarian in talking of welfare rights as natural rights. There have been all sorts of positions in between.[20] As Richard Miller argued, we seem at least to have too many rights, many of which conflict with no (apparent) way of making a further appeal to natural rights in order to determine which rights override when they conflict.[21] We seem, at least, if we remain in a hermeneutical circle of rights-talk, to have no way of knowing which of our putative rights, if any, are genuinely natural rights.

Cohen and Nozick, philosophers of no mean intellect, asserted exactly opposed things as natural rights. Each seemed to imply that if we would carefully reflect, it would be clear what our natural rights are, at least in determinate circumstances. Cohen and Nozick did argue in the idiom of rational intuitionism. Within that kind of framework they did try to provide convincing moral argumentation for one view or another, but they appealed to the very notions that seem to be in question, or at least to be problematic.

It is anything but clear whether we should expect anything very decisive here. Certain intuitions just seem without much in the way of rationalization to be unquestionably taken as foundational. Yet it seems very late in the day to try running such a moral Cartesianism. We seem to be at a loss here to ascertain what our natural rights really are. We are, as Bernard Williams pointed out, relying very heavily on intuition in a world where we know there are many and conflicting intuitions.[22]

When we reflect on this and on Marx's talk about morality being ideological, it is difficult, to put it mildly, to sustain a belief in natural rights. This is reinforced when we reflect on Marx's claims that rights claims are ideological (on a rational reconstruction—'pervasively tend to be ideological'); that what is standardly taken to be a right, either juridically or morally, in a given society during a given epoch will be determined or strongly conditioned by the mode of production at the time; and that our very understanding of ourselves, including our moral self-understanding, is deeply conditioned by the dominant ideology of the time. This sort of awareness inclines thoughtful people to be very wary indeed of talk about what in our heart of hearts we recognize to be a natural right or even to be fair or unfair. This awareness leads us to be very cautious about rational intuitionism. Our understanding of the way ideology functions gives us very good reasons to believe that our society, as every class society, cooks the books here. This should lead us to be very suspicious of our own self-consciousness—that is, of our own moral intuitions. Perhaps in some way—say by a very careful application of what John Rawls and Norman Daniels called the method of *wide* reflective equilibrium—we could winnow out these intuitions.[23] But this kind of fallibilism is distant from Cohen's, or for that matter Nozick's, confident reliance on relatively untutored moral intuitions.

There is, moreover, something worrisome about Cohen's initially attractive, streamlined way of talking about what it is for something to be a natural right. Recall Cohen's minimalist conception of what a natural right is: "Natural rights are rights which are not merely legal ones. We say that we have them on moral, not legal, grounds" (11). But suppose J. L. Mackie was right, and it is the case that moral beliefs, including beliefs in rights, are merely social demands, a conception with which some Marxists would sympathize. If that is so, what contrasts with something that is *just* a legal right? What is not *merely* a legal right is not just customary in the way legal rights are customary but is customary in some other way as well. If Mackie's account of moral beliefs is near to the mark, 'being customary' comes in this context to being the social demand of a determinate society, with a distinctive mode of production. That is surely not what Cohen wanted to call a 'natural right,' but the social demand is a right that is not merely a legal one or perhaps not a legal one at all, and so it fits Cohen's conception of a natural right. The social demand is a reading, albeit a reductionist one, of what a moral right is. Moral rights are social demands that are not merely legal or perhaps legal demands at all. But surely Cohen wanted to say something more, or at least people who have wanted to defend natural rights have wanted to assert something more robust.

The point—perhaps the whole point—of asserting natural rights is to assert something that people have in virtue of being human beings, something that allegedly does not depend on the legal code, the set of conventions, the customary conceptions of what is right or morally required or on any other customs, or on the social demands of a particular society, no matter how strongly or pervasively expressed. Natural rights were meant to be something that moral agents could assert in the face not only of legal social demands but in the face of any social demands at all, no matter how much social pressure there was behind them. But Cohen's characterization of a natural right as a moral right that is not merely legal does not entitle us to set natural rights against such social demands or to contrast them with such social demands. Cohen's characterization does not give us a higher tribunal, as the natural rights tradition thought it was doing, to assess our social demands, whether legal or nonlegal. With what, in effect, is a low redefinition of a 'natural right,' we are no longer able to make the very strong kind of claims that defenders of natural rights wished to make and that gave such talk point.[24]

It is unhelpful to say that, the foregoing notwithstanding, it really does make such a strong claim because for Cohen natural rights are rights we have on moral grounds. For such a counter to be persuasive, Cohen would have to make out that anti-realists in morality, such as Mackie or Westermarck, were mistaken in identifying morality with social demands. But to do so he would have to argue in the face of Marxist claims about ideology, the class bias of moral conceptions, and historical materialism. Marxist sociology of morals and Mackian-Westermarkean anti-moral realism claims seem at least to fit like hand and glove. I do not believe a Marxist has to have a Mackie-like conception of ethics, but it is a very natural resting place and fits at least on the surface, far better with a Marxist sociology than does a Cohen-like, Nozick-like Cartesian moral rationalism about natural rights clear to the light of reflective moral reason. No one who has a good sense, which we get from Marx and the Marxist tradition, about how ideology prone we are in such domains should have such a firm confidence in our capacities to be able, through intuition and moral reflection, to capture what it is that is right and morally required of us. Marxist immoralism jettisons too much, but natural rights Marxist moralism is far too rationalistically confident about our unschooled moral capacities.

VIII

These criticisms of a Marxist moralism that takes a natural rights turn may be too much of the guise and not probing enough of the substance of a rights-based Marxist moralism.[25] The confident assertiveness of Cohen's account could be dropped, and a fallibilistic tentativeness befitting any philosophical claim could be assumed without anything of its content being changed. What looks like an appeal to rational intuitionism or received opinion could be firmly set aside and the method of wide reflective equilibrium utilized.[26] Perhaps the natural rights Cohen appealed to could be sustained by such a procedure while the natural rights claims about private productive property made by Nozick and other right-wing libertarians are rejected.[27] Perhaps my criticisms reflect a meta-ethical nervousness about talk of natural rights more than anything substantive.

To illustrate, consider a possible response of Cohen. He could say that given his definition of 'natural rights' or any plausible emendation of it, natural rights could have any foundation you like. Natural rights might be founded on a utilitarian basis or on some egalitarian principle. Moreover, why shouldn't this meta-ethical nervousness also be extended to talk of justice and of things being good or bad? Why be more skeptical about natural rights than about any other moral norm, deontological or teleological? If a meta-ethical nervousness about rights is in part rooted in beliefs about how much of our moralizing is ideological, we need to temper this trepidation with the recognition that if any moral belief is to be ideological, not every moral belief can be. (If 'ideological' is to qualify 'moral belief,' it must make a non-vacuous contrast.) Cohen could well ask me, "of what normative belief pertinent to socialist action could you be more confident than the belief that we have a natural right to productive property that belongs to all of us in common?"

While taking the point about a need for a non-vacuous contrast, I would respond that the belief he mentioned is not one of the normative beliefs relevant to socialist action about which I am most confident and that I do not think other socialists should be either. I am far more confident (a) that in our time capitalism, at least in its present form, gives rise to unnecessary suffering, to a needless denial of opportunities, to alienated labor, to degradation of people, to an undermining of human autonomy, and to an unfair division of benefits, burdens, and life chances; and (b) that these are evils than I am that we have a *natural right* to productive property, which is to be held in common rather than owned privately as it must be in a capitalist society.[28] It could be a desirable thing that we hold such property in common rather than it being something to which we have a natural right. Even if we think the latter just might be true, we are, or at least should be, much more confident of the former. If more autonomy, more equality of condition and of opportunity, and less misery all around were to emerge from a social system that has the private ownership of productive property than could arise from feasible socialist alternative possibilities, then I would be for such capitalist property relations. As is almost always the case where live moral issues are involved, a lot turns on what the facts actually are. In almost all cases it is to the facts, theory dependent though they be, that we principally should direct our attention. I hold that what Cohen took to be a natural right is in fact a dependent, somewhat derivative moral belief, although not an unimportant moral belief for a socialist.

Marxists, as well as others, in seeking to make a moral critique of capitalism and a defense of socialism, would do well to focus on the harm capitalism does to people, the misery it creates and sustains, how it dehumanizes labor, the way it undermines autonomy, and how it militates against the possibility of a world where people could be *moral* equals. Such a view does not suffer from the criticisms I made of natural rights accounts, for the nature of these harms and the inequalities capitalism sustains are *comparatively* easy to ascertain. It is even easier to establish that these harms are unnecessary than it is to establish what we do or do not have natural rights to. Even considerations of justice, linked with conceptions of what is fair and what is not, rather than to considerations about the violations of natural rights, may very well be more amenable to rational assessment than will claims about natural rights. Marxists should focus their attention on considerations about needless suffering, the denial of autonomy and inequality, and the like rather than on the comparatively problematic conception of natural rights.

Cohen's account, as I have remarked, sounds like a form of rational intuitionism. He remarked about views like those of Westermarck or Mackie that if moral anti-realism is true, then rights are nonsense.[29] For Cohen, natural rights appear not to be something we construct but something that reflection reveals to us. We, that is, just discover it on reflection to be true that there are natural rights. But that is a very mystifying notion. Let me come at this indirectly. I have criticized his way of defining a natural right. He could amend his definition to avoid my criticism by saying that what makes a right natural is that its existence does not depend on its being in any sense recognized or established by law, custom, or whatever. Plainly, we would want to say, to use his example, that when the last Jew, in a society otherwise consisting entirely of Nazis, is dragged off, that this person can correctly say that his rights are being violated. Certainly, we must say and mean that. Still the 'we' that say 'we must' is not the 'we' of humankind at large but a certain sort of people, with certain traditions, socialized in certain ways, with certain socially acquired beliefs, with a certain understanding of the world, and the like. The very same 'we' will respond that *recognition* of this natural right may depend on our being a certain people but its *justification* does not. We—this particular 'we'—hope that anyone with anything like a reasonable understanding of the world and who reflects and takes the matter to heart would so respond. Perhaps by implicit, *persuasive* definition we are making this true by definition. But if this is so, then what we have accomplished is not very considerable. Cohen seemed to think that any rational being can just see or come to appreciate that such moral beliefs are true. But if when pressed we *just* have to rely on our intuitions or considered judgments, then we have something that is very historically and culturally variable, something that is too much like received opinion. Yet Cohen like Nozick seemed at least to rely very heavily on intuitions.

Cohen did indeed disavow any claim that in speaking of natural rights he was appealing to anything he claimed to be true because self-evident. He is not a kind of Marxist Henry Sidgwick or C. D. Broad. Still, Cohen did take certain moral beliefs to be something that on reflection we appreciate to be just obviously true, and he was confident that they require moral realism as a philosophical foundation. But both of these claims, to understate it, are very problematical philosophical claims. Cohen, like Nozick and unlike Rawls or Norman Daniels (both of whom were wary of such claims), was quick to appeal to intuition.

To such an appeal, my routine, if you will, ho-hum arguments against natural rights do apply, and nothing has proven them wrong for all of their ho-humedness. Perhaps if Cohen would utilize the coherentist methodology of wide reflective equilibrium, he could show that an account of natural rights with the content he gave to it would be the most adequate account of morality presently available.[30] He indeed might be able to show that wide reflective equilibrium would rationalize convictions about natural rights in a way that would yield a rationally justified Marxist moralism. I have not been concerned to deny that possibility but to argue (a) that it is something Marxists have good reasons to be wary of; (b) that it requires considerable careful elucidation and justification if it is to overcome such scruples; and (c) that there might be a far simpler way to defend a Marxist moralism. This defense could eschew giving natural rights a central place, or perhaps even any place, in moral deliberation and stress instead harms, unnecessary suffering, inequalities, the undermining of autonomy and fraternity, and the impeding of human flourishing.

Such an approach fits better with the naturalism of Marxism than does any appeal to natural rights. There are in our society also a motley of goods and rather divergent conceptions of what is fair and what is not. (This is something that Marxist anti-moralists have rightly stressed, as did Marx himself.) But that notwithstanding, the good ties in more straightforwardly with naturalistic notions of needs and wants than do rights.[31] Conceptions of fairness, which can be uncoupled from a stress on rights, are linked clearly, coupled or uncoupled, with a central moral belief held across the political and moral spectrum by people touched by modernity—namely, a belief in *moral* equality, a very deep-seated conviction that the life of everyone matters and matters equally. Modern defenders of natural rights believe this, but so do people who will have neither truck nor trade with natural rights. It is a part of modern moral sensibility, but this is not to say that this belief must be taken as an intuition and cannot be placed in a wide reflective equilibrium with other beliefs, moral and otherwise, that are part of a modern *Sittlichkeit.*[32] This gives us a kind of objectivity (a rationalized and informed intersubjectivity) but hardly the objectivity the rational intuitionist looks to have or the kind that would require, as Cohen required, moral realism. But such a moral objectivity is not unproblematic and may very well be unnecessary to make sense of our moral lives. There are reasons, perhaps compelling reasons, as Bertrand Russell believed, for regarding moral realism as a deeply entrenched philosophical myth. A Marxist moralism requiring such foundations and a Marxist anti-moralism may be taking in each other's dirty linen.[33] Marxists may be able to get on very well indeed without taking sides on such arcane matters as moral realism or moral anti-realism and that without lapsing into Marxist anti-moralism.[34]

Notes

1. Robert Tucker, *The Marxian Revolutionary Idea* (New York: Norton, 1969), Chapter 2; Robert Tucker, *Philosophy and the Myth of Karl Marx*

(Cambridge: Cambridge University Press, 1961), pp. 11–27; Allen W. Wood, "The Marxian Critique of Justice," *Philosophy and Public Affairs* 1 (1972–73):224–282; and Allen W. Wood, "Marx on Right and Justice," *Philosophy and Public Affairs* 8 (1978–79):267–295; Ziyad Husami, "Marx on Distributive Justice," *Philosophy and Public Affairs* 8 (1978–79):27–64; Gary Young, "Justice and Capitalist Production: Marx and Bourgeois Ideology," *Canadian Journal of Philosophy* 8 (1978):421–454; Gary Young, "Doing Marx Justice," *Canadian Journal of Philosophy*, Supplementary vol. 7 (1981):251–268; Richard Miller, *Analyzing Marx* (Princeton, N.J.: Princeton University Press, 1985), pp. 3–97; Richard Norman, *The Moral Philosophers* (Oxford: Clarendon Press, 1983), pp. 173–201; Steven Lukes, *Marxism and Morality* (Oxford: Clarendon Press, 1985); Jon Elster, *Making Sense of Marx* (Cambridge: Cambridge University Press, 1985), pp. 196–233. For an important review article (a) that has a thorough grasp and an illuminating categorization of the literature and (b) that provides a defense of Marxist moralism, see Norman Geras, "On Marx and Justice," *New Left Review* 150 (March/April 1985):47–89.

2. On the side I characterize, following Wood, as Marxist immoralism there are Allen W. Wood, Richard W. Miller, Andrew Collier, and Anthony Skillen. On the Marxist moralist side there are G. A. Cohen, William Shaw, Norman Geras, Jon Elster, and Gary Young. Yet in their overall philosophical approaches these philosophers have much in common. They are all, broadly speaking, in the analytical tradition. For a description of the phenomena of analytical Marxism see Richard W. Miller, "Marx in Analytic Philosophy: The Story of a Rebirth," *Social Science Quarterly* 4, no. 4 (December 1983):846–861.

3. Allen W. Wood, *Karl Marx* (London: Routledge & Kegan Paul, 1982); G. A. Cohen, "Review of Wood's *Karl Marx*," *Mind* 92, no. 367 (July 1983):440–445; G. A. Cohen, *Karl Marx's Theory of History: A Defence* (Oxford: Oxford University Press, 1978); G. A. Cohen, "Freedom, Justice and Capitalism," *New Left Review* (March/April 1981):3–16; and G. A. Cohen, "The Critique of Private Property: Nozick on Appropriation," *New Left Review* (March/April 1985):89–108.

4. This was argued with particular force by Allen W. Wood in two recent articles. Allen W. Wood, "Marx's Immoralism," in Bernard Chavance (ed.), *Marx en Perspective* (Paris: Editions de l'Ecole des Haute Etudes en Sciences Sociales, 1985), pp. 681–698; and in his "Justice and Class Interests," *Philosophica* 33, no. 1 (1984):9–32. I shall particularly be concerned to examine the latter article in this chapter.

5. Wood, "Marx's Immoralism," pp. 695–698; and Miller, *Analyzing Marx*, pp. 94–97.

6. Wood, "Justice and Class Interests."

7. See Wood, "The Marxian Critique of Justice"; "Marx on Right and Justice"; and *Karl Marx*, pp. 125–156.

8. Ibid., p. 11. This article will take close textual analysis in my text. Future page references to it will be given in the text.

9. Miller, *Analyzing Marx*, pp. 15–97. Was Miller being realistic here? Is it plausible for people to think that Marx thought the horrors he described in the first volume of *Capital* or the ones that Engels described in writing about Manchester would look horrible only if one identified with the proletarian standpoint? Did Miller think that Marx believed there could not be an impartial reason for adopting that very standpoint? It would hardly seem credible to answer either question in the affirmative. But this looks very much like a reductio.

10. Wood, *Karl Marx,* pp. 125–156. There is some suggestion that Wood might have been confusing an attempt to advance the common interests of all society with defending an impartial principle of justice. But what can be impartially defended, particularly in an unjust society, need not be the same thing as what is in the common interests of the whole society.

11. See Wood, "Marx's Immoralism."

12. Kai Nielsen, "On Taking Historical Materialism Seriously," *Dialogue* 22 (1983):319–338.

13. Miller, *Analyzing Marx,* pp. 15–50. Cohen thought that in a way Marx believed the very reverse—that no large-scale historical action ever takes place except under the banner of the general interest of society. He further believed that in the socialist case that what the banner proclaims is also non-evanescently true. See G. A. Cohen, "Peter Mew on Justice and Capitalism," *Inquiry* 29, no. 3 (September 1986):315–324. I am indebted to Cohen here as I am for the substantive remarks in notes 9 and 10.

14. Joel Feinberg, "The Nature and Value of Rights," in S. Gorovitz et al. (eds.), *Moral Problems in Medicine* (Englewood Cliffs, N.J.: Prentice-Hall, 1976), pp. 454–467. I have argued that Marx believed, and rightly so, that what furthers the cause of the proletariat also furthers the cause of justice. It could be argued that it is not so obvious that the two could not conflict (in real life situations). If, for example, Stalin was generally correct in identifying proletarian interests and acted effectively in their interests, then it would seem that morality and proletarianism have conflicted over and over again in actual human history. Perhaps the starving of the Ukrainian kulaks was in the long-term interests of the proletariat. That is surely a conceptual possibility, but it is also thoroughly evident that nothing like this actually obtaining is even remotely plausible. It is political fiction. What is needed to undermine my claim is a plausible case of where long-term proletarian interests conflict with the good of humankind. I do not think there are any. If I am mistaken about that empirical issue, then things are more difficult than I supposed.

15. Andrew Levine, *Arguing for Socialism* (London: Routledge & Kegan Paul, 1984), pp. 65–76.

16. Karl Marx, *Marx-Engels Werke,* vol. 3 (Berlin: Dietz, 1961–66), p. 443.

17. John Rawls, "The Independence of Moral Theory," *Proceedings and Addresses of the American Philosophical Association* 47 (1974–75):5–22; and his "Justice as Fairness: Political Not Metaphysical," *Philosophy and Public Affairs* 14, no. 3 (Summer 1985):223–251.

18. An important defense of it from a variety of criticisms was made by Cohen in his "Reply to Four Critics," *Analyse & Kritik* 5, no. 3 (December 1983):195–222. The article with the strange natural rights thesis I am concerned critically to inspect is his "Freedom, Justice and Capitalism," *New Left Review* 126 (1981):3–16. Future page references to it will be given in the text. I think *in this domain* that Cohen's work suffers from taking Nozick too seriously.

19. Kai Nielsen, *Equality and Liberty: A Defense of Radical Egalitarianism* (Totowa, N.J.: Rowman and Allanheld, 1985).

20. H.L.A. Hart, "Are There Any Natural Rights?" *The Philosophical Review* 64 (1985); and Rodney Peffer, "A Defense of Rights to Well-Being," *Philosophy and Public Affairs* 8 (1978–79).

21. Miller, *Analyzing Marx,* pp. 22–30. See also his "Rights or Consequences," in *Midwest Studies in Philosophy* 7 (1982):151–174; and his "Rights and Reality," *The Philosophical Review* 90, no. 3 (July 1981):383–407. This

was discussed in Chapter 9 where the possibility of their being a 'super-right' to break conflicts was trotted out to give the rights-based theorist a little more *Lebensraum.*

22. Bernard Williams, "The Moral View of Politics," *The Listener* (June 3, 1986).

23. Rawls, "The Independence of Moral Theory," pp. 5–22; Norman Daniels, "Wide Reflective Equilibrium and Theory Acceptance in Ethics," *The Journal of Philosophy* 76 (1979):256–282; and Norman Daniels, "Reflective Equilibrium and Archimedean Points," *Canadian Journal of Philosophy* 10, no. 1 (March 1980):83–103.

24. Paul Edwards, *The Logic of Moral Discourse* (Glencoe, Ill.: Free Press, 1955), explained the term of art 'low redefinition.'

25. In what follows I address, among other things, myself to a host of queries and criticisms made by G. A. Cohen. I am grateful for his perceptive criticisms, and I hope I have gone some way toward meeting them.

26. John Rawls, *A Theory of Justice* (Cambridge, Mass.: Harvard University Press, 1971), pp. 19–21, 48–51, 577–587; "The Independence of Moral Theory," *Proceedings and Addresses of the American Philosophical Association* 47 (1974-75):7–10. Daniels, "Wide Reflective Equilibrium and Theory Acceptance in Ethics," pp. 256–282; "Moral Theory and Plasticity of Persons," *The Monist* 62 (1979):265–287; "Some Methods of Ethics and Linguistics," *Philosophical Studies* 37 (1980):21–36; "Reflective Equilibrium and Archimedean Points," pp. 83–103; "Two Approaches to Theory Acceptance in Ethics" in David Copp and David Zimmerman (eds.), *Morality, Reason and Truth* (Totowa, N.J.: Rowman and Allanheld, 1985), pp. 120–140; and "An Argument about the Relativity of Justice," *Revue Internationale de Philosophie* (1989). Jane English, "Ethics and Science," *Proceedings of the XVI Congress of Philosophy.* Kai Nielsen, "On Needing a Moral Theory: Rationality, Considered Judgements and the Grounding of Morality," *Metaphilosophy* 13, no. 12 (1982):97–116; "Considered Judgements Again," *Human Studies* 6 (1982):109–118; and *Equality and Liberty,* Chapter 2.

27. G. A. Cohen, "The Critique of Private Property"; and his "Robert Nozick and Wilt Chamberlain: How Patterns Preserve Liberty," *Erkenntnis* 2 (1977):5–23.

28. I am, of course, more confident that they are evils than I am that they or at least some of them are *unnecessary* evils. What level and what type of productive advance we need to be able equitably to meet needs are not easy to ascertain. There is a whole cluster of factual-cum-theoretical questions that make a developed Marxist sociology and political economy something we very much need in such contexts if moral theorizing is to have much in the way of a practical point. See here Andrew Collier, "Scientific Socialism and the Question of Socialist Values," *Canadian Journal of Philosophy,* Supplementary volume 7 (1981):121–154; Kai Nielsen, "Coming to Grips with Marxist Anti-Moralism," *Philosophical Forum* 19, no. 1 (Fall 1987):1–22; and Kai Nielsen, "On the Poverty of Moral Philosophy," *Studies in Soviet Thought* 33 (1987):39–56.

29. It is instructive to contrast J. L. Mackie's view here. He did not think that moral anti-realism required the repudiation of a rights-based theory. J. L. Mackie, *Persons and Values* (Oxford: Clarendon Press, 1985), pp. 105–119.

30. See references in note 21.

31. The extensive relevance of needs here was powerfully argued by David Braybrooke, *Meeting Needs* (Princeton, N.J.: Princeton University Press, 1987).

32. Chapter 11 herein.

33. My criticisms of Cohen are not meant to show that a sound rights-based defense of Marxist moralism could not be articulated. I only seek to show that an account so freely appealing to intuitions and so ready to invoke moral realism will not do without very extensive supplementary argument. It is, however, very questionable whether such a supplementary argument can be successfully carried out. Similar arguments could be used against such a deployment of intuitions concerning what is good and what is just. But my criticisms of Marxist immoralism do not rely on such an appeal.

34. It was Wood's claim that a consistent Marxist must accept the class interest thesis. This entails putting class interests first, and this, for a clear-headed and reasonable socialist militant or someone unequivocally taking the standpoint of labor, means giving pride of place in contemporary circumstances to proletarian class interests, even if they conflict with what are generally regarded as correct moral claims. This is not merely because of the revolutionary efficacy of proletarian interests (nor did Wood claim that), but this is what we should do if we care about human emancipation and think that historical materialism is roughly correct. For Wood, paradoxically, this 'should' would have to be some non-moral but still rationally and normatively justifiable use of 'should.' I argue, alternatively, that the 'should' here is a moral should; that there is no conflict in contemporary circumstances between proletarian class interests and the moral point of view in real life situations; and that we can safely ignore desert island situations. I add 'contemporary circumstances' because in the very early stages of capitalism, horrible as the very contemplation of that is, the everything-considered morally correct thing to do was to favor the development of capitalism, even though that was not in the short-term interests of the proletariat or in the long-term interests of the proletarians then alive. This was necessary to build up the productive forces, which in turn was necessary to achieve human emancipation. To will the end is to will the necessary means to the end, although this does not mean that we will it without ambivalence or sorrow. This streak of consequentialism, incidentally, by no means commits me to utilitarianism.

11

Marxism and the
Moral Point of View

Marxists, I shall argue, are best understood not as rejecting morality per se, as jettisoning moral belief *holus bolus,* but as rejecting something very pervasive in class societies—namely, moral ideology, those false moral conceptions that have the appearance of universality but in reality only answer to the interests of a determinate class.[1] Allen Wood, by contrast, saw Marx "as a critic or opponent of morality, and not merely of false moral ideas but of all morality."[2] Marx, Wood told us, was an immoralist (683). Wood, of course, realized and indeed stressed what is patently evident anyway—that Marx's "writings are filled with bitter denunciations of the capitalist system and its defenders, as well as extravagant praise for the radical working class movement and for those whom he views as its legitimate representatives" (681). However, it is not clear, Wood went on to say, what "norms or values . . . lay behind his critique of capitalism and his advocacy of communism or socialism" (681). But it is clear that Marx did have an "attitude of extreme and open hostility to moral theorizing, to moral values . . . even to morality itself" (682). Given that Marx himself was quite prepared, without the slightest hesitation or ambivalence, to make firm moral judgments, why (pace Wood) is it not more plausible to believe that Marx was not rejecting morality itself but its false coinage in the *moralism* of moral ideology—an ideology that does its subterranean work in the oppression of the working class, the peasantry, and the like? The very passion of Marx's denunciation of morality is explained by the moralist's hatred and contempt for the misuse of genuine morality in a moral *ideology* that serves repressive ruling-class interests.

Wood, however, staunchly maintained that matters run deeper than that. Notions such as justice and rights (the very concepts themselves), Wood argued, cannot, in a manner consistent with what is canonical in Marxist theory, have the kind of transhistorical validity that most people, including most philosophers, believe they have. Put differently, if Marxist theory is correct, Wood contended, claims of justice and rights cannot have any transhistorical validity. Indeed, he would have it, they cannot on a consistent Marxist account have any critical rational force at all. They only have, and can only have, a sociological, juridical reality. What is right or what is just is mode-of-production relative. Conceptions of rights or of justice are superstructural notions dependent on the mode of production of the time. What is just—and not merely what is *thought* to be just—is what helps facilitate or stabilize the dominant mode of production of the time, and what rights we have, what conceptions we have of them, and what weight we give to conflicting rights are similarly functional for the dominant mode of production. Where for a time the class struggle is intense and where there is no dominant mode of production, there are and can be no accepted, culturally authoritative standards of justice or of rights. These notions in such circumstances will at best be essentially contested concepts. There is no reality to which they can answer.

In criticizing capitalism, to talk of violation of the rights of workers is to substitute verbal mystification for a scientific analysis of the workers' situation and their prospects. Such moralizing has no genuine emancipatory force. What is needed instead are scientific analyses, both abstract ones and concrete ones, that will enable members of the working class to know who they are, what their class interests are, who they were, and who they might become. This scientific analysis— not moral philosophy, analysis of moral conceptions, or moralizing— is what the working class needs, particularly when the reality of moral beliefs is mode-of-production dependent and has no transhistorical or critical reality.

As J. L. Mackie would put it, there is no objective prescriptivity to moral beliefs.[3] People mistakenly believe in morals. That is, they believe in some objective, transhistorical reality to which moral notions answer, but this belief rests on a mistake, for there is no such transhistorical moral reality. If we have a good scientific understanding, which historical materialism and a Marxist theory of classes will arguably give us, we will see that there can be no rational Archimedean point that will enable us to assess societies and say which are just and which not or what the inalienable rights of human beings are or what the good life for a human being is. As Wood put it, "According to *The German Ideology*, the discovery by historical materialism of the connection between moral ideology and material class interests has 'broken the staff of all morality' whatever the content of that morality might be" (682). Morality—all morality, "and not just bourgeois ideology about morality"—has, Wood maintained, been scientifically and rationally described and analyzed in such a way that anyone who understands what is going on will come to see that believing in morals is rationally on a par with believing in God where it is clear enough that God is some sort of reified human projection. Neither God nor morality can be what their faithful take them to be. Neither answer, nor can answer, to any objective reality. Belief in God or in morals rests on illusions.

II

I do not mean to deny that Marx sometimes had some such meta-belief, and I do not mean to deny that some acute philosophers, both Marxist and non-Marxist, have thought something like this as well.[4] What I do want to query is whether the Marxist canon commits us to a rejection of morality.

Wood believed that the destruction of the foundations of morality or indeed of any reasonable rationale for believing in morals is one of the achievements of historical materialism (682). That is to say, he believed that if historical materialism is a correct scientific account of epochal social change, then morality can have no rational foundation. One way the argument could go is like this: Historical materialism (the materialist conception of history) requires that all moral beliefs and conceptions be ideological, be beliefs and conceptions that wittingly or unwittingly represent, or at least answer to, class interests, while through the distorting lens of ideology these beliefs are represented in class ideology (a pleonasm) as answering to the interests of everyone alike in an even-handed way. Morality just is, and can only be, moral ideology, and ideological conceptions necessarily distort our understanding of ourselves and our class situation in the interests of the hegemony of some class. Such conceptions will not help liberate us from oppression, but will help to continue to shackle us to that very oppression. Historical materialism and a Marxist theory of ideology show us why moral ideas can answer to nothing objective and why they are, and must be, merely vehicles of class interests, typically of dominant class interests.

Historical materialism and a Marxist theory of ideology, I shall now argue, do not establish any such thing. They in effect tender a sociology of morals.[5] They show us, if they are approximately correct conceptions themselves, how morality *typically* functions in class society, how moral notions massively and pervasively affect people's lives in class society. Historical materialism and a Marxist theory of ideology show us the dark, oppressive underside of morality in our lives in class societies. It is the analogue in the public domain of what Freud, another stern critic of moralism, showed in the domain of so-called private morality.

But this Marxist sociology of morals is not, even implicitly, an epistemology or a meta-ethic. This sociology of morals requires no epistemology of ethics or a meta-ethic, let alone an error-theorist meta-ethic, such as Edward Westermarck's or J. L. Mackie's, or some other subjectivist account to set against moral realism or quasi-moral realism. Historical materialism is neutral with respect to these arcane disputes. It enjoins neither subjectivism, moral realism, quasi-moral realism, anti-moral realism, or anti-anti-moral realism.

Moral ideas are, of course (and trivially so), a part of the superstructure, if historical materialism is true, but from this it does not follow that moral ideas must be ideological, for while all ideological conceptions are superstructural, not all superstructural conceptions are ideological. For, if they were, then all ideas, including many if not all of Marx's own ideas, would be ideological and Marx would have hoisted himself by his own petard. However, principles of interpretive charity will hardly allow this reading, particularly if we can find an equally plausible reading that does not require it. A refusal to identify superstructural and ideological notions does just that and has a solid textual base as well. However, even if this refusal did not have such a textual base, there is no reason why contemporary Marxists should not draw this distinction in the superstructure between ideological beliefs and non-ideological superstructural beliefs.[6] This distinction allows Marxists to go on saying what a Marxist understanding of the sociology of morals and ideology requires—namely, that morality is *ideology prone*—but this distinction does not require the stronger claim that all moral ideas, because they are superstructural, *must* be ideological or that they must be ideological *sans phrase*.

This saves the phenomena. We can see why Marxists have rightly said, as a remark in the sociology of morals, that morality is ideology while also allowing Marx, Engels, and others to condemn capitalism as oppressive and dehumanizing and to speak consistently, particularly in private correspondence, of what common human decency and socialist duty require and of what the contours of a truly human society would look like.

III

Even if we do not distinguish between superstructural considerations and ideological ones, as one species of superstructural considerations, a good understanding of ideology would give us a reading that would allow us consistently and non-pejoratively to speak, as Lenin and Trotsky did, of a socialist ideology. That reading will make the mark (the determining criterion) of the ideological that it answer to class interests, not that it distorts our understanding of social reality. A 'non-class ideology' on such a conception is a contradiction in terms. Marxists can, and I believe should, define 'an ideology' as a cluster of beliefs, conceptions, or practices that function, or at least purports to function, to serve the interests of a class or sometimes of several classes (this is a theory-justified stipulative definition, a reformative definition, if you will). On that conception there can be dominant class ideologies and challenging class ideologies.

The foregoing conceptualization, while squaring well with Marxist texts, has a number of other distinct advantages. It does not set Lenin, with his talk of 'socialist ideology,' into conflict with Marx; it does not make an ideology something that must, in however a disguised or an elliptical way, be a form of propaganda distorting our understanding of ourselves and our world; and it does not set science and ideology on a collision course by holding that if a belief is ideological, it cannot be a true scientific belief. An ideological belief need not distort and that it answers to class interests need not make it unscientific. Some of Keynes's economic theories could have served capitalist interests and no doubt did; nevertheless, these theories could have been correct or partially correct scientific accounts or at least genuinely scientific accounts. And Marx certainly thought his economic doctrines in *Capital* were true scientific accounts; yet he also believed they plainly served proletarian interests. Moreover (to state the obvious), that they did so was extremely important to him. Somewhat parallel things can be said of morality. The moral belief 'Capitalism robs the workers' could serve the interests of the working class and thus be a bit of working-class ideology and still be a justified moral belief—justifiable, that is, from a disinterested point of view.

However, if we read the Marxist slogan 'Morality is ideology' as saying that all morality must be ideological like all cats must be feline, then even on the foregoing reading of 'ideology,' we make Marxists say something that (to put it charitably) has to be implausible. This would make it impossible in the future communist society for there to be moral relations among human beings. Morality would simply drop out in a classless society. Marx, in his wilder utopian fantasies, did talk of morality, along with law, disappearing in the future communist society.[7] But Jon Elster was surely right in saying that in a perfectly Marxist sense that is bad utopianism.[8]

We will never have such abundance that people will be able to take whatever it is they need, and although in the future communist society conflicts among people will be fewer and people will no longer be so prone to pursue such self-interested directions, there still will be some conflict of interests. Couples will sometimes split up, and they will both want the child or the dog for the preponderance of the time. There will be situations where, between two thoroughly competent persons, both persons cannot get the chair in Micronesian studies at the same university at the same time. In fine, sometimes—although not so pervasively and no longer across class lines—people will be at cross purposes. Moreover, no matter how altruistic people may turn out to be, they will still need some impartial device to adjudicate conflicts of interests, and this is one of the fundamental things for which we have morality and law. In a classless society and a stateless society there would be fewer such conflicts, but it is totally unrealistic not to believe that some will remain. We would, even with the withering away of the state, need some state-like devices for law, and even if we could dispense with law, we would still need morality impartially to adjudicate such conflicts. Imaginative alterations of elements in the situation could rid us of some conflicts of interest. We might, for a conveniently easy example, have two chairs at the same place at the same time in Micronesian studies. But some conflicts, it is safe to predict, would remain in any society, and we need morality or law backed up by morality fairly to adjudicate such conflicts.

We must take care that we do not so characterize ideology and morality such that we end up making it logically (conceptually) impossible for there to be morality in a classless society, where there will be extensive clarity in the social relations between people. To claim there can be no morality in a classless society is absurd. We should not want so to gerrymand our ways of talking and conceiving that we make it impossible for us to speak of there being a morality in a classless society. To do so is merely to play with words. We can with every bit as much fidelity to the core conceptions of Marxism give a sociological reading to the claim that morality is ideology rather than an epistemological reading that would make 'morality is ideology' parallel to the claim that cats are feline. This sociological reading makes sense of Marx and Marxism. It obviates what would otherwise be paradoxes, and it fits with the Marxist core. Although this reading does indeed conflict with Marx's remark about morality coming to an end in a classless society, that remark is (a) not even remotely a part of the Marxist core or entailed by that core and (b) it is in itself wildly implausible.

IV

There is another way that historical materialism might be thought to undermine morality. Historical materialism, it has been said, requires historical determinism, and historical determinism, it has also not infrequently been claimed, undermines genuine human agency and with that moral responsibility. Knowledge of historical necessity and knowing in a determinate historical circumstance what is the right thing to do are, given historical determinism, one and the same. The moral *is* what is historically necessary, whatever that is; those who have a correct understanding of the laws of social development will also, and automatically, know what is right and wrong, good and bad, desirable and undesirable for humankind.[9] But if there were such necessities, this would undermine our very conception of moral agency and thus, paradoxically, of morality.

This hard, determinist line fits badly with Engels's remark in *The Holy Family* that "there is no independent entity called 'history' using mankind to attain its ends; history is simply the purposeful activity of human beings" and with Marx's famous remark that "men make their own history but do not make it irrespective of the conditions they are in." It may, however, be replied that Marx's stress on praxis and class struggle (in general, on human agency) to the contrary notwithstanding, if historical materialism is true, it requires historical determinism, and determinism of any sort requires the belief that there are causal links beyond human agency that are both necessary and sufficient for human beings doing what they do and for their not doing what they do not do. Moral responsibility and genuine human agency, Marx's pious hopes to the contrary notwithstanding, must be an illusion if historical materialism is true.

To this there are at least two things to be said. First, historical materialism is not so tightly formulated that it requires historical determinism, economic determinism, or anything so determinate and deterministic. Historical materialism does not say that for any event, including, of course, any historical event, of type A, there is some set of initial conditions of type B and C such that when such initial conditions occur an event of type A will occur. Historical materialism makes no such tight claim. Marx's account here is not as fine grained as that. It only asserts, in a theory of epochal social change, that when the productive forces are so developed that they tend to clash with the productive relations, it becomes increasingly probable that sooner or later a social revolution will occur that will bring on stream-changed relations of production. The relations will better match with the forces of production, and with that change an altered superstructure will in time appear that will better match with the relations of production. Talk of inevitability is hyperbolic for what is very, very probable. In short, we need not read historical materialism in a deterministic fashion. We need not stick Marx, who wished to set aside philosophy, with such a philosophical doctrine.

However, for those like myself who find determinism, at least for macroscopic objects, a very plausible conception indeed, we can, as Richard Rorty is wont to put it, be good compatibilists as were Thomas Hobbes, Benedict de Spinoza, David Hume, and J. S. Mill. So we can agree that historical materialism is best understood as requiring determinism, but given that determinism is compatible with human agency and the only kind of freedom that really matters to human beings, we can read Marx and Engels as what they probably were anyway (given the influence on them of Hegel and through Hegel, Spinoza)—compatibilists who maintained there is no conflict between determinism and freedom. Talk of determinism and talk of human agency are different vocabularies that go on in different, non-competing language games used for different and non-conflicting purposes.

In the long history of philosophical disputes about determinism and moral responsibility, compatibilism is perhaps not a clear winner, but particularly in some of its recent sophisticated and nuanced formulations, it has been made very plausible indeed in spite of its initial counter-intuitiveness to someone first coming to philosophy.[10] Everything considered, compatibilism has fewer paradoxes and non-explanatory elements than do its incompatibilist rivals. There is no reason why historical materialists cannot avail themselves of the more sophisticated compatibilist accounts and set aside the claim that if historical determinism is true, historical necessity and moral judgment are one and the same and that, as Paul Henri Holbach maintained, human agency and moral responsibility are illusions.

V

Allen Wood made an argument that was different from any of those that we have previously canvassed.[11] It is an argument (a) that has considerable plausibility for what he regarded as Marx's immoralism and (b) in which he showed that Marx's immoralism was a consistent and plausible doctrine fully compatible with the Marxist core. Indeed, the Marxist core may, Wood claimed, even require it. I am not much concerned to deny that a Marxist immoralism—a view of Marx as a critic of morality who also rejected morality at least in political domains—is *consistent* with Marxist core beliefs.[12] Rather, I am concerned to give rational grounds for denying the claim that the Marxist core *requires,* or even clearly favors, Marxist immoralism.

Marxist immoralism cannot even be consistent with the Marxist core if G. A. Cohen's powerful criticism of Wood is sound, but Steven Lukes and Jon Elster in turn raised problems about Cohen's arguments that may have some force.[13] I do not want to crawl again into that thicket in this chapter (although I shall in the next); my intent is to consider here whether the Marxist core requires a Marxist immoralism or even whether the account that is most evidently in accordance with that core is a Marxist immoralism.[14]

Let me first set out Wood's arguments. Wood saw "Marx's immoralism as a repudiation of moral values in favour of certain nonmoral ones" (686). Wood thought, not implausibly, that Marx "derived his conception of morality from Hegel, but modified it in certain ways in accordance with his materialist theory of history" (686). When we see that Hegel's conception was a deep repudiation of the tradition in moral philosophy coming down to us from the utilitarians and from Kant, we will see, if taken with historical materialism, a plausible rationale for Marx's immoralism. As Wood put it:

> I think that someone who held a basically Hegelian conception of morality and its role in human life together with a Marxian materialist conception of history and a Marxian preoccupation with freedom and rational

transparency in social relationships might have quite strong reservations about morality, strong enough to motivate the anti-moral pronouncements we find in Marx's writings" (686).

In contrast with Mill and Kant, and indeed with the tradition in moral philosophy, Hegel believed there are two complimentary concepts of morality, not one. For Hegel there is morality as *Moralität* and, in contrast, morality as *Sittlichkeit*. *Moralität*, as Wood nicely put it, "is the reflective attitude of an active agent seeking to actualize the idea of autonomy or subjective freedom" (686).[15] By contrast, "*Sittlichkeit* is the set of institutions and objective norms, sanctioned by custom, through which the members of a living and rational social order fulfill the demands of the social whole to which they belong" (686).[16] In Hegel's theory *Moralität* and *Sittlichkeit* are importantly and closely interrelated, although in important ways *Moralität* is parasitic on *Sittlichkeit*. The parasitic side is this: Without the customary morality of *Sittlichkeit*, "derived from the social order, the conscientious individual self would have no content, no specific duties through which to express itself" (686).[17] Morality as *Sittlichkeit* provides *the actual content of the moral order* because its norms represent to individuals what Hegel called a rational or universal life and interest. Moreover, without this social order the individual would be rudderless and "doomed to impotence and frustration in its attempts to realize the moral good" (686).[18] The achievement of individual autonomy, for Hegel, "consists precisely (*sic*) in the actualization of the universal by the individual" (686).

However, the relation of *Moralität* to *Sittlichkeit* is not entirely parasitical. As societies move toward the Enlightenment, an element of reciprocity between *Moralität* and *Sittlichkeit* grows steadily stronger. To be rational in form, *Sittlichkeit* needs *Moralität*. As we move toward the Enlightenment, individuals in such cultures begin to see themselves as autonomous, and they begin to demand that what they, as individuals, will—or at least will in a universalizable way—be seen by their culture, indeed the whole social world, as good. *Moralität* and *Sittlichkeit* come, for Hegel, to fit like hand and glove. As Wood put it, "For Hegel . . . the norms of morality are the demands a social order makes on individuals in order to sustain its life and impose its rational form on the world. And these norms have rational validity for the individual because their fulfillment enables the individual self to attain rational autonomy and self mastery" (686).

How would someone, as Marx presumably did, who started with that Hegelian conception of morality come to see morality (assuming this person had a good understanding of what he or she was doing), once he or she accepted what I have called the Marxist core set of beliefs, particularly historical materialism? Wood's answer emerged in the following crucial passage:

Let us now try to imagine how morality, conceived along Hegelian lines, ought to strike a Marxian historical materialist. A historical materialist conceives of a social order not as a form of spirit but as a form of commerce or mode of production. For nearly the whole of past social history, moreover, society has been divided into hostile classes whose interests are fundamentally divided by relations of oppression or exploitation. If objective moral norms represent the demands of the current social order, then most fundamentally they represent the economic needs of the prevailing mode of production. They enjoin conduct from each individual which corresponds to that mode, which is harmonious or functional in relation to it. Thereby, they enjoin from each individual the behavior which is on the whole advantageous to the ruling and exploiting classes within the society. Thus if the Hegelian conception of morality as *Sittlichkeit* is correct, then the *Sittlichkeit* of bourgeois society will indeed be what *The Communist Manifesto* says it is, merely bourgeois prejudices masking bourgeois interests (687).

Whatever Marx may or may not have believed here—and Wood recognized that our claims must remain speculative for we have no texts to seize on—a Marxist, starting from the Marxist core, need not accept such a Hegelian account of ethics. He or she can, and in my view should, recognize that Hegel was gesturing at something important with his distinction between morality as *Sittlichkeit* and as *Moralität,* but he or she need not accept Hegel's rationalist and politically naive rendering of *Sittlichkeit. Sittlichkeit,* as we have seen, is conceived by Hegel as "the set of institutions and objective norms, sanctioned by custom, through which the members of a living and rational social order fulfill the demands of the social world to which they belong" (686). But a Marxist, or for that matter a non-Marxist empiricist, might simply excise the rationalistic elements in Hegel's conception of the concept of *Sittlichkeit* (remember it is not meant to be a term of art) and keep what at least is arguably insightful. What we need to do is to excise the phrases 'objective norms' and 'rational' from the preceding characterization, and then, by making some realistic substitutions, we will gain a far less tendentious characterization of *Sittlichkeit.* In the de-mythologized characterization it reads: "*Sittlichkeit* is the set of institutions and, culturally speaking, deeply embedded norms, sanctioned by custom, through which the members of the social order in question fulfill the demands of the social whole to which they belong." Without bringing in contentious philosophical claims, or being in any other way tendentious, we have here a less philosophically loaded characterization of *Sittlichkeit* that still brings out its vital social function in society. Indeed, without Hegel's obscurities about rationality, *Sittlichkeit* tells us something important about the social role of morality.

Given such a conception of *Sittlichkeit*—that is, of the *sociological* foundations of morality—the historical materialist does not need to say anything about the *necessity* for a belief in objective rational moral norms, which Marxists then proceed to debunk and quite properly expose as illusory. The historical materialist need not (and should not) say that the social order recognized by *Sittlichkeit* is to be regarded as a *rational* social order, which Marxists, continuing with their ideology critique, expose as an irrational, repressive, and dehumanizing social order. Whether it is such an irrational social order depends on whether it is a class society and if so, which class has control and how this control works. In a workers-controlled society in the early stages of socialism, the society would still be a class society, and there would be in it a distinctive, but hopefully not irrational, *Sittlichkeit.*

I have given a more neutral charcterization of *Sittlichkeit* than Hegel's. Mine is the kind of *Sittlichkeit* that would have to be in any social order, including a classless society. In my more neutral characterization, morality as *Sittlichkeit* need not make such Hegelian claims to validity, although Marxists will point out that in class-divided societies prior to the advent of socialism the dominant ideologies of the society will be such that most people will be mystified into believing something that at least bears a family resemblance to what Hegel believed—namely, that the set of institutions to which they are heir contain the objective norms of a living rational order. They have, it will generally be believed, in some mysterious way objective pre-scriptivity.

Marxists, given their core theory, which is in its relevant respects an empirical sociological account, will expose this Hegelian talk about a rational social order and objective norms as ideology, which in the typical situation and most surely in bourgeois societies obfuscates. Marxists will show how bowdlerized conceptions of Hegelian *Sittlichkeit* will get infused into how people think their morality—here plainly a moral ideology—will function in class societies. But it is plausible to believe that classless societies—even on the communist end of the transition—would still have a *Sittlichkeit,* although in thinking through what this would be it is important to keep in mind the de-mythologized, philosophically unfreighted, sociological characterization I gave it.

In this way, morality, while no longer being moral ideology, could remain perfectly intact in a classless society. As individuals, as moral agents, we would still start, as always and unavoidably, from morality as *Sittlichkeit.* We would start from our culturally speaking deeply embedded norms that go with our interlocked set of institutions. These norms are what John Rawls characterized as our firmest considered judgments.[19] Now, starting with them and then turning a Rawlsian trick by utilizing a coherentist model of justification and rationalization, we would seek to get them into *wide* reflective equilibrium. This would involve, in our reasoning from such a *Sittlichkeit,* considerable win-nowing out of these culturally received norms. Moreover, because we are seeking a *wide* reflective equilibrium (and will not be content with anything narrower), we will appeal not only to the abstract moral principles emerging out of *Moralität* in its reciprocal relations with

Sittlichkeit, but to the very best social theories we have (empirical-cum-theoretical theories that are both descriptive-explanatory and interpretive).[20]

If the Marxist core social theory is correct, these will be largely Marxist theories. What we will do, utilizing the method of wide reflective equilibrium, will be to shuttle back and forth between those three elements until, for a time, we gain a coherent package of beliefs and principles, what Rawls called a stable equilibrium. It will, almost certainly, be an equilibrium that will require us to modify and in some instances weed out some of the norms from the cluster of culturally inherited norms of our *Sittlichkeit.* This equilibrium will also require us to either abandon or reshape some of our (individually concocted) abstract norms; devise new ones; put new questions to social theory; and perhaps in various ways modify that social theory where it is not sufficiently established to be plausibly considered factually validated. In Otto Neurath's famous metaphor, we rebuild the ship at sea.

This coherentism of wide reflective equilibrium will give us a demythologized sense of the way in which morality could come, in the distinctive constructivist sense John Rawls spoke of, to have an objective justification and where its norms could be said (although in a thoroughly fallibilistic spirit) to be rational and objectively valid. In this case, objectivity would come to a certain kind of inter-subjectivity that rests on the consensus attained in wide reflective equilibrium.[21] Recall that we are talking about what morality could come to, and predictably would come to, if Marx's political sociology is near to the mark, in a classless society. By contrast, morality, as the long quotation by Wood brings out, would remain ideology, or largely ideology, in class-divided societies that were not (as is socialism in the transition) even on their way to becoming classless societies.

Starting with a streamlined Hegelian conception of morality, I have shown (a) what it would be like in a classless society to have a non-ideological morality and (b) how, as things stand in class-divided societies, morality is going to be very largely ideological in the pejorative ways in which Marxists characteristically speak. In a classless society morality, as the morality and the moral conceptions of any society, gets much of its content from the customary norms, from the shared considered judgments of the society. Without such a cluster of norms, individuals would not be recognizably human, let alone capable of achieving rational autonomy (rational self-direction), but as *Moralität* recognizes and would fully recognize in classless societies, this is not all to which rational autonomy and self-mastery come. Morality is not just our station and its duties. What finally would obtain, with material abundance, would be a mode of production committed to the satisfaction of needs and the achievement of a society no longer divided into classes with antagonistic interests where a dominant class oppresses and exploits a weaker class. We would at least have achieved material conditions propitious for the attainment of individual autonomy and self-mastery (if they do not come to the same thing). And in such circumstances some will successfully avail themselves of the available conditions for attaining such autonomy, thus making, for the first time in history, universal human emancipation a real possibility. There would, however, still be some conflicts of interest. Steven Lukes to the contrary notwithstanding, we would not only have a morality of emancipation; a morality as *Sittlichkeit* would remain as well and would have, as a proper part, a morality of *Recht,* although it is not unreasonable to expect that this element of morality would become increasingly less prominent as classlessness sinks in.[22]

VI

What I have shown here is how someone, starting with historical materialism and the roughly Hegelian understanding of morality Wood adverted to, could very plausibly come out with a rejection of Marxist immoralism (of Marx's immoralism, *if* it was that) and claim instead that in the circumstances of a thoroughly classless society, we could, and would, come to have a non-ideological morality. (Given what ideology is, we logically could not have an *ideological* morality in a classless society.) We could on Marxist premises draw these conclusions while at the same time remaining firmly wedded to the Marxist sociological thesis that in class societies moral ideology is the order of the day. In class-divided societies only an *appearance* of universal interests is represented by *Sittlichkeit.* What we have here, distorted by ideology, is a false picture of a system of norms answering to universal human interest. But in classless societies, with the clarity of social relations and with the undistorted discourse that would obtain, (if Marxist social theory is on the mark), it will be possible for universal interests to be represented in the *Sittlichkeit* and thus for us to have a rational morality that is not an ideology. The demands of morality need no longer be subversive of rationality. Under such circumstances, we could rightly speak of the *Sittlichkeit* of such a society and of its norms roughly as Hegel did, and the society in Rawls's sense would be a well-ordered society.

However, this is not to gainsay Wood's powerful and correct point that as a matter of sociological fact, morality will and must, in most of its employments, continue to function as a form of ideology in class societies. A lucky few will be able, more or less clearly, to see through these ideological constructions. Moreover, it is also not unreasonable to believe that there are some particular moral judgments that are not hobbled by ideological deformation—for example, that friendship carries with it commitments and that friendship between human beings is a precious thing. Indeed, some of the moral judgments that dot Marx's and Engels's texts and the texts of other classical Marxists are hopefully examples of non-ideologically distorted moral judgments. But all that notwithstanding, in class societies morality, as a set of social institutions, fundamentally and pervasively works to subvert the self-understanding of those who follow it, whatever their class position. In the process, morality works against the very rationality and autonomy it professes to fulfill. To achieve autonomy, what we really need to do (among other things) is to see through the deception and to see the needs and interests misrepresented by moral demands precisely for what they are. Our task is to "relate to these needs and interests directly instead of relating to them in the glorified form they assume to moral consciousness" (687). It is in this sense that communism should abolish morality and historical materialism should "break the staff of all morality" by exposing the real meaning of moral demands in class society (687–688). This is the forcefully underlying claim of Marxist immoralism.

VII

In spite of what I have argued, it might be said that at best I have established that a consistent Marxist, accepting the canonical core of Marxist social theory, could have a morality of emancipation but not a consistent morality of *Recht.* Justice is a purely juridical and ideological notion that will drop out in the communist society of the future. Justice, when applied to economic transactions, is, as Wood argued, a purely functional notion. As Marx put it in *Capital,* "The justice of transactions which go on between agents of production rests on the fact that these transactions arise out of the production relations as their natural consequences. [The content of such transactions] is just whenever it corresponds to the mode of production, is adequate to it. It is unjust whenever it contradicts it" (288–289).[23]

To try using justice as a critical social tool, Marx argued, is worse than useless. Moral-talk is actually antithetical to these class interests for it tends to pervert the understanding workers have of their personal interests and their class interests and the relation between them. Instead of helping workers clearly to see their situation, moral-talk fills their heads with a lot of "obsolete verbal rubbish" about rights and justice.[24] What is important to instill in workers, Marx argued, "is not moral blame directed against the bourgeoisie but rather a clear-sighted recognition that their own interests are deeply opposed to those of the bourgeoisie" (691). Proletarian revolutionaries should be, on Marx's account, resolute, disillusioned individuals who understand what class society is like; know the line of march and the steps to be taken; and comprehend how in capitalist societies law, morality, and religion are no more than bourgeois prejudices masking bourgeois interests.[25] Morality generally and justice in particular requires "in principle an equal concern and respect for the interests of all" (693).

But Marx claimed that to accept this vantage point of impartiality and disinterestedness, which is associated with taking the moral point of view, is to fail to understand the nature of class society and, in effect, to sell out the interests of the proletariat. Well-informed proletarians, who are clearly aware of their class interests and individual interests, will not take this disinterested path of justice. They will put class interests first and will struggle to protect and further proletarian class interests and to further "the interests of other classes (such as the peasantry or the petty bourgeoisie) only to the degree that they are temporarily coincident with or incipiently identical to the interests of the proletariat."[26] Militants should not distract themselves with extensive worries about what is just or fair or with attempts to take into account, in an impartial and Olympian way, the interests of everyone alike. To rally oneself around much moralistic positioning will only stand in the way of revolution and human emancipation.

Although this position could be accepted as a guideline for what most militants and most proletarians, militants or non-militants, should do in the midst of a determinate class struggle, it would still remain unclear whether this should be their theoretical practice in all contexts, including contexts in which the struggle is well disguised and most people do not see the situation as one of class struggle. It is not evident what all Marxist theoreticians who may also be militants are to do in such contexts. In the familiar context—indeed, the pervasive semi-theoretical and somewhat academic contexts of our societies—in which Marxists have been painted by anti-Marxists as unprincipled amoralists or nihilists who are theoretically defenseless in the face of totalitarianism, talk about principled amoralism may not sound, or perhaps even be, very convincing.

Wood, in this context, mentioned a possible Marxist justificatory move that he then quickly set aside on the ground that there is no sign that Marx was ever concerned with such a justification. But if the question is what a consistent Marxist could plausibly maintain, particularly given at least the prima facie unsatisfactoriness of sticking with amoralism, Wood's suggestion might be well worth pursuing. He suggested that it might be moral and indeed just, in a quite objective and non-ideological sense of those terms, "to countenance differential concern with the interests of different groups, if such a concern could be justified by some general principles of justice or the greatest good of all" (693). Thus, John Rawls, for example, in a manner compatible with his overall conception of justice as fairness, justified the greatest concern, in certain ways and certain circumstances, for the most disadvantaged stratum of society. Similarly a Marxist could, and in my view should, justify differential concern for the proletariat on the basis that proletarians are the most oppressed and dehumanized class but are nevertheless able, through their own emancipation, to bring about a state of affairs where there will be a general emancipation. The classless society that would result will enable us in time to act on the maxim, 'From each according to his ability, to each according to his needs' and thereby finally meet (as far as possible) everyone's needs impartially.

Thus, each person will be treated as an equal member of a kingdom of ends where there at last can be an equal respect for all people, which will manifest itself as a concern for the needs of all. The concern will be that the needs of everyone be satisfied as far as possible at the highest level of which each person is capable. This satisfaction will occur in the context of a similar maximal satisfaction of needs for everyone alike. Individual differences will lead to differences in need satisfaction here—this is inescapable—but we are to be guided by the maxim that there are to be no social impediments to maximal satisfaction of needs for each person, compatible, as far as this is possible, with a similar treatment of everyone alike.

Such Kantian principles are not, in class societies, the principles with which we are *directly* to act in accordance. Rather, in such societies, we should act to further and protect proletarian class interests. That should be the direct maxim of our actions whether we are workers or we take the standpoint of labor. But in addition to the intrinsic desirability of satisfying those class interests, they are also the means to classlessness and to a more general (more universal) emancipation, which, a Marxist can consistently assert, is also a central desideratum of his or her struggles.

Where interests intractably conflict, some interests must take pride of place, but that is a familiar situation morally. Indeed, it is principally for such situations that (beyond its ideological functions) we have a morality at all, and where proletarian interests conflict with other interests, Marxists say that the proletarian interests trump the other interests. But this siding with labor need not imply an indifference to the other interests; that trumping may be perfectly in accordance with the moral point of view. What there is instead is a moral recognition that in certain circumstances justice not only countenances but requires a differential treatment of different people differently situated. This is something that is perfectly universalizable and impartially justifiable. And it has, as a background assumption, a belief in the desirability and indeed in the moral requirement of a more general emancipation where that can be attained.

Proletarian militants, particularly when they are not also theoreticians, need not engage in such complicated reasoning. In the midst of class struggle, furthering proletarian class interests should be their aim. Nothing I have said is meant to deny or obscure that, but if Marxist social theory is approximately true, with a proletarian victory the interests of the vast majority will be furthered, and with the coming of classlessness far more interests can and will be satisfied and satisfied more equitably than has been the case ever before in history. The move from capitalism to socialism is a move to social systems that are increasingly humane, meet more fully human aspirations, and are increasingly more just societies.

Wood to the contrary notwithstanding, Marxists can consistently assert contextually objective critical principles of justice. And I think (pace Wood) the best way of reading *The Critique of the Gotha Programme* is by reading Marx as doing just this. Whatever Marx's motivations, it is important to note that he did see, as Wood acknowledged, that the proletarian movement, in a way "no other movement as fully could, is a movement which will further the long-term good of humanity generally, insofar as its destiny is to liberate humanity from class society" (693). Indeed on Marx's theory, and unproblematically, that is its destiny. If Marx's empirical account of the world is correct, or nearly so, if he understood correctly the direction of epochal social change and the nature of the new mode of production that he believed will come into existence, and if that new mode of production actually does come into existence and comes to have the structure that Marx predicted it will, then the communist society of the future will be a better society than the capitalist society we live in now and better than the transitional socialist society, which in turn will be better than the capitalist society that preceded it.

Wood would say 'better' but not 'morally better or less unjust.' But as almost all his critics have chorused, this is merely playing with words and sticking with an arbitrarily narrow conception of morality.[27] It surely would be logically odd and conceptually anomalous to deny, if Marx's empirical descriptions are near to the mark, that the communist society of the future would be, morally speaking, although not only morally speaking, preferable to the previous societies. So it appears at least to be the case that Marxists cannot only coherently and consistently make moral judgments, but they can make contextually objective moral judgments. The core arguments between Marxists and conservatives and liberals should *not* be between, on the one hand, Marxist amoralism and, on the other, conservativism or liberalism, which both stick consistently with the moral point of view. Instead, the crucial debate will be between, on the one hand, the respective accuracy of these competing accounts of who we were, are, and are likely to become (if a nuclear war does not send us all to heaven) and, on the other hand, who, without drifting into utopian fantasy, gives us the more reason to find hope in the world, who has the most adequate vision of what that hoped for world would look like, and who has the best conception of the modalities for its achievement. (Of course, to complicate matters, one account might be better along one of these dimensions and not so good along another.) This, of course, in a broad sense is a moral conception, a moral vision of our human life together.

I believe Marxism does better, or at least has the resources for doing better, along all of these dimensions, although I have not tried to argue that here. Rather, I have tried to show that Marxist amoralism is not the most plausible Marxist position and that someone, accepting unreservedly beliefs that are at the canonical core of Marxism, could consistently believe in morals and argue in evaluative terms, including moral terms, for the objective superiority of communism and socialism over capitalism. The actual argument for the superiority of socialist principles and conceptions of justice over conservative or liberal ones still has to be made. I have here, as a prolegomenon, tried to give grounds for setting aside some prima facie powerful Marxist roadblocks to the making of it. It is important to recognize that this 'moralized' Marxism is not a 'Marxism within the limits of morality alone,' for accepting a Marxism in accordance with the moral point of view does not, as we have seen, entail giving up the class interests thesis (the idea that proletarian interests come first). Such an acceptance does not entail or in any way establish that Marxists need construct an ethical theory to add to the foundations of Marxism, and this acceptance certainly does not mean that Marxists should cease being historical materialists and become instead historical idealists who believe we can make fundamental changes in the world through moralizing. Marxists, while remaining historical materialists and sticking with the moral point of view, should also in a certain way be Marxist anti-moralists and deride or debunk the idealist and utopian view that we can fundamentally change the world by gaining correct moral views and presenting them in clear, sympathetic, and charismatic ways. Marx always was bitterly contemptuous of such *moralism,* and rightly so. There is too much at stake to place our trust in such utopianism. (Note this itself, paradoxically, is a normative judgment.) In this way, Marxists are, and should be, hostile to morality, but this does not mean they should reject morality or turn away from the belief—a firm belief among socialists—that the capitalist system is an exploitative and thoroughly unjust social system that robs and dehumanizes vast masses of people in a quite unnecessary way.

Notes

1. Kai Nielsen, "Marx and Moral Ideology," *African Philosophical Inquiry* 1, no. 1 (January 1987):71–86. See also Chapter 2.

2. Allen W. Wood, "Marx's Immoralism," in Bernard Chavance (ed.), *Marx en Perspective* (Paris: Editions de l'Ecole des Haute Etudes en Sciences Sociales, 1985), pp. 682–83. Future references to this article will be given in the text.

3. J. L. Mackie, "A Refutation of Morals," *Australasian Journal of Philosophy* (1946):77–90. For a more nuanced statement of what is essentially the same view, see his *Ethics: Inventing Right and Wrong* (Harmondsworth, England: Penguin Books, 1977). For some probing discussions of Mackie's account see Ted Honderich (ed.), *Morality and Objectivity* (London: Routledge & Kegan Paul, 1985).

4. In addition to the text of Wood's under scrutiny here, there are other relevant Marxist anti-moralist texts, including some further texts by Wood. Allen W. Wood, "Justice and Class Interests," *Philosophica* 33, no. 1 (1984):9–32; Allen W. Wood, "The Marxian Critique of Justice," *Philosophy and Public Affairs* 8 (1978-79):267–295; Allen W. Wood, *Karl Marx* (London: Routledge & Kegan Paul, 1982), pp. 125–156; Derek Allen, "Marx and Engels on the Distributive Justice of Capitalism," *Canadian Journal of Philosophy,* Supplementary volume 7 (1981):221–250; Robert Tucker, *The Marxian Revolutionary Idea* (New York: Norton, 1969), Chapter 2; Robert Tucker, *Philosophy and the Myth of Karl Marx* (Cambridge: Cambridge University Press, 1961), pp. 11–27; Richard W. Miller, *Analyzing Marx* (Princeton, N.J.: Princeton University Press, 1985), pp. 15–97; Andrew Collier, "Truth and Practice," *Radical Philosophy,* no. 5 (1973):9–16; Andrew Collier, "The Production of Moral Ideology," *Radical Philosophy,* no. 9 (1974):5–15; Andrew Collier, "Scientific Socialism and the Question of Socialist Values," *Canadian Journal of Philosophy,* Supplementary vol. 7 (1981):121–154; Andrew Collier, "Positive Values," *The Aristotelian Society,* Supplementary vol. 57 (1983):37–54; Kai Nielsen, "Coming to Grips with Marxist Anti-Moralism," *The Philosophical Forum* 19, no. 1 (Fall 1987):1–22; Anthony Skillen, "Marxism and Morality," *Radical Philosophy* 8 (1974):11–15; Anthony Skillen, "Worker's Interests and the Proletarian Ethic: Conflicting Strains in Marxian Anti-Moralism," *Canadian Journal of Philosophy,* Supplementary vol. 7 (1981):155–170; Anthony Skillen, *Ruling Illusions: Philosophy and the Social Order* (Brighton, England: Harvester Press, 1977).

5. This was well argued by Williams Shaw in "Marxism and Moral Objectivity," *Canadian Journal of Philosophy,* Supplementary vol. 7 (1981):19–44. See also Chapter 7 herein.

6. This has been well argued, along with appropriate documentation to the texts of Marx and Engels, by John McMurty, *The Structure of Marx's World-View* (Princeton, N.J.: Princeton University Press, 1978), pp. 123–156.

7. Karl Marx, *The Portable Karl Marx,* Eugene Kamenka (ed.) (Harmondsworth, England: Penguin Books, 1983), pp. 509–557.

8. Jon Elster, *Making Sense of Marx* (Cambridge: Cambridge University Press, 1985), pp. 231–233, and 526–527. See also A. Nove, *The Economics of Feasible Socialism* (London: Allen and Unwin, 1983), pp. 15–17.

9. Steven Lukes, *Marxism and Morality* (Oxford: Clarendon Press, 1985), pp. 100–139.

10. See, for example, Harry Frankfurt, "Freedom of Will and the Concept of a Person," *The Journal of Philosophy* 68 (1971):5–20; and his "Coercion and Moral Responsibility" in T. Honderich (ed.), *Essays on Freedom of Action* (London: Routledge & Kegan Paul, 1980), pp. 63–86.

11. See here not only his "Marx's Immoralism" but also his "Justice and Class Interests." See the discussion of "Justice and Class Interests" in the previous chapter.

12. Miller, *Analyzing Marx,* pp. 15–97.

13. G. A. Cohen, "Review of Wood's *Karl Marx,*" *Mind* 92, no. 367 (July 1983):440–445; Elster, *Making Sense of Marx,* pp. 224–227; and Lukes, *Marxism and Morality,* pp. 47–59. I discuss these arguments in the next chapter.

14. I do come to grips with Cohen's arguments in the next chapter.

15. Frederich Hegel, *Philosophie des Rechts, Werke,* vol. 7 (Frankfurt, 1970), paragraphs #105–107.

16. Ibid., paragraph #144.

17. Ibid., paragraphs #135, #153.

18. Ibid., paragraphs #141–143, and #149.

19. John Rawls, "Justice as Fairness: Political Not Metaphysical," *Philosophy and Public Affairs* 14, no. 3 (Summer 1985):223–251; and his "Kantian Constructivism in Moral Theory," *The Journal of Philosophy* 77, no. 9 (1980):515–572.

20. John Rawls, "The Independence of Moral Theory," *Proceedings and Addresses of the American Philosophical Association* 47 (1974–75):5–22; Norman Daniels, "Wide Reflective Equilibrium and Theory Acceptance in Ethics," *The Journal of Philosophy* 76 (1979):256–282; and Kai Nielsen, *Equality and Liberty: A Defense of Radical Egalitarianism* (Totowa, N.J.: Rowman and Allenheld, 1985), Chapter 2.

21. See here his "Kantian Constructivism in Moral Theory."

22. Lukes, Marxism and Morality, Chapter 4.

23. Karl Marx, *Marx-Engels Werke,* vol. 25 (Berlin: Dietz Verlag, 1961–66), pp. 351–352.

24. Karl Marx, *Marx-Engels Werke,* vol. 19 (Berlin: Dietz Verlag, 1961–66), p. 22.

25. Karl Marx, *Marx-Engels Werke,* vol. 4 (Berlin: Dietz Verlag, 1961–66), p. 472.

26. Ibid.

27. Allen E. Buchanan, *Marx and Justice* (Totowa, N.J.: Rowman and Littlefield, 1982), pp. 52–60, 80; Ziyad Husami, "Marx on Distributive Justice," *Philosophy and Public Affairs* 8 (1978-79):27–64; George Brenkert, "Freedom and Private Property in Marx," *Philosophy and Public Affairs* 8 (1978-79):122–147; Gary Young, "Justice and Capitalist Production: Marx and Bourgeois Ideology," *Canadian Journal of Philosophy* 8 (1978):421–454; Norman Geras, "On Marx and Justice," *New Left Review,* no. 150 (March/April 1985):47–89.

12

Marxism and
Arguing for Justice

I

Arguing for justice is arguing for principles and practices that are to be justified on the basis of disinterested or impartial considerations. This, of course, is not all such argument is, although it is irreducibly at least that. Now, as we turn to Marx in order to fix ideas about justice, it is important to realize that it is very difficult and indeed perhaps impossible to establish what he thought about justice. Indeed, in recent years, as we have seen amply in this book, there has come into existence a minor growth industry that has tried to establish what his views about justice and, more broadly, about morality were.

It is agreed on all sides that Marx, one of the great denouncers of all time, condemned capitalism as a brutalizing social system that dehumanizes, exploits and oppresses human beings, although he also stressed capitalism's prodigious productive capacities. Marx also believed, it is further agreed, that capitalism does this even in the face of objective possibilities for radical social change, even where a change to socialism in the developed countries would render such brutalization unnecessary. It is further agreed by many that if (a) Marx's description of how capitalism works and (b) his assessment of what the alternatives are and what they are like are close to being correct, then Marx would be justified in those criticisms and that harsh condemnation.

Nevertheless, there is a deep and seemingly intractable dispute among sophisticated, conceptually astute thinkers very knowledgeable about Marx's texts as to whether Marx thought capitalism was unjust or whether he thought any whole social system could be properly appraised in terms of the justice or injustice of the whole system where those terms were taken, as people arguing for justice take them, as terms of critical appraisal. I do not intend to step into this thicket and try to establish what Marx's views about justice really were (although I did say something about it in Chapters 4 and 8). However, I think we should at least entertain the possibility that Marx, who disdained writing systematically about justice or any other moral conception, had no consistently thought out view here.

What does concern me, and what seems to me far more important to ascertain than the Marxological point, is whether we can, given certain commonplace and thoroughly unproblematic considered convictions, plausibly draw out from his central views about history, about how capitalism is structured, and about the nature of society *implicit* principles of justice of a reasonable sort that can be of some value in the critique of capitalism and other whole social formations. Put differently, and extended slightly, can contemporary Marxists who are knowledgeable about moral philosophy and who share such unproblematic considered moral convictions find implicit in the Marxist canon a basis for consistently articulating principles of justice that are (a) critical principles of justice capable of assessing in those terms whole social formations and (b) are compatible with core canonical Marxist social theory and practice? Can contemporary Marxists discover or construct such principles, and can these very principles play a modest and rationally justified role, compatible with the full acceptance of historical materialism, in a critique of capitalism and a defense of socialism that includes a moral critique and defense? Again there is deep and knowledgeable disagreement about the prospects here among contemporary philosophers who are also Marxists or Marxologists. Allen Wood and Richard Miller, for example, thought such a project is un-Marxian and, Marxian or un-Marxian, thoroughly mistaken, while G. A. Cohen and Jon Elster believed that this is just what contemporary Marxists should set about doing.[1]

I want to investigate here whether Marxists, operating with what I shall characterize as core Marxist beliefs, can consistently make transhistorical assessments of the justice or injustice of whole social systems and whether, if this can be done, it should be done. (That Marxists can, if they make such transhistorical assessments, does not entail that there are transhistorical, context-independent principles of justice.) Can Marxists reasonably claim, particularly if their descriptive-explanatory-interpretive claims are approximately true, that capitalism is unjust and that socialism is just or at least less unjust? Can Marxists argue that it is reasonable to expect that the communist society of the future, in being what Marx called a truly human society, will also be thoroughly just, or will it be 'beyond justice'? Or does it even make much sense to talk of a society being 'beyond justice'?

It might seem to some that Marxism allows such judgments and that socialism cannot make much sense without such judgments. But we should also remember that such astute and knowledgeable students of Marx and Marxism as Allen Wood and Richard Miller argued that Marx made no such transhistorical assessments of justice. Wood and Miller claimed that Marx did not use 'justice' (more accurately, '*Gerechtigkeit*') as a critical normative term, and they argued that a good understanding of what I have called the core conceptions of Marxism should dissuade contemporary Marxists from doing so themselves.[2] Turning the screw one more notch against moralistically inclined Marxism, Wood and Miller contended that in reality it is unnecessary and undesirable to moralize Marxism even if it were possible to do so. It is, as Wood put it, "Quite possible for an immoralist to possess a rational, humane outlook, as indeed Marx did" and, without inconsistency, believe that it is a mistake to think that one must appeal to morality in order to oppose tyranny, brutality, and inhumanity. Indeed, such a belief is worse than a mistake—it is "a superstition, a first cousin in fact of the superstition that one must believe in God in order to be morally good."[3]

If we take the point that people can be decent and humane without believing in morals, the question remains: Why, particularly in political contexts, should Marx and Marxists reject taking the moral point of view? Why should they steadfastly set their face against the very possibility of the assessment of the justice or injustice of whole social systems? This is particularly puzzling when such Marxist immoralists as Wood and Miller readily admitted that Marx critically assessed whole social systems. He was, as is patently and uncontroversially evident, perfectly willing to use evaluative concepts in his appraisals of capitalism and socialism. Indeed, he was lavish in the use of these concepts. He did not, in the way Max Weber was later to recommend, think of himself as a normatively neutral social scientist. What Wood and Miller were concerned to deny is that Marx made these assessments in *moral* terms, in terms of moral values. They further believed (Miller more unqualifiedly than Wood) that contemporary Marxists should follow Marx here, for, as Wood claimed, "it will prove difficult, for instance, to combine a materialist conception of history and society with a critique of capitalism on moral grounds."[4]

Principles of justice, Wood reminded us in his "Justice and Class Interests" and I noted initially, "must be advanced on impartial considerations."[5] However, Wood claimed that Marx "refused to evaluate social institutions from an impartial or disinterested standpoint, and regarded the whole enterprise of doing so as ensnared in ideological illusions."[6] That refusal, both Wood and Miller argued, is a matter of Marxists being faithful to their own deepest beliefs. A belief in the division of society into antagonistic classes is one such deep belief within Marxist theory; so is a belief in the necessity of class struggle.

In our time, Marxists believe, the class interests of the two principal opposing classes are in conflict. (That some members of either class are not aware of it does not gainsay it.) They have no alternative but to fight it out until the proletarian class, or so Marxists believe, is victorious. There is no realistic way of resolving these conflicting class interests by an appeal to the impartial considerations of justice.

What from a consistently Marxian point of view should be struggled for, Wood claimed, is "the achievement of the immediate interests of the working class."[7] We should not attempt to justify, according to Miller and Wood, the overthrow of capitalism from a disinterested standpoint. We should argue instead for the desirability of its overthrow and its replacement by socialism from the standpoint of the proletariat; and from what is in accordance with the interests of those classes whose interests coincide with the interests of the proletariat in this respect (such as the peasantry), or from the standpoint of classes whose members are (in his opinion) destined to become proletarians (such as the petty bourgeoisie).[8]

II

In asking whether a consistent Marxist should be such a Marxist immoralist or should, make moral assessments—including assessments in terms of the justice/injustice—or capitalism, socialism, and communism as well as earlier social formations, we need to spell out what I have called the core canonical conceptions of Marxism. Without such conceptualization we will not have any reasonable understanding of what it is to take a Marxist standpoint, and thus we can have scant grounds for asserting or denying that Marxists can consistently and coherently make such assessments.

What are these canonical core conceptions? They are constituted by

An acceptance of historical materialism and its allied conception of ideology

An acceptance of class as an objective reality where one's class position is determined by one's relation to the means of production

A stress on the pervasiveness and necessity of class struggle, which will culminate in a social revolution that will institute a fundamental change in the modes of production and its attendant social relations

A conception of the transition from capitalism to socialism

A conception of the future communist society

A conception of the role of the party

A conception of democracy

A belief that communism is at least feasibly on the historical agenda and that its advent is desirable

A stress on the viability of something called dialectical method

A belief in the unity of theory and practice
A conception of human nature (that is, a conception of the needs
    and capacities of human beings)
An acceptance of the labor theory of value

These core conceptions played a prominent part in the theories of all classical Marxists. That is to say, to treat the notion extensionally, they were accepted by Marx, Engels, Lenin, Luxemburg, Bukharin, Trotsky, Lukács, Gramsci, and Mao. Different Marxists gave these conceptions somewhat different readings (compare Gramsci and Bukharin on historical materialism) and different stresses (compare Lenin and Luxemburg on the role of the party). Moreover, contemporary Marxists not only give these core beliefs different readings, which usually reflect different cultural backgrounds (compare contemporary French or Italian Marxists with English or Scandinavian Marxists); contemporary Marxists make different non-canonical additions to this core, and some reject or at least distance themselves from some elements of the core. Analytical Marxists, for example, tend to distance themselves from talk of dialectics, Lenin's admonitions to the contrary notwithstanding. And three major analytical Marxists (G. A. Cohen, John Roemer, and Jon Elster) have rejected the labor theory of value. Some (Cohen and Elster) have even come to doubt the approximate truth of historical materialism, and another, Andrew Levine, has only accepted a reduced version of historical materialism that he called its rational kernel.[9]

All this notwithstanding, what makes them all Marxists is that they take a sympathetic departure from these core canonical beliefs; and in doing so they take them very seriously indeed, and not just as theses to be refuted but as possible sources of truth. Moreover, contemporary Marxists link their own analyses of social phenomena to those of Marx and the classical Marxists and find, as did Jon Elster, who departed very extensively indeed from Marx, that most of the views about society they hold to be true and important they can trace back to Marx.[10] If the departure goes too far, where 'too far' can surely not usefully or indeed reasonably be defined precisely, it is reasonable to wonder (as is the case with Elster) why that person continues to describe him- or herself as a Marxist.

Marxism is, thankfully, not written in stone. It should not be treated like a theological or a metaphysical system. Indeed, if it is, it could have no claim to being a scientific account of social reality. Marxism is, rather (in a good scientific spirit), a developing account of social reality in which some of the core elements will drop out, others will get modified, and new elements will be added. Talk of either 'orthodox Marxism' or 'revisionism' should be rejected as being more appropriate to theology than to a scientific social theory. That Marxism is also, and integrally, a revolutionary praxis should make no difference to this judgment.

Still, these core conceptions are the central elements in 'orthodox Marxism,' and contemporary Marxism must take its departure from a very extensive relation to them, including an attempt to see their force in our present attempts to interpret the world and to change it. What I most centrally want to do here is to see if that core or reasonable extensions or retractions of that core require an acceptance of Marxist immoralism or whether instead they are compatible with some defense of transhistorical principles of justice that neither collapses into ideological twaddle or into the pointless vacuities of 'eternal justice' so aptly satirized by Engels.[11] (It is important to recognize that a political conception of justice such as John Rawls's has no more use for 'eternal principles of justice' than did Engels.[12])

III

There is one very short way dissenters developed by G. A. Cohen in explicit criticism of Marxist immoralism.[13] If sound, Cohen's critique would, in a snappy set of arguments, give us good grounds for condemning capitalism as unjust and for (morally) preferring socialism to capitalism. Cohen started with Wood's startling claim that if Marx's account of capitalist society is on the mark, it remains true that although, "capitalist exploitation alienates, dehumanizes and degrades wage laborers, it does not violate any of their rights, and there is nothing about it which is wrongful or unjust."[14] This surprising claim is so, it is argued, because in capitalist societies there are, if Marxist theory is right, "no rights beyond those which capitalist exploitation honors."[15] Cohen responded by pointing out that in many places Marx said the capitalist has robbed the worker and that capitalism is based on theft, "since capitalists pay wages with money they get by selling what workers produce."[16] Moreover, Marx could not mean by 'robbery' simply that the worker has, according to the rules of capitalism, been robbed because in the cases that Marx took to be the most paradigmatic of robbery, the transaction obeys the exchange of what in the capitalist system is the exchange of equivalents. But Marx's central point in this context is that this very exchange—although in a perfectly straightforward sense it is 'an equal exchange'—enables the capitalist to rob the worker because it allows the capitalist to appropriate surplus labor from the worker. This extraction of what comes, in a Marxist way of characterizing things, to surplus value—newly created value from surplus labor—is the source of the capitalist's profits. The capitalist gains from the labor power of the workers beyond what the labor power produces that is equivalent to the commodities the worker must consume to remain alive and to be able to work. This, according to the rules of capitalism, is a fair exchange; so, *given the rules of capitalism,* the worker is not robbed. However, Marx said, the worker is robbed, although not by capitalist standards, when surplus value is extracted from him or her. The capitalist, on Marx's view, is like a conqueror "who buys commodities," as Marx put it in the *Grundrisse,* "from the conquered with the money he has robbed them of, since capitalists pay wages with money they get by selling what workers produce."[17]

It is clear here, Cohen claimed, that Marx was using 'rob' in some transhistorical mode-of-production-non-relative sense because Marx agreed that according to the rules of capitalism, the worker is not robbed but still insisted that nevertheless he is robbed. Then, Cohen went on to remark in a passage that received some attention from Steven Lukes and Jon Elster,

> since, as Wood will agree, Marx did not think that by capitalist criteria the capitalist steals, and since he did think he steals, he must have meant that he steals in some appropriately non-relativist sense. And since to steal is, in general, wrongly to take what rightly belongs to another, to steal is to commit an injustice, and a system which is 'based on theft' is based on injustice.[18]

So there we have it. Marx, whatever he might at other times have thought, did clearly, as a direct consequence of a central part of his theory, believe that capitalism is unjust, and he thereby thought that (pace Wood and Miller) transhistorical and non-mode-of-production-relative moral judgments concerning justice and injustice could be made. This, it is tempting to say, establishes quite unequivocally that Marx at least sometimes in his actual social criticism showed that he regarded capitalism as unjust, and, more importantly, it shows that such a belief in the injustice of capitalism is linked to, or is at least not incompatible with, core elements of Marxist social theory.

Cohen remarked that Marx could only "lack the belief that capitalism was unjust because he failed to notice that robbery constitutes an injustice."[19] But it is implausible to believe that on most occasions Marx would have done this, for, after all, the logical (conceptual) relationship between "robbery and injustice is so close that anyone who thinks capitalism is robbery must be treated as someone who thinks capitalism is unjust, even if he does not realize that he thinks it is."[20]

The existence of texts that show, or at least seem to show, that when writing them "Marx thought all non-relativist notions of justice and injustice were moonshine," also show, if that is really the import of those texts, "that, at least sometimes, Marx *mistakenly thought that Marx did not believe that capitalism was unjust, because he was confused about justice.*"[21] But it is clear from Cohen's argument in the immediately preceding paragraph that in his actual practice of social criticism Marx believed that capitalism is unjust and that a consistent application of his theory committed him to this position. The upshot of Cohen's argument then is to uphold, against Wood and in effect against Miller (against Marxist anti-moralism generally), the conventional idea that Marx thought, and rightly so, that capitalist exploitation is unjust.

IV

However, even if we can thus set the conflicting exegetical passages aside, there are theoretical difficulties involved that perhaps keep Cohen's argument from being as decisive as he believed it to be. (Remember here our concern is not with *Marx* exegesis but with what *Marxists* can consistently say in this domain.) First, as Elster noted, "the robbery involved differs from the standard cases of theft."[22] In standard contexts, as when I steal your pen, the stolen object exists prior to the act of stealing it. Suppose you have a pen that I want that either I cannot afford or I cannot find in a store. I steal your pen when I proceed to take it without your permission. Something exists that is not mine that I want, and this provides the incentive to steal. In all the standard cases of stealing there must be something there to be taken prior to the act of stealing. But, Elster pointed out, this is not the case with Marx's and Cohen's cases of capitalists stealing from workers. Indeed, in Cohen's case, and cases like it, it is the other way around, and this raises some worries about whether what is going on is properly described as stealing or robbery. As Elster put it, "In capitalist exploitation it is the other way around: it is because the surplus can be appropriated and robbed that the capitalist has an incentive to create it. Had there been no capitalist, the workers would not have been robbed, but they also have nothing that anyone could rob them of."[23]

This weakens, or at least appears to weaken, Cohen's case, for given the differences here we may not be justified in assimilating capitalist exploitation to straightforward theft. But it is straightforward theft that is unproblematically wrong and unjust because it is, among other things, a violation of others' rights. However, that this is so for this extended use of 'theft' appears at least not to be so unproblematically evident. Perhaps we can successfully argue that it is unjust, but then we must produce that argument. It appears at least that we cannot so straightforwardly and decisively establish that Marx believed capitalism to be unjust or that Marxist theory requires that claim from the consistent Marxist.

V

Steven Lukes in his *Marxism and Morality* made, at the end of his discussion of Marxism and rights and after his own attempt to unravel the conundrum of Marx and Marxism on justice, a criticism of Cohen's argument, which if well taken would be far more damaging than Elster's. According to Lukes, Cohen assumed that Marx believed that on these matters we can have a perspective that is non-relativistic and that enables us to say that the capitalist steals in some appropriately non-relativist sense. But, Lukes claimed, Marx, and indeed all consistent Marxists, will deny that there is any coherent sense in accordance with which we can make such a judgment. For Marx all such judgments, Lukes claimed, "are perspective relative."[24] It was Lukes's belief that Marx was committed, and that contemporary Marxists should likewise be committed, to the belief that in such matters "objectivity, in the sense of perspective-neutrality," is "an illusion, indeed an ideological illusion."[25] There just is no perspective-free, appropriately objective sense in which the capitalist can be said to rob the worker and violate his or her rights. What is appropriate to say depends on the perspective from which we look at the matter, and there is no such thing, on Marx's account, as a privileged perspective. As Lukes saw it, "Marx's view on capitalism's justice was both internally complex and hierarchically organized."[26]

Depending on the perspective from which we are viewing it, Marx's theory sanctions (1) the belief that the relation between the capitalist and the worker is just, or at least not unjust, (2) that the relation is unjust, (3) that the relation is just in one respect and unjust in another, and (4) that the relation is "neither just nor unjust."[27] When Marx stressed a functionalist account of how juridical norms serve to stabilize and rationalize the relations of production, he was viewing things from the first perspective. This is the perspective to which Wood repeatedly drew our attention. But Marx also stressed that when we are looking at things from the perspective of the socialism of the transition, we will make an external critique of the functional capitalist norms. This includes the norms of justice employed in capitalist society. When we do this we will say that from *this* perspective capitalism is unjust. But in doing so we are now judging these norms according to the socialist norm, 'To each according to his labor contribution.'

Marx, however, also made an internal critique of the functional norms of capitalist society, which showed how they are the mere appearance of an equivalent exchange of commodities. This is a third perspective. When we look just at the transaction between capitalist and worker, ignoring background conditions and what goes on in production, we will say that the transaction is just. Alternatively, when we look at the background conditions we will see how the worker is forced to sell his or her labor to some capitalist or other. Moreover, in the sphere of production, when we look at the vital situation of the workplace, we will see how workers fall under the control of capitalists. We should say that system is unjust.[28] So from this third perspective, Lukes maintained, we will say that in certain respects capitalism is just and in other respects it is unjust. Moreover, from this perspective, there is no way—or so Lukes maintained—of summing it up and saying it is just or unjust *sans phrase*.

Finally, from a fourth perspective, we will say that capitalism and indeed socialism as well are neither just nor unjust. According to Lukes, this is how we will view capitalist functional norms from the perspective of communism's higher phase. In communism, with the great abundance brought about by the development of the productive forces and with the creation of communist human beings with more cooperative, more work-oriented, less acquisitive personalities, we will come to live and cooperate together in society in a situation that is effectively beyond what Hume and Rawls referred to as the circumstances of justice. It is a circumstance where (on Lukes's and Wood's understanding) 'the non-justice principle'—'From each according to his abilities, to each according to his needs'—guides our relations with one another. From this fourth perspective the very attribution of justice and injustice is a mark of class society, a flawed society, which is transcended in communist society where no attributions of either justice or injustice are made. From this perspective (to put it paradoxically), a well-ordered society will be neither just nor unjust; it will be beyond justice.

Such a fourfold analysis reveals the internal complexity, the multi-perspectival quality, the hierarchical organization of Marx's view of capitalism's justice or lack thereof. This analysis also reveals the justifiability, if Lukes is right, of 'going beyond justice' in a successor social formation to both capitalism and socialism. Marx, Lukes claimed, consistently maintained all these perspectives. In nuanced ways Marx brought them all to bear in his analysis and critique of capitalist society. But according to Lukes, Marx steadfastly denied that any one of these perspectives is a privileged perspective. There is no all-things-considered perspective here. Cohen's error, Lukes claimed, was in failing to see the perspectival quality of Marx's account and how Marx denied that any perspective had a privileged or authoritative place that would give us an Archimedean point or a non-relativistic conception of justice. Cohen's mistake, Lukes would have it, was to take uncritically and without justification the second perspective as the authoritative perspective, which would give us such an Archimedean point, an objective, non-decentered perspective from which to appraise capitalism in moral terms. Lukes's counter was that there is no such single perspective on Marx's account that would, with respect to norms and values, afford an Archimedean point or any single, authoritative, fully objective critical perspective.

VI

When we reflect on that portion of Lukes's account expounded previously, some remarks about Marx's conception of dialectics are in order. However, before I turn to that, there are two things that should be said about Lukes's claims. First, vis-à-vis the Marxist canonical core, there may be nothing with respect to either Lukes's or Cohen's claims that would lead us to favor one view rather than another, with the possible exception that *perhaps* Lukes's view of Marx might fit better with Marx's conception of the dialectic and dialectical method. But the part about dialectics needs in turn to be balanced against the greater simplicity and direct plausibility of Cohen's claim. Perhaps Lukes multiplied perspectives beyond need. On the other hand, Lukes's hierarchical and alternative perspectival account does have distinct advantages. It puts together, in at least a putatively, complimentary, and coherent account, the rival accounts of Marx's scattered remarks about justice. With Lukes's account they are not longer seen as simply rival accounts. Indeed, they are not rival accounts at all, but are complimentary accounts placed in a wider perspective. Cohen's account, by contrast, set the putative alternatives to Marx's accounts aside on the grounds that Marx, who was not a moral philosopher and did not think carefully and systematically about justice or other moral values, could very well have been confused about justice. According to Cohen, our task is to try instead to ascertain what plausible view of justice fits best with a Marxist core social theory. Cohen, in this vein, and in contrast with Lukes, took something really central in the Marxist core—namely, Marx's labor theory of value and his related conception of capitalist exploitation—and working from that tried to show that given those theories, in order to be consistent Marx must say that the capitalist robs the worker and therefore that the capitalist treats the worker unjustly.

The only way I can see for Lukes to resist Cohen's alternative (apart from a turn to dialectics, which I shall consider in the next section) is for him to try making out, as Wood no doubt would, that neither the labor theory of value nor the theory of capitalist exploitation allied to it commit one to saying the capitalist robs the worker. However, here I think, given Cohen's careful arguments, the burden of proof lies with Lukes and Elster to show that the capitalist either does not, full stop, rob the worker or that, in robbing the worker, the capitalist somehow thereby does not do him or her an injustice. But here, or at least so it seems, Lukes and Elster will have an uphill battle, and this will remain true even if, à la Elster, the use of 'rob' in this context is not exactly paradigmatic. (This will remain true even if we reject the labor theory of value, as Cohen did, for, as he showed, in Marx's account there is a powerful conception of exploitation that does not depend for its force on the labor theory of value.[29])

The second thing to be said is that given the very Hegelianism that Lukes stressed in Marx and indeed in Marxism, it is not plausible to believe that Marx would take all of these perspectives as being equally valid or, if 'valid' is not the right word here, equally adequate. After all, the dialectical account was a developmental account that stressed that we attain progressively more comprehensive and more adequate perspectives, which transcend the earlier or less-nuanced ones. For Hegel no one could overleap history, but looking back on previous epochs, we can come to comprehend them in a more adequate way.

There is the dialectical method, which is so much at the Marxist core, and there is Lukes's stress on an internally complex, hierarchically organized, multi-perspective conceptualization of justice. Neither leads us to a relativism where all these perspectives are taken to be equally valid but to the developmental view I have just described. Lukes appeared at least to believe that Marx thought that all these perspectives are equally valid or at least that there is no reason to say that some are more comprehensive and more adequate than others. But that seems to be not the way one would expect Marx or a Marxist to look at things. We should expect, rather, that given Marx's method (here a good coherentist methodology), the different perspectives would lead to progressively higher syntheses so that the fourth perspective, that of the future communist society with its distinctive norms, would provide the most adequate perspective.

VII

For many contemporary philosophers, including some Marxists, talk of dialectics or dialectical method is embarrassing. Talk of 'dialectical logic' as a replacement for logic as we have come to know it is (to put it minimally) a non-starter. Yet a notion of dialectics is a canonical element of Marxism. J. N. Findlay, Charles Taylor, and, most importantly as far as Marx is concerned, Allen Wood gave us de-mythologized readings of dialectics that do not set it in conflict with logic and that reveal dialectics to be a reasonable, perhaps useful, conception to employ in coming to understand the social world, including those aspects of the social world that have to do with justice and morality more generally.[30] Such thinking may apply to Lukes's analysis, for I think Lukes was in effect employing a dialectical conception when he gave his perspectival reading of Marx on justice. A more explicit use of dialectical conceptions may very well strengthen such an account.

Marx was clearly indebted to Hegel for his conception of dialectics. Marx was critical of the Hegelian dialectic, although he considered himself to be working with a dialectic related to the Hegelian one. Marx wanted to expose the 'mystical' nature of dialectics and to save its 'rational kernel.' Marx never got around to saying straightforwardly what its rational kernel is or to giving a clear articulation of what dialectics and the dialectical method come to, but some commentators have given a clear and plausible interpretation of what Marx was about here.[31] I shall simply use elements of their readings to help elucidate and strengthen my claims about a Marxian understanding of justice that is responsible to the Marxist canon.

Dialectic, in either a Hegelian or Marxist form, should be understood as a general conception of the type of intelligible structure that is to be found in the world, and a dialectical conceptual system or a dialectical method should be thought of as a program for the sort of theoretical structure that would best display that intelligible structure. Both Hegel and Marx saw the dialectic as a process of organic development. For Hegel that organic development was fundamentally a process of 'cosmic reason.' It is the process by which *Geist* tests and refutes the imperfect forms of its embodiment as it rises successively to higher forms. For Marx the dialect was the organic development of the productive forces and the consequent changes of relations of production over whole epochs in a manner that is ever more adequate to our needs and that affords us an ever greater control over our lives.[32] In the Hegelian conception, the dialectical method does not typically or paradigmatically proceed by way of inferences or entailments but by way of a notational deepening of what has gone before.[33] For Marx and Marxists there also is a search for genuine causal connections, although Marxists want to see causal connections placed in a wider framework than empiricists are wont to do. For Marx, unlike for Hegel, our thought processes, as we gain an ever more adequate notational grip on things, do not generate the known reality out of our conceptions, but our thought processes, as our notational grip improves, ever more adequately grasp the inner connections of an independent reality given to us empirically. (Here we see a crucial difference between idealism and realism.) But Marx agreed with Hegel that a theory that captures the structure of reality must conceive of things as organized totalities. This theory will perspicuously display the developmental tendencies and will explicate that organic structure of reality through a hierarchy of conceptions or viewpoints on this whole, which will display all the levels or stages belonging to its nature.

Where Hegel in an a priori fashion looked for a necessary movement of thought, Marx looked for real (empirically discerned) causal connections. Still, they both thought of the world as something that is characterized by inherent tendencies to develop and subject periodically to radical changes in its basic structure. As Allen Wood well put it:

> The 'rational kernel' is his [Hegel's] vision of reality as structured organically and characterized by inherent tendencies to development. The 'mystical shell' is Hegel's logical pantheistic metaphysics which represents the dialectical structure of reality as a consequence of thinking spirit's creative activity. Marx's 'inversion' of Hegel consists in viewing the dialectical structure of thought not as a cause or explanation for the dialectical structure of reality, but merely as a consequence of the fact that it is thought's function to mirror a dialectically structured world.[34]

Marx, as a historical materialist, took the social world (society) to be an organic whole whose economic relations pass through definite stages of historical development and are driven by basic tendencies to change. Historical materialism sees the underlying dynamic of this change in the conflict between the economic relations and the productive forces as they develop throughout history and in the resulting class conflict. "Historical materialism," as Wood put it, "is animated by Hegel's philosophical vision, even if there is nothing specifically Hegelian about the explanatory factors it postulates."[35]

In both Hegel and Marx there are two species of dialectic. They have been usefully labeled a 'temporal dialectic' and a 'hierarchical dialectic.'[36] I have so far been principally talking about a temporal dialectical process (as in epochal changes in social formations brought about by the development of the productive forces over time), but the dialectic à la Lukes's talk of justice is a hierarchical one, as is the dialectical development displayed in Marx's *Capital*.[37] Where we have a hierarchical dialectic we have, not a temporal process, but a series of successively more adequate viewpoints on a subject matter. Our notational scheme and with it our general understanding successively improve with our changed and ever more comprehensive and probing viewpoints.

Lukes's four perspectives, from which we can understand justice on a Marxian account, should be understood as such a hierarchical dialectic. For Marx, as Lukes remarked, there was no perspective-neutral viewpoint in such contexts, but nevertheless we are not mired in relativism because each successive perspective gives us an increasingly more adequate viewpoint from which to understand and make judgments about justice. There is no privileged perspective, but some perspectives are more adequate than others.

Marx did not believe that with this dialectical hierarchy of viewpoints we will finally get to 'the truth' or the absolute, as if we even understood what we were talking about here. Marx was as much a fallibilist as was John Dewey or Willard van Quine. But this does not gainsay that some of these viewpoints will not enable us to make truer or more approximately truer statements that are more coherently, perspicuously, and comprehensively arranged than we can from other viewpoints. In that way one viewpoint can without any mystification be said to be more adequate than another. But our knowledge will never be final and complete. Even our best scientific knowledge will always be no more than an approximate grasp of reality and will be subject to development, revision, and periodic theoretical revolution.[38] And the same will be true for our moral understanding, including our judgments about what is just and unjust.

Lukes in effect gave us a typology of a hierarchical development of our thinking concerning justice. I do not think he had either the stages or the number of stages right (as I will gesture at in the next section), but the sense of how a Marxist conception of justice should be dialectical that is implicit in his conceptualization does seem to me to be right. Moreover, it is fallibilistic and perhaps even historicist without (whatever Lukes may have thought he was establishing) being relativist. From the fact (if it is a fact) that we cannot, at least in such domains, obtain perspective neutrality and from the further fact (if it is a fact) that all such judgments are perspective relative, we do not get relativism or subjectivism. We do not get the belief that all moral beliefs are equally valid or that one moral judgment is as good as another. These relativistic or subjectivistic beliefs do not follow from the foregoing Marxist beliefs about perspectivism. The Marxist conception of a hierarchical dialectic helps us see why.

VIII

As I have just suggested, it might readily be accepted that Marx's dialectical approach led to increasingly higher and more adequate perspectives while denying, as I would, that the highest, most adequate perspective was a 'beyond justice perspective.' It might be said, alternatively, that the perspective Cohen in effect adopted, where capitalism is said to be unjust full stop, is the more adequate perspective. Here I think what should be said is that while Lukes was right about there being a hierarchical account in Marxism—a hierarchical dialectical account if you will—he was nonetheless mistaken in not seeing (a) that the perspective at the pinnacle of the hierarchy (to keep the metaphor) affords a more adequate perspective than do those further down the hierarchy (stage four gives a more adequate perspective than stage one); and (b) that Elster was right in believing that at the pinnacle of the hierarchy we do not move 'beyond justice' but to its highest form in a hierarchy of conceptions of justice, which shows us what an increasingly more just society would look like. Elster's reading of *The Critique of the Gotha Programme* (a reading I have also independently given in Chapter 4) enabled him reasonably to impute to Marx a hierarchical theory of justice with the needs principle taking priority over the contribution principle when the forces of production are so developed that social wealth flows very freely and when the last vestiges of class divisions disappear. When such a state of affairs obtains (if it ever obtains), then we will have communistically inclined human beings without the slightest inclination to commit capitalist acts.[39] When it becomes possible to act on the needs principle, rather than on the contribution principle, because the world will have turned, our societies will have become more just than previous societies. (The conservative claim that this can never come about is an empirical claim about what is feasibly possible and must be argued on empirical grounds. Here it is useful to recall the dictum about the pessimism of the intellect and the optimism of the will.)

It is, as Elster pointed out, one of Marx's wilder, more utopian scenarios to think that we could ever attain such abundance that we could just take what we need.[40] There always will remain some scarcities (although these scarcities, as always, in part will be socially defined) and some conflicts of interest. We need, for such circumstances of abundance, a nuanced statement of the needs principle. It will assert something like, 'To each according to his or her needs that are compatible with others similarly satisfying their needs.' But we also need to supplement this with the principle 'Where two needs, had by two different persons, conflict and it is impossible to satisfy both needs and where both needs are equally compatible with satisfying the needs of others, to the person whose need is greater, where this can be ascertained.' Where, in turn, there is no ascertaining this or where the needs are the same, the guiding principle should be, 'To others whose needs would be the most extensively satisfied by satisfying the needs of the one rather than the other of the two persons.' To put roughly the same general point differently, where satisfying A's need is more fecund for satisfying the needs of others than is satisfying B's need, and where A's need is itself no greater than B's or we cannot ascertain the difference, then satisfy A's needs rather than B's, where they both cannot be satisfied. And where A and B are both as previously, but there is no way of ascertaining that the satisfaction of one person's needs is the more fecund for others, then the operative principle should be, 'To the person who wins with something like a fair flip of a coin.'

I am not saying that a Marxist should be committed to just this modification of the needs principle. It is much too slapdash and a kind of initial trying things out for that. But I am saying a Marxist should be committed to something of this sort, something that tries to capture both an equal consideration of the needs of everyone and, as far as it is compatible with such an equal consideration of needs, the maximal satisfaction of needs all around at the highest level of need satisfaction of which human beings are capable.

This modulation of a stress on maximization—the determined building up of the productive forces—makes good sense in a society that has sufficiently developed productive forces to make social wealth extensive, but this is the only sort of society in which the needs principle should gain operative force. Elsewhere it is just a heuristic. But in a world of abundance, it is the principle to be used. However, we are not, even in a developed communist society, beyond the circumstances of justice. Rather, in different societies with different modes of production, we have distinct principles of justice that are uniquely applicable to that society with that mode of production. In a capitalist society we have something like, 'From each according to his or her contribution and to each according to the assets he or she owns and controls.' In the transitional socialist society it is, 'From each according to his or her labor contribution and to each according to his or her labor contribution.' In the communist society of the future, ignoring the preceding complications for the nonce, it is, 'From each according to his or her ability and to each according to his or her needs.'

These principles are hierarchically arranged in a developmental scheme, and these societies are progressively higher forms of social existence that are progressively more just. From the perspective of a communist society of the future, capitalism is unjust, where it is possible for a higher form of society to replace it. However, even when capitalism first came into existence or where its mode of production is extremely stable with no conflict between the forces of production and relations of production, it would still have been possible, coherently and correctly, to say that capitalism is unjust. Not many in that context would have said it or even have thought it. People do not think beyond the grid of their culture very readily. Still, it is possible even in such circumstances to envision a better, a more just, society that could come into existence in the future under changed conditions. A person who has such thoughts would see capitalism as a necessary evil that people in this world order are not at present able to overcome. They know that they will not be able to overcome it until the productive forces are sufficiently developed so that socialism becomes a possibility. For a time—and in some circumstances for a very long time—people will have to settle for something very inferior indeed.

Most people in most societies do not have such an awareness. They, more or less, do the thing done and believe in most of the mores of their society. But there are in every society always a few nay-sayers who are not utterly, culturally, and conceptually imprisoned. Some people in some cultural circumstances may well be able to see that such a society, with the development of the productive forces and with determined class struggle, will in time become possible and that such a society is the more desirable society. When (or indeed if) such a society comes into existence, it will be a society in which there will be more justice than in the old society, and by comparison the old society will seem morally and humanly inadequate indeed. With such an understanding, to persist in a defense of the old society is to act wrongly, for it is in reality to support a reign of injustice. If this new society (a) is a feasible possibility and (b) is not likely to have unintended consequences that would make life worse than the life people have in the old society, then an agent who understands this has, morally speaking, very good reason indeed to favor the new society. If Marxist theory has got it roughly right about the social world's actualities and empirical possibilities, then capitalism is an unjust social system and, moreover, this is a claim that is objectively justified in the appropriate sense in which moral claims can be objectively justified.

This account, like John Rawls's, is contextualist in denying that there is a single principle of justice or set of principles of justice that applies in all circumstances, but this account is objectivist and emancipatory in maintaining that it is sometimes better to be in one situation with its determinate principle or principles of justice with their associated practices than in another situation with its determinate principle or principles of justice with their associated practices. This account also argues that in principle at least anyone in either situation can come to see that. Extreme historicists and conceptual relativists, not Karl Marx, are those who come up with theses of conceptual imprisonment, with the belief that all perspectives are equally adequate, or at least with the somewhat weaker belief that we can have no good reasons for thinking one perspective is more adequate than another.[41]

Notes

1. Allen W. Wood, "The Marxian Critique of Justice," *Philosophy and Public Affairs* 1 (1971-72):224–282; Allen W. Wood, "Marx on Right and Justice," *Philosophy and Public Affairs* 8 (1978-79):267–295; Allen W. Wood, *Karl Marx* (London: Routledge & Kegan Paul, 1982), pp. 125–156; Allen W. Wood, "Marx's Immoralism," in Bernard Chavance (ed.), *Marx en Perspective,* (Paris: Editions de l'Ecole des Haute Etudes en Sciences Sociales, 1985), pp. 681–698; Allen W. Wood, "Justice and Class Interests," *Philosophica* 33, no. 1 (1984):9–32; Richard W. Miller, *Analyzing Marx* (Princeton, N.J.: Princeton University Press, 1985), pp. 15–97; G. A. Cohen, "Freedom, Justice and Capitalism," *New Left Review* (March/April 1981):3–16; G. A. Cohen, "Review of Wood's *Karl Marx,*" *Mind* 92, no. 367 (July 1983):440–445; Jon Elster, "Exploitation, Freedom, and Justice," J. R. Pennock and J. W. Chapman (eds.), *Marxism, Nomos* 26 (New York: New York University Press, 1983), pp. 277–304; and Jon Elster, *Making Sense of Marx* (Cambridge: Cambridge University Press, 1985), pp. 196–233. For an important review article (a) with a good grasp and an illuminating categorization of the literature and (b) that provided a defense of Marxist moralism, see Norman Geras, "On Marx and Justice," *New Left Review* 60 (March/April 1985):47–89. He also provided a useful bibliography.

2. See the references to Wood and Miller in the previous footnote.

3. Wood, "Marx's Immoralism," pp. 696–697.

4. Ibid., p. 696.

5. Wood, "Justice and Class Interests," p. 15. See also Miller, *Analyzing Marx,* pp. 15–97.

6. Wood, ibid.

7. Karl Marx, *Marx-Engels Worke,* vol. 4 (Berlin: Dietz Verlag, 1961–66), p. 492.

8. Ibid., p. 471.

9. Andrew Levine, *Arguing For Socialism* (London: Routledge & Kegan Paul, 1984), pp. 192–196.

10. Elster, *Making Sense of Marx,* p. 531.

11. Frederick Engels, *Anti-Dühring,* Emile Burns (trans.) (New York: International Publishers, 1939), Chapters 9–11. See also Chapter 3.

12. John Rawls, "Justice as Fairness: Political Not Metaphysical," *Philosophy and Public Affairs* 14, no. 3 (Summer 1985):223–251.

13. G. A. Cohen, "Review of Wood's *Karl Marx,*" *Mind* 92, no. 367 (July 1983):440–445.

14. Wood, *Karl Marx,* p. 43.

15. Cohen, "Review of Wood's *Karl Marx,*" p. 442.

16. Ibid., p. 445.

17. Karl Marx, *Grundrisse,* Martin Nicolaus (trans.) (Harmondsworth, England: Penguin Books, 1973), p. 705.

18. Cohen, "Review of Wood's *Karl Marx,*" p. 443.

19. Ibid.

20. Ibid.

21. Ibid., p. 444 (italics in original).

22. Elster, *Making Sense of Marx,* p. 225.

23. Ibid.

24. Steven Lukes, *Marxism and Morality* (Oxford: Clarendon Press, 1985), p. 59.

25. Ibid.

26. Ibid., p. 58.

27. Ibid., p. 48.

28. Gary Young, "Justice and Capitalist Production: Marx and Bourgeois Ideology," *Canadian Journal of Philosophy* 8 (1978):421–454; and Gary Young, "Doing Marx Justice," *Canadian Journal of Philosophy,* Supplementary vol. 7 (1981):251–268.

29. G. A. Cohen, "The Labour Theory of Value and the Concept of Exploitation," *Philosophy and Public Affairs* 8, no. 4 (1979), 338–360; and his "More on Exploitation and the Labour Theory of Value," *Inquiry* 26, no. 3 (September 1983):309–331.

30. J. N. Findlay, *Language, Mind and Value* (London: George Allen and Unwin, 1963), pp. 217–231; his *Hegel: A Re-Interpretation* (London: George Allen and Unwin, 1965); Charles Taylor, *Hegel* (Cambridge: Cambridge University Press, 1979); and Wood, *Karl Marx,* pp. 189–234.

31. Wood, ibid., pp. 207–218. See, as well, the chapters by Richard Norman, in Richard Norman and Sean Sayers, *Hegel, Marx and Dialectic: A Debate* (Atlantic Highlands, N.J.: Humanities Press, 1980).

32. Wood, *Karl Marx,* pp. 207–211; and G. A. Cohen, *Karl Marx's Theory of History: A Defense* (Oxford: Clarendon Press, 1978), pp. 1–27.

33. Findlay, *Language, Mind and Value,* p. 225.

34. Wood, *Karl Marx,* p. 209.

35. Ibid., p. 214. Also see Cohen, *Karl Marx's Theory of History,* pp. 1–27.

36. Wood, *Karl Marx,* p. 197.

37. Ibid., pp. 216–234.

38. Ibid., p. 215.

39. Chapter 4 herein.

40. Elster, *Making Sense of Marx,* pp. 230–233. See also pp. 526–527.

41. The hierarchical dialectic I have deployed here for justice causally depends on the temporal dialectic of the epochal transformation of whole modes of production and with them other social formations. This dialectic requires, that is, movement in the social world. The socio-economic conditions necessary to make feasible the application of the communist principle of justice do not exist when a capitalist, to say nothing of a feudal, mode of production is stable. However, it is possible to say how a socialist mode of production and a communist principle of justice are prefigured in the capitalist mode of production. Perceptive people can see how the capitalist mode of production is developing the capacities to be transformed into a socialist mode of production and how this in turn will in time produce the conditions necessary for the communist principle of justice actually to appropriately guide our human interactions. It is not that we have an *Aufhebung* of the principle of justice of capitalism. It is not transformed while still being preserved in socialism

or in communism. Rather, in both socialism and communism we have distinct principles of justice appropriate to the transformed socio-economic structures made possible by the development of the forces of production. A hierarchical dialectic gives us the conceptual grid adequately to understand and perspicuously to display something of what it would be like to attain this more adequate perspective. However, if my de-mythologized account of the dialectic in Section VII seems worrisome, forget about dialectics and attend to my adoption and development of Lukes's hierarchical account of justice as a stating of principles of justice that, as the world changes, make seriatim their use feasible in their various contextually appropriate circumstances. Moreover, as we move upward in the hierarchy, we will get principles of justice that increasingly answer more fully to the interests of ever widening groups of human beings.

Index

DATE DUE

NOV 11 1991			
GAYLORD			PRINTED IN U.S.A.